ZAGAT

Paris Restaurants 2012/13

LOCAL EDITOR
Alexander Lobrano

LOCAL COORDINATOR
Mary Deschamps

STAFF EDITOR
Josh Rogers

Published and distributed by
Zagat Survey, LLC
76 Ninth Avenue
New York, NY 10011
T: 212.977.6000
E: paris@zagat.com
www.zagat.com

ACKNOWLEDGMENTS

We thank Jeff Aguero, Axel Baum, Sabine Brassart, Chloé Broughton, Catherine Brownstone, Gilbert Brownstone, François Cornu, Bryant Detwiller, Alexandra Ernst, Raphael Goumain, Solange Herter, Anne Liebmann, Mike Lima, Anne and Gerard Mazet, Yves Nespoulous, Tita Scuba, Garret Siegel, Boi Skoi, Peter and Susan Solomon and Alex Torres, as well as the following members of our staff: Caitlin Miehl (editor), Brian Albert, Sean Beachell, Maryanne Bertollo, Reni Chin, Larry Cohn, Nicole Diaz, Kelly Dobkin, Kara Freewind, Jeff Freier, Alison Gainor, Matthew Hamm, Danielle Harris, Justin Hartung, Marc Henson, Karen Hudes, Ryutaro Ishikane, Natalie Lebert, Mike Liao, Vivian Ma, James Mulcahy, Polina Paley, Hilary Sims, Amanda Spurlock, Alice Urmey, Chris Walsh, Jacqueline Wasilczyk, Yoji Yamaguchi, Sharon Yates, Samantha Zalaznick, Anna Zappia and Kyle Zolner.

The reviews in this guide are based on public opinion surveys. The ratings reflect the average scores given by the survey participants who voted on each establishment. The text is based on quotes from, or paraphrasings of, the surveyors' comments. Phone numbers, addresses and other factual data were correct to the best of our knowledge when published in this guide.

Our guides are printed using environmentally preferable inks containing 20%, by weight, renewable resources on papers sourced from well-managed forests. Deluxe editions are covered with Skivertex Recover® Double containing a minimum of 30% post-consumer waste fiber.

ISBN-13: 978-1-60478-445-9
ISBN-10: 1-60478-445-8
Printed in the
United States of America

Contents

Ratings & Symbols

Zagat Top Spot	Name	Symbols	Cuisine	Zagat Ratings

	FOOD	DECOR	SERVICE	COST
Z Tim & Nina's ◐ *French/Thai*	▽ 23	9	13	€15

Area, Address, Métro Stop & Contact*

6e | 604, rue de Buci (Odéon) | 01-23-45-54-32 | www.zagat.com

Review, surveyor comments in quotes

Jamais fermé, this "crowded" 6th-arrondissement cafe started the "French-Thai craze" (e.g. foie gras in pad Thai or lychee bouillabaisse); though it looks like a "historic garage" and T & N "never heard of credit cards or reservations" - or service, for that matter - the "*merveilleuse* Bangkok-Brest cuisine" draws delighted diners due to decidedly downmarket tabs.

Ratings

Food, Decor & **Service** are rated on a 30-point scale.

- 0 - 9 poor to fair
- 10 - 15 fair to good
- 16 - 19 good to very good
- 20 - 25 very good to excellent
- 26 - 30 extraordinary to perfection
- ▽ low response | less reliable

Cost

The price of dinner with a drink (tipping is not expected in France); lunch is usually 25% to 30% less. For unrated **newcomers** or **write-ins,** the price range is as follows:

- I 35€ and below
- M 36€ to 55€
- E 56€ to 90€
- VE 91€ or above

Symbols

- Z highest ratings, popularity and importance
- ◐ serves after 11 PM
- S M closed on Sunday or Monday
- ≠ no credit cards accepted

Maps

Index maps show restaurants with the highest Food ratings in those areas.

* When calling from outside France, dial the country code +33, then omit the first zero of the number listed.

About This Survey

Here are the results of our **2012/13 Paris Restaurants Survey,** covering 714 eateries in the Paris area. Like all our guides, this one is based on input from avid local consumers - 8,015 all told. Our editors have synopsized this feedback, highlighting representative comments (in quotation marks within each review). To read full surveyor comments - and share your own opinions - visit **zagat.com,** where you will also find the latest restaurant news, special events, deals, reservations, menus, photos and lots more, **all for free.**

ABOUT ZAGAT: In 1979, we started asking friends to rate and review restaurants purely for fun. The term "user-generated content" had yet to be coined. That hobby grew into Zagat Survey; 33 years later, we have over 375,000 surveyors and cover airlines, bars, dining, fast food, entertaining, golf, hotels, movies, music, resorts, shopping, spas, theater and tourist attractions in over 100 countries. Along the way, we evolved from being a print publisher to a digital content provider, e.g. **zagat.com** and Zagat mobile apps (for Android, iPad, iPhone, BlackBerry, Windows Phone 7 and Palm webOS). We also produce marketing tools for a wide range of blue-chip corporate clients. And you can find us on Google+ and just about any other social media network.

UNDERLYING PREMISES: Three simple ideas underlie our ratings and reviews. First, we believe that the collective opinions of large numbers of consumers are more accurate than those of any single person. (Consider that our surveyors bring some 1.2 million annual meals' worth of experience to this survey, visiting restaurants regularly year-round, anonymously - and on their own dime.) Second, food quality is only part of the equation when choosing a restaurant, thus we ask our surveyors to rate food, decor and service separately and then report on cost. Third, since people need reliable information in an easy-to-digest, curated format, we strive to be concise and we offer our content on every platform - print, online and mobile. Our Top Ratings lists (pages 7-18) and indexes (starting on page 149) are also designed to help you quickly choose the best place for any occasion, be it for business or pleasure.

MERCI: We're grateful to our Paris-based local editor, Alexander Lobrano, a food and travel writer; our local coordinator, Mary Deschamps, a freelance Franco-American writer and translator; and contributors Barbra Austin, a Paris food writer, and Corinne LaBalme, editor of *La Belle France*. Thank you, guys. We also sincerely thank the thousands of people who participated in this survey - this guide is really "theirs."

JOIN IN: To improve our guides, we solicit your comments - positive or negative; it's vital that we hear your opinions. Just contact us at **nina-tim@zagat.com.** We also invite you to join our surveys at **zagat.com.** Do so and you'll receive a choice of rewards in exchange.

New York, NY
May 23, 2012

Nina and Tim Zagat

What's New

Despite the Eurozone's recent economic volatility, appetite for Paris' dining scene remains healthy overall: 62% of surveyors report eating out as frequently as they did a year ago, 17% say more often and 21% less. This, despite the fact that the average cost of a meal in Paris is a whopping 61.64€, well ahead of London (51.89€) and almost double NYC (32.76€).

TOP TICKETS: While some of Paris' most venerable culinary names are among this Survey's winners – **Taillevent** ranks No. 1 for Food and Service while **L'Atelier de Joël Robuchon** is the Most Popular – recent arrivals are also generating considerable buzz. Dial now to land a seat at talked-about tables like top-rated newcomer **Septime**; **Agapé Substance,** David Toutain's small-platery; Left Bank power spot **L'Affable**; or Ménilmontant's foodie favorite **Chatomat.** Though Parisians are split on whether a famous chef makes them more inclined to dine at a restaurant (48% say yes; 49% say it has no effect), crowds are tuning in to *Top Chef* winner Romain Tischenko's market-driven **Le Galopin.** And despite steep prices, **Shang Palace,** the luxe Cantonese at the Shangri-La, is booked solid too.

IMPORTED TALENT: La Ville-Lumière still shines as a beacon for ambitious young chefs from abroad. Laura Adrian and Braden Perkin checked in with American **Verjus,** while Japan's Kei Kobayashi (**Kei**) and Mexico's Beatriz Gonzalez (**Neva**) are dishing up modern French fare. Yankees spreading burgermania in Paris include pastry chef Camille Malmquist (baking buns for **Blend**) and Kristin Frederick, who rolls down the rues in the city's first food truck, **Le Camion Qui Fume.**

UNCORKING A TREND: In many of the hippest *quartiers,* wine bars are the new bistros (i.e. local go-to places), with trendy nook **Au Passage** and **Le Dauphin** (near big brother **Le Chateaubriand**) ruling the roost in the 11th, and Pierre Jancou's **Vivant** packing in bon vivants in the 10th. The Latin Quarter's **Dans les Landes** serves Southwestern tapas, while in the Marais, **Jaja** (a **Glou** offshoot) pairs interesting *vins* with organic bites.

CASUAL AND CONCISE: Parisians are bellying up to counters, balancing on tall stools or otherwise deviating from tried-and-true tables/chairs/banquettes at casual perches like Antoine Westermann's rotisserie **Le Coq Rico, Gyoza Bar** (a **Passage 53** spin-off) and the Basque-esque **Pottoka.** Also, toques are ditching long à la carte menus for more focused offerings. Examples include **Chatomat** (limited menu), **Le Galopin** (seven-course tasting menu) and **Verjus** (tasting menus).

SURVEY STATS: Respondents report dining out an average of 3 times per week, on par with NYC but ahead of London (2.4) and behind Tokyo (4) . . . Service is the city's top dining-out irritant, cited by 76%, with noise a distant second (17%) . . . 52% say it's rude to text, tweet or talk on a mobile phone in a restaurant, but only 13% are averse to diners snapping photos.

Paris, France
May 23, 2012

Alexander Lobrano

Most Popular

Plotted on the map at the back of this book.

1. Atelier Joël Robuchon | *Haute*
2. Taillevent | *Haute*
3. Guy Savoy | *Haute*
4. Jules Verne | *Haute*
5. Alain Ducasse | *Haute*
6. Tour d'Argent | *Haute*
7. Bofinger | *Brasserie*
8. Grand Véfour | *Haute*
9. 144 Petrossian | *Seafood*
10. Arpège | *Haute*
11. Coupole | *Brasserie*
12. Train Bleu | *Classic French*
13. Bar à Huîtres | *Seafood*
14. Cinq | *Haute*
15. Pied de Cochon | *Brasserie*
16. Pierre Gagnaire | *Haute*
17. Lasserre | *Haute*
18. As du Fallafel | *Israeli*
19. Epicure (Le Bristol) | *Haute*
20. Relais/l'Entrecôte | *Steak*
21. Ami Louis | *Bistro*
22. Café de Flore | *Classic French*
23. Meurice | *Haute*
24. Brass. Lipp | *Brasserie*
25. Pré Catelan | *Haute*
26. Chez L'Ami Jean | *Basque*
27. Ze Kitchen Galerie* | *Eclectic*
28. Fontaine de Mars | *Southwest*
29. Comptoir/Relais | *Bistro/Brass.*
30. Procope | *Classic French*
31. Apicius | *Haute*
32. Senderens* | *New French*
33. Ambroisie | *Haute*
34. Hélène Darroze | *New Fr./SW*
35. Deux Magots | *Classic Fr.*
36. Benoît | *Lyon*
37. Chez Georges | *Bistro*
38. Astrance | *Haute*
39. Villa Corse | *Corsica*
40. Ambassadeurs | *Haute*
41. 6 New York | *New French*
42. Spring | *New French*
43. Café Constant | *Bistro*
44. Brass. Flo | *Brasserie*
45. Epi Dupin | *Bistro*
46. Vin et Marée | *Seafood*
47. Dôme | *Seafood*
48. Café de la Paix | *Classic French*
49. Fouquet's | *Classic French*
50. Ambassade/Auvergne | *Auv.*

Many of the above restaurants are among the Paris area's most expensive, but if popularity were calibrated to price, a number of other restaurants would surely join their ranks. To illustrate this, we have included two pages of Best Buys starting on page 17.

* Indicates a tie with restaurant above

Key Newcomers

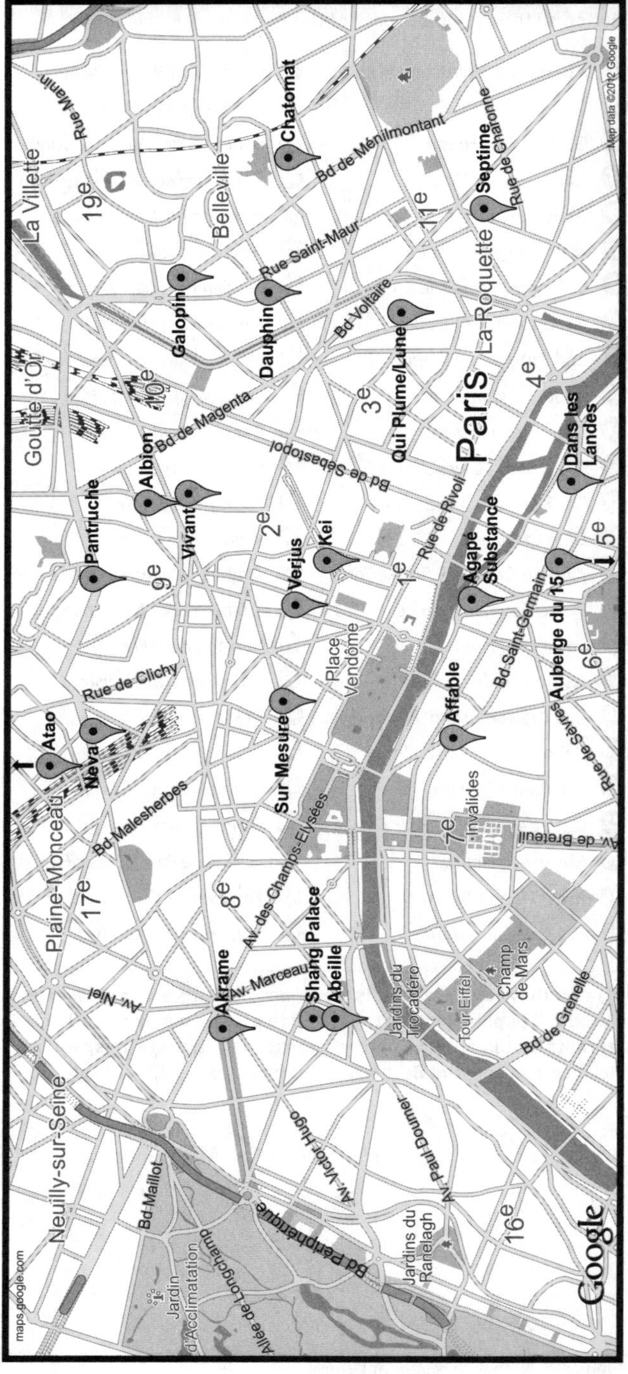
Chatomat
Septime
Galopin
Dauphin
Qui Plume/Lune
Albion
Vivant
Pantruche
Verjus
Kei
Dans les Landes
Agapé
Substance
Auberge du 15
Affable
Sur Mesure
Atao
Neva
Akrame
Shang Palace
Abeille
Paris
La Villette
Belleville
Goutte d'Or
La Roquette
Plaine-Monceau
Neuilly-sur-Seine
Place Vendôme
Invalides
Champ de Mars
Tour Eiffel
Jardins du Trocadéro
Jardins du Ranelagh
Jardin d'Acclimatation
Rue Manin
Bd de Ménilmontant
Rue de Charonne
Rue Saint-Maur
Bd Voltaire
Bd de Magenta
Bd de Sébastopol
Rue de Rivoli
Bd Saint-Germain
Rue de Sèvres
Av. de Breteuil
Bd de Grenelle
Rue de Clichy
Bd Malesherbes
Av. des Champs-Elysées
Av. Marceau
Av. Niel
Av. Victor Hugo
Av. Paul-Doumer
Bd Périphérique
Bd Maillot
Allée de Longchamp
19e
10e
11e
3e
4e
2e
9e
1e
5e
6e
7e
8e
17e
16e
Map data ©2012 Google
maps.google.com
Google

Key Newcomers

Our editors' picks among this year's arrivals. See full list at p. 195.

Abeille | *Haute* | Philippe Labbé creates a buzz at the Shangri-La

Affable | *Bistro* | Chic Left Bank power spot

Agapé Substance | *New French* | Tapas in Saint-Germain

Akrame | *New Fr.* | Modern techniques in sleek digs in the 16th

Albion | *Wine Bar/Bistro* | Anglo owners go French in the 10th

Atao | *Brittany/Seafood* | Breton bivalves by way of Batignolles

Auberge du 15 | *Classic Fr.* | Country classics in the 13th

Chatomat | *New Fr.* | Ménilmontant mints a hipster bistro

Dans les Landes | *Wine Bar/Bistro* | Small plates, big ham in the 5th

Dauphin | *New Fr.* | Inaki Aizpitarte's ultramodern tapas joint

Galopin | *Bistro* | *Top Chef* champ's brilliant, out-of-the-way bistro

Kei | *New French* | Talented Japanese student of French gastronomy

Neva | *New Fr.* | A young crowd stationed near Gare Saint-Lazare

Pantruche | *Bistro* | Good buy below Sacré Coeur

Qui Plume/Lune | *New Fr.* | Asian accents in a former convent

Septime | *Bistro* | Ex–L'Arpège chef's minimalist nook in the 11th

Shang Palace | *Chinese* | Shangri-La's high-end Cantonese stunner

Sur Mesure | *Haute* | Thierry Marx checks into Mandarin Oriental

Verjus | *Amer./Wine Bar* | An American in Paris, next to the Palais-Royal

Vivant | *Wine Bar/Bistro* | In the gentrifying 10th, a hopping bar scene

---

As we go to press, Spanish star Sergi Arola is opening **Arola** at the brand-new W Paris Opéra Hotel, and star butcher Yves-Marie Le Bourdonnec is about to debut **The Beef Club,** a steakhouse near Les Halles specializing in rare-breed meat. Yannick Alléno is readying **Terroir Parisien,** a casual bistro in the Latin Quarter. And the wine-bar craze continues, with the next pour being **Youpi et Voilà** from Patrice Gelbart in the 10th near the Canal Saint-Martin.

Springtime in Paris heralds the arrival of Anne-Sophie Pic, of the celebrated **Maison Pic** in Valence, to the capital. Also on tap is **Il Circolo,** a trattoria in the 9th, and Joe Allen catches up with Paris' new-found love of American eats with an entry in the 10th. Restaurateur Massimo Mori (**Emporio Armani Caffè, Mori Venice Bar**) is slated to launch a 'ciceteria' (Venetian-style tapas bar), and chef Flora Mikula returns after closing her **Les Saveurs de Flora** with a sunny Mediterranean venue in the 11th.

The year will also see Alain Ducasse retooling the currently shuttered **Spoon Paris** with a new look, concept and menu, plus the transfer of Guy Savoy's eponymous Haute Cuisine table to quarters designed by Jean-Michel Wilmotte in the Hôtel de la Monnaie.

Top Food

29 Taillevent | *Haute*

28 Pierre Gagnaire | *Haute*
Guy Savoy | *Haute*
Grand Véfour | *Haute*
Cinq | *Haute*
Alain Ducasse | *Haute*
Duc | *Seafood*
Astrance | *Haute*
Meurice | *Haute*
Pramil | *Bistro*

27 Lasserre | *Haute*
Spring | *New French*
Ambroisie | *Haute*
Atelier Joël Robuchon | *Haute*
Comptoir/Relais | *Bistro/Brass.*
Guilo-Guilo | *Asian*
Apicius | *Haute*
Epicure (Le Bristol) | *Haute*
Ambassadeurs | *Haute*
Passage 53 | *Haute*
Hiramatsu | *Haute/New French*
Jean-François Piège | *Haute/New Fr.*
Michel Rostang | *Classic French*
Bigarrade | *New French*
Arpège | *Haute*
Carré des Feuillants | *Haute*

26 Caviar Kaspia | *Russian*
Senderens | *New French*
Table d'Eugène | *New French*
Pré Catelan | *Haute*
Oulette | *New French/SW*
Divellec | *Seafood*
Relais Louis XIII | *Haute*
Grand Venise | *Italian*
Huîtrerie Régis | *Shellfish*
Quinzième | *New French*
Severo | *Steak*
Quincy | *Bistro*
Hélène Darroze | *New Fr./SW*
Truffière* | *Classic French*
Yam'Tcha | *Asian/New French*
Frenchie | *Bistro*
Chamarré Montmartre | *Mauritian/New French*

25 Fakhr el Dine | *Lebanese*
Pavillon Ledoyen* | *Haute*
Relais Plaza | *Brass./Eclectic*
Fables/Fontaine | *Seafood*
Clos/Gourmets | *New French*
Relais d'Auteuil* | *Haute*
Septime* | *Bistro*

BY CUISINE (FRENCH)

BISTRO (CONTEMP.)

28 Pramil
27 Comptoir/Relais
26 Frenchie
25 Septime
Maison du Jardin

BISTRO (TRAD.)

26 Quincy
25 Chez L'Ami Jean
Violon d'Ingres
Petit Pontoise
Régalade

BRASSERIE

27 Comptoir/Relais
25 Relais Plaza
24 Dessirier
Chez Les Anges
23 Pétrus

CLASSIC

27 Michel Rostang
25 Ourcine
Gourmand
Papilles
Joséphine/Dumonet

CONTEMPORARY

28 Pramil
27 Spring
Hiramatsu
Jean-François Piège
Bigarrade

HAUTE CUISINE

29 Taillevent
28 Pierre Gagnaire
Guy Savoy
Grand Véfour
Cinq

Excludes places with low votes, unless otherwise indicated

LYON

24 Aub. Pyrénées Cévennes
23 Benoît
22 Lyonnais
Opportun▽
19 Chez René

OTHER REGIONS

25 Chez L'Ami Jean (Basque)
Petites Sorcières (Northern)
24 Chez Michel (Brittany)
Troquet (Basque)
23 Tante Louise (Burgundy)

PROVENCE

25 Marius
23 Casa Olympe
21 Chez Janou
20 Bastide Odéon
Petit Niçois▽

SEAFOOD

28 Duc
26 Divellec
25 Fables/Fontaine
Ecailler du Bistrot
Marius

SHELLFISH

28 Duc
26 Huîtrerie Régis
25 Ecailler du Bistrot
Marius
23 Marée

SOUTHWEST

26 Oulette
Hélène Darroze
25 Trou Gascon
24 D'Chez Eux
Aub. Pyrénées Cévennes

STEAK

26 Severo
23 Boeuf Couronné
Relais de Venise
Gourmets des Ternes
Relais/l'Entrecôte

WINE BARS/BISTROS

25 Bourguignon/Marais
24 Baratin
23 Caves Pétrissans
Cave Schmidt
22 Enoteca

BY CUISINE (OTHER)

ASIAN/CHINESE

27 Guilo-Guilo
26 Yam'Tcha
23 Chez Vong
Oth Sombath
22 Tsé-Yang

ECLECTIC

25 Relais Plaza
Ze Kitchen Galerie
22 Market
19 Café Rouge
18 Fumoir

ITALIAN

26 Grand Venise
24 Sormani
Ostéria
23 Chez Vincent
Casa Bini

JAPANESE

25 Isami
Aida
Benkay
Foujita
24 Kinugawa

MIDDLE EASTERN

25 Fakhr el Dine
24 Liza
23 As du Fallafel
22 Al Dar
19 Chez Marianne

MOROCCAN

22 Timgad
21 Mansouria
El Mansour
Atlas
20 404

SPANISH/LATIN AMER.

23 Fogón
Anahuacalli
22 El Palenque
19 Anahi
- Candelaria

THAI

22 Chieng Mai
Lao Siam
21 Diep
Khun Akorn
19 Tricotin

BY SPECIAL FEATURE

BRUNCH

22 Market
21 Findi
Flora Danica
20 404
18 Fumoir

BUSINESS DINING

24 Dessirier
Chez Les Anges
23 Marius et Janette
Drouant
19 Montalembert

CHILD-FRIENDLY

23 Anahuacalli
22 Rôtiss. du Beaujolais
Relais/l'Entrecôte
Sébillon
20 Rôtiss. d'en Face

HOTEL DINING

28 Cinq (George V)
Alain Ducasse (Plaza Athénée)
Meurice (Meurice)
27 Atel. Joël Robuchon (Pont Royal)
Comptoir/Relais (Relais)

LATE DINING

27 Atelier Joël Robuchon
26 Caviar Kaspia
25 Fakhr el Dine
Relais Plaza
Chez L'Ami Jean

LIVE ENTERTAINMENT

25 Fakhr el Dine
Chez Cécile
23 Annapurna
20 Maxim's
18 Boeuf sur le Toit

MEET FOR A DRINK

26 Frenchie
25 Bourguignon/Marais
23 Café Lenôtre
Cave Schmidt
22 Enoteca

NEWCOMERS (RATED)

25 Septime
Agapé Substance
24 Auberge du 15
23 Abeille
Akrame

PEOPLE-WATCHING

22 Stresa
20 Fouquet's
19 Opéra Rest.
18 Costes
16 Café de Flore

SUNDAY DINING

28 Pierre Gagnaire
Cinq
Pramil
27 Atelier Joël Robuchon
Comptoir/Relais

TRENDY

28 Astrance
27 Spring
Comptoir/Relais
Guilo-Guilo
Quinzième

WINNING WINE LISTS

29 Taillevent
28 Pierre Gagnaire
Guy Savoy
Grand Véfour
Cinq

BY ARRONDISSEMENT

1ST

28 Grand Véfour
Meurice
27 Spring
Carré des Feuillants
26 Yam'Tcha

2ND

27 Passage 53
26 Frenchie
24 Pur'
Liza
Gavroche

3RD

28 Pramil
24 Ami Louis
23 Petit Marché
Bascou
Hangar

4TH

27 Ambroisie
25 Isami
Bourguignon/Marais
24 Ostéria
Gaigne

5TH

- 26 Truffière
- 25 Papilles
- Tour d'Argent
- Petit Pontoise
- 24 Agrume

6TH

- 27 Comptoir/Relais
- 26 Relais Louis XIII
- Huîtrerie Régis
- Hélène Darroze
- 25 Maison du Jardin

7TH

- 27 Atelier Joël Robuchon
- Jean-François Piège
- Arpège
- 26 Divellec
- 25 Fables/Fontaine

8TH

- 29 Taillevent
- 28 Pierre Gagnaire
- Cinq
- Alain Ducasse
- 27 Lasserre

9TH

- 23 Casa Olympe
- 22 Rose Bakery
- Petit Riche
- 21 Bistro/Deux Théâtres
- Boule Rouge

10TH

- 24 Chez Michel
- 20 Verre Volé
- 19 Brass. Julien
- Brass. Flo
- 18 Terminus Nord

11TH

- 25 Septime
- Rino
- Ecailler du Bistrot
- 24 Aub. Pyrénées Cévennes
- 23 Villaret

12TH

- 26 Oulette
- Quincy
- 25 Trou Gascon
- 24 Gazzetta
- Ebauchoir

13TH

- 25 Ourcine
- 24 Auberge du 15
- 23 Avant Goût
- Petit Marguery
- 22 Cailloux

14TH

- 28 Duc
- 26 Severo
- 25 Petites Sorcières
- Régalade
- 23 Cagouille

15TH

- 26 Grand Venise
- Quinzième
- 25 Beurre Noisette
- Benkay
- 24 Troquet

16TH

- 28 Astrance
- 27 Hiramatsu
- 26 Pré Catelan
- 25 Fakhr el Dine
- Relais d'Auteuil

17TH

- 28 Guy Savoy
- 27 Michel Rostang
- Bigarrade
- 24 Sormani
- Dessirier

18TH

- 27 Guilo-Guilo
- 26 Table d'Eugène
- Chamarré Montmartre
- 21 Café Burq
- Sale e Pepe

19TH & 20TH

- 24 Baratin
- 23 Chez Vincent
- Boeuf Couronné
- 22 Allobroges
- Lao Siam

OUTSIDE PARIS

- 22 Rest. Manufacture
- Romantica
- Sébillon
- 21 Bistrot/Côté La Boutarde
- 19 Ile

Top Decor

29 Cristal Room

28 Cinq
Grand Véfour
Taillevent
Meurice
Ambassadeurs
Lasserre

27 Jules Verne
Epicure (Le Bristol)
Train Bleu
Alain Ducasse
Grande Cascade
Pré Catelan
Tour d'Argent

26 Maison de l'Amér. Latine
Pavillon Ledoyen
Ralph's*
Minipalais
Ambroisie
Maison Blanche
Guy Savoy

25 Ombres
Brass. Julien
Bouillon Racine
Ile
Lapérouse
Apicius
Georges
Grand Colbert
Fermette Marbeuf
Costes
Chalet des Iles
Pavillon Montsouris
Relais Louis XIII
1728
Coupe-Chou
Vagenende

24 Derrière
Kong*
Pierre Gagnaire
Jardins de Bagatelle
Procope
Bofinger
Maxim's
Quai
Café de la Paix
Coupole
Pavillon du Lac
Café Marly
Rosa Bonheur

HISTORIC SPACES

Ambassadeurs
Aub. Nicolas Flamel
Bofinger
Charpentiers
Deux Magots
1728
Fermette Marbeuf
Grande Cascade
Grand Véfour
Jules Verne
Lapérouse
Lasserre
Laurent
Maxim's
Pavillon Ledoyen
Pré Catelan
Procope
Relais Louis XIII
Tour d'Argent
Train Bleu

OUTDOORS

Absinthe
Arc
Avenue
Café Lenôtre
Chez Gégène
Closerie des Lilas
Epicure (Le Bristol)
Grande Cascade
Jardins de Bagatelle
Laurent
Maison de l'Amér. Latine
Méditerranée
Pavillon du Lac
Pavillon Montsouris
Petite Cour
Rest. du Palais Royal
Romantica
Rosa Bonheur
Saut du Loup
Terrasse Mirabeau

ROMANCE

Abeille
Alain Ducasse
Ambassadeurs
Ambroisie
Astrance
Caviar Kaspia
Coupe-Chou
Epicure (Le Bristol)
Grande Cascade
Grand Véfour
Guy Savoy
Joséphine/Dumonet
Jules Verne
Lapérouse
Lasserre
Meurice
Pavillon Ledoyen
Pré Catelan
Restaurant Paul
Tour d'Argent

ROOMS

Ambassadeurs
Ambroisie
Boeuf Couronné
Brass. Mollard
Brass. Printemps
Chez Jenny
Cristal Room
1728
Grand Véfour
Guy Savoy
Lapérouse
Maison Blanche
Maison Prunier
Market
Meurice
Mori Venice Bar
Oth Sombath
Pré Catelan
Senderens
Train Bleu

VIEWS

Bouquinistes
Caviar Kaspia
Cinq
Epicure (Le Bristol)
Fontaine de Mars
Fontaine Gaillon
Georges
Grande Cascade
Grand Véfour
Jules Verne
Lapérouse
Lasserre
Maison Blanche
Méditerranée
Ombres
Pavillon Ledoyen
Petite Cour
Quai
Rest. du Palais Royal
Tour d'Argent

Top Service

28 Taillevent
Epicure (Le Bristol)
Meurice
Cinq
Ambassadeurs
Guy Savoy
Grand Véfour
Pierre Gagnaire
Alain Ducasse

27 Astrance
Lasserre

26 Pré Catelan
Tour d'Argent
Florimond
Table du Lancaster
Apicius
Arpège
Ambroisie
Pramil
Michel Rostang
Hiramatsu

25 Relais Plaza
Grande Cascade
Dominique Bouchet
Laurent
Benkay
Carré des Feuillants
Caviar Kaspia
Bigarrade

24 Jules Verne
Relais Louis XIII
Septime
Atelier Joël Robuchon
Chiberta
Auguste
Divellec
Gourmand
Quinzième
Il Vino
Spring
Azabu
Chamarré Montmartre*
Grand Venise*
Lapérouse*
Pavillon Ledoyen*
Truffière*
Jamin
Guilo-Guilo
Oulette
Stella Maris

Best Buys

1. As du Fallafel
2. Higuma
3. Chartier
4. Al Taglio
5. Baron Rouge
6. Rose Bakery
7. Chieng Mai
8. Rosa Bonheur
9. Breizh Café
10. Lao Lane Xang
11. Tricotin
12. Bistrot du Peintre
13. Maharajah
14. Chez Marianne
15. Temps des Cerises
16. Bistrot des Dames
17. Domaine de Lintillac
18. Nouveau Village Tao
19. Petit Marché
20. Petit St. Benoît
21. Perraudin
22. Cave Schmidt
23. Bistrot du Passage
24. Café des Musées
25. Sale e Pepe
26. Cul de Poule
27. Coin/Gourmets
28. Table d'Eugène
29. Ebauchoir
30. Chez Prune
31. Café du Commerce
32. Lozère
33. Café Burq
34. Bistro/Deux Théâtres
35. Baratin
36. Pizza Chic
37. Trumilou
38. Boulangerie
39. Pramil
40. Foujita

OTHER GOOD VALUES

Affranchis
Albion
Atlas
Biche au Bois
Bistro du 17ème
Bistrot d'Henri
Buisson Ardent
Café Constant
Cailloux
Cantine/Tontons
Chatomat
Chez Paul
Cinq Mars
Cocottes
Couleurs/Vigne
Dans les Landes
Fines Gueules
Flore en l'Ile
Fontaines
Fourchette/Printemps
Galopin
Grille St-Germain
Hangar
Jeanne A
Lao Siam
Lescure
Lilane
Mémère Paulette
Mesturet
Pantruche
Papilles
Passage
Petit Cheval/Manège
Philou
Pré Verre
P'tit Troquet
Régalade
Régalade St-Honoré
Verre Bouteille
Vins des Pyrénées

GOOD-VALUE PRIX FIXES

Please call ahead to confirm.

DINNER (40€ & UNDER)

Absinthe 32
A et M .34
Beurre Noisette 35
Cantine/Troquet 30
Chez Cécile. 29
Chez Les Anges 35
Clocher Péreire. 35
Clos des Gourmets. 37
Fakhr el Dine. 33
Florimond 35
Fougères 36
Frenchie 34
Gourmand. 35
Hide. .22
Kei 38
Lilane 35
Maison du Jardin 27
144 Petrossian 35
Ourcine. 34
Pantruche 34
Papilles 22
Petite Sirène/Copenhague . . . 38
Petit Pontoise 35
Pramil 30
Régalade. 34
Rest. de la Tour 27
Rest. Le Pergolèse 38
Rino. .38
Shu 38
Troquet 32

LUNCH (30€ & UNDER)

Agrume 19
Ambassade/Auvergne. 30
Aromatik. 18
Auberge du 15 26
Bélisaire 24
Biche au Bois. 28
Café Constant. 16
Chamarré Montmartre 29
Chez Ly 26
Christophe 19
Ecailler du Bistrot 18
Fables/Fontaine 30
Fish La Boissonnerie. 27
Foujita 14
Gaigne. 18
Grand Pan 29
Hide. .20
Kai. 25
KGB. .27
Liza 21
Lyonnais 30
Moissonnier. 24
Moulin à Vent. 25
Ostéria 20
Ourcine. 26
Père Claude 29
Petites Sorcières 20
Philou 25
Septime 21
Timbre 22
Truffière 28
Vaudeville. 26
Yam'Tcha 30
Ze Kitchen Galerie. 27

RESTAURANT DIRECTORY

	FOOD	DECOR	SERVICE	COST

NEW Abeille (L') *Haute Cuisine* 23 | 21 | 21 | €96

16e | Shangri-La Hotel | 10, av d'Iéna (Iéna) | 01-53-67-19-90 | www.shangri-la.com

A buzz-worthy addition to the Haute Cuisine scene, this gastronomic table at the new Shangri-La Hotel in the 16th showcases chef Philippe Labbé's "refined" cuisine; a "superb" Pierre-Yves Rochon-designed room with bold-yellow accents ('*abeille*' means 'bee', a Napoleonic symbol and a wink to the building's first owner, Bonaparte's grandnephew), along with professional service and "elevated prices" complete the picture.

Absinthe (L') [S] *Bistro* 21 | 20 | 20 | €52

1er | 24, pl du Marché St-Honoré (Pyramides/Tuileries) | 01-49-26-90-04 | www.michelrostang.com

Fashionable masses take shopping breaks for "good-value" "traditional" bistro fare with "spots of trendiness" at Caroline Rostang's "well-run" refueling station facing the Marché Saint-Honoré; the loftlike interior has plenty of "warm ambiance", but "sit outside" on the "agreeable terrace" for "good people-watching."

Accolade (L') [S] [M] *Bistro* 20 | 20 | 20 | €42

17e | 23, rue Guillaume Tell (Pereire) | 01-42-67-12-67 | www.laccolade.com

"Evolved bistro cooking" via a "varied", midpriced menu that "follows the seasons" awaits at this husband-and-wife-run spot at the far edge of the 17th; the "bare-bones" setup is "a little tight" and "noisy", but "charming" nonetheless, thanks in part to the "pleasant" staff; P.S. the prix fixe is a "great value."

A et M, Restaurant [M] *Classic French* 21 | 19 | 20 | €50

16e | 136, bd Murat (Porte de St-Cloud) | 01-45-27-39-60 | www.am-restaurant.com

A rare "great buy" in the 16th, this "neighborhood" bistro (a sibling of Apicius) is considered "an exceptional value" for its "imaginative cooking within the classic repertoire"; a "charming" staff warms up the sleek, simple interior, and there's also sidewalk seating.

Afaria [S] [M] *Basque/New French* 23 | 17 | 18 | €45

15e | 15, rue Desnouettes (Convention) | 01-48-56-15-36

"Inventive" Basque-Southwest "*cuisine de terroir*" (think Bayonne ham, boudin noir, tapas) keeps Julien Duboué's rustic-chic "neobistro" in the 15th "filled with locals" who "return regularly" on account of "reasonable" prices that add up to "one of the better values in Paris"; if "the rest is no miracle", the staff is "friendly" enough and there's a "buzzy bar area."

NEW Affable (L') [S] [M] *Bistro* - | - | - | E

7e | 10, rue de St-Simon (Rue du Bac/Solférino) | 01-42-22-01-60 | www.laffable.fr

You'll rub (cashmere) shoulders with the Left Bank power elite in the ruby-red banquettes of this chic new bistro, where of-the-moment touches – foamy sauces, exotic spices – inflect the otherwise classic

FOOD | DECOR | SERVICE | COST

Gallic fare by a former Apicius chef; it's all *très* 7th arrondissement, including the price, though the lunch prix fixe is affable enough.

NEW Affranchis (Les) Ⓢ Ⓜ *Bistro* | - | - | - | M

9e | 5, rue Henri Monnier (St-Georges) | 01-45-26-26-30 | www.restaurantlesaffranchis.fr

Fab flea-market finds fill this old-meets-new neighborhood bistro that recently debuted near Pigalle, where classics like terrine de campagne, calf's liver and coddled eggs get a contemporary, large-white-plate makeover; savvy locals like that the prices are reasonable, if not entirely retro.

Affriolé (L') Ⓢ Ⓜ *Bistro* | 23 | 17 | 21 | €46

7e | 17, rue Malar (Invalides/La Tour-Maubourg) | 01-44-18-31-33

The "creative cuisine" is "always different and always good" at this "animated" bistro in the 7th, whose moderate prices make it an "excellent value"; the "likable" staff creates a "congenial" atmosphere in the "contemporary" space, but be forewarned: its "small size and popularity" mean booking is "a must."

Agapé (L') Ⓢ *New French* | 24 | 19 | 22 | €86

17e | 51, rue Jouffroy d'Abbans (Wagram) | 01-42-27-20-18 | www.agape-paris.fr

Laurent Lapaire (see also Agapé Substance) is the boldface name behind this table in the 17th, known for the "inventive" New French cuisine coming out of its "high-level kitchen", now overseen by chef Yohann Lemonnier; "young French couples" love the "warm" service and the "tasteful" room's subdued earth tones, even if it's "*un peu cher*" (business diners appreciate the "bargain" prix fixe lunch).

NEW Agapé Substance Ⓢ Ⓜ *New French* | 25 | 18 | 22 | €102

6e | 66, rue Mazarine (Odéon) | 01-43-29-33-83 | www.agapesubstance.com

It's "food as theater" at this "exciting", ultramodern Saint-Germain newcomer, where "brilliant" young chef David Toutain, a L'Arpège alum, wows with his "intellectual" New French cuisine, served in a series of small plates (cryptically described only by their principal ingredient) from an open kitchen that extends to one long, communal table – where you may very well "make new friends" while perusing the iPad wine list; just beware the "outrageous" prices, "rocking stools with no backs" and robotic Japanese toilet.

Agrume (L') Ⓢ Ⓜ *New French* | 24 | 16 | 21 | €51

5e | 15, rue des Fossés St-Marcel (St-Marcel) | 01-43-31-86-48

"Book way in advance" for one of the few seats in chef Franck Marchesi-Grandi's "culinary heaven" deep in the 5th, where his "remarkable, personal" New French creations and "magic act"/ "cooking lesson" in the open kitchen distract from "distressed"-minimalist digs; the chef's wife/co-owner, Karine Perrin, leads the "kindly" staff, and the (not cheap but) "unbelievable bargain" prices put this place "on every foodie's list", "judging from the mostly non-French clientele."

	FOOD	DECOR	SERVICE	COST

Aida [S][M] *Japanese* — 25 | 20 | 24 | €160

7ᵉ | 1, rue Pierre Leroux (Duroc/Vaneau) | 01-43-06-14-18 | www.aidaparis.com

"The show is magnificent" at the counter of this minimalist 20-seat Japanese jewel in the 7th, where the "tasteful omakase" menus are prepared with "first-quality ingredients" and complemented by an "impeccable" Burgundy-focused wine list; "meticulous" service further justifies the "high prices"; P.S. jackets suggested; it's dinner only, except Friday when lunch is also served.

Aimant du Sud (L') [S] *Classic French* — ▽ 21 | 19 | 21 | €42

13ᵉ | 40, bd Arago (Les Gobelins) | 01-47-07-33-57

The *terroir* of the South permeates the Classic French chalkboard menu at this "relaxed" Gobelins neighborhood spot; locals appreciate its "warm welcome" and its list of "little-known but excellent" Basque country wines, not to mention the "good price/quality ratio."

NEW Akrame [S] *New French* — 23 | 20 | 20 | €68

16ᵉ | 19, rue Lauriston (Charles de Gaulle-Etoile) | 01-40-67-11-16 | www.akrame.com

Up-and-comer Akrame Benallal applies ultramodern technique (his former bosses include Pierre Gagnaire and Ferran Adrià) to create "beautiful" dishes at his "perfectly realized" modern French table in the 16th; the sleek, black-and-white setting is "agreeable" and the service "friendly" enough, but the daily changing, no-choice tasting menus mean that the "real surprise comes from the plate" – literally; P.S. closed weekends.

[Z] Alain Ducasse au Plaza Athénée [S] *Haute Cuisine* — 28 | 27 | 28 | €195

8ᵉ | Plaza Athénée | 25, av Montaigne (Alma Marceau/ Franklin D. Roosevelt) | 01-53-67-65-00 | www.alain-ducasse.com

"If heaven is half this perfect, it's worth being good" claim those who've made the pilgrimage to Alain Ducasse's "temple of Haute Cuisine" in the Plaza Athénée, which "dazzles" diners "with course after course" of "brilliant" delectables, served by a "beyond fabulous" staff that makes surveyors feel at ease in the "beautiful, hushed" setting; it's an "over-the-top" experience that's the perfect way to celebrate "if your very wealthy aunt has just left you her fortune"; P.S. reservations and jackets (for gents) are required; closed weekends.

NEW Albion [S][M] *Wine Bar/Bistro* — - | - | - | M

10ᵉ | 80, rue du Faubourg Poissonnière (Poissonnière) | 01-42-46-02-44 | www.restaurantalbion.com

The name may be Anglo and the owners (former teammates at Fish La Boissonnerie) hail from the Commonwealth, but the midpriced menu at this new bistro/wine shop in the 10th is pure French with a soupçon of a southern accent; a Franglish crowd has quickly colonized the roomy, pewter-hued space, dressed simply with wooden-plank floors, large wine racks and a zinc bar.

	FOOD	DECOR	SERVICE	COST

Alcazar ◐ *New French* — 18 | 22 | 18 | €58

6e | 62, rue Mazarine (Odéon) | 01-53-10-19-99 | www.alcazar.fr
"Atmosphere beats food" at Brit design magnate Terence Conran's "cavernous", "Soho-like" Saint-Germain lair, a "noisy", "trendy" (maybe "too trendy") late-'90s "landmark" that still draws "lots of beautiful young people"; the New French fare is deemed "average" to "good" and the service uneven, but occasional live music and a stop at the mezzanine bar help make it worth the euros.

Al Dar ◐ *Lebanese* — 22 | 16 | 19 | €43

5e | 8, rue Frédéric Sauton (Maubert-Mutualité) | 01-43-25-17-15
16e | 93, av Raymond Poincaré (Victor Hugo) | 01-45-00-96-64
"Succulent" mezes and other "high-quality", moderately priced options await at this pair of "traditional" Lebanese tables in the 5th and 16th; service is "friendly" but can be "hurried" and the decor is rather "simple", which might be why some consider carryout to be a "better value."

Allard ◐ *Bistro* — 21 | 20 | 20 | €64

6e | 41, rue St-André-des-Arts (Odéon) | 01-43-26-48-23 | www.restaurant-allard.com
"Nothing ever changes" and that's "as it should be" at this "quaint" Saint-Germain "time warp", where "quintessential" French bistro fare ("duck with olives is why one comes here") is delivered by "competent" servers to a "bustling", often "touristy", crowd; it may be expensive and look "a little shopworn", but it's an "authentic" experience that "merits the reservation."

Allobroges (Les) [M] *Classic French* — 22 | 19 | 21 | €49

20e | 71, rue des Grands-Champs (Buzenval/Maraîchers) | 01-43-73-40-00 | www.lesallobroges.com
In the "very out-of-the-way" 20th, this relatively "affordable" Classic French spot continues to win fans with a seasonal menu of "good-quality" fare served in a "hushed", butter-toned room; all that plus a "warm" welcome make it "worth the trek" to this decidedly "non-trendy" part of town.

Al Taglio *Pizza* — 22 | 16 | 19 | €26

11e | 2 bis, rue Neuve Popincourt (Oberkampf/Parmentier) | 01-43-38-12-00
This "*très bonne*" Oberkampf pizzeria does as the Romans do, selling slices of its large, rectangular pies by weight – with over 30 choices of toppings, which change daily; it's popular with hip, young locals and families, who appreciate the "cheerful" staff and "value" tabs.

Ambassade d'Auvergne *Auvergne* — 22 | 18 | 21 | €49

3e | 22, rue du Grenier St-Lazare (Rambuteau) | 01-42-72-31-22 | www.ambassade-auvergne.com
"Go for the *aligot*" (potatoes whipped with cheese and garlic) – it's "the real thing" – and stay for the "enormous" chocolate mousse at this "old reliable" Beaubourg bistro dishing up "hearty", midpriced Auvergnat fare; a "dedicated" staff presides over a series of

"rustic" "hunting lodge"-like rooms that, if "dated", retain their "picture-postcard charm."

Ambassadeurs (Les) *Haute Cuisine* 27 | 28 | 28 | €170

8ᵉ | Hôtel de Crillon | 10, pl de la Concorde (Concorde) | 01-44-71-16-16 | www.crillon.com

"The epitome of luxurious dining" awaits at the landmark Hôtel de Crillon, where diners are regaled by young chef Christopher Hache's "sublime" Haute Cuisine and made to feel "like Louis XV" thanks to service that's "as close to being hand-fed as one can get" ("never have so many waited on so few"); one look at the "amazing vintages" on the wine list or the "gorgeous golden, mirrored" 18th-century room and it's clear that you should carry "two credit cards" - you "may need them both"; P.S. jackets suggested.

Ambroisie (L') *Haute Cuisine* 27 | 26 | 26 | €184

4ᵉ | 9, pl des Vosges (Bastille/St-Paul) | 01-42-78-51-45 | www.ambroisie-paris.com

This "grande dame" of Haute Cuisine, "discreetly situated" on the Place des Vosges, is "still one of the best", with chef-owner Bernard Pacaud offering "exquisite seasonal" dishes in an "elegant", intimate setting that evokes 17th-century France; reservations are "tough" and prices "lavish", especially for the "amazing" wines, but everyone should allow the "pampering" staff to "spoil" them rotten at least "once in a lifetime"; P.S. jacket and tie required.

Ami Louis (L') *Bistro* 24 | 16 | 19 | €108

3ᵉ | 32, rue du Vertbois (Arts et Métiers/Temple) | 01-48-87-77-48

"Legendary roast chicken", "amazing" foie gras and "gargantuan" portions keep "lots of Americans" and "famous" folk, among others, coming back to this "mythic", "pre-war" bistro in the 3rd, which may be "well worn" but is "comfortable, like a favorite pair of slippers"; service is of the "brusque Parisian" variety and reservations can be "impossible", but it's "worth" the "exorbitant" prices; P.S. closed Monday and Tuesday.

Anahi *Argentinean/Steak* 19 | 17 | 18 | €59

3ᵉ | 49, rue Volta (Arts et Métiers/Temple) | 01-48-87-88-24

"Trendy" types favor this professionally run dinner-only Argentinean steakhouse in the 3rd for late-night bites of "succulent" beef, looking past "pricey" tabs and slightly offbeat decor (think "old butcher shop"); despite the "unusual" surroundings, it's a likely place "to meet models" and other fashion types from the quarter.

Anahuacalli *Mexican* 23 | 17 | 21 | €43

5ᵉ | 30, rue des Bernardins (Maubert-Mutualité) | 01-43-26-10-20

One of the few "true Mexicans" (*ce n'est "pas du* Tex-Mex") in the capital, this "typical"-looking cantina in the Latin Quarter has a "likable" staff that dispenses "authentic" "grandmother" fare and "excellent" cocktails to a "packed" house, making "reservations obligatory, even during the week"; it's "a little expensive" for food that might be had "at home" for cheap, "but for Paris . . ."

FOOD	DECOR	SERVICE	COST

Annapurna ◐ Ⓢ *Indian* — 23 | 21 | 20 | €62

8e | 32, rue de Berri (George V/St-Philippe-du-Roule) | 01-45-63-91-62

"Marvelous smells" of "spices and more spices" clue you in to the "savory" flavors that await at this "excellent" Indian near the Champs-Elysées, one of Paris' oldest subcontinentals; some find it "expensive", but its colonial "club"-style atmosphere, "pleasant" service and "magnificent sitar player" help make amends.

Antoine ◐ *Bistro/Seafood* — 22 | 18 | 22 | €71

16e | 10, av de New York (Alma Marceau) | 01-40-70-19-28 | www.antoine-paris.fr

"Wonderful fish" dishes, a "charming" staff and "an amazing view of the Eiffel Tower" make this posh, airy Golden Triangle bistro a place to "quietly impress" on a "romantic evening"; it's "*très cher*", "but then fish is very expensive", especially when it's this "remarkably good."

AOC (L') Ⓢ Ⓜ *Bistro* — 23 | 19 | 22 | €47

5e | 14, rue des Fossés St-Bernard (Cardinal Lemoine/Jussieu) | 01-43-54-22-52 | www.restoaoc.com

A "meat-lover's heaven", this "rustic" Latin Quarter bistro transports diners to "the provinces" via its "simple", "honorable", "old-style" country cooking starring "quality" ingredients; "prices are reasonable", and the "gracious" couple that runs the place makes some feel like part of a "true French family."

Ⓩ Apicius Ⓢ *Haute Cuisine* — 27 | 25 | 26 | €149

8e | 20, rue d'Artois (George V/St-Philippe-du-Roule) | 01-43-80-19-66 | www.restaurant-apicius.com

"Maestro" Jean-Pierre Vigato achieves near-"culinary perfection" with his "sublime" Haute Cuisine accompanied by "intuitive" service at this 8th arrondissement "gem"; despite being in the middle of Paris, the setting (a former private mansion) is a "haven of peace" thanks to its "incredible" lush grounds, making it perfect for a "romantic evening" "if you have the means" - and have scored a "difficult-to-get" reservation; P.S. jacket suggested; closed weekends.

Arc (L') Ⓢ *New French* — 16 | 22 | 18 | €82

16e | 12, rue de Presbourg (Charles de Gaulle-Etoile) | 01-45-00-78-70 | www.larc-paris.com

A "hip" crowd gathers for after-work cocktails and after-hours clubbing in the '70s-style lounge and sprawling garden areas of this "grandiose" multitasking mansion in the 16th, while business-lunchers appreciate that it's "ideally located for meetings", with "efficient" service; the weak link is the contemporary French cooking, seemingly priced for "Russian millionaires", though it's hard to argue with the "magnificent view" of the Arc de Triomphe.

Ardoise (L') Ⓜ *Bistro* — 23 | 16 | 20 | €48

1er | 28, rue du Mont-Thabor (Concorde/Tuileries) | 01-42-96-28-18 | www.lardoise-paris.com

"Well located" next to the Tuileries, this "little box of a room" turns out "big, rich" bistro favorites that are deemed a "great value" for the "high-priced neighborhood"; "tourists abound" and the decor is rather "plain", but service is "charming" and being "open on Sunday is a huge plus."

Aromatik (L') *New French* ∇ 18 | 19 | 19 | €41

9e | 7, rue Jean-Baptiste Pigalle (Trinité) | 01-48-74-62-27 | www.laromatik.com

The "agreeable" art deco dining room is "retro" in style, but the cooking is contemporary at this New French below Pigalle, where divergent global influences meet with "original", if sometimes "uneven", results; still, prices are moderate, the welcome is "warm" and it was a former hang of Josephine Baker.

Z Arpège (L') S *Haute Cuisine* 27 | 23 | 26 | €192

7e | 84, rue de Varenne (Varenne) | 01-47-05-09-06 | www.alain-passard.com

"Vegetable lovers make the pilgrimage" to this posh corner of the 7th to sample the "pristine" Haute Cuisine of chef-owner Alain Passard, whose "creativity" with "pure", "from-the-garden" produce shows how simple ingredients "can be elevated" to the "realm of art"; the "understated elegant" decor received a recent upgrade (so might your credit limit given "exorbitantly expensive" tabs), but the "impeccable" service and "formidable" wine list are fine as is; P.S. closed weekends; reservations required.

Z As du Fallafel (L') ◐ *Israeli* 23 | 8 | 15 | €14

4e | 34, rue des Rosiers (St-Paul) | 01-48-87-63-60

"Nothing compares" to the "craveable", "messy" falafel sandwiches at this Marais "institution", served by a "ruthlessly efficient" staff and best eaten on the "street" rather than in the "spartan" interior; although they can seem "endless", the "lines are there for a reason" - it's the No. 1 deal in Paris; P.S. it closes Friday at sundown, reopening Sunday.

Assaggio (L') *Italian* ∇ 22 | 21 | 22 | €56

1er | Hôtel Castille | 33, rue Cambon (Concorde/Madeleine) | 01-44-58-45-67 | www.castille.com

A "petite oasis from the hustle of the city" in the Castille Hôtel, this luxe Italian pleases a "lovely" crowd that doesn't mind spending a pretty penny on pasta (housemade, *naturalmente*) and other "fine" fare served by a "helpful" staff; in warm weather, the frescoed garden is pure Florentine elegance.

Assiette (L') M *Bistro/Southwest* 19 | 17 | 20 | €56

14e | 181, rue du Château (Gaîté/Mouton-Duvernet) | 01-43-22-64-86 | www.restaurant-lassiette.com

"Thoughtful", "traditional cuisine" - from cassoulet and quenelles to "deadly" desserts - graces the plates at this "unpretentious" Southwestern bistro in Montparnasse; tabs can be "more expensive than one imagines", but old-fashioned decor and "gracious" hosts contribute to an overall "comfortable", "relaxed" experience; P.S. closed Monday and Tuesday.

	FOOD	DECOR	SERVICE	COST

Astier *Bistro* 21 | 17 | 20 | €44

11e | 44, rue Jean-Pierre Timbaud (Oberkampf/Parmentier) | 01-43-57-16-35 | www.restaurant-astier.com

"If you're a cheese lover, this is what heaven tastes like" say fromage fanatics who visit this "out-of-the-way" Oberkampf stalwart from Frédéric Hubig (Café Le Moderne) not so much for its "solid", mid-priced bistro fare as for the "extraordinary" meal-ending cheese platter; "warm" service and a "movie-set" Parisian ambiance (think "checked tablecloths") make up for being packed "too close together"; P.S. Hubig's Jeanne A and Sassotondo are right next door.

Astor (L') ⊠ *Classic French* 24 | 20 | 22 | €88

8e | Hôtel Astor | 11, rue d'Astorg (St-Augustin) | 01-53-05-05-20 | www.hotel-astor.net

"Very correct" Classic French cuisine, updated by an infusion of global flavors at the hands of chef Nicolas Clavier, distinguishes this "elegant and refined" 1930s-style hotel table in the 8th; the quarter's business crowd shrugs off the expensive prices and finds special appeal in drinks at the attached bar; P.S. jacket suggested.

Z Astrance (L') ⊠ M *Haute Cuisine* 28 | 23 | 27 | €210

16e | 4, rue Beethoven (Passy) | 01-40-50-84-40

In the 16th, chef Pascal Barbot's "modern, elegant" Haute Cuisine reaches the "pinnacle of grace" in his "incredibly imagined and prepared" plates "accompanied perfectly" by "well-chosen wines"; the tasting menu (no à la carte) is "frightfully expensive" and the "smallish" dining room, which features "almost-private" balcony seating, is "not as grand" as some might prefer, but the chef's "genius" combined with "faultless" service make for "a miracle of perfection" – though the real miracle might be scoring an "impossible reservation"; P.S. closed Saturday-Monday; reservations and jackets required.

NEW Atao M *Brittany/Seafood* - | - | - | E

17e | 86, rue Lemercier (Brochant/La Fourche) | 01-46-27-81-12

A former fashion designer from an oyster-farming family reclaims her heritage, bringing beautiful Breton seafood (raw and cooked) to the table at this airy, blue-and-white Batignolles arrival, where you might start with bivalves and finish with a buttery crêpe, all served with filial pride; it's not cheap, but still less than a round-trip TGV ticket to Brest.

Z Atelier de Joël Robuchon (L') ● *Haute Cuisine* 27 | 23 | 24 | €116

7e | Hôtel Pont Royal | 5, rue de Montalembert (Rue du Bac) | 01-42-22-56-56

8e | Publicis Drugstore | 133, av des Champs-Elysées (Charles de Gaulle-Etoile/George V) | 01-47-23-75-75

www.joel-robuchon.net

"Each course is more taste-bud-popping than the previous" at Joël Robuchon's "casually chic" Saint-Germain and Etoile duo (Paris' Most Popular dining destinations) known for offering "the best counter dining on the planet" – patrons perch on stools "observing the kitchen" while savoring "artful" Haute Cuisine enhanced by "perfectly paired" wines and "informative" service; both branches are "sleek", "modern" and "hip" ("there are even some tables" in the 8th), and while tabs are steep, the setup delivers a "great show" as well as a "superb" meal; P.S. no reservations at peak times.

Atelier Maître Albert (L') ◐ *Bistro* 23 | 23 | 23 | €63

5e | 1, rue Maître-Albert (Maubert-Mutualité) | 01-56-81-30-01 | www.ateliermaitrealbert.com

"Don't even think of ordering anything" but the "wonderful roast chicken" at this "expensive" Guy Savoy–run rotisserie/bistro in the 5th, across from Notre Dame; the crowd is "trendy", service is "agreeable" and the exposed-stone walls combine with "contemporary" accents to "chic" yet "cozy" effect, especially "by the fireplace."

Atlas (L') M *Moroccan* 21 | 20 | 20 | €43

5e | 12, bd St-Germain (Maubert-Mutualité) | 01-46-33-86-98 | www.latlas.fr

"Terrific tagines" and "correct couscous" are on the "authentic" menu at this long-standing Latin Quarter Moroccan, which evokes its homeland with a "pretty" setting fit with elaborately carved white walls that are more Fez than 5th arrondissement; an "efficient" staff, "reasonable" prices and sidewalk tables with a view of the busy boulevard are added appeals that make booking ahead a must; P.S. Tuesday is dinner only.

Auberge Bressane (L') *Classic French* 22 | 18 | 21 | €57

7e | 16, av de la Motte-Piquet (Ecole Militaire/La Tour-Maubourg) | 01-47-05-98-37 | www.auberge-bressane.fr

"Copious" quantities of "invigorating", "hearty" classic fare – including many specialties from Lyon and Burgundy that are "often hard to find in Paris", like the "exceptional" soufflé au fromage – really hit the spot ("especially in winter") at this pricey place near Invalides; the 1950s/Gothic château-style decor is "equally as old-fashioned" as the service, both of which "satisfy those who are nostalgic for an age they never knew"; P.S. reservations are "a must."

Auberge Dab (L') ◐ *Brasserie* 20 | 20 | 19 | €57

16e | 161, av de Malakoff (Porte Maillot) | 01-45-00-32-22 | www.rest-gj.com

"The absence of surprise" is "an art" at this "immutable" "institution" near Porte Maillot in the 16th – from the "typical" brasserie look (leather banquettes, wood paneling) to the "traditional", rather "expensive", menu that includes standout seafood; "quality" service also appeals to the "upscale", "beautiful" and sometimes "famous" diners who flock here, making "reservations absolutely necessary."

Auberge du Champ de Mars *Classic French* 23 | 21 | 22 | €57

7e | 18, rue de l'Exposition (Ecole Militaire) | 01-45-51-78-08 | www.aubergeduchampdemars.fr

"Frequented by knowing locals", this well-run svelte storefront in the 7th (near the Eiffel Tower, no less) serves "traditional food" "with a flair" in a handsome setting that "harks back to days gone by"; prices have spiked, but rising scores in all areas give credence to early champions of chef Philippe Excoffier and his wife, Michèle, whom they say have given the place "new life."

Auberge Nicolas Flamel *Classic French* 21 | 23 | 20 | €52

3e | 51, rue de Montmorency (Arts et Métiers/Rambuteau) | 01-42-71-77-78 | www.auberge-nicolas-flamel.fr

Set in the oldest house in Paris (it "existed before Columbus arrived in America"), this "magical" Beaubourg table transports diners to the early 15th century for a "charming", "candlelit" evening amid exposed beams and stone walls; the moderately priced Classic French dishes are "well prepared" and service is equally solid, but it's worth booking a table mainly "to share in the historical experience."

Auberge Pyrénées Cévennes (L') [S] *Lyon/Southwest* 24 | 18 | 22 | €48

11e | 106, rue de la Folie-Méricourt (République) | 01-43-57-33-78

"Big appetites" give big applause to what may be the "best" cassoulet in Paris at this Southwestern-Lyonnais specialist known for "large portions" and "outstanding value" that lure followers to the "out-of-the-way" Oberkampf; those who make the trek feel like they're "walking into a country home" on account of the "hunting-lodge" decor and "warmhearted", "personal" service.

NEW **Auberge du 15 (L')** [S] [M] *Classic French* 24 | 19 | 22 | €48

13e | 15, rue de la Santé (Port-Royal) | 01-47-07-07-45 | www.laubergedu15.com

What a "pleasant surprise" say surveyors who've checked into this "promising" new Classic French spot in the 13th arrondissement; the updated "home cooking" is *très bon* and available at an old-fashioned price, while the retro country inn digs (wood paneling, stone walls, patterned drapes) are "nice" and "calm."

Auguste [S] *Classic French* 24 | 20 | 24 | €95

7e | 54, rue de Bourgogne (Varenne) | 01-45-51-61-09 | www.restaurantauguste.fr

Chef Gaël Orieux's "passion is abundantly apparent" in his "inventive" takes on French classics and "meticulously prepared" seafood, much of it sustainable, offered at this elegant table in the 7th; the sleek, red-and-white space is "intimate", and service "irreproachable", making for "a real find" that's "pricey" but "still within reach", particularly the prix fixe lunch; closed weekends.

Avant Goût (L') [S] [M] *New French* 23 | 15 | 20 | €43

13e | 26, rue Bobillot (Place d'Italie) | 01-53-80-24-00 | www.lavantgout.com

Chef Christophe Beaufront's "innovative" French dishes – including the signature pot-au-feu de cochon – have garnered a loyal fan base for this "friendly" "hangout" in Butte-aux-Cailles, helped further by an "excellent price/quality ratio"; the room may be "charmless" but it's "nicely untouristed" and therefore "often full" of "locals" (hint:

FOOD | DECOR | SERVICE | COST

"reserve, or else!"); P.S. across the street is its on-the-go sibling, Avant-Goût Côté Cellie, a prepared-foods and wine shop.

Avenue (L') ◐ *New French* 16 | 20 | 15 | €63

8e | 41, av Montaigne (Franklin D. Roosevelt) | 01-40-70-14-91 | www.avenue-restaurant.com

"Grab a table outside" and "watch the charming creatures" saunter by this all-day-and-late-night Golden Triangle mainstay, a high-design canteen for "couture customers" for whom "see and be seen is the motto" (even the "haughty" servers "take your breath away, they're so pretty"); the "average", "international"-tinged contempo French fare includes "choices good when dieting", though the "prohibitive" prices will make your wallet leaner too; P.S. reservations are advised.

Azabu Ⓜ *Japanese* 24 | 17 | 24 | €51

6e | 3, rue André Mazet (Odéon) | 01-46-33-72-05

Japanese teppanyaki – "as superb as it is inventive" – awaits at this "little" midpriced "gem" near Odéon, along with "exemplary" service in a "minimalist" setting; devotees say "you must eat at the counter" so you can watch the grill cook in action (even if it means that "your clothes might remember certain plates" too) and recommend washing everything down with one of the "*très bons* sakes" on offer.

Bacchantes (Les) ◐ ⊠ *Wine Bar/Bistro* 21 | 17 | 21 | €46

9e | 21, rue de Caumartin (Havre-Caumartin/Opéra) | 01-42-65-25-35 | www.lesbacchantes.fr

"Well-prepared" French classics (with a "special mention for beef" dishes) are served forth by "smiling" waiters at this "reasonably priced" wine bar/bistro in the 9th; diners are seated "almost on top of each other" in the narrow, "noisy", simply dressed space, but proximity to the Opéra Garnier, late-night hours and a large selection of wines by the glass team up to make it a popular post-show tipple.

Ballon des Ternes (Le) ◐ *Brasserie* 19 | 18 | 19 | €58

17e | 103, av des Ternes (Porte Maillot) | 01-45-74-17-98 | www.leballondesternes.fr

A "consistent standard", this Porte Maillot brasserie offers "copious" amounts of "sincere" fare, including "wonderful" seafood (it's known for shellfish), in an "authentic" "belle epoque" dining room; if it's "a little expensive for the quality", the "attentive", "expeditious" service combined with a location near the convention center make it a "practical" choice for business dining.

Ballon et Coquillages ◐ *Seafood* - | - | - | M

17e | 71, bd Gouvion-St-Cyr (Porte Maillot) | 01-45-74-17-98

With just 14 stools ringing a circular bar, this "convivial" seafood spot in the 17th (an annex of Le Ballon des Ternes) makes it easy for newcomers to make friends with "regulars"; its seaside shack-chic look pairs perfectly with the Utah Beach oysters, langoustines and other sparkling specimens from the midpriced *fruits de mer* platters on offer; P.S. no reservations.

	FOOD	DECOR	SERVICE	COST
Bar à Huîtres (Le) ◐ *Seafood*	21	19	19	€52

3e | 33, bd Beaumarchais (Bastille) | 01-48-87-98-92
5e | 33, rue St-Jacques (Cluny La Sorbonne) | 01-44-07-27-37
14e | 112, bd du Montparnasse (Raspail/Vavin) | 01-43-20-71-01
17e | 69, av de Wagram (Ternes) | 01-43-80-63-54
www.lebarahuitres.fr

When you "just want oysters, a bit of bread and a good wine", "any of these superb" addresses in this "consistent chain" of seafood specialists provides "good-quality" *fruits de mer,* "beautifully served" in glittering, aquariumlike digs; prices are middling, service is "friendly" and "the iPad menus are a cute touch."

Baratin (Le) ◐ *Wine Bar/Bistro* 24 | 17 | 21 | €40

20e | 3, rue Jouye-Rouve (Belleville) | 01-43-49-39-70

"Wonderful" "home cooking" at an "awesome price", along with an "audacious selection of natural wines", is on the menu at chef Raquel Carena's "unpretentious" Belleville *bistrot à vins;* the setup is "simple" and "intimate" ("expect to make new friends at the next table" - perhaps some of the top toques who hang out here), and service is generally "friendly"; P.S. reservations are "indispensable", by the way.

Bar des Théâtres ◐ *Bistro* 17 | 16 | 18 | €41

8e | 44, rue Jean Goujon (Alma Marceau) | 01-47-23-34-63

Though still known for its "delightful" steak tartare, a standout on the otherwise "reliable" midpriced bistro menu, this gathering spot in the 8th strikes some as "a shadow of its former self" since part of its space was "amputated" (the former main dining room and entrance on the Avenue Montaigne, across from the Théâtre des Champs-Elysées); yet if nostalgists are content to "cherish the memories", supporters say it's still "perfectly suited" for a "quick dinner" before or after a show - after all, the current entrance *is* just around the corner.

Baron Rouge (Le) Ⓜ *Wine Bar/Bistro* 18 | 20 | 21 | €28

12e | 1, rue Théophile Roussel (Ledru-Rollin) | 01-43-43-14-32

"Arrive early if you want a place to sit" (no reserving) or stand around one of the crates or "barrels that serve as tables" at this "hopping post-work meeting place" near the Marché d'Aligre that's "friendly" "even when packed"; "wine definitely comes first", but it's also "super" for an affordable "plate of cheese or charcuterie among friends" and, in season, "fresh oysters" with the crowd spilling out "on the sidewalk."

Bartolo ◐ Ⓜ ⊄ *Pizza* 20 | 14 | 15 | €43

6e | 7, rue des Canettes (St-Germain-des-Prés) | 01-43-26-27-08

This Saint-Germain Italian may serve some of "the best pizzas in Paris" - hot from a wood-burning oven - but it requires "patience" to deal with the sometimes "surly" staff and a cash-only policy that's surprising for such a relatively "expensive" place; on warm days, skip the very "Neapolitan", 1950s-vintage dining room and take a seat on the "little terrace."

	FOOD	DECOR	SERVICE	COST

Bascou (Au) ☒ *Basque* 23 | 17 | 21 | €44

3e | 38, rue Réaumur (Arts et Métiers) | 01-42-72-69-25 | www.au-bascou.fr

The name is simple and straightforward, but the regional cooking is "imaginative" and "generous" at this "excellent" Basque enclave in the 3rd; middling prices, unfussy bistro decor and very good service put diners at ease, encouraging them to "arrive early and leave late"; closed weekends.

Bastide Odéon (La) *Provence* 20 | 17 | 18 | €56

6e | 7, rue Corneille (Odéon) | 01-43-26-03-65 | www.bastide-odeon.com

Under new direction since early 2011, this "comfortable" standby near the Luxembourg Gardens remains "skilled in the language" of Provence, and its "eggplant, olives and seafood" still "transport" diners to the South of France; it's so "popular", particularly with "tourists", that booking is essential, but locals needn't fear: the "assiduous" staff tends "to separate Francophones and Anglophones", dividing them among the different "simple", "sunny"-hued rooms.

Beaujolais d'Auteuil (Le) *Classic French* 19 | 17 | 19 | €44

16e | 99, bd de Montmorency (Porte d'Auteuil) | 01-47-43-03-56 | www.beaujolaisdauteuil16.com

"Solid, hearty meals" built of French classics are the foundation of this "unpretentious" "neighborhood" bistro in the 16th that pleases regulars with "efficient", "welcoming" ("even with kids!") service and "affordable" prices; the "typical" 1930s "bistro" decor is well preserved, notably the tiled floor, though the sidewalk terrace is perhaps a more "interesting" perch in the summer.

NEW Bélisaire (Le) ☒ *Bistro* ▽ 23 | 17 | 22 | €46

15e | 2, rue Marmontel (Convention/Vaugirard) | 01-48-28-62-24 | www.lebelisaire.free.fr

"Everything is perfect in this little corner of the 15th" say early adopters of this fledgling bistro and its "superbly" prepared "traditional" fare that's right at home in the old-fashioned, '30s-style setting; the "small" digs are "crowded, but that's only proof of the value", and for what it's worth, there's "not an American to be found" – for now.

Bellini *Italian* ▽ 21 | 19 | 21 | €61

16e | 28, rue Le Sueur (Argentine) | 01-45-00-54-20 | www.restaurantbellini.com

For a "change of pace", diners dive into the "quality comfort food" at this Italian in the 16th, where the wines come from the other side of the Alps, but the signature pasta and cheese flambéed with cognac, has a decidedly French accent; it's not cheap, but service is "friendly" and the atmosphere "charming."

Benkay *Japanese* 25 | 21 | 25 | €99

15e | Hôtel Novotel Tour Eiffel | 61, quai de Grenelle (Bir-Hakeim/Charles Michels) | 01-40-58-21-26 | www.restaurant-benkay.com

True "happiness is the sashimi" at this "exceptional" hotel Japanese in the 15th (the teppanyaki is "amazing" too), though opinion splits on the '70s-style decor: "*très* chic" vs. "a little passé"; still, the kitchen's "culinary refinement" combined with "impeccable service" and a "wonderful view" of the Seine from some tables make it a natural, if "expensive", choice "for business dinners" or "to celebrate a special event"; P.S. reservations required.

Benoît *Lyon* — 23 | 22 | 21 | €82

4e | 20, rue St-Martin (Châtelet/Hôtel de Ville) | 01-42-72-25-76 | www.benoit-paris.com

A "veritable icon", this century-old address in the 4th that was "revived" by Alain Ducasse several years ago is "still one of the most dependable" for "high-class bistro" fare with a Lyonnais bent served by a "professional" crew; "luxury" tabs leave some fuming, and non-natives balk at being exiled to the "foreigners' ghetto" of the back room, but the "classic" brass-trimmed decor is picture-perfect everywhere.

Beurre Noisette (Le) *Bistro* — 25 | 16 | 22 | €46

15e | 68, rue Vasco de Gama (Lourmel/Porte de Versailles) | 01-48-56-82-49 | www.lebeurrenoisette.com

Gourmets "in the know" rave it's "worth the trip" to chef-owner Thierry Blanqui's "neighborhood jewel" of a bistro "deep" in the 15th for a menu that's "full of imagination" (and "reasonable" prices too); tight but "homey" quarters and service that comes with a "smile" contribute to the "buzzing", "convivial" atmosphere, especially around the communal table.

Biche au Bois (A la) *Bistro* — 22 | 15 | 21 | €41

12e | 45, av Ledru-Rollin (Gare de Lyon) | 01-43-43-34-38

"If you like wild game" in season, "run immediately" (with a reservation) to this traditional "neighborhood" bistro near Gare de Lyon for "copious portions" of "old-fashioned" cooking, seasoned with a "warm welcome" and served at "value" prices - especially the prix fixe; seating is "a little tight in the "small", "rustic" room, but "that facilitates the conviviality"; closed weekends.

Bien Décidé (Le) *Wine Bar/Bistro* — - | - | - | M

6e | 117, rue du Cherche Midi (Duroc/Falguière) | 01-45-48-39-28

There's little to decide at this bare-bones bistro and wine bar in the less traveled part of the 6th, owned by actor (and winemaker) Gérard Depardieu, where "the menu is short" but portions of the simple, midpriced fare are "generous" and served by a "pleasant" staff in the "tiny" green-and-pink space; it's a retail shop too, if you're looking to take a bottle home; P.S. closed weekends.

Bigarrade (La) *New French* — 27 | 19 | 25 | €99

17e | 106, rue Nollet (Brochant) | 01-42-26-01-02

"Wow!" says the stylish set that has eaten its way through the "creative, incisive" New French tasting menus at what some call "one of the most exciting kitchens of Paris" (indeed, it's an open kitchen) at this mod white-and-lime-green storefront in the 17th; "well-synchronized" service caps the "pleasurable" experience, leading fans to declare it "worth" the high prices; P.S. at press time, a chef change was reportedly in the works; closed Saturday–Monday.

NEW Big Fernand Ⓢ *Burgers* | - | - | - | I

9e | 55, rue du Faubourg-Poissonnière (Cadet/Poissonnière) | 01-47-70-54-72 | www.bigfernand.com

Freshness rules at this new burger joint in the 9th, where you can order from the menu or build your own from a bevy of meats (beef, chicken, lamb), cheeses and gourmet garnishes - yes, you want fries with that - and wash it all down with an organic soda; eat in the narrow, bare-bones-chic space (stone walls, bare bulbs) and watch the plaid-shirted, mustachioed types fry and flip behind the long counter, or take it to go.

Bistral (Le) Ⓢ Ⓜ *Bistro* | 22 | 17 | 21 | €50

17e | 80, rue Lemercier (Brochant) | 01-42-63-59-61 | www.lebistral.com

"When it's good it's very good" say fans of this "friendly" Batignolles "sleeper", a contemporary kitchen offering an ever-changing slate of "upscale" bistro fare at moderate prices; cellarlike stone walls wrap the "petite" space, a nod to the "incredible" list of organic wines.

Bistro au Vieux Chêne Ⓢ *Bistro* | 23 | 16 | 19 | €48

11e | 7, rue du Dahomey (Faidherbe-Chaligny) | 01-43-71-67-69 | www.vieuxchene.fr

You might "wish that all neighborhoods had" a bistro like this after a trip to the 11th for the "simple" but "lovely", product-driven fare at this "cute" time capsule ("that zinc bar!"); all in all, it's a "solid value" with a "friendly" vibe that's conducive to "everyday good feelings"; P.S. closed weekends.

Bistro 121 *Bistro* | 22 | 17 | 21 | €57

15e | 121, rue de la Convention (Boucicaut) | 01-45-57-52-90 | www.bistro121.fr

The "original" French cooking is "well realized" at this contemporary bistro in the 15th that sports a mod white-and-gray look enlivened with bold splashes of color; a "friendly" staff and "fair prices" further please neighborhood denizens, who find it a "sure value."

Bistro de Breteuil (Le) *Bistro* | 18 | 18 | 19 | €43

7e | 3, pl de Breteuil (Duroc) | 01-45-67-07-27 | www.bistrocie.fr

There's only "one price" on the all-inclusive menu, but a "large choice" of dishes guarantees that there's "something for everybody" at this "reliable" classic bistro in the 7th that's trimmed in plush red velvet and golden-hued accents; it's "among the best deals in Paris" say the "locals" who favor it - and who know to "eat outside in summer" on the "pretty" terrace; P.S. it's "always busy", so make reservations.

Bistro des Deux Théâtres (Le) ◐ *Bistro* | 21 | 20 | 21 | €40

9e | 18, rue Blanche (Trinité) | 01-45-26-41-43 | www.bistrocie.fr

Diners like the "varied menu" of "classic products" at this "convivial" bistro in the 9th, part of a restaurant group that runs on an "excellent-value" one-price-fits-all system, drinks included; antique posters and other stage memorabilia will please "show lovers" as will the location and late-night hours, plus the "attentive" staff makes a first-timer feel "like a regular" among the "always interesting" Right Bank crowd.

NEW Bistro des Gastronomes (Le) *Bistro* ▽ 23 | 22 | 22 | €50

5e | 10, rue Cardinal Lemoine (Cardinal Lemoine/Jussieu) | 01-43-54-62-40 | www.bistrodesgastronomes.com

"This is the real deal" gush fans of this "wonderful" new bistro in the 5th, where the chef-owner brings his former experience at Bistro Volnay to bear on a midpriced menu of updated classics; the "friendly" staff wins points too, though devotees would prefer to keep it a secret, since it's "hard enough" to get a seat in the simple, blond-wood-paneled environs.

Bistro du 17ème (Le) *Bistro* 19 | 18 | 18 | €42

17e | 108, av de Villiers (Pereire) | 01-47-63-32-77 | www.bistrocie.fr

Locals like the "accessible", reliably "correct" cooking at this "friendly" bistro in the 17th - part of a chain - where the "complete and efficient", moderately priced formula includes an "interesting" choice of wines; the mirrored, faux-luxe rooms strike some as "cold", but as long as you "don't go expecting gastronomy" it adds up to an "unbeatable" deal.

NEW Bistronomes (Les) S *Bistro* - | - | - | E

1er | 34, rue de Richelieu (Palais Royal-Musée du Louvre/Pyramides) | 01-42-60-59-66 | www.lesbistronomes.fr

A "contemporary yet classically based" chef, who has cooked under Eric Frechon and Michel Rostang, crafts a "routinely changing" menu at this "wonderful" but pricey new bistro tucked next to the Palais-Royal; the brown-and-taupe space is "cozy" and "low-key", but service is plenty professional thanks to a maître d' with the Ritz and Crillon on his résumé.

Bistro Poulbot S M *Bistro* ▽ 23 | 18 | 18 | €42

18e | 39, rue Lamarck (Lamarck-Caulaincourt) | 01-46-06-86-00 | www.bistropoulbot.com

After a revamp, the classic cooking at this Montmartre bistro now carries an Italian accent (possibly outdating the Food score), courtesy of a new chef-owner whose menu might feature a terrine de campagne next to a zucchini carpaccio; prints by illustrator Francisque Poulbot still hang in the "cozy" old-fashioned space, and service remains as down to earth as the prices, making it "stand out" in a quarter dominated by "tourist traps."

Bistro St. Ferdinand ◐ *Bistro* 19 | 18 | 18 | €42

17e | 275, bd Pereire (Porte Maillot) | 01-45-74-33-32 | www.bistrocie.fr

Like its siblings in the Bistro & Cie chain, this bistro in the 17th offers a "well-thought-out" all-inclusive formula that diners routinely cite for its "excellent price-to-quality ratio"; "efficient" service and its Palais des Congrès location make it a "good" choice for conducting "business", while its wide-ranging seating options - "flashy" main dining room, cozy library, glassed-in winter garden, outdoor terrace – cover every occasion.

Bistrot à Vins Mélac ⊠ *Wine Bar/Bistro* 18 | 19 | 19 | €41

11e | 42, rue Léon Frot (Charonne) | 01-43-70-59-27 | www.melac.fr

"The best mustache in Paris" – attached to its "delightful" owner, Jacques Mélac – greets all comers to his 11th-arrondissement *bistrot à vins,* known for dishes that are steeped in the "terroir" of the Auvergne and offered at "populist" prices; the "friendly" staff is happy to ply oenophiles with wine from the Languedoc, and if the "rustic" interior is "nothing fancy" it's still an "authentic" slice of "Vieux Paris."

Bistrot d'à Côté La Boutarde *Bistro* 21 | 17 | 20 | €52

Neuilly-sur-Seine | 4, rue Boutard (Pont-de-Neuilly) | 01-47-45-34-55 | www.michelrostang.com

Michel Rostang is behind this "pleasant", "friendly" bistro in Neuilly, which offers daily rotisserie specials on its "traditional" menu; seating may be "tight" in the wood-paneled room decorated with an assortment of antique coffee grinders, but that allows for good "eavesdropping", especially during lunch, which draws "advertising people" and other biz types who like the good-deal prix fixe menu.

Bistrot d'à Côté Flaubert *Bistro* 21 | 18 | 19 | €61

17e | 10, rue Gustave Flaubert (Pereire/Ternes) | 01-42-67-05-81 | www.bistrotflaubert.com

A "warm welcome" greets arrivals at this "cozy little hideaway" in the 17th, offering a Lyon-leaning bistro menu "of old-fashioned quality"; the setting, featuring a collection of whimsically decorative *barbotines* (ceramic mugs) lining the pumpkin-hued walls, is "charming", and if tabs are pricey, it's still "Michel Rostang food at a fraction of the price" of his flagship around the corner.

Bistrot d'André (Le) ⊠ *Bistro* 20 | 18 | 20 | €45

15e | 232, rue St-Charles (Balard) | 01-45-57-89-14 | www.lebistrotdandre.fr

Across from the Parc Citroën, and named for the iconic car company's founder, this "great little" bistro in the 15th serves both "modern" French fare and "classics" at "attractive" prices that appeal to "business"-lunchers, as does the solid service; car buffs get revved up sitting "where the workers" from the former plant used to eat and gazing at the vintage memorabilia that festoons the walls, though there are "nice outside tables" too.

Bistrot de l'Oulette ⊠ *Southwest* 22 | 15 | 20 | €47

4e | 38, rue des Tournelles (Bastille) | 01-42-71-43-33 | www.l-oulette.com

"Excellent" Southwestern cooking (e.g. a "perfect" cassoulet) is "just the right medicine" on a "winter night" in Paris say supporters of this "tiny" bistro close to the Place des Vosges; there's "not much atmosphere" in the "unassuming" room (and "every American in town" seems to be here), but service is "helpful" and the prices "[won't] break the bank."

	FOOD	DECOR	SERVICE	COST
Bistrot de Paris (Le) ◐ Ⓢ Ⓜ *Bistro*	19	19	20	€52

7ᵉ | 33, rue de Lille (Rue du Bac/St-Germain-des-Prés) | 01-42-61-16-83

"A favorite year after year" – long ago as a hangout for Left Bank literati, now as a power-lunch spot for local politicos – this "classic *bistrot*" in the 7th retains its rep for "honest", "dependable" eats at middling prices; service is "always friendly" too, but it's the "classic" belle epoque decor that keeps the tourist bloc streaming in for a "quintessential Paris" experience.

Bistrot des Dames (Le) ◐ *Bistro* — 18 | 23 | 17 | €34

17ᵉ | Hôtel El Dorado | 18, rue des Dames (Place de Clichy) | 01-45-22-13-42 | www.eldoradohotel.fr

The "enchanted garden" at this "typically Parisian"-looking Batignolles bistro provides "trendy thirtysomethings" from the quarter with a "little corner of calm greenery" amid the urban bustle; its cut-rate fare is "without great scope" but is "well prepared" and served by a "friendly" crew – all in all, it's a "perfect summer spot" as long as you "arrive early", since reservations aren't taken for the outdoor tables.

Bistrot des Vignes (Le) *Bistro* — 20 | 18 | 20 | €41

16ᵉ | 1, rue Jean Bologne (La Muette/Passy) | 01-45-27-76-64 | www.bistrotdesvignes.fr

"*Très bons*" classics like roast chicken and duck confit are on the table at this "most pleasant" bistro in the 16th, where there's "nothing unexpected except the price": the "value really shines"; a contemporary but "cozy" setting and an "excellent" staff make it quite a "serviceable" choice when shopping on the nearby Rue de Passy (especially for parents, since there's a kids' menu).

Bistrot d'Henri (Le) ◐ *Bistro* — 22 | 16 | 21 | €40

6ᵉ | 16, rue Princesse (Mabillon/St-Germain-des-Prés) | 01-46-33-51-12 | www.bistrotdhenri.com

"One of the best deals in town" is this "cute", "casual" bistro in the 6th say savvy savers who find "value" in its "down-to-earth" French "home cooking" and "warm" service; it's "cramped" sitting at the wooden tables in the leather-banquette-lined space, but the "mob scene" is proof that most feel this "teeny" place is "worth the lack of elbow room" for the equally teeny tabs.

Bistrot du Dôme (Le) Ⓜ *Seafood* — 22 | 19 | 20 | €55

14ᵉ | 1, rue Delambre (Vavin) | 01-43-35-32-00

Dôme Bastille (Le) *Seafood*

4ᵉ | 2, rue de la Bastille (Bastille) | 01-48-04-88-44

"It's hard to beat the freshness and quality" of the fish and shellfish at this pair of "old Parisian" bistros in the 4th and 14th, where the "terrific" seafood should come as no surprise, considering they're related to ("but cheaper than") legendary Le Dôme; the "efficient" crews staffing the "pleasant" rooms, which are both decorated in ocher hues and piscine-themed tilework, offer "good advice" on the day's catch, and the "wines are well selected" and "reasonably priced."

	FOOD	DECOR	SERVICE	COST

Bistrot du Passage ⊠ *Bistro* | 23 | 18 | 21 | €37

17e | 14, passage Geffroy Didelot (Villiers) | 01-43-87-28-10 | www.bistrot-du-passage.com

Given the "quality and quantity on the plate" at this contemporary French bistro on a pedestrian alley in the 17th, it's an "unbeatable value" – especially "for the neighborhood"; the modern red-white-and-black setting has few frills but is ably serviced by a "warm" staff, making it "ideal" for "groups" or a "simple meal" with a friend.

Bistrot du Peintre (Le) ◐ *Bistro* | 18 | 22 | 20 | €31

11e | 116, av Ledru-Rollin (Bastille/Ledru-Rollin) | 01-47-00-34-39 | www.bistrotdupeintre.com

"Stunning 1900s decor" wins raves at this Bastille-area bistro aswirl with "vintage" art nouveau touches, and the "basic" meat-and-potatoes menu ("tasty starters", "real" french fries) also gets kudos for its "excellent value"; a "friendly" crew sees to diners' "enjoyment", whether inside or out on a "pleasant" terrace that is only marginally "marred by noisy" traffic.

Bistrot du Sommelier ⊠ *Wine Bar/Bistro* | 22 | 18 | 24 | €78

8e | 97, bd Haussmann (St-Augustin) | 01-42-65-24-85 | www.bistrotdusommelier.com

Cork dorks love to "test their wine skills" against an "enthusiastic" staff (waiters have you "guess the wine after you drink it"), making for a "fun way" to discover new labels at star-sommelier Philippe Faure-Brac's *bistrot à vins* in the 8th; given the "simple" wine-cellar digs and fare that's "reliable" but perhaps "not memorable", detractors say the "price-quality ratio" is "not great", but viticulturists pile on for events like the "wonderful" tastings with wine-growers on Fridays; P.S. closed weekends; reservations required.

Bistrot Paul Bert (Le) ⊠ M *Bistro* | 21 | 17 | 19 | €48

11e | 18, rue Paul Bert (Faidherbe-Chaligny) | 01-43-72-24-01

"Off the beaten path" in the 11th lies this "boisterous" bistro serving a "solid", midpriced menu "with beef the star" ("best steaks in town" claim many) plus "interesting" wines; the old-school look is straight "out of central casting", as are the "brusque" waiters, adding up to "everything" one "imagined a French bistro would be."

Bistrot Vivienne ⊠ *Bistro* | 19 | 21 | 18 | €41

2e | 4, rue des Petits-Champs (Bourse/Palais Royal-Musée du Louvre) | 01-49-27-00-50 | www.galerie-vivienne.com

This "hidden" bistro tucked into the "lovely" Galerie Vivienne shopping arcade balances its "cozy" and "cute" "retro" look with "a touch of trendiness", making it "perfect for an afternoon tea"; "reasonable prices" match the "simply prepared food" and solid service; P.S. make reservations, especially for the popular lunch.

Bistro Volnay ⊠ *Bistro* | 21 | 18 | 20 | €58

2e | 8, rue Volney (Opéra) | 01-42-61-06-65 | www.bistrovolnay.fr

"Careful" market cooking (look for wild game on the menu in autumn) is on the slightly pricey menu at this bistro with "modern" art deco looks situated between the Opéra Garnier and the Madeleine; the "superb" wine list, including many by the glass, merits a mention, as does the fact that it's run - with "great professionalism" - by two women; P.S. closed weekends.

Bizan ⊠ Ⓜ *Japanese* | - | - | - | E

2e | 56, rue Ste-Anne (Quatre-Septembre) | 01-42-96-67-76 | www.isse-et-cie.fr/bizan

"Refinement and tradition reign supreme" at this "expensive" Japanese spot situated in the Little Tokyo district around the Rue Sainte-Anne, serving top-drawer sushi, rarefied bento boxes and elegant kaiseki-style dinners; the "Zen" minimalist decor (think lots of "blond wood") and "discreet" service appeal to Japanese expats and French fashion-industry types.

NEW Blend ⊠ *Burgers* | - | - | - | I

2e | 44, rue d'Argout (Etienne Marcel/Sentier) | 01-40-26-84-57 | www.blendhamburger.com

The burgers at this Sentier newcomer are made with beef from marquee meat man Yves-Marie Le Bourdonnec, topped with gourmet condiments and served on buns made by an American pastry chef; a younger crowd seems to have no trouble sliding into the wooden benches of the nifty, mod space - or paying the lean tabs.

Boeuf Couronné (Au) ◐ *Classic French* | 23 | 19 | 23 | €52

19e | 188, av Jean Jaurès (Porte de Pantin) | 01-42-39-44-44 | www.boeuf-couronne.com

"Carnivores" claim this "classic"-looking meat palace in the 19th (near the "former abattoirs of La Villette") "never disappoints" with "beautifully cooked" beef served by "professional", "old-school" waiters who will "tell you where each cut of meat comes from - even the cow's name"; tabs are "a bit expensive" but "not excessive", and regulars note "the best deal is the set menu", which includes a cocktail and half bottle of wine.

Boeuf sur le Toit (Le) ◐ *Brasserie* | 18 | 21 | 19 | €58

8e | 34, rue du Colisée (Franklin D. Roosevelt/St-Philippe-du-Roule) | 01-53-93-65-55 | www.boeufsurletoit.com

"Roaring Twenties" decor (is that "Scott" and "Zelda" at the next table?) and "enjoyable" jazz piano are the major draws at this "mythic" Flo-owned brasserie near the Champs-Elysées - though aside from a few "excellent" seafood options, the fare is strictly "no surprises"; even if the "scenery is its main asset" (it was recently freshened up, possibly outdating the Decor score), the staff is "competent" and the high prices are still a "value" for the neighborhood.

Z Bofinger ◐ *Brasserie* | 19 | 24 | 19 | €56

4e | 5-7, rue de la Bastille (Bastille) | 01-42-72-87-82 | www.bofingerparis.com

"No, you're not in an [old] MGM movie", though the decor at this circa-1864 brasserie near the Opéra is certainly "spectacular" - especially the "beautiful glass cupola" - and if the pricey Alsatian-influenced fare "doesn't inspire" to the same degree, it also "does

	FOOD	DECOR	SERVICE	COST

not disappoint", thus tourists and residents alike still deem it a "favorite", especially for shellfish; though large it gets "quite crowded", so book ahead and trust in the "quick and friendly" staff.

Bon Accueil (Au) *Bistro* — 23 | 19 | 22 | €52

7e | 14, rue de Monttessuy (Alma Marceau/Ecole Militaire) | 01-47-05-46-11 | www.aubonaccueilparis.com

"In the shadow of the Eiffel Tower" – with a "killer view" of it from the sidewalk tables – this "cozy"bistro offers "innovative" takes on the classics, "with an emphasis on game and fish"; a "preponderance of tourists" dampens some Parisians' amour, but most find it a "good value" and report "not only a 'good welcome', but a fine goodbye."

Bonne Franquette (La) *Bistro* — - | - | - | M

18e | 2, rue des Saules (Abbesses) | 01-42-52-02-42 | www.labonnefranquette.com

Go "back in time" and channel the ghosts of Renoir, Monet, Van Gogh and other past residents of this former *auberge* in Montmartre, now well run as a classic bistro with a midpriced menu showcasing "quality" "products *du terroir*"; in good weather, the tree-"shaded" terrace is the place to be.

Bon Saint Pourçain (Le) *Classic French* — 19 | 15 | 20 | €42

6e | 10 bis, rue Servandoni (Odéon/St-Sulpice) | 01-43-54-93-63

"Lovingly prepared", "down-home" French classics are "popular with the locals" at this "reasonably priced", "no-frills" "hole-in-the-wall" down a "narrow cobblestone street" in the stylish Saint-Sulpice neighborhood; it's run by a father/daughter team that makes all comers "feel welcome", but bring cash because "old-time Left Bank" ambiance also translates as "no credit cards."

Bons Crus (Aux) *Wine Bar/Bistro* — ▽ 21 | 15 | 20 | €45

1er | 7, rue des Petits-Champs (Bourse/Palais Royal-Musée du Louvre) | 01-42-60-06-45

"Jovial" is the watchword for this "unpretentious" wine bar near Palais-Royal that serves "simple, hearty" bistro dishes "with an accent on the Southwest" along with plates of cold cuts; "good value" and "hospitality" make up for a lack of decor.

Botanistes (Les) *Bistro* — ▽ 19 | 16 | 19 | €55

7e | 11 bis, rue Chomel (Sèvres-Babylone/St-Sulpice) | 01-45-49-04-54

This "pleasant neighborhood" bistro in the 7th is frequented by the area's publishing trade and shoppers from the nearby Bon Marché department store, all of whom appreciate the moderate prices for the "inventive" yet "real French" cuisine turned out by chef-owner Jean-Baptiste Gay; his charming wife, Virginie Gay, and the "friendly" staff add cheer to the cozy digs, which are outfitted with a red-and-white checkerboard tile floor and custard-yellow walls.

Boucherie Roulière *Bistro* — ▽ 26 | 18 | 23 | €52

6e | 24, rue des Canettes (St-Sulpice) | 01-43-26-25-70

There's "first-rate", "simply grilled" beef and fish at this "wonderful local steakhouse", which, despite its central Left Bank location near

Saint-Sulpice, remains "under the radar"; the narrow, "typical bistro"-looking room may be "short on space", but "prompt", "pleasant" service and middling tabs broaden its appeal.

Bouchon et L'Assiette (Le) *Bistro* ▽ 22 | 19 | 22 | €43

17e | 127, rue Cardinet (Ternes/Villiers) | 01-42-27-83-93

"Honest" prices, which extend to "very affordable" wines by the glass, are the hallmark of this "reliable" bistro on the northern edge of the 17th, serving "dependably interesting" Basque and modern French dishes; the professional staff guides diners through ever-changing chalkboard menus, which, along with a few colorful vintage posters, are the only decoration punctuating the simple, gray interior.

Bouillon Racine *Classic French* 18 | 25 | 17 | €42

6e | 3, rue Racine (Cluny La Sorbonne/Odéon) | 01-44-32-15-60 | www.bouillonracine.com

The "magnificent art nouveau" embellishment in this heavily "gilded", "mirrored" 1890s-era bi-level Classic French spot near the Odéon is something to see; ok, so it outshines the "average" fare and "mediocre" service, but who cares when the prices are "reasonable" and the beer is "fantastic"?

Boulangerie (La) *Bistro* 22 | 18 | 19 | €39

20e | 15, rue des Panoyaux (Ménilmontant) | 01-43-58-45-45

A "big smiling man behind the bar" (the chef and part-owner) welcomes "regulars" and visitors alike to this "folksy" corner bistro housed in a converted bakery in the "offbeat" and "off-the-beaten-track" Ménilmontant neighborhood; best of all, the "pleasurable", sometimes "inventive", French fare doesn't cost a lot of bread.

Boule Rouge (La) *North African* 21 | 15 | 20 | €39

9e | 1, rue de la Boule-Rouge (Grands Boulevards) | 01-47-70-43-90

What fans call "the most authentic couscous in Paris" provides a taste of Tunisia via métro at this oasis of North African "family-style" cooking in the 9th; the decor – featuring a ceiling fresco of a desert scene – is equally evocative, if less favored, but "reasonable" tabs and "*très bien*" service add to its attractions.

Bouquinistes (Les) *New French* 23 | 21 | 22 | €74

6e | 53, quai des Grands-Augustins (St-Michel) | 01-43-25-45-94 | www.lesbouquinistes.com

The "affordable version" (relatively speaking) of Guy Savoy's brand of "unstuffy", seasonal New French cuisine can be had at this "chic", "modern" table in the 6th staffed by an "attentive but not intrusive" crew; try to ignore the "tourists" and sit by the "front windows and watch the parade of cars and people along the Seine."

NEW Bourgogne Sud *Burgundian* - | - | - | I

9e | 14, rue de Clichy (Liège/Trinité-d'Estienne d'Orves) | 01-48-74-51-27

Snails, boeuf bourguignon and all sorts of Burgundian goodies are on the menu at this bargain-priced newcomer near the Casino de Paris theater district, the debut effort from Gilles Breuil (formerly director at Petit Riche and Procope); the simple digs are brightened by blond-wood paneling and many mirrors reflecting the light from a large bank of windows.

Bourguignon du Marais (Au) ☒☒ *Wine Bar/Bistro* 25 | 19 | 22 | €49

4e | 52, rue François Miron (Pont-Marie/St-Paul) | 01-48-87-15-40

"Outstanding traditional" Burgundian fare (e.g. "trademark boeuf bourguignon") matched by "phenomenal" wines from the region puts this "convivial" wine bar/bistro "a cut above most Marais eateries "without the attitude or relentless chicness" often found here; professional service and moderate prices are further pluses, so nab a table on the [heated] terrace and "you're king of the world."

NEW **Braisenville** ☒ *Eclectic* - | - | - | M

9e | 36, rue de Condorcet (Anvers) | 09-50-91-21-74

This trendy, moderately priced South Pigalle newcomer offers an ever-changing menu of globally inspired small plates, most of which are grilled over hot coals in the showpiece Spanish-style brazier that's visible from the counter seats or orange-cushioned wire chairs in the casual, contemporary room.

Brasserie Balzar ◐ *Brasserie* 18 | 20 | 19 | €50

5e | 49, rue des Ecoles (Cluny La Sorbonne/St-Michel) | 01-43-54-13-67 | www.brasseriebalzar.com

This "picture-perfect" Parisian brasserie ("smoky mirrors, brass fixtures") near the Sorbonne offers "honest" French "comfort food" and "people-watching" – "especially male profs with much younger female students"; it's often "elbow to elbow", but the staff is "friendly" and "funny" and the prices are "fair" (watch for late-night bargains).

Brasserie de la Poste ☒ *Brasserie* ∇ 22 | 19 | 20 | €40

16e | 54, rue de Longchamp (Trocadéro) | 01-47-55-01-31

"Reliable", if "not new and trendy", cooking is perfectly suited to the "mom-and-pop" feel of this "cute and cozy" '50s-style brasserie off the Place du Trocadéro; everyone from business-lunchers to families are put at ease by the "personable" staff and the "affordable" tabs.

Brasserie de l'Ile St-Louis ◐ *Brasserie* 19 | 19 | 18 | €41

4e | 55, quai de Bourbon (Cité/Pont-Marie) | 01-43-54-02-59 | www.labrasserie-isl.fr

Given such "gorgeous" views of Notre Dame from the "terrific terrace" one might "expect a tourist trap", but this all-day Alsatian brasserie on the Ile Saint-Louis is full of "locals and tourists" alike who find the "gratifying country fare" a solid "value"; if outside seating is unavailable (due to weather or the no-reserving policy), the "atmospheric" interior offers a "slice of Old Paris" – but in or out, you're "well situated for a lovely post-dinner stroll" along the Seine; P.S. closed Wednesday.

Brasserie du Louvre *Brasserie* 19 | 21 | 20 | €49

1er | Hôtel du Louvre | Pl André Malraux (Palais Royal-Musée du Louvre) | 01-44-58-37-21 | www.hoteldulouvre.com

This "elegant" hotel brasserie "conveniently" located across from the Louvre racks up more praise for its ambiance ("the people-watching alone is worth the visit") than for its "refined" cuisine; still, the staff is "friendly" and the tabs are moderate, making it especially "good for tourists."

Brasserie Flo ◐ *Brasserie* | 19 | 21 | 18 | €51

10e | 7, cour des Petites-Ecuries (Château d'Eau) | 01-47-70-13-59 | www.flobrasseries.com

"Exactly what a brasserie should be" – "fun, loud" and foaming with "good beer" – this "archetype" of the genre in the 10th (owned by Groupe Flo) let's you "know you're in Paris" with its remarkable atmosphere and "all those mirrors and moldings" transporting diners back to "a different era"; the fare is "classic" and "consistent" and served "efficiently" by a "polite" staff, adding up to a "good value for the money."

Brasserie Julien ◐ *Brasserie* | 19 | 25 | 21 | €58

10e | 16, rue du Faubourg St-Denis (Strasbourg-St-Denis) | 01-47-70-12-06 | www.flobrasseries.com

"The decor is something to behold" at this "stunning" "bastion of art nouveau", an "expensive" Groupe Flo-owned "gem" of a brasserie in a rough-around-the-edges part of the 10th that causes some surveyors to sigh "were the neighborhood only better"; still, most brave the trip and deal with the "noise" inside the huge space (it "actually adds to the ambiance"), enjoying "correct" cuisine served by a "lovely" staff; P.S. "chocoholics delight" in the profiteroles here.

Brasserie La Lorraine ◐ *Brasserie* | 18 | 18 | 17 | €64

8e | 2, pl des Ternes (Ternes) | 01-56-21-22-00 | www.brasserielalorraine.com

"Amazing seafood platters" are the standouts on the otherwise "typical" brasserie menu at this "classic" address on the Place des Ternes; service gets mixed marks ("pro" vs. "pretentious"), the bright art deco-esque space is often "noisy" and prices are "equal to the high ceilings", but late-night hours make it "perfect after a concert."

Z Brasserie Lipp ◐ *Brasserie* | 18 | 21 | 17 | €56

6e | 151, bd St-Germain (St-Germain-des-Prés) | 01-45-48-53-91 | www.brasserie-lipp.fr

"Everybody should go at least once" to this "archetypical brasserie" in Saint-Germain aver tourists and locals alike – "after all, it is *The Moveable Feast*", even if its "history" is "more appetizing" than its just-"decent", premium-priced cuisine; expect "waiters with real character" (some "pleasant", others "grumpy"), and take care not to be seated in "Siberia" upstairs.

Brasserie Lutetia *Brasserie* | 19 | 20 | 20 | €64

6e | Hôtel Lutetia | 23, rue de Sèvres (Sèvres-Babylone) | 01-49-54-46-76 | www.lutetia-paris.com

"Convenient" if you're "staying at the Lutetia" or shopping at the Bon Marché, but otherwise, the culinary consensus on this all-day hotel spot "known for its seafood" is "good but unremarkable" – andthe prices are "high for a brasserie"; still, the dining room is rather "beautiful" and patrolled by a "gracious", "accommodating" staff.

Brasserie Mollard ◐ *Brasserie* 18 | 23 | 17 | €58

8e | 115, rue St-Lazare (St-Lazare) | 01-43-87-50-22 | www.mollard.fr
The "primary reason to visit" this all-day brasserie near the Gare Saint-Lazare "is the landmarked decor", which includes "beautiful hundred-year-old art nouveau" mosaics; that, along with "legitimately famous" seafood choucroute and other "quality" fish specialties justify "high" prices, even if service is merely "acceptable."

Brasserie Printemps ☒ *Classic French* 15 | 21 | 14 | €37

9e | Printemps | 64, bd Haussmann (Auber/Havre-Caumartin) | 01-42-82-58-84 | www.printemps.com
The "magnificent" 1923 stained-glass dome that hangs over an "urban-chic" dining area is the major selling point for Printemps' in-store Classic French canteen; it's a "convenient" and "affordable" place to "rest between shopping bouts" due to "rapid" waiters (that is, "if you can find them"), but otherwise, those unimpressed with the food wonder "why eat in a department store?"; P.S. dinner Thursdays only.

Breizh Café M *Brittany* 22 | 16 | 20 | €29

3e | 109, rue Vieille-du-Temple (Filles du Calvaire/St-Paul) | 01-42-72-13-77 | www.breizhcafe.com
"*Vive la Bretagne*" cry cravers of the "novel" crêpes and galettes - washed down by an "incredible array of ciders" - at this "tiny", wood-paneled all-day diner in the Marais; its "cool" rep, "gentle prices" and "charming" staff mean it's "prudent to reserve", but even then there may be a "long wait"; P.S. closed Monday and Tuesday.

Briciola (La) ☒ *Pizza* ▽ 19 | 12 | 18 | €30

3e | 64, rue Charlot (Filles du Calvaire/République) | 01-42-77-34-10
It's not your typical "red-checked-tablecloth pizzeria" say fans of this shabby-chic hangout in the northern Marais dishing up "tasty" pizzas of "real Italian quality"; everyone from "bobo" couples to families with bambinos appreciates the "fast" service, but note that, "unfortunately", it's "as expensive as pizzas always are in Paris."

Buisson Ardent (Le) ☒ *Bistro* 22 | 19 | 23 | €43

5e | 25, rue Jussieu (Jussieu) | 01-43-54-93-02 | www.lebuissonardent.fr
"It's hot" at this "burning bush" (as the name translates) in the Latin Quarter university district say followers who claim its "modern" bistro menu "gets more ambitious each season" (the Food score is up by three points) and is "one of the best deals in town"; traces of the '20s linger in the wine-and-absinthe-hued space whose "intimate" air is enhanced by the "enthusiastic, young staff."

Café Burq ◐☒ *Wine Bar/Bistro* 21 | 17 | 20 | €37

18e | 6, rue Burq (Abbesses/Blanche) | 01-42-52-81-27
"Hipster ambiance" puts this "cool little" Montmartre wine bar/bistro on the "trendy" map as much as its "original", midpriced nosh, like the "must"-have honey-roasted Camembert; it's especially "fun"

late nights when people pack in "like sardines" to meet "friends", enjoy the "great bar" and ogle the "attractive" staff.

Café Cartouche Ⓢ *Bistro* — | - | - | - | M |

12e | 4, rue de Bercy (Bercy/Cour St-Émilion) | 01-40-19-09-95

This spin-off of the popular Repaire de Cartouche, "tucked away" in the Bercy neighborhood of the 12th, lives up to that area's past as a wine warehouse district with an "interesting" cellar that complements "carefully prepared", moderately priced bistro classics; there's "no decor" to speak of but the staff is "efficient", so focus on your dining companion and discuss the films screening at the nearby Frank Gehry–designed Cinémathèque de Paris.

Café Constant *Bistro* — | 24 | 16 | 21 | €47 |

7e | 139, rue St-Dominique (Ecole Militaire) | 01-47-53-73-34 | www.cafeconstant.com

"Sublime" yet "deceivingly simple French comfort food" draws droves down a "charming side street" near the Eiffel Tower to chef Christian Constant's "good-value", "no-frills" bistro counterpart to Le Violon d'Ingres; the decor may have grown a bit "shabby" and tables are "inches apart", but service is "crisp" and it's always "filled with the buzz of people having a great time"; P.S. no reservations.

Z Café de Flore ◐ *Classic French* — | 16 | 22 | 17 | €44 |

6e | 172, bd St-Germain (St-Germain-des-Prés) | 01-45-48-55-26 | www.cafedeflore.fr

A "classic haunt of literary giants" and intellectuals like Jean-Paul Sartre, this art deco "Left Bank landmark" is now "overrun by tourists" despite "so-so", "overpriced" Classic French fare ("marvelous" omelets excepted) served by waiters who can be "cold" and "testy"; even so, fans say "may it never change", advising you to "relax", sip "the greatest hot chocolate in the world" and "watch the self-conscious preeners" (or even the likes of Karl Lagerfeld or Sonia Rykiel) "dying for you to notice them" – it may just "bring out your inner philosopher"; P.S. no reservations.

Café de la Jatte *Italian* — | 18 | 21 | 18 | €51 |

Neuilly-sur-Seine | 60, bd Vital-Bouhot (Pont-de-Levallois) | 01-47-45-04-20 | www.cafelajatte.com

"Bravo!" bray the "*branché*" Neuilly neighbors who flash their "bling-bling" at this "fashionable" Ile de la Jatte "institution" that recently made the switch from Eclectic fare to a midpriced Italian menu, which is deemed "better than before" (its Food score is up by four points); everything else remains unchanged: the child-friendly Sunday brunch, service that gets mixed marks, the "beautiful" terrace and "immense" dinosaur sculpture suspended above the gargantuan dining room.

Café de la Musique ◐ *Brasserie/New French* — | 17 | 18 | 15 | €38 |

19e | Cité de la Musique | 213, av Jean Jaurès (Porte de Pantin) | 01-48-03-15-91 | www.cite-musique.fr

"Notable" mainly for its "convenience" – it's across from the Parc de la Villette and close to the Médiathèque and the Zénith concert hall - this eatery in the Cité de la Musique hits some less-pleasing notes with its "basic", "unexciting" nuevo brasserie menu and service that's "not up to par"; still, the tabs are "fair", leading culture vultures to perch all day long on the huge terrace or on the plush "velvet" seats inside the "cool", mod space.

Café de la Paix ◐ *Classic French* 19 | 24 | 19 | €67

9e | InterContinental Le Grand Hôtel | 12, bd des Capucines (Auber/Opéra) | 01-40-07-36-36 | www.cafedelapaix.fr

The gilded Napoleon III decor is "spectacular" and so are the pastries (the "best you will ever eat") at this Classic French grande dame in the InterContinental Le Grand; but given a menu that's "not mind-blowing" overall, it's "on the expensive side", which is why wallet-watchers gravitate to the more affordable and casual sidewalk terrace cafe with its views of the "passing parade" and the Opéra Garnier.

Café de l'Esplanade (Le) ◐ *Classic/New French* 18 | 21 | 17 | €63

7e | 52, rue Fabert (Invalides/La Tour-Maubourg) | 01-47-05-38-80

A "beautiful view of Les Invalides" from sidewalk tables sets apart this late-night outpost of the trend-conscious Costes empire, and although the Classic and New French cooking that's deemed "expensive for the quality" and a staff that at times seems "snobby" don't quite live up to the "pleasant" Napoleon-inspired decor, a gorgeous crowd still makes it a "cool" place to "see and be seen."

Café des Musées *Bistro* 20 | 17 | 20 | €35

3e | 49, rue de Turenne (Chemin-Vert/St-Paul) | 01-42-72-96-17

Bargain prices - the "nightly prix fixe is a steal" - at this hip Marais bistro have hot young designers rubbing shoulders with museumgoers (it's near the Picasso Museum, etc.); "well-chosen wines" and a "friendly and familial" staff help keep the "bare-bones" interior "packed and lively" at all times.

Café du Commerce (Le) ◐ *Bistro* 17 | 21 | 17 | €35

15e | 51, rue du Commerce (Emile Zola) | 01-45-75-03-27 | www.lecafeducommerce.com

"Magnificent period decor" revs history buffs' motors at this bistro in the 15th that was daringly built around a "breathtaking" multilevel sky-lit atrium in 1921 and first functioned as an auto workers' canteen; critics suggest the kitchen is resting "on its laurels" and say they would like "more attention" from the staff, but most agree it's an "affordable" "feast for the eyes"; P.S. the glass roof retracts in good weather.

Café du Passage (Le) ◐ ☒ *Wine Bar/Bistro* - | - | - | I

11e | 12, rue de Charonne (Bastille/Ledru-Rollin) | 01-49-29-97-64

Cozy armchairs and soft lighting provide a "comfortable atmosphere" at this apartmentlike bistro/wine bar located in a former furniture atelier in the ultrahip neighborhood east of the Bastille; it's a "must for exploring new wines" (the list numbers almost 400) and a haven for whiskey hounds (40 selections) who nosh on casual platters of cheese and charcuterie between rounds; P.S. open evenings only, till 2 AM.

Café Le Moderne ☒ *Bistro* 22 | 20 | 22 | €47

2e | 40, rue Notre-Dame-des-Victoires (Bourse) | 01-53-40-84-10

"Original" cuisine showcasing "imagination backed up with real skill" matches the tastefully "contemporary" decor at Frédéric Hubig's "stylish", "softly lit" bistro near the Bourse; a "friendly" staff and "one the best quality/value ratios in the city" round out the rah-rahs for this restaurateur who also owns the more casual Astier in the 11th.

Café Lenôtre (Le) *New French* 23 | 23 | 22 | €57

8e | Pavillon Elysée | 10, av des Champs-Elysées (Champs-Elysée-Clémenceau) | 01-42-65-97-71 | www.lenotre.fr

A "perfect post-Champs-Elysées stroll reward" is digging into the "exquisite" desserts or "delightful", light savory fare at this New French cafe outpost of the famed catering company; prices are "high", but the "attentive" staff and "sublime setting" in and around a glass pavilion built for the 1900 World's Fair make the "parklike" respite "hard to pass by."

Café Marly ◐ ☒ *Classic/New French* 17 | 24 | 16 | €52

1er | 93, rue de Rivoli (Palais Royal-Musée du Louvre) | 01-49-26-06-60

The "priceless view" of the Louvre's I.M. Pei-designed pyramid far surpasses the "predictable" but moderately priced classic and contemporary Costes-chain fare at this Empire-style "escape from the museum's prodigious visitors"; if the staff seems "more worried about their own looks than service", most just sigh and say "sipping champagne" under the "beautiful" terrace's colonnades "just never gets old."

Café Rouge *Classic French/Eclectic* 19 | 21 | 20 | €48

3e | 32, rue de Picardie (République/Temple) | 01-44-54-20-60

This "stylish", loft-style duplex serving "reliable" Classic French and Eclectic cuisine in the northern Marais is appreciated for its "fast" service and "decent" value; the BYO policy, particularly, is a good way of saving money, but be forewarned: the corkage fee is €15; P.S. its wine bar sibling, Bar Rouge, is next door.

Café Ruc ◐ *Bistro* 15 | 17 | 14 | €51

1er | 159, rue St-Honoré (Palais Royal-Musée du Louvre) | 01-42-60-97-54

Yet "another link in the Costes chain" yawns a passel of Parisians none too enamored of this 1st-arrondissement bistro that churns out "unexceptional" fare considered "more expensive that it needs to be" (delivered by an often-"rude" staff); but culture vultures point out positives like late-night hours and a "strategic" location "a stone's throw from the Louvre" and the Comédie-Française; P.S. there's "good people-watching" in the plush red-and-green interior and on the sidewalk.

	FOOD	DECOR	SERVICE	COST

Café Salle Pleyel *New French* ▽ 16 | 20 | 17 | €40

8e | 252, rue du Faubourg St-Honoré (Ternes) | 01-53-75-28-44 | www.cafesallepleyel.com

The "mythic" Salle Pleyel concert hall schedules an eclectic musical mix - philharmonic to pop divas - but the midpriced menu at this "friendly" French eatery on-site is strictly modern (and is "renewed" yearly by a celeb chef - at press time, it's Mauro Colagreco from Le Mirazur in Menton); the "art deco" space is open for lunch weekdays but dinner is available only before performances, so book ahead.

Café Terminus *Brasserie* 19 | 22 | 22 | €49

8e | Hôtel Concorde St-Lazare | 108, rue St-Lazare (St-Lazare) | 01-40-08-43-30 | www.concordestlazare-paris.com

At this "timeless" Parisian brasserie in the Concorde Hotel near the Gare Saint-Lazare, "traditional" classics at "reasonable" prices are served by a "friendly" staff, which makes it a safe bet for "business lunches"; an additional selling point is the "beautiful" but ersatz belle epoque decor, designed by the fashion world's Sonia Rykiel.

NEW Caffe Burlot Thierry Costes *Italian* - | - | - | VE

8e | 9, rue du Colisée (Franklin D. Roosevelt/St-Philippe-du-Roule) | 01-53-75-42-00 | www.maisonthierrycostes.com

Two Thierrys - Burlot (ex Zébra Square) and Costes (Thoumieux, etc.) - have partnered to create this *molto* chic Italian near the Champs, where pan-peninsular pastas are delivered by *bellissima* waitresses, and the dark and leafy room, meant to evoke midcentury Italian cool (think Marcello Mastroianni), gives diners a dose of la dolce vita - though you might have to pawn your Prada to pay for it.

Caffé dei Cioppi *Italian* ▽ 25 | 17 | 20 | €37

11e | 159, rue du Faubourg St-Antoine (Ledru-Rollin) | 01-43-46-10-14

The "sunny" welcome at this Bastille-area mom-and-pop trattoria draws diners in, but it's the "authentic", moderately priced cuisine "made with care, love and knowledge" right in the open kitchen that keeps them glued to their seats; fans say the "tiny" space "deserves to accommodate more people", but at least in summer there's additional seating outside adjacent to a "pretty" pedestrian-only cul-de-sac; P.S. odd dinner hours make "booking advised."

Caffé Toscano *Italian* ▽ 19 | 17 | 20 | €49

7e | 34, rue des Sts-Pères (St-Germain-des-Prés) | 01-42-84-28-95

Reasonably priced options are at a premium in the chic gallery/shopping district of the 7th, so pasta purists recommend this "pleasant" trattoria run by "real Italians" for its "flavorful" fare at relatively "cheap" prices, which makes up for the "simple", even "spare", terra-cotta decor.

Cagouille (La) *Seafood* 23 | 13 | 19 | €70

14e | 10, pl Constantin Brancusi (Gaîté/Montparnasse-Bienvenüe) | 01-43-22-09-01 | www.la-cagouille.fr

Always "filled with people who are delighted they are eating so well", this "hidden gem" lures afishionados to the "unexciting" 14th with the promise of "extremely fresh seafood" (no meat); "high" prices and "kitschy nautical" trappings are soon forgotten after letting the "diligent" staff guide you through the "amazing" cognac collection.

Cailloux (Les) *Italian* 22 | 19 | 19 | €39

13e | 58, rue des Cinq-Diamants (Corvisart/Place d'Italie) | 01-45-80-15-08

In the trendy, relatively "bucolic" Butte aux Cailles district, this "very good" if "not overly original" Italian attracts a "noisy" crowd clamoring for "fresh pasta"; macaroni mavens moan that the menu could benefit from "occasional updates", though moderate tabs and "attentive" (even "cute") servers satisfy all but the wettest noodles.

Caïus [S] *New French* 24 | 20 | 22 | €51

17e | 6, rue d'Armaillé (Charles de Gaulle-Etoile) | 01-42-27-19-20 | www.caius-restaurant.fr

This "solid little performer" south of the Etoile is a "well-deserved success" for "talented" chef-owner Jean Marc Notelet, "a whiz with herbs and spices" as evidenced in his daily changing menu of "creative" French cuisine; a sober wood-paneled room, "good-humored" staff and moderate prices draw a healthy business crowd for lunch; P.S. closed weekends.

NEW Camélia *New French* - | - | - | E

1er | Mandarin Oriental | 251, rue St-Honoré (Concorde) | (33-1) 70-98-74-00 | www.mandarinoriental.com/paris

Molecular master Thierry Marx is the man behind the curtain at this open-all-day modern French in the new Mandarin Oriental in the 1st, where a contemporary, white-on-white dining room leads on to a lush garden (the place to be in fine weather); the 45-minute/45-euro midday menu caters to business-lunchers, but otherwise you'll need a few more bills in your Birkin bag for this blossom.

Camélia (Le) [S] [M] *New French* ▽ 21 | 19 | 24 | €63

Bougival | 7, quai Georges Clemenceau (La Défense RER) | 01-39-18-36-06 | www.lecamelia.com

"On the outskirts of Paris" in suburban Bougival, chef-owner Thierry Conte "finesses" a "delicious" menu that walks the line between regional and New French cuisine at this "calm" respite attended by a "discreet" staff; literary lovers enjoy "*un bon moment*" in this lemon-hued country auberge that's forever remembered as the meeting place that inspired Dumas' *La Dame aux Camélias*.

NEW Camion Qui Fume (Le) [M] *Burgers* - | - | - | I

Location varies; see website | 06-23-19-74-92 | www.lecamionquifume.com

The food truck trend roars into Paris, driven by a young American named Kristin Frederick, who slings thick and juicy burgers with all the fixings, plus BBQ pulled pork sandwiches, from her four-wheeled fryer; the wait can be long but it won't take much of your hard-earned cash (sorry, no credit cards), and it's worth it just to see proper Parisians take a stab at *le street food*; P.S. see its website for scheduled locations and times.

	FOOD	DECOR	SERVICE	COST

NEW Candelaria *Mexican* | - | - | - | I |

3e | 52, rue de Saintonge (Filles du Calvaire) | 01-42-74-41-28 | www.candelariaparis.com

Get in line (or go early) for *muy auténtico* tacos and tostadas, served with serious salsas and gorgeous guac (and a surprising black bean brownie) in a stark, white storefront that's skinnier than the jeans worn by the young, upper Marais crowd who cram in along the counter; if you're thirsty, sneak through the hidden door at the back for a perfectly crafted margarita or shot of mezcal in the low-lit, cavelike lounge area.

Cantine de Quentin (La) Ⓜ *Wine Bar/Bistro* | - | - | - | I |

10e | 52, rue Bichat (Jacques Bonsergent/République) | 01-42-02-40-32

In the "ultratrendy" Canal Saint-Martin district, this down-to-earth wine bar/bistro serves "real food" to those on a budget; folks also like being able to purchase artisanal prepared foods and wines from the on-site market - a "nice concept", even if the stocked shelves do double duty as decor.

Cantine des Tontons (La) Ⓢ *Classic French* | 17 | 19 | 15 | €33 |

15e | 36, rue de Dantzig (Convention/Porte de Versailles) | 01-48-28-23-66

"Dinner with friends" - be they bosom buddies or strangers you just rubbed elbows with at the communal tables - is the *raison d'être* of this "convivial" canteen with "mismatched" flea-market trimmings in the far 15th, near Convention métro; there's no menu, just two *plats du jour* sandwiched between trips to the self-service buffet for "simple but tasty" old-fashioned French appetizers and desserts just like "*grand-mère*'s" - and almost as cheap.

Cantine du Troquet (La) Ⓢ *Basque* ▽ | 25 | 18 | 23 | €41 |

14e | 101, rue de l'Ouest (Pernety) | no phone

NEW Cantine du Troquet Dupleix *Basque*

15e | 53, bd de Grenelle (Dupleix) | 01-45-75-98-00

Christian Etchebest's "bustling" Basque bistro in Montparnasse takes "no reservations" - and his fans have no reservations either, citing "perfectly prepared" Southwestern cuisine (think grilled pigs' ears) "served with generosity and verve"; a "convivial" sports bar-like setting and an "eclectic" list of "reasonably priced" wines equal "no stress", "no attitude, just fun"; P.S. closed weekends; there's a new spin-off in the 15th.

Z Carré des Feuillants Ⓢ *Haute Cuisine* | 27 | 22 | 25 | €153 |

1er | 14, rue de Castiglione (Concorde/Tuileries) | 01-42-86-82-82 | www.carredesfeuillants.fr

Alain Dutournier creates the "perfect alliance" between Haute Cuisine and the "discreet" flavors of the Southwest at this "quiet, calm" affair with an "excellent" wine list, midway between the Place Vendôme and the Tuileries; the "modern", some say "cold", interior is graced by contemporary art as well as "impeccable", "stylish" servers, but be warned: prices are "celestial" - non-millionaires are advised to try the lunch prix fixe, a relative "bargain"; P.S. jacket and tie required.

	FOOD	DECOR	SERVICE	COST

Cartes Postales (Les) 🅂 *Japanese/New French* | - | - | - | M |

1er | 7, rue Gomboust (Opéra/Pyramides) | 01-42-61-02-93

Roughly the size of a postage stamp, this "quiet", bare-bones storefront behind the Place du Marché Saint-Honoré isn't much to look at, but a small cadre of connoisseurs claims it "deserves wider recognition" for chef-owner Yoshimasa Watanabe's "simple but exquisite" New French-Japanese cuisine that's "value"-priced; "attentive" servers guide patrons through the menu, and there's a "half-plate" policy when it's "impossible to choose" between two options.

Casa Bini *Italian* | 23 | 16 | 19 | €52 |

6e | 36, rue Grégoire de Tours (Odéon) | 01-46-34-05-60

"Not overly complicated in any way" - just "straightforward" "real Italian" fare "impeccably executed" and priced moderately - is the house style of this Odéon-area ristorante with "warm" service and cozy but "no-frills" digs; "chances are good you'll spot a celeb or two" playing with the "tasty" beef carpaccio and tipping back vino from the northern part of The Boot.

Casa Olympe 🅂 *New French/Provence* | 23 | 16 | 18 | €67 |

9e | 48, rue St-Georges (Notre-Dame-de-Lorette/St-Georges) | 01-42-85-26-01 | www.casaolympe.com

A "favorite of locals", including French showbiz personalities, Olympe Versini's Pigalle bistro serves "tasty" though "pricey" New French-Provençal cuisine in "man-sized portions"; seating is "cramped" in the pair of rooms (one mustard-colored, one ox-blood), but given the "friendly" service, it shakes out as "a real gem"; P.S. closed weekends.

Casse-Noix (Le) 🅂 *Bistro* | - | - | - | M |

15e | 56, rue de la Fédération (Dupleix) | 01-45-66-09-01 | www.le-cassenoix.fr

It may look "authentically" old-fashioned, but this Eiffel Tower-area bistro is a relative newcomer that wins praise for a "smooth" staff that ferries "huge servings" of French bistro fare considered "reasonably priced for Paris"; don't miss the unique collection of nutcrackers (hence the name) owned by chef-owner Pierre-Olivier Lenormand (ex Régalade); P.S. closed weekends.

Cave Schmidt (La) 🅂🄼 *Wine Bar/Bistro* | 23 | 18 | 18 | €36 |
(fka Cave de l'Os à Moëlle)

15e | 181, rue de Lourmel (Lourmel) | 01-45-57-28-28

Stéphane Schmidt (ex Violon d'Ingres) hasn't made many tweaks to the "cozy" communal tables, "unbeatable prices", "family-style" self-service or the budget-conscious retail wine boutique that distinguish this wine bar in the 15th, which he took ownership of (along with its big papa Schmidt - L'Os à Moëlle) in late 2011; the Food score may not reflect the change, but the early word is that it still offers the same "fine" bistro fare, with the addition of some items from Schmidt's native Alsace.

FOOD	DECOR	SERVICE	COST

Caves Pétrissans [S] *Wine Bar/Bistro*

23	18	19	€49

17e | 30 bis, av Niel (Pereire/Ternes) | 01-42-27-52-03 | www.cavespetrissans.fr

French "classics" made with "ingredients sourced from regional and reputable" producers are priced right at this "family-owned" and warmly run *bistrot à vins* in the 17th - though oenophiles make the trip more for the "terrific selection of wines" that are offered at retail prices from the in-house boutique; the "yesteryear" decor, with its wood paneling and checkered floors, evokes the 1930s; P.S. closed weekends.

[Z] Caviar Kaspia ◐ [S] *Russian*

26	23	25	€122

8e | 17, pl de la Madeleine (Madeleine) | 01-42-65-33-32 | www.caviarkaspia.com

"Exceptional" caviar, blini and smoked fish - washed down with "ice-cold vodka" - provide "decadent fun" for the well-heeled at this "intimate" "jewel box" that "brings Russia to the table in creative (and pricey) ways"; "reserve a window table" to have the best views of the neoclassical Madeleine church across the street; P.S. for roe on the run, there's a boutique on the ground floor.

Céladon (Le) *Classic French*

23	22	23	€93

2e | Hôtel Westminster | 15, rue Daunou (Opéra) | 01-47-03-40-42 | www.leceladon.com

"Hospitality" is the watchword of the "discreet" staff as it transports the "refined", "up-to-date" French classics of chef Christophe Moisand (ex Meurice) to the tables in the Hôtel Westminster's "traditionally elegant" (jackets suggested), "feminine" Regency-style dining room; while it's "expensive" on weekdays, it morphs into the "bargain" 'Petit Céladon' on weekends, serving affordable fixed-price meals that include wine; P.S. a "quick-witted" barman makes The Duke's Bar worthy of a tipple.

[Z] 144 Petrossian (Le) [S][M] *Seafood*

24	22	23	€104

7e | 144, rue de l'Universite (Invalides/La Tour-Maubourg) | 01-44-11-32-32 | www.petrossian.fr

This classic "temple" to fish eggs in the posh 7th arrondissement offers what may be "the perfect champagne-and-caviar meal in Paris", though the rest of chef Rougui Dia's "refined" seafood menu, served in "comfortable, luxe" surroundings, also gets high marks; it's "not cheap", but the prix fixe options are a "wonderful deal", and the "considerate", "efficient" staff helps make it "worth" a visit.

Cerisaie (La) [S] *Southwest*

23	16	21	€48

14e | 70, bd Edgar Quinet (Edgar Quinet) | 01-43-20-98-98 | www.restaurantlacerisaie.com

"A lovely young couple" runs this weekdays-only Montparnasse venue that's known for its "warm welcome" and "excellent" Southwestern fare (it's "foie gras heaven") well matched by a "thoughtful", reasonably priced wine list; booking ahead is a must to secure some of the "tight seating" in the "tiny", "spare" room.

	FOOD	DECOR	SERVICE	COST
▽	21	21	21	€32

Chalet (Le) *Alpine/Classic French*

Neuilly-sur-Seine | 14, rue du Commandant Pilot (Les Sablons/ Porte Maillot) | 01-46-24-03-11 | www.lechaletdeneuilly.com

"Very rich" and "very good" describes the cheese raclette, fondue, tartiflette and other Montagnarde specialties served in "copious" portions by a "pleasant" staff at this peak of Alpine cooking rising in the heart of Neuilly; the wood-paneled, pseudo ski lodge digs are *très montagne,* but the tabs hit rock bottom; P.S. the menu rotates to lighter Classic French cuisine in summer.

18 | 25 | 18 | €59

Chalet des Iles (Le) *Classic French*

16e | Lac Inférieur du Bois de Boulogne (La Muette/Rue de la Pompe) | 01-42-88-04-69 | www.chaletdesiles.net

Straight out of a "Renoir painting", this "magical" island enclave "beautifully situated" in the Bois de Boulogne is accessed by a "charming" boat ride, making the experience a "romantic must" ("lunch alfresco among strolling peacocks is a pure dream"); however, even the most impressed Impressionists concede that the Classic French fare is merely "adequate" and "a little expensive" for what it is; P.S. closed for dinner on Sunday; closed Monday in winter.

26 | 22 | 24 | €72

Z Chamarré Montmartre *Mauritian/New French*

18e | 52, rue Lamarck (Lamarck-Caulaincourt) | 01-42-55-05-42 | www.chamarre-montmartre.com

Thanks to jovial Mauritian chef Antoine Heerah's "original" use of unusual fruits and veggies, it's "worth going to Montmartre" for his "superb fusion" of French and Indian Ocean flavors, served by true professionals indoors amid sea-green walls with a "fun" view of the kitchen action or outdoors on a "pretty" shaded terrace; save up your euros because it's expensive - and save room for sweets because "desserts are almost better than the meal."

- | - | - | M

Chantairelle S *Auvergne*

5e | 17, rue Laplace (Maubert-Mutualité) | 01-46-33-18-59 | www.chantairelle.com

"As close as you can get to the countryside in Paris", this moderately priced Auvergnat bistro near the Sorbonne sports a rustic interior trimmed with wood and stone, plus there's a trellised back garden; "large portions" of "savory regional cuisine", like poached eggs or stuffed cabbage, mean it's earmarked for those "with hearty appetites"; P.S. cat fanciers mourn the recent passing of the restaurant's resident mouser, Maurice, but are making friends with Simone, a new gray-and-white tabby.

23 | 21 | 21 | €57

Chardenoux (Le) *Bistro*

11e | 1, rue Jules Vallès (Charonne/Faidherbe-Chaligny) | 01-43-71-49-52 | www.restaurantlechardenoux.com

Best known from reality TV cooking shows, southern-accented chef Cyril Lignac also owns this real-world bistro in the 11th, which turns out "honest", "updated" dishes with "not a false note" on the menu; fans say "you can't beat" the circa-1900 "gilded decor" or the "impeccable" service, and the weekday lunch prix fixe is a way around pricey tabs.

NEW Chardenoux des Prés *Bistro* ▽ 21 | 17 | 23 | €63

6e | 27, rue du Dragon (St-Germain-des-Prés/St-Sulpice) | 01-45-48-29-68 | www.restaurantlechardenouxdespres.com

Cyril Lignac's new Saint-Germain spin-off of his popular Right Bank bistro Chardenoux has a more "cozy" interior featuring dark patterned walls, cognac-colored banquettes and swivel chairs lining a zinc bar, but its Southwestern-leaning menu looks similar to its big brother's, as do the high prices – though they come off as a better value in this comparatively spendy neighborhood; "exemplary" hospitality and a pooches-allowed policy are additional selling points.

Charlot - Roi des Coquillages ◐ *Brasserie* 21 | 17 | 19 | €65

9e | 12, pl de Clichy (Place de Clichy) | 01-53-20-48-00 | www.charlot-paris.com

"Excellent" oysters take top billing at this art deco brasserie "institution" adorned with actors' headshots in the slowly gentrifying Place de Clichy theater district; upstairs tables "overlooking the square" make the "good-value" shellfish platters feel positively "royal", as does the "service with a smile."

Charpentiers (Aux) ◐ M *Bistro* 20 | 17 | 20 | €45

6e | 10, rue Mabillon (Mabillon/St-Germain-des-Prés) | 01-43-26-30-05 | www.auxcharpentiers.fr

This "historic" Saint-Germain bistro was established by the Carpenter's Guild in 1856 and retains that relationship today, along with its equally ageless, "solid and dependable" cuisine for "fair prices"; the "old-fashioned" decor dovetails perfectly with the "mature" clientele that favors it; closed Monday and Tuesday.

Chartier *Classic French* 15 | 24 | 17 | €25

(aka Bouillon Chartier)

9e | 7, rue Faubourg Montmartre (Grands Boulevards) | 01-47-70-86-29 | www.restaurant-chartier.com

The masses wait in line to "jump back to 1900" at this "timeless" canteen off the Grands Boulevards delivering "passable" Gallic classics (fit for "a high school cafeteria" say critics); food aside, fans enjoy sharing the communal tables (and the "chaos") in the enormous, "gorgeous" belle epoque space, and like watching the "good-humored" waiters "tote up the bill" on the paper tablecloths – it never amounts to much, making it "unbeatable" "when you're broke."

Chateaubriand (Le) ◐ S M *New French* 23 | 16 | 18 | €65

11e | 129, av Parmentier (Goncourt/Parmentier) | 01-43-57-45-95

"Rock-star" chef Inaki Aizpitarte's "daring and challenging" contemporary French cuisine makes this pricey Oberkampf "kingdom of the bobos" one of "the most inventive" tables in Paris; critics say the experience can be undermined by "long lines", "uninviting" minimalist decor and having dishes from the no-options set menu "thrown at you like you are in a cafeteria" (by the admittedly "handsome", "young" waiters), but acolytes claim it's "worth the battle" - just "arrive with patience and a little attitude of your own."

NEW Chatomat *New French* - | - | - | E

20e | 6, rue Victor Letalle (Ménilmontant) | 01-47-97-25-77

Paris food scenesters are flocking to this freshly minted, brick-and-bare-bulb bistro, perched (way) up the hill in Ménilmontant, where a young couple brings impressive international experience to bear on their light, contemporary French creations; the menu is limited and not cheap, but the price is right for the quality.

Chen Soleil d'Est ⊠ *Chinese* - | - | - | VE

15e | 15, rue du Théâtre (Charles Michels) | 01-45-79-34-34

The "best Peking duck in Paris" (and possibly "the most expensive" as prices would only approach "acceptable if they were two times lower") and other Chinese dishes of "unvarying quality" are the calling card of this Sino survivor in the 15th; it may be located in nowheresville, but the dining room's rather baroque Chinoiserie transports diners to that famous duck's hometown.

Cherche Midi (Le) ◐ *Italian* 22 | 16 | 17 | €48

6e | 22, rue du Cherche-Midi (Sèvres-Babylone/St-Sulpice) | 01-45-48-27-44

"Outstanding authentic Italian" cuisine prepared "without bells or whistles" but with "quality products" from Italy gets *molto* praise from fans of this midpriced trattoria with a marble-topped bar in the slick Sèvres-Babylone shopping district; the "tiny", "unassuming" space gets "crowded" and "noisy" once the "good house wines" start flowing, so "reserve early" or chat up one of the "friendly" waiters.

Chéri Bibi ◐ ⊠ *Bistro* ▽ 20 | 20 | 18 | €69

18e | 15, rue André-del-Sarte (Anvers/Château Rouge) | 01-42-54-88-96

"Hipsters" haunt this "trendy" bistro in Montmartre, its "friendly" staff making them feel at home in a "pleasant" space outfitted with flea-market furnishings; the wines are organic and the "attractively presented" vintage eats "change regularly" based on the season, keeping the well-heeled bobos coming back for more.

Chez André ◐ *Bistro* 22 | 18 | 20 | €55

8e | 12, rue Marbeuf (Franklin D. Roosevelt) | 01-47-20-59-57 | www.chez-andre.com

"Yes, the tables are packed" close together at this "old-fashioned bistro" near the Champs, but it offers a "glimpse" of a "bygone era" when food was "simple" but "delicious" and waitresses "smiled" and wore "white aprons"; it's also "unbeatable for price" in "such an expensive" area, another reason why it's always "abuzz."

Chez Cécile (La Ferme des Mathurins) ⊠ *Classic French* ▽ 25 | 21 | 22 | €62

8e | 17, rue Vignon (Madeleine) | 01-42-66-46-39 | www.chezcecile.com

Lively owner Cécile Desimpel often picks up the mike on Thursday "jazz nights" at this sleek, crimson-and-sand-colored dining room, a "peaceful haven" near the Madeleine serving "carefully prepared traditional" French classics; service is also "well done" here, helping to justify the "expensive" tabs.

Chez Denise - La Tour de Montlhéry *Bistro* 23 | 18 | 20 | €52

1er | 5, rue des Prouvaires (Châtelet-Les Halles) | 01-42-36-21-82

A "taste of old Les Halles", this "rollicking" "meatfest" stays open all night serving "dinosaur-sized steaks and lots of offal" from a blackboard menu of "classic, artery-stopping" bistro fare that's best when washed down with "excellent and cheap" house Brouilly; don't expect pampering from the "gruff but harmless" staff, and plan on making many new friends over red-checked tablecloths at the "cramped" tables; P.S. closed weekends.

NEW Chez Flottes *Brasserie* - | - | - | M

1er | 2, rue Cambon (Concorde/Tuileries) | www.chezflottes.com

In an area of sky-high rents near the Tuileries, this *très* popular brasserie stands out with its reasonably priced traditional eats, which include a few Aveyronnais items, a nod to the heritage of the family who runs it; skylights and stained-glass windows lend an airy feel to the family-friendly digs (tots dig the kids' menu; adults gravitate to the bar); P.S. its upstairs New French sibling, Flottes O. Trement, has a hip, supper club vibe.

Chez Francis *Brasserie* 18 | 20 | 18 | €58

8e | 7, pl de l'Alma (Alma Marceau) | 01-47-20-86-83 | www.chezfrancis-restaurant.com

"Reserve in advance" for the coveted terrace and its "unmatched", "unobstructed views of the Eiffel Tower" (particularly "gorgeous at night") at this large brasserie on swanky Place de l'Alma that's popular with shoppers, theatergoers, "tourists", "romantics" and businesspeople; taking a back seat to the alfresco vista are the "solid traditional" eats, "very French" service and "classic" red-plush interior, and if tabs are "expensive", remember: "you pay for the view."

Chez Françoise *Classic French* 20 | 17 | 21 | €53

7e | Aérogare des Invalides (Invalides) | 01-47-05-49-03 | www.chezfrancoise.com

A somewhat "disconcerting" location beneath the Air France terminal at Les Invalides is the setting for "quality-but-no-surprises" traditional French cuisine that's priced well and served with "professionalism" at this "politician's hangout" (the National Assembly is nearby); its underground space is decorated in a vaguely 1950s style and features a "pleasant" sunken terrace that's blissfully "free of traffic noise."

Chez Fred *Bistro* ▽ 19 | 16 | 18 | €57

17e | 190 bis, bd Pereire (Pereire/Porte Maillot) | 01-45-74-20-48

Behind a neon-lit facade in the 17th, this dark and intimate spot outfitted in traditional bistro decor serves "amazing" steaks and "good-value" wines from an "exceptionally wide" list; however, those who used to come here for its *bouchon*-style bites contend that the menu has lost much of its regional edge and needs to be "re-Lyonized."

Chez Gégène Ⓜ *Classic French* 16 | 19 | 18 | €40

Joinville-le-Pont | 162 bis, quai de Polangis (Joinville-le-Pont RER) | 01-48-83-29-43 | www.chez-gegene.fr

Boogie-woogie "into the last century" at this "adorably outdated" but "friendly" *guinguette* located on the Marne River in suburban Joinville-le-Pont; just remember that it's all about the dancing here, not the "banal" Classic French fare (at least it's not expensive); P.S. closed January–March, open weekends only October–December.

Z Chez Georges ☒ *Bistro* 23 | 20 | 21 | €62

2e | 1, rue du Mail (Bourse) | 01-42-60-07-11

"Butter, cream and sauces" aren't stinted on at this "bastion of tradition" near the ultrafashionable Place des Victoires, a "boisterous" bistro hidden behind a sedate wooden facade that "charms" with its "delicious" eats, e.g. "excellent" sole meunière and a "lethal" baba au rhum; it's "not cheap" and folks are "crammed" together in the "old-fashioned" room, but those worries recede as "doting" waitresses attend to your every need; P.S. closed weekends.

Chez Georges ◐ *Brasserie* 22 | 18 | 21 | €57

17e | 273, bd Pereire (Porte Maillot) | 01-45-74-31-00 | www.restaurant-chezgeorges.fr

This "convivial" Porte Maillot brasserie gets a thumbs-up for its "generous portions of classic" dishes, including "excellent" meat, from a somewhat "expensive" menu; a "professional" staff ushers people through dinner in the simple, "comfortable" dining room, and the location is "convenient" for a meal "after the cinema."

Chez Géraud ☒ *Classic French* ▽ 20 | 17 | 19 | €65

16e | 31, rue Vital (La Muette) | 01-45-20-33-00

"A lovely experience from the welcome to the coffee" is to be had at this "neighborhood place" in the 16th, "where good unpretentious" joints are hard to find; it's especially enjoyable in cold weather when "exceptional" game is sighted on the menu of Gallic classics, but in any season, oenophiles pore over the "excellent" wine list while art-lovers appreciate the Longwy ceramic decoration; P.S. closed weekends.

Chez Grenouille ☒ *Bistro* ▽ 21 | 16 | 19 | €49

9e | 52, rue Blanche (Blanche/Trinité) | 01-42-81-34-07 | www.restaurant-chezgrenouille-paris.com

In super-trendy Pigalle, Alexis Blanchard's bistro bucks low-cal diet trends with a "vive le cholesterol!" menu that includes "exceptional" offal dishes; despite the no-frills decor and tight quarters, a "good atmosphere" prevails on account of the "friendly" staff, while moderate prices seal its no-brainer status; P.S. closed weekends.

Chez Janou ◐ *Provence* 21 | 20 | 19 | €43

3e | 2, rue Roger Verlomme (Bastille/Chemin-Vert) | 01-42-72-28-41 | www.chezjanou.com

"You can only say '*mais, oui*!'" to this popular provider of Provençal provender on a "charming backstreet" behind the Place des Vosges, where the "delicious" regional fare, "incredible list of pastis" and "cheerful" service transport the "hip" Marais crowd to sunnier climes; always "buzzing" and easy on the wallet, it's "a perfect place for dinner with friends", especially on the "pleasant" terrace; P.S. don't miss its "crowning glory", the all-you-can-eat chocolate mousse.

Chez Jenny ◐ *Alsace* | 19 | 20 | 19 | €48

3e | 39, bd du Temple (République) | 01-44-54-39-00 | www.chezjenny.com

The choucroute is "seriously awesome" - and the "fish and *fruits de mer*" are "equally" good - at this "classic" 1930s brasserie near République, owned by the Frères Blanc group; mirroring the menu's regional emphasis, real "Alsatian ambiance" radiates from the "magnificent" old space (check out the Spindler marquetry), and though it feels "a little factorylike" to some, most are "happy" here - service is "affable" and "you can even bring your kids."

Chez Julien *Bistro* | 21 | 23 | 19 | €55

4e | 1, rue du Pont-Louis-Philippe (Hôtel-de-Ville/Pont-Marie) | 01-42-78-31-64

Whether seated in the "spectacular" Napoleonic dining room or on the "pretty" patio overlooking a picturesque old church, diners swoon over the "to-die-for" decor at this "romantic" Marais bistro near the Seine; it's under the Costes umbrella and "seemingly touristic, but the food is first rate", the service solid and the prices "reasonable."

Z Chez L'Ami Jean ◐ S M *Basque* | 25 | 17 | 21 | €59

7e | 27, rue Malar (Invalides/La Tour-Maubourg) | 01-47-05-86-89 | www.amijean.eu

"An adventure in dining" awaits at this "lively", "value"-driven Basque bistro near Les Invalides, where chef Stéphane Jego's "flavorful" cooking wows surveyors; a graffitied wall and exposed ducts vie with wood paneling and cured ham hanging from the ceiling in the city-vs.-country space that's *très* "cramped" - "if the tables were any closer together, you'd be French kissing" your neighbor - still, the "skilled and cheeky" servers make it work.

Chez la Vieille S *Bistro* | ▽ 23 | 16 | 19 | €64

1er | 1, rue Bailleul (Louvre-Rivoli) | 01-42-60-15-78

"*La vieille*" Adrienne is long gone, "but her spirit lingers in the menu" of "traditional" fare in "generous" portions (you may want to "starve yourself" beforehand) at this "legendary" bistro near Les Halles; service is "attentive", and though the setting is "spartan", it's a "time capsule", an all-in-all "*très bonne*" experience, albeit "not a cheap" one.

Chez Léna et Mimile S M *Bistro* | 21 | 24 | 19 | €51

5e | 32, rue Tournefort (Censier-Daubenton/Place Monge) | 01-47-07-72-47 | www.chezlenaetmimile.com

"One of the most beautiful terraces in Paris", overlooking a "quiet" square in the 5th, attracts diners to this "undiscovered treasure" serving classic bistro standards plus occasional "molecular" dishes; the staff is "professional" and "unobtrusive", and it's a sure "value" to which regulars "return with pleasure" - even in poor weather, when the "cozy, comforting" circa-1930s interior beckons.

Chez Les Anges Ⓢ *Brasserie* 24 | 20 | 23 | €58

7e | 54, bd de la Tour-Maubourg (La Tour-Maubourg) | 01-47-05-89-86 | www.chezlesanges.com

Diners are in heaven at this "modern brasserie" in the 7th, which offers "a great take on the classics" next to contemporary items, plus a "deep wine list", at an "excellent price/quality ratio"; the service, led by proprietors Jacques and Catherine Lacipiere, shows "elegance and hospitality", and the sleek, "spacious" setting works as well for a "business lunch" as a "calm evening" out; P.S. closed weekends.

Chez Ly ◐ *Chinese/Thai* ▽ 25 | 20 | 23 | €52

17e | 95, av Niel (Pereire) | 01-40-53-88-38

Hong Kong–born Sy Ly presides over this "delicious" spot in the 17th, where "classic and inventive recipes" from the Chinese and Thai repertoires get the "high-end" treatment; service is "diligent", and the Chinoiserie-filled room is agreeable, adding up to a "sure value."

Chez Marianne *Mideastern* 19 | 15 | 13 | €27

4e | 2, rue des Hospitalières St-Gervais (St-Paul) | 01-42-72-18-86

The Middle Eastern mezes "fill you up quickly but with delight" at this "classic" of the old Jewish quarter also specializing in cut-rate Eastern European eats; the "animated" crowd is what passes for decor in the "cramped" interior, so the "patio is an alfresco favorite" - assuming you can pin down one of the "moody" servers to seat you - or just grab a falafel from the window to go.

Chez Marie-Louise Ⓢ Ⓜ *Bistro* - | - | - | M

10e | 11, rue Marie-et-Louise (Goncourt/Jacques Bonsergent) | 01-53-19-02-04 | www.chezmarielouise.com

Mediterranean touches dot the menu of updated bistro classics at this "friendly" Canal Saint-Martin hang that's "worth the visit" to the 10th; the bobo crowd is attracted by the easygoing prices and looks at home in the narrow space stocked with cool flea-market finds.

Chez Michel ◐ Ⓢ *Brittany* 24 | 16 | 20 | €53

10e | 10, rue de Belzunce (Gare du Nord/Poissonnière) | 01-44-53-06-20

The "beautiful" bounty of Brittany is on full display in the "traditional, serious" fare (including, in season, "some of the best game in Paris") at chef-owner Thierry Breton's "bustling" bistro near Gare du Nord; service is "friendly", and though some diners are nonplussed by the "simple" ye olde plaster-and-exposed-beams trim, it's still "worth" a trip; P.S. closed weekends.

Chez Nénesse Ⓢ *Classic French* ▽ 21 | 15 | 19 | €31

3e | 17, rue de Saintonge (Filles du Calvaire/République) | 01-42-78-46-49

There's "unexpected pleasure" in the "unfussy" homestyle cooking at this well-priced, "old-school" bistro in the Marais, where the tiled interior - complete with a heating stove - appears "untouched for many years"; service is "retro" too, with a special mention for the "wry wit" of the "inimitable" proprietor; P.S. closed weekends.

	FOOD	DECOR	SERVICE	COST
Chez Omar ◐ *Moroccan*	19	14	18	€37

3e | 47, rue de Bretagne (République/Temple) | 01-42-72-36-26
"Couscous is king" at this "busy, noisy and fun" Moroccan - always in season with the fashion-industry crowd - in the "super-trendy" 3rd, where the "welcoming" Omar is supported by a solid staff; the vast, Old Paris room is "good" for "group dining" and also for celeb-spotting, so long as you don't mind waiting in line and bringing a little cash (neither reservations nor credit cards are accepted).

	FOOD	DECOR	SERVICE	COST
Chez Paul ◐ *Bistro*	22	19	19	€42

11e | 13, rue de Charonne (Bastille/Ledru-Rollin) | 01-47-00-34-57 | www.chezpaul.com
A "true Parisian vibe" pulses at this 1940s-era bistro near the Bastille favored by locals and "well-informed tourists", where the resolutely "traditional", "no-frills" cooking (eggs with mayo, marrow bones, steak with shallots) is "*comme à la maison*", "only better" - and not all that much more expensive; a "competent" staff works a "classic" space so perfectly preserved it'd please a "location scout" for a "WWII" film.

	FOOD	DECOR	SERVICE	COST
Chez Paul ◐ *Bistro*	22	18	21	€42

13e | 22, rue de la Butte aux Cailles (Corvisart/Place d'Italie) | 01-45-89-22-11
Take a "trip into deep France" when you slide into one of the red banquettes at this Butte aux Cailles bistro, where the meaty, "traditional" "cuisine de terroir" is "updated to today's tastes"; "charming waiters" cater to the "diverse" crowd of locals, which appreciates the "reasonable" (read: non-touristy) tabs.

	FOOD	DECOR	SERVICE	COST
Chez Prune ◐ *Eclectic*	15	16	14	€28

10e | 36, rue Beaurepaire (Jacques Bonsergent/République) | 01-42-41-30-47
"Grab a seat outside" and "enjoy the scene" - and the view of the Canal Saint-Martin - at this "canteen for all the trendy people" of this "arty" *quartier*; it's "about the people more than the food", but the "hip", "young" things that hang here all day until late at night don't seem to mind it for a "sip" of wine or a "simple" bite to eat from the "inexpensive" Eclectic menu.

	FOOD	DECOR	SERVICE	COST
Chez Ramulaud ◐ *Bistro*	-	-	-	M

11e | 269, rue du Faubourg St-Antoine (Faidherbe-Chaligny/Nation) | 01-43-72-23-29 | www.chez-ramulaud.fr
The "interesting" bistro fare is both "traditional" and "modern" at this "casual", "typically Parisian" "neighborhood charmer", a good "budget choice" near Place de la Nation, where "the welcome is always warm"; its "great" wine list, peppered with some "unusual finds", merits a mention too.

	FOOD	DECOR	SERVICE	COST
Chez René *Lyon*	19	18	20	€45

5e | 14, bd St-Germain (Maubert-Mutualité) | 01-43-54-30-23
"Keep it simple" and you'll "enjoy" this no-frills but "friendly" "time warp" of a bistro (like a Lyonnais *bouchon,* really) in the 5th, a "favor-

FOOD | DECOR | SERVICE | COST

ite" "haunt" of a clientele that "spans the ages"; all said, it's an "enduring" classic where prices are as "soothing" and stable as the food.

Chez Savy ☒ *Aveyron* — 20 | 17 | 20 | €58

8e | 23, rue Bayard (Franklin D. Roosevelt) | 01-47-23-46-98

"Ah, that lamb shoulder" sigh contented clients of this "convivial" Aveyron address, one of the few "true neighborhood bistros" in the tony 8th, where "spot-on" service and a preponderance of regulars (mostly "radio and media professionals") make for a "familial" feel in the "narrow", booth-filled art deco room; P.S. closed weekends.

Chez Vincent ◐☒ *Italian* — 23 | 19 | 21 | €61

19e | Parc des Buttes Chaumont (Botzaris/Buttes Chaumont) | 01-42-02-22-45

The "ever-present" and "passionate" Vincent dishes up "colorful and generous" Italian fare along with "huge portions of hospitality" that make guests "feel like family" at his ristorante, housed in one of the cottagelike pavilions of the Parc des Buttes Chaumont; it's *molto* pricey but "worth a visit", especially if you "sit outside" surrounded by lush park views.

Chez Vong ◐☒ *Chinese* — 23 | 22 | 23 | €65

1er | 10, rue de la Grande Truanderie (Etienne Marcel/Les Halles) | 01-40-26-09-36 | www.chez-vong.com

Make "a Cantonese stopover" in "the heart of Old Paris" at chef-owner Vai Kuan Vong's "elegant", "refined" (and "expensive") Chinese table near Les Halles, where the "magical Peking duck" is "a must"; the "attentive" staff is always "smiling", as is the centerpiece of the dining room: a 90-kg. Buddha made of butter.

Chiberta (Le) ☒ *New French* — 24 | 22 | 24 | €110

8e | 3, rue Arsène Houssaye (Charles de Gaulle-Etoile) | 01-53-53-42-00 | www.lechiberta.com

It's "perfect to the last detail" claim devotees of this New French table off the Champs, where the "alert", "inventive" cooking style is at home in the "very modern" space, a series of rooms whose "subdued lighting" and "austerity" contribute to a sense of "calm"; service is worthy of "a grand restaurant" and so, perhaps, are the prices (no surprise, considering it's a Guy Savoy venture).

Chieng Mai ☒ *Thai* — 22 | 17 | 20 | €28

5e | 12, rue Frédéric Sauton (Maubert-Mutualité) | 01-43-25-45-45

"Authentic", "aromatic" Thai food draws diners to this long-standing Latin Quarter address that has shown "remarkable consistency" over the years; there's "little atmosphere", but prices are "reasonable" and the service "smiling."

Christine (Le) ◐ *Classic French* — 21 | 20 | 22 | €57

6e | 1, rue Christine (Odéon/St-Michel) | 01-40-51-71-64 | www.restaurantlechristine.com

The "smart and delicious" updated French classics at this Saint-Germain gathering spot are "perfectly portioned", seasoned by "courteous" service and come at an "excellent" value if you go with the prix fixe; what's more, the neo-"rustic" dining room – with exposed beams and stone walls offset by "eye-catching" tangerine accents – is "romantic" despite "numerous tourists who have discovered its charm."

Christophe *Bistro* ▽ 24 | 17 | 22 | €55

5e | 8, rue Descartes (Cardinal Lemoine) | 01-43-26-72-49 | www.christopherestaurant.fr

"The food is the only star" – besides chef-owner Christophe Philippe perhaps – at this Latin Quarter bistro where the "best ingredients", sourced from some of France's finest suppliers, are employed in the "excellent", "simply prepared" meat-centric dishes ("if you love offal, go"); "the incongruity of the food and the decor can be disorienting" – the teensy room is "no-frills" – but it's a real "deal"; P.S. closed Wednesday and Thursday.

Cibus ☒ *Italian* - | - | - | M

1er | 5, rue Molière (Palais Royal-Musée du Louvre/Pyramides) | 01-42-61-50-19

The menu is "never the same", the mostly organic "products are fresh" and the staff are real "characters" at this moderately priced "true" Italian near the Palais-Royal; it's a minimalist and "minuscule" 20-seater, where "everyone can hear each other", but "that's also what makes it charming."

Cigale Récamier (La) ☒ *Classic French* 22 | 19 | 19 | €54

7e | 4, rue Récamier (Sèvres-Babylone) | 01-45-48-86-58

"A soufflé-lover's fantasy", satisfying dreams both sweet and savory, awaits at this Classic French table down a tiny pedestrian alley in the 7th, "just the spot" "after shopping" at the Bon Marché thanks to its "calm, contemporary" decor (the bookcase centerpiece is *très* "nerd chic"); the staff alternates between "casual" and "professional", but prices are "correct" for the neighborhood, and a crowd of beau monde regulars means the "people-watching isn't bad either" (*bonjour,* Jacques Chirac).

Z Cinq (Le) *Haute Cuisine* 28 | 28 | 28 | €179

8e | Four Seasons George V | 31, av George V (Alma Marceau/George V) | 01-49-52-71-54 | www.fourseasons.com/paris

"Dine like royalty" at this Haute Cuisine landmark in the Four Seasons George V, where "brilliant" chef Eric Briffard's "flawless", "sybaritic" cooking is matched by the "marvelous" service and "opulent", "floral" surroundings (it's one of the city's "most beautiful rooms"), resulting in a "sublime" experience for "all your senses"; yes, you will pay "dearly for the privilege", but this is "*le top du top*": a "meal of a lifetime" that's "worth the splurge"; P.S. jacket required.

Cinq Mars ☒ *Bistro* 21 | 20 | 20 | €43

7e | 51, rue de Verneuil (Rue du Bac/Solférino) | 01-45-44-69-13

Don't miss the "lick-the-bowl-good" chocolate mousse at this "charming neighborhood" bistro near the Musée d'Orsay offering a "simple menu" of French "comfort food" and "warm" service; it draws "cool, young" Left Bankers who pack into the "cute", "dimly lit" old-meets-new room for a reasonably priced "dinner with friends."

Citrus Etoile ☒ *Classic/New French* 24 | 20 | 23 | €81

8e | 6, rue Arsène Houssaye (Etoile) | 01-42-89-15-51 | www.citrusetoile.fr

Surveyors swoon over chef-owner Gilles Epié's "inventive" takes on Classic French cuisine as well as the "charming welcome" of his "vivacious" wife, who directs the "attentive" service at this "premier", if pricey, destination for "gastronomy" that's "close to the Champs, but not too touristy"; as befits the name, the "spacious", "modern" room is accented by orange hues (e.g. the live goldfish swimming atop many tables); P.S. closed weekends.

Claude Colliot ☒ M *New French* ∇ 23 | 16 | 21 | €61

4e | 40, rue des Blancs Manteaux (Hôtel-de-Ville) | 01-42-71-55-45 | www.claudecolliot.com

Chef Claude Colliot is "in his element" at this "hip" Marais laboratory, a minimalist showcase for the "of-the-moment" refined techniques - "his foam infusions are a revelation" - that make him "one of a kind"; service is "friendly" and "unaffected", and while it all "comes at a price", the trend-conscious crowd thinks it's "worth a trip."

Cloche des Halles (La) ☒ *Wine Bar/Bistro* ∇ 18 | 14 | 20 | €30

1er | 28, rue Coquillière (Les Halles/Louvre-Rivoli) | 01-42-36-93-89

The market at Les Halles is long gone, but the bell that once heralded its openings and closings still hangs at this "old-timer" wine bar and bistro, good "for a glass of cru Beaujolais", "some cheese and charcuterie", or maybe a "simple" lunch; the corner location is full of "typical Parisian ambiance", and the prices are nostalgic too.

NEW **Clocher de Montmartre (Au)** *Bistro* - | - | - | I

18e | 10, rue Lamarck (Château Rouge) | 01-42-64-90-23 | www.auclocherdemontmartre.fr

Antoine Heerah's new Montmartre crowd-pleaser offers casual free-form feeding all day long on cafe and bistro favorites - savory tarts, omelets, salads, etc. - with sweet prices in playful, eye-popping digs (e.g. juxtaposing black-and-white checkerboard floors with toile wallpaper and teal chairs); P.S. design geeks note the Ingo Maurer and Marcel Wanders fixtures.

Clocher Péreire (Le) ☒ *New French* ∇ 24 | 16 | 23 | €51

17e | 42, bd Pereire (Pereire) | 01-44-40-04-15 | www.clocher-pereire.fr

The "inventive", "top-quality" cooking at this New French table in the 17th approaches "true gastronomy" - unsurprising, considering the chef-owners' previous stints at Le Bristol, Taillevent et al. - but the "unbeatable" prices are more bistro-like; service is "agreeable" too, rendering the "slightly boring" (i.e. taupe) contemporary decor easy enough to forget; P.S. closed weekends.

	FOOD	DECOR	SERVICE	COST

Clos des Gourmets (Le) *New French* 25 | 21 | 23 | €58

7e | 16, av Rapp (Alma Marceau/Ecole Militaire) | 01-45-51-75-61 | www.closdesgourmets.com

"Go, go, go!" urge fans of this "hot reservation" near the Eiffel Tower, where the "imaginative" French cuisine is "consistently excellent" and customers "feel at home" in the "quiet, elegant" dining room; "while not inexpensive", the quality/price ratio is among "the best in the neighborhood", something even the "upscale" clientele appreciates.

Closerie des Lilas (La) *Classic French* 20 | 23 | 20 | €69

6e | 171, bd du Montparnasse (Port Royal/Vavin) | 01-40-51-34-50 | www.closeriedeslilas.fr

"Ah, the ambiance!" sigh lovers of this "timeless" multitasker - and erstwhile Hemingway haunt - in the Port Royal area, with its "romantic", "unchanged" interior and arboreal terrace, both attended by a "professional" staff; those who find prices "excessive" for the Classic French fare served in the restaurant section opt instead for oysters and other "typical" fare in the brasserie or head for the "wonderful bar" and its live piano; P.S. reservations suggested in the restaurant, not taken in the brasserie.

Clown Bar *Wine Bar/Bistro* ∇ 15 | 24 | 18 | €35

11e | 114, rue Amelot (Filles du Calvaire) | 01-43-55-87-35 | www.clown-bar.fr

Sure, "there is better food" to be had elsewhere, "but the place remains adorable" say fans of this "charming" wine bar/bistro almost next door to the Cirque d'Hiver, a "vintage" art nouveau shrine to - what else? - the clown; service is "*bon*", and it's perfect for "a drink and a simple meal" of "solid"-enough grub, making for a "great bargain", no fooling; P.S. open Wednesday–Saturday; cash only.

NEW **Cobéa** *New French* - | - | - | VE

14e | 11, rue Raymond Losserand (Gaîté/Pernety) | 01-43-20-21-39 | www.cobea.fr

Chef Philippe Belissent recently unveiled this ambitious New French near Montparnasse, where market ingredients get the modernist treatment in a prix fixe–only format of three courses at lunch (plus an amuse-bouche - a relative bargain), and limited-choice menus of four, six or eight courses at dinner; tables are well spaced in the contemporary, pewter-and-bone-hued room, which allows ample elbow room to sign the ample bill; P.S. reservations required.

Cocottes (Les) *New French* 24 | 19 | 21 | €43

7e | 135, rue St-Dominique (Ecole Militaire) | www.maisonconstant.com

Christian Constant's "casual but chic" "'diner'" concept "just keeps getting better" rave regulars about this "fun", "affordable" address in the 7th, where the "precise" New French comfort food is served in personal-sized "casseroles" (Staub, *bien sûr*) by a "cordial" staff to a "convivial" crowd seated at communal high-top tables or on stools at the counter; reservations aren't accepted, so forget about "the French proclivity to eat late" and "come early" to minimize the wait.

	FOOD	DECOR	SERVICE	COST

Coin des Gourmets (Au) *Cambodian/Vietnamese* | 23 | 16 | 22 | €38

1er | 38, rue du Mont-Thabor (Concorde) | 01-42-60-79-79 ⊠
5e | 5, rue Dante (Cluny La Sorbonne/Maubert-Mutualité) | 01-43-26-12-92
A "great change from everyday ordinary" Parisian fare is the promise of the "full-flavored", "authentic" Cambodian and Vietnamese specialties at this pair of "unprepossessing" family-run eateries, where "hospitality" rules; decor is "more classic in the 5th, more designy in the 1st", but both offer "a beautiful [culinary] voyage at a reasonable price."

Comédiens (Les) ◐ ⊠ *Classic French* ▽ 19 | 18 | 19 | €65

9e | 7, rue Blanche (Trinité) | 01-40-82-95-95 | www.lescomediensparis.fr
The Classic French cooking is "generous and good" (albeit "expensive") at this "simple and convivial" spot in the 9th, which sports a contemporary loftlike look with plenty of seating at the long bar; the real "strong point" is that "they serve late", satisfying the post-performance prandial needs of thespians and theatergoers.

Comme à Savonnières ◐ ⊠ Ⓜ *Bistro* - | - | - | M

6e | 18, rue Guisarde (St-Germain-des-Prés) | 01-43-29-52-18
There's a slight nod to the food and wine of the Loire Valley, but not everything on the otherwise typical menu is 'as in Savonnières' at this "bustling" Saint-Germain bistro, which hosts a "very friendly" crowd of "young professionals" in a stone-walled duplex; a "convivial" crew and easy prices, especially at lunch, make it one "to recommend."

NEW Compagnie de Bretagne (La) *Brittany* - | - | - | M

6e | 9, rue de l'Ecole de Médecine (Cluny-La Sorbonne/Odéon) | 01-43-29-39-00 | www.compagnie-de-bretagne.com
Galettes go chic at this Saint-Germain crêperie, where premium Breton products, including artisanal ciders, are showcased in a preppy Bridgehampton-meets-Brest room designed by Pierre-Yves Rochon; service is as well behaved as the Bonpoint-clad kids who accompany their parents here on weekends, and prices remain family-friendly (for the quarter).

NEW Comptoir de Brice (Au) Ⓜ *New French* - | - | - | I

10e | 2 Marché Couvert Saint-Martin | 31-33, rue du Château-d'Eau (Château-d'Eau/Jacques Bonsergent) | 07-87-36-77-38 | www.aucomptoirdebrice.com
Telegenic *Top Chef* semifinalist Brice Morvent can now be seen surrounded by fans at the counter of his casual canteen in the covered Marché Saint-Martin, where he's cooking up affordable Med-accented modern French fare, plus a signature burger that's achieved cult status; natural light illuminates the open kitchen, which is the focal point of the fresh-looking avocado-and-white space; P.S. bonuses abound: takeout is available, there's an on-site boutique and the chef gives cooking classes too.

FOOD	DECOR	SERVICE	COST

Comptoir des Mers (Le) *Seafood* ▽ 23 | 18 | 20 | €58

4e | 1, rue de Turenne (St-Paul) | 01-42-72-66-51 | www.livraison-fruitsdemer.com

"Fresh fish is guaranteed" – and you'll pay for it – at this sleek Marais seafood market-cum-restaurant, where the simple, "cooked to perfection" preparations highlight the quality of the product; a fleet of "helpful" servers assists diners navigating the waters in the mod, mirrored room that features a large aquarium.

Z Comptoir du Relais (Le) *Bistro/Brasserie* 27 | 17 | 21 | €58

6e | Hôtel Relais Saint-Germain | 9, carrefour de l'Odéon (Odéon) | 01-44-27-07-97 | www.hotel-paris-relais-saint-germain.com

Yves Camdeborde "defines haute bistro cooking" at his Odéon "gem", offering "innovative" dishes distinguished by "amazing ingredients" and "incredible execution" on both the brasserie menu (served daytime/weekends) and no-options prix fixe format (served weeknights); tables are "cramped", service can be "brusque" and you may need to "sell your soul for a dinner reservation" ("hint: stay at the hotel") or "wait in line for lunch", but fans say it's "worth it", especially since most are "thrilled with the quality for the price."

Comptoir Marguery (Le) *Burgundian* ▽ 21 | 17 | 21 | €44

13e | 9, bd de Port-Royal (Les Gobelins) | 01-42-17-43-43 | www.comptoirmarguery.com

"A friendly smile" awaits at this "cozy" brick-walled Burgundian bistro (little sister to Le Petit Marguery next door) in the 13th, whose "attention to ingredients" is evident in its "hearty" fare; it's a "fabulous value" too, a fact that is not lost on loyal "locals" who have made it their "little canteen."

Concert de Cuisine (Le) ⊠ *Japanese/New French* - | - | - | M

15e | 14, rue Nélaton (Bir-Hakeim) | 01-40-58-10-15 | www.leconcertdecuisine.com

"Sit at the counter and observe the dancing movements" of chef-owner Naoto Masumoto as he turns out his "sophisticated" Franco-Japanese fare at this tiny teppanyaki in the far 15th, where the griddle is the centerpiece of the minimalist Zen dining room; all in all, it's a "fabulous" culinary experience at a "remarkable value" (it's prix fixe only).

Congrès Maillot (Le) ◐ *Brasserie* 20 | 18 | 20 | €59

17e | 80, av de la Grande-Armée (Porte Maillot) | 01-45-74-17-24 | www.congres-maillot.com

"The oysters are divine" at this vast, plushly decorated brasserie in the 17th with a "reputation for shellfish" and otherwise "correct" cooking; staffed by "competent personnel" and open all day until 2 AM, it's a "*bon* business address", favored by conventioneers from the nearby Palais des Congrès, who consider the "copious" all-inclusive option an "unbeatable" deal.

FOOD | DECOR | SERVICE | COST

Copenhague Danish | 23 | 20 | 20 | €77

8e | 142, av des Champs-Elysées (Charles de Gaulle-Etoile/George V) | 01-44-13-86-26 | www.floradanica-paris.com

"The herring is a delight, the smoked salmon perfect" and the other Nordic dishes "highly refined" at this "modern, sober and elegant" Dane on the Champs, perched above its more affordable sibling Flora Danica; some find little warmth in the "prim" but able staff and rather "cold" interior design, but the "hidden gem of a garden" is a decidedly un-chilly alternative in summer; P.S. closed weekends.

NEW Coq Rico (Le) *Bistro* | - | - | - | E

18e | 98, rue Lepic (Lamarck-Caulaincourt) | 01-42-59-82-89 | www.lecoqrico.com

Antoine Westermann recently hatched this all-bird bistro in the 18th, where pedigreed poultry, both part (livers, hearts) and parcel (whole roasted birds), is the prime ingredient; the bright, barnyard-moderne room is clad in white clapboards and countrified plank floors, and the well-plumed crowd pecking at their food don't seem to mind the high-flying prices.

NEW Cornichon (Le) *Bistro* | - | - | - | M

14e | 34, rue Gassendi (Denfert-Rochereau/Mouton-Duvernet) | 01-43-20-40-19 | www.lecornichon.fr

There's a Chez l'Ami Jean alum behind this contemporary bistro recently installed in the 14th, where hearty but sophisticated market-based cuisine is accompanied by a standout wine list; moderate tabs have locals puckering up to the handsomely lit room, with its dark wood and clean, contemporary lines.

Corte (La) *Italian* | - | - | - | M

1er | 320, rue St-Honoré (Tuileries) | 01-42-60-45-27

Both the cuisine and the charming owner have a Neapolitan accent at this blink-and-you'll-miss-it Italian table, hidden down a "tranquil" courtyard off the Rue Saint-Honoré; it draws chic locals who maintain their *bella figure* on a diet of "fine" antipasti, housemade pastas and fish dishes from an always-changing menu.

Costes *Eclectic* | 18 | 25 | 15 | €76

1er | Hôtel Costes | 239, rue St-Honoré (Concorde/Tuileries) | 01-42-44-50-25 | www.hotelcostes.com

"Dine with the glitterati" at this "sexy" hotel eatery on Rue Saint-Honoré, where the cosmopolitan Eclectic cuisine ("overpriced, of course") is "ok" but "forgettable in the finest Costes tradition"; "be beautiful or be ignored" could be the motto of the "snooty" "models" on staff, but it's worth a pilgrimage to the "people-watching center of the world" to enjoy a slice of the "high-fashion lifestyle."

Cottage Marcadet (Le) *New French* | - | - | - | E

18e | 151 bis, rue Marcadet (Lamarck-Caulaincourt) | 01-42-57-71-22 | www.cottagemarcadet.com

Young chef-owner Cyril Choisne "strives to please" with his "inventive" New French cuisine at this "overlooked" "jewel" on the quiet side of Sacré Coeur; reservations are necessary to snag one of the 15 seats in the "calm", "romantic" dining room, and though the furniture is straight out of Versailles, you won't lose your head over the (relative) "bargain" pricing.

Cotte Rôti (Le) *Bistro* | - | - | - | M

12^e^ | 1, rue de Cotte (Gare de Lyon/Ledru-Rollin) | 01-43-45-06-37

Chef-owner Nicolas Michel's contemporary bistro near the Aligre market draws loyal locals who appreciate his creatively presented, seasonal dishes (an intense mushroom lasagna, a tender seven-hour lamb) plus the list of biodynamic wines; gone is the garish red-and-gray color scheme after a recent redo in neutral tones, but the "personalized" service and wallet-friendly prices remain intact.

Cou de la Girafe (Le) *New French* | ∇ 13 | 16 | 14 | €51

8^e^ | 7, rue Paul Baudry (Franklin D. Roosevelt/St-Philippe-du-Roule) | 01-56-88-29-55 | www.restaurantlecoudelagirafe.com

Warm earth tones frame the chic faces who frequent this sleek corner resto-lounge where the "pleasant" ambiance boosts the appeal of the "passable" New French cuisine; service can be lackluster, and it's a little "*cher*" for what it is, but this is "the heart of the 8th", after all.

Couleurs de Vigne *Wine Bar/Bistro* | - | - | - | I

15^e^ | 2, rue Marmontel (Convention/Vaugirard) | 01-45-33-32-96 | www.couleurs-de-vigne.com

The word through the grapevine is that oenophiles can ogle a large and "excellent" assortment of "not-expensive" bottles arrayed on the walls in what passes as decor at this *demi*-sized, no-frills neighborhood *bistrot à vins* in the 15th; the "friendly" staff supplies the perfect pairings - charcuterie, cheese and the like - from a "correct" and ultra-cheap menu that's as full of terroir as the wine; P.S. closed weekends.

Coulisses (Les) *Bistro* | - | - | - | M

9^e^ | 19, rue Notre Dame de Lorette (St-Georges) | 01-45-26-46-46 | www.restolescoulisses.fr

This "surprising" theater district bistro pulls off a successful balancing act between old-school fare like tartare and pot-au-feu, and more contemporary creations, all driven by the market, priced well and thoughtfully accompanied by a biodynamic wine list; though relatively new, it already feels like a classic, thanks to the smart, retro decor, and the fact that it remains "pretty much undiscovered" by anyone but locals.

Coupe-Chou (Le) *Classic French* | 20 | 25 | 19 | €56

5^e^ | 9-11, rue de Lanneau (Maubert-Mutualité) | 01-46-33-68-69 | www.lecoupechou.com

"Go with your sweetheart" to this "romantic" Classic French in the 5th, housed in "a warren of delightfully small rooms" that feels "more like a country inn than a restaurant"; "copious" portions of "authentic" Gallic fare, served by a "helpful and patient" staff, make it a relatively "good-value" destination "on a cool Paris evening" - especially with "a table next to the fireplace."

	FOOD	DECOR	SERVICE	COST

Coupe Gorge (Le) ◐ *Bistro* | - | - | - | M |

4e | 2, rue de la Coutellerie (Hôtel-de-Ville) | 01-48-04-79-24 | www.coupegorge.fr

The "Old Paris" feeling is what attracts a "noisy" crowd to the red banquettes of this "fun little bistro" for "simple, good food" like steak tartare and duck confit at moderate prices; service is "friendly", and an "excellent location" in the Marais doesn't hurt, either.

Z Coupole (La) ◐ *Brasserie* | 18 | 24 | 18 | €58 |

14e | 102, bd du Montparnasse (Vavin) | 01-43-20-14-20 | www.flobrasseries.com/coupoleparis

"Central casting waiters" have their shrugs down pat at this "mythical" Montparnasse brasserie owned by Groupe Flo, a "sumptuous" art deco palace that's "charged with history" and always overflowing with tourists, pretty Parisians and "their little dogs" too; the food has perhaps "declined in quality over the years" – and the prices are definitely "modern" – but the *fruits de mer* platters remain "superb", and besides, it's a "quintessential Paris experience."

Crabe Marteau (Le) ☒ *Brittany/Seafood* | 20 | 18 | 20 | €39 |

17e | 16, rue des Acacias (Argentine) | 01-44-09-85-59 | www.crabemarteau.fr

"You'd think you were in Brest" as you hammer away (literally) at "enormous" crabs and pick at the other "fresh" *fruits de mer* at this casual seafood specialist in the 17th, where the "warm" service is as "adorable" as the kitschy seaside decor; bonus: the bill won't sink your bank balance.

Crémerie (La) ☒ *Wine Bar/Bistro* | ▽ 21 | 18 | 18 | €38 |

6e | 9, rue des Quatre-Vents (Odéon) | 01-43-54-99-30 | www.lacremerie.fr

The natural and organic *vins* and "*beaux*" charcuterie and cheese at this "cute boutique" wine bar and shop in the 6th make for a perfect, moderately priced "apéritif or light lunch"; it's housed in a former dairy and retains the original painted ceiling, which, combined with "convivial" service, lends an "old-world" feel.

Cristal de Sel ☒ M *New French* | ▽ 27 | 17 | 25 | €45 |

15e | 13, rue Mademoiselle (Commerce/Félix Faure) | 01-42-50-35-29 | www.lecristaldesel.fr

"Shhh, don't tell anyone about this place" beg acolytes who happily make the pilgrimage to the "deep" 15th for the "exquisitely presented" New French cuisine of chef and part-owner Karil Lopez, whose gastro-bistro style is informed by years at Le Bristol; co-owner Damien Crepu leads the "absolutely charming" staff, and tables are "well spaced" in the "simple but elegant" room, making for an almost "fine-dining experience" without the high price.

Z Cristal Room ☒ *New French* | 20 | 29 | 20 | €90 |

16e | Baccarat | 11, pl des Etats-Unis (Boissière/Iéna) | 01-40-22-11-10 | www.baccarat.fr

Baccarat chandeliers illuminate this "striking", grand siècle-inspired space designed by Philippe Starck – voted Paris' tops for

Decor - housed in a former aristocratic residence in the 16th; the staff is "courteous" and the kitchen's New French offerings are "good" but, according to some, "too expensive" for "minimalist" portions, leading critics to say "skip the food and see the crystal" - if nothing else, it's a "superb showroom" for the famous crystal company, whose offices and museum are here.

Crudus [S] *Italian/Wine Bar* — - | - | - | M

1er | 21, rue St-Roch (Pyramides/Tuileries) | 01-42-60-90-29

The "simple Italian way" of cooking emphasizes the quality of the organic ingredients used at this midpriced, "mini"-sized restaurant/ wine bar in the 1st, an almost all-white nook with a big wood bar, clear-topped tables and wooden chairs filled by swanky Saint-Honoré locals who like the "professional and friendly" service.

Crus de Bourgogne (Aux) [S] *Bistro* — ▽ 20 | 21 | 21 | €38

2e | 3, rue Bachaumont (Les Halles/Sentier) | 01-42-33-48-24 | www.auxcrusdebourgogne.com

"Delicious, traditional" fare - mostly Burgundian, with wines to match - is what's cooking at this gently priced, "typically Parisian" 1930s-era bistro in the Montorgueil *quartier,* staffed by waiters who are "always smiling" and "available"; P.S. closed weekends.

Cuisine (La) *New French* — ▽ 22 | 20 | 21 | €85

8e | Royal Monceau | 37, av Hoche (Ternes) | 01-42-99-98-80 | www.leroyalmonceau.com

The *haute bourgeois* meets high design in the 8th at this new flagship table of the refurbished Royal Monceau Hotel (now part of the Raffles group), where chef Laurent André's "hyper-fresh" New French cooking, and desserts by pastry demigod Pierre Hermé, feed an international, recession-immune crowd in a "splendid", library-like room with low leather chairs, Murano glass and a color-streaked ceiling, signed by Philippe Starck.

Cuizine (La) [S][M] *Bistro* — - | - | - | E

11e | 73, rue Amelot (Chemin-Vert) | 01-43-14-27-00 | www.lacuizine.fr

Run by a charming couple, this neighborhood bistro brings a little sunshine to the stretch between Bastille and République, with a seasonal, Mediterranean-leaning menu and a bold, orange-and-black color scheme; local office workers take advantage of the prix fixe deal at lunch (otherwise, it's pricey), and the crowd veers a little younger and hipper at night.

Cul de Poule *Bistro* — 20 | 16 | 18 | €34

9e | 53, rue des Martyrs (Pigalle) | 01-53-16-13-07

This funky Rue des Martyrs bistro uses seasonal ingredients from marquee producers, resulting in "original" dishes that - along with a natural and organic wine list - please the "trendy" bobos who like to know where their food comes from; prices are "cheap", mismatched midcentury-modern chairs furnish the place and the hip *serveuses* are "charming" too.

Dali (Le) *Classic French* | - | - | - | VE

1er | Hôtel Meurice | 228, rue de Rivoli (Concorde/Tuileries) | 01-44-58-10-44 | www.lemeurice.com

More sumptuous than surreal, this "elegant" room in the Hôtel Meurice offers all-day dining via a menu of "superb" Classic French fare from the playbook of head chef Yannick Alléno; though less expensive than the hotel's flagship table (Meurice), tabs "soar" nonetheless, but it's "a treat on every level" that leaves diners feeling "like royalty"; P.S. reservations required.

NEW **Dans les Landes** *Wine Bar/Bistro* | ∇ 23 | 17 | 18 | €38

5e | 19 bis, rue Monge (Censier-Daubenton) | 01-45-87-06-00

"Go with friends and share" the "excellent" Southwestern tapas at this ham-heavy wine bar/bistro that recently set up shop in the 5th, a second address from Julien Duboué of Afaria; it gets "noisy" at the high-top communal tables (e.g. when rugby's on TV), but the price is right, service is "quick" and it's a "fun stop" for a "convivial" bite.

Da Rosa *Eclectic/Wine Bar* | 21 | 16 | 17 | €40

6e | 62, rue de Seine (Mabillon/Odéon) | 01-40-51-00-09 | www.darosa.fr

"For some wine and ham in the afternoon, it doesn't get any better" than this chic eat-in épicerie, a sort of wine bar where you can snack on a selection of "nice little tidbits" like charcuterie - Spanish *jamon,* in particular - delivered by "friendly" servers to tables on the pretty "hedged terrace" or in the "shadowy" cellar; it's an affordable "way to cap a day of art-gallery hopping" in Saint-Germain.

Daru ⊠ *Russian* | ∇ 19 | 16 | 19 | €91

8e | 19, rue Daru (Courcelles/Ternes) | 01-42-27-23-60 | www.daru.fr

Trade *vin* for vodka at this Russian redoubt in the 8th, where caviar, blini, borscht and other "delicious" specialties are served in a "cozy", red-hued dining room; it's priced more for petro-oligarchs than the proletariat, but party loyalists say "go" anyway.

NEW **Dauphin (Le)** ⊠ M *New French* | 22 | 16 | 18 | €54

11e | 131, av Parmentier (Goncourt) | 01-55-28-78-88

If you can't get a table at Le Chateaubriand in the 11th, consider its new heir apparent a few doors down operating at "the same high level", where enfant terrible Inaki Aizpitarte's "inventive" New French cooking gets the small-plates treatment; professional hipster waiters manage the crowd of foodies and creatives, whose conversations reverberate in the "noisy", ultramodern "cube of marble" (designed by Rem Koolhaas and Clément Blanchet).

Davé ⊠ *Chinese/Vietnamese* | ∇ 17 | 12 | 21 | €53

1er | 12, rue de Richelieu (Palais Royal-Musée du Louvre) | 01-42-61-49-48

It's "fashionistas", "not foodies", who frequent this "fabulous" Chinese-Vietnamese "hole-in-the-wall" next to the Palais-Royal, where the biggest draw might be monsieur Davé himself, a "divine" "character" who always "has some pretty great stories" about the famous faces he's fed; "it doesn't matter" that the semi-pricey food is only "fine" or the decor nonexistent - it's a "Parisian institution."

	FOOD	DECOR	SERVICE	COST

D'Chez Eux Ⓢ Ⓜ *Southwest* — 24 | 18 | 21 | €71

7e | 2, av de Lowendal (Ecole Militaire) | 01-47-05-52-55 | www.chezeux.com

"Authentic *cuisine campagnarde*" – i.e. country cooking "like your French *grand-mère*" used to make – awaits at this Southwestern in the 7th, where you're greeted "with a basket of sausages" by "great waiters" who give this place "real personality"; "checkered tablecloths" and "comfortable tables complete the homey picture", and while some find it "high priced", you "won't leave here hungry."

Délices d'Aphrodite (Les) *Greek* — 20 | 15 | 16 | €43

5e | 4, rue de Candolle (Censier-Daubenton) | 01-43-31-40-39 | www.mavrommatis.fr

There's "sunshine on the plates" at this Hellenic haven in the Latin Quarter that's "almost as good as" mother ship Mavrommatis, but "cheaper"; thanks to "personalized" service, "calm and tranquility" flow in the Aegean-accented room and on the "pretty terrace" too.

Derrière *New French* — 15 | 24 | 15 | €48

3e | 69, rue des Gravilliers (Arts et Métiers) | 01-44-61-91-95 | www.derriere-resto.com

Welcome to "hipsterville": you might "eat dinner while the next table plays Ping-Pong" at this "apartment"-like hangout in the 3rd (behind sibling Le 404) that appeals to a "young", "trendy" crowd with "funky" mismatched decor; it's "a little expensive" for New French fare that's "forgettable but not bad" and service that's "not professional", but it's a fine place to "kick off a fun night."

Dessirier ◐ *Brasserie/Seafood* — 24 | 22 | 23 | €88

17e | 9, pl du Maréchal Juin (Pereire) | 01-42-27-82-14 | www.restaurantdessirier.com

"Top of the line" seafood of "extraordinary freshness" is "delicately prepared" at this sleek, Michel Rostang-run brasserie in the 17th, a go-to for business diners who appreciate the "discreet service" and "isolated tables" in a curvilinear, gray room that's brightened with coral-colored accents and whimsical sculptures; the catch is that it's "expensive", especially "if you don't take the set menu", but otherwise, "everything is perfect."

Desvouges Ⓢ *Bistro* — - | - | - | M

5e | 6, rue des Fossés St-Marcel (Les Gobelins/St-Marcel) | 01-47-07-91-25 | www.restaurantdesvouges.fr

A veteran journalist gave up reporting to follow his gastronomic dreams, and the result is this well-priced "little" lace-curtained bistro on the far side of the 5th, where the "simple but good" food has won a small following; it's recommended "for wine lovers" too, and the "convivial welcome gives it a particular soul"; P.S. closed weekends.

Deux Amis (Aux) Ⓢ Ⓜ *Wine Bar/Bistro* — 21 | 18 | 21 | €50

11e | 45, rue Oberkampf (Oberkampf) | 01-58-30-38-13

"Delicious tapas" with "delicate flavors" come at "reasonable prices" at this casual wine bar/bistro in Oberkampf, where the small plates - and a few heartier *plats du jour* - strike some as "a lot fresher" than the Atomic Age diner decor; it's "trendy" all the same, packed with hipsters and foodies who gather at the old zinc bar for "boisterous" evenings over bottles of natural wine or something stronger.

Z Deux Magots (Les) ◐ *Classic French* 17 | 21 | 17 | €45

6e | 6, pl St-Germain-des-Prés (St-Germain-des-Prés) | 01-45-48-55-25 | www.lesdeuxmagots.fr

"What a show!" cry those who "savor Paris street life" in all its glory at this "iconic", "grand" all-day cafe in Saint-Germain - even if the parade of tourists, "pseudo-literati" and "Prada models" would make a former habitué like Sartre "roll in his grave"; so what if the Classic French eats are "secondary", "overpriced" and served by waiters who "could be nicer" - just grab a table outside, "splurge on a coffee" and "while away the day."

Diep ◐ *Asian* 21 | 15 | 18 | €64

8e | 55, rue Pierre Charron (George V) | 01-45-63-52-76 | www.diep.fr

"The Peking duck is still delicious" at this Asian elder statesman "near the fashion houses" of the 8th, where the kitchen turns out "*très bons*" Chinese, Thai and Vietnamese dishes and the room "drips Chinese kitsch" (some say it's "starting to date itself"); it's all "a little bling-bling", and "the prices correspond to the clientele" who prefer to be seated "by the entrance, to see and be seen."

Z Divellec (Le) ⓢ *Seafood* 26 | 21 | 24 | €138

7e | 107, rue de l'Université (Invalides) | 01-45-51-91-96 | www.le-divellec.com

"It's true, they know how to cook fish" at this "elegant, upscale" seafood restaurant in the 7th, famous for its "amazing" pressed lobster; the "exquisite service" satisfies "your every need", and while some wish it were "a little more festive", the sober feel is fine for the fleets of politicians - and others "with the means" - who dock in the "imposing" room for power dining; P.S. reservations required; closed weekends.

1728 ⓢ *New French* 21 | 25 | 20 | €81

8e | 8, rue d'Anjou (Concorde/Madeleine) | 01-40-17-04-77 | www.restaurant-1728.com

The "royal" decor at this "princely" restaurant, housed in Lafayette's "historic" former mansion near La Madeleine, is a "lovely" backdrop for a "romantic" dinner of "inventive" French cuisine "refined with an Asian tint" and served by a "professional" staff; many come "more for the exceptional setting than for the food" - and it's "a little bit expensive" at that - but Americans, at least, consider it a chance to "repay the debt" they owe France.

NEW Dodin de Mark Singer (Le) ⓢ Ⓜ *New French* - | - | - | E

17e | 42, rue des Acacias (Argentine/Charles de Gaulle-Etoile) | 01-43-80-28-54

American-in-Paris chef Mark Singer has been cooking in France for nearly three decades (most recently at the erstwhile Cave

Gourmande), and now he's taken over the old Petit Colombier space in the 17th, contemporizing its look with pale oak floors, red accents and Chinese-style lanterns, and offering finely wrought New French cooking while breathing new life into some classics; the prix fixe menus offer good value (though à la carte prices are steep).

Domaine de Lintillac *Southwest* 20 | 14 | 19 | €32

2e | 10, rue St-Augustin (Quatre-Septembre) | 01-40-20-96-27 | www.lintillac-paris.com
7e | 20, rue Rousselet (Duroc/Vaneau) | 01-45-66-88-23 | www.restaurant-lintillac.com
9e | 54, rue Blanche (Blanche/Trinité) | 01-48-74-84-36 | www.lintillac-paris.com ☒
16e | 7, av de Versailles (Mirabeau/Passy) | 01-42-88-42-42 | www.lintillac-paris.com

Everything is "just ducky" at these Southwestern spots, where a "spectacular cassoulet" and other dishes based on products direct from the Périgord please "lovers of foie gras and canard"; their basic setups offer "no frills", but they're all "warm, little" places staffed by "attentive" crews and are a "stunning value" to boot.

Dôme (Le) ◐ *Seafood* 22 | 22 | 20 | €76

14e | 108, bd du Montparnasse (Vavin) | 01-43-35-25-81

Whether you go for the "superb sole" or "straight to the oysters" and a bottle of Chablis, "there isn't better seafood anywhere" claim connoisseurs of this packed-to-the-gills Montparnasse "institution", a "belle epoque beauty" of a brasserie; "energetic" service helps it work equally well "for a family outing or a business lunch" - depending, perhaps, on who's paying the "expensive" bill.

Dôme du Marais (Le) ◐ *New French* 19 | 21 | 17 | €54

4e | 53 bis, rue des Francs-Bourgeois (Hôtel-de-Ville/Rambuteau) | 01-42-74-54-17 | www.ledomedumarais.fr

A recent change of owner and chef, plus a mild renovation, may outdate the scores, but in essence nothing has truly changed here: a "dramatic setting" still makes this onetime pawnbrokers' auction house a "top choice for a romantic dinner in the Marais", whether seated under the glass-and-cast-iron dome in the circular main room or in the luminous winter garden; the "refined" New French cuisine still comes at a "not-outrageous price" and service remains as "efficient" as ever.

Dominique Bouchet ☒ *Haute Cuisine* 25 | 21 | 25 | €105

8e | 11, rue Treilhard (Miromesnil) | 01-45-61-09-46 | www.dominique-bouchet.com

"Magnificent" meals that are "always intelligent" and "stylishly prepared" please both "locals and tourists" at this Haute Cuisine haven in the high 8th, where the "warm" but consummately pro staff is "very helpful with the menu"; even the "lovely" owner, Dominique Bouchet, is "personally involved", often visible "at the pass" from the kitchen to the "modern", exposed-stone and white-linen dining room, to which deep-pocketed fans "return at every opportunity."

	FOOD	DECOR	SERVICE	COST

Drouant ◐ *Classic French* | 23 | 22 | 22 | €80 |

2e | 16-18, rue Gaillon (Opéra/Quatre-Septembre) | 01-42-65-15-16 | www.drouant.com

Chef Antoine Westermann puts a "modern twist on the French classics" at this long-standing favorite near the Opéra Garnier, offering "pricey", thematically grouped gastronomic declensions alongside more straightforward, "sure-value" plats du jour; the "elegant" but comfortable rooms and the "warm, attentive" staff make it a "first-class" choice "for business", "couples" or – thanks to the 'young gastronomes' menu – "the family."

Z Duc (Le) S M *Seafood* | 28 | 18 | 24 | €114 |

14e | 243, bd Raspail (Raspail) | 01-43-20-96-30

"Extraordinary fish" is "refined" to great heights at this Montparnasse mariner, where "the menu doesn't change nor does the crowd" nor, seemingly, has the ocean-liner decor during the last "30 years"; passengers are further pacified by "professional service", and though "expensive", it's a "sure thing, where constancy is a joy."

Duc de Richelieu (Le) ◐ S *Lyon* | ▽ 22 | 19 | 21 | €52 |

12e | 5, rue Parrot (Gare de Lyon) | 01-43-43-05-64

"Simple but good" Lyonnais fare and "terrific Beaujolais crus" are served by an "adorable" staff and come at "reasonable" prices at this "classic" ruby-red 1930s bistro in the 12th; it's just the ticket for a no-frills fill-up before catching a train at the nearby Gare de Lyon.

Ebauchoir (L') S M *Bistro* | 24 | 18 | 22 | €40 |

12e | 43, rue de Cîteaux (Faidherbe-Chaligny) | 01-43-42-49-31 | www.lebauchoir.com

"Don't miss their famous *riz au lait*" counsel fans of this "welcoming" bistro offering denizens of the 12th "refined" seasonal fare; the yellow-wall-and-tile-floor setting is old-timey but "trendy" all the same, thanks to the "noisy", young folks who clearly agree that it's a "great place to have dinner with friends" (at a "very good" price) – in other words, *"pensez à réserver"* (consider booking); P.S. check out its sister wine bar across the street, Siffleur de Ballons.

Ebouillanté (L') *Classic French/Tearoom* | ▽ 22 | 21 | 21 | €26 |

4e | 6, rue des Barres (Pont-Marie/St-Paul) | 01-42-74-70-52 | www.restaurant-ebouillante.fr

For something "different", try this "friendly" Marais tearoom for a "quick, light meal" such as salads and *briques* (Tunisian crêpes) filled with "high-quality" ingredients; it's "not so expensive" either, but its biggest "advantage" is the "super terrace" on the "quiet", cobbled pedestrian-only street.

Ecaille de la Fontaine (L') S *Shellfish* | - | - | - | E |

2e | 15, rue Gaillon (Opéra/Quatre-Septembre) | 01-47-42-02-99 | www.la-fontaine-gaillon.com

The *fruits de mer* are "always impeccable" at this lower-priced (but no less chic) seafaring sibling to Fontaine Gaillon in the 2nd; the "intimate" green-and-red interior has a "clublike" feel, and service remains "agreeable" even when "overwhelmed" by demands of the regulars and perhaps the celeb friends of owner Gérard Depardieu; P.S. reservations are "a must."

Ecailler du Bistrot (L') S M *Seafood* 25 19 20 €55

11e | 20-22, rue Paul Bert (Faidherbe-Chaligny) | 01-43-72-76-77 | www.lecaillerdubistrot.fr

For "a good dose of iodine", dive into the "flawless oysters, as big and briny as you could ever want" at this unassuming seafooder in the 11th (the all-fish *frère* to Bistrot Paul Bert next door), where "fish tastes like fish and that's enough in itself" thanks to its "great freshness and quality"; service is "discreet" but "convivial", and the wine is "*très bon*" too, though the check can be a bit harder to swallow.

Ecluse (L') ◐ *Wine Bar/Bistro* 17 17 18 €46

1er | 34, pl du Marché St-Honoré (Pyramides/Tuileries) | 01-42-96-10-18
6e | 15, quai des Grands-Augustins (St-Michel) | 01-46-33-58-74
8e | 15, pl de la Madeleine (Madeleine) | 01-42-65-34-69
8e | 64, rue François 1er (George V) | 01-47-20-77-09
17e | 1, rue d'Armaillé (Charles de Gaulle-Etoile) | 01-47-63-88-29
www.leclusebaravin.com

This "smooth-running franchise" of wine bars pleases with its "attentive" servers full of "good advice" for choosing from the Bordeaux-leaning wine lists that "marry well" with "decent" classic bistro dishes like foie gras and steak tartare; the "rustic, comfortable" settings are conveniently open all day, every day, until late, and prices are something of a "bargain."

Ecume Saint-Honoré (L') S M *Shellfish* ▽ 23 16 21 €63

1er | 6, rue du Marché St-Honoré (Pyramides/Tuileries) | 01-42-61-93-87

Those who like it raw know that the sparkling-"fresh" seafood on display at this "cozy" *poissonnerie* in the 1st is also available for eating on the spot, including "sublime oysters" shucked before your eyes (perhaps by the "charming owner" himself); the goods are served at high-top tables under a ceiling painted with seagulls, with piped-in sounds of the surf to complete the illusion of dining "at a seashore town."

Editeurs (Les) ◐ *Brasserie* 14 21 16 €41

6e | 4, carrefour de l'Odéon (Odéon) | 01-43-26-67-76 | www.lesediteurs.fr

There's "always a buzz" at this Odéon "literary haunt", a "sumptuous" spot where you'll be "surrounded by books" in a "comfortable", librarylike room trimmed with dark wood and red leather; service can be "slow" and the "ordinary" brasserie fare leaves something to be desired, but prices are moderate and the well-read find it "a perfect location to meet for a drink."

El Mansour S M *Moroccan* 21 20 20 €70

8e | 7, rue de la Trémoille (Alma Marceau) | 01-47-23-88-18 | www.elmansour.fr

This Moroccan "takes you on a gastronomic voyage" with its fragrant couscous and tagines judged "*très bons*" for both "quality and quantity"; the luxe, jewel-toned room is straight out of "*One Thousand and One Nights*", an "efficient" staff metes out the mint tea and prices are "reasonable" – that is, given the Golden Triangle location.

El Palenque ☒Ⓜ⇥ *Argentinean/Steak*   22 | 14 | 19 | €43

5ᵉ | 5, rue de la Montagne Ste-Geneviève (Maubert-Mutualité) | 01-43-54-08-99 | www.el-palenque.fr

"Tender" grilled meats, plus empanadas to start and dulce de leche for dessert, make diners "nostalgic for the pampas" at this mid-priced Argentinean steakhouse in the Latin Quarter, where the service is "warm" and "familial" – "especially if you speak Spanish"; the only beef is with the "tiny" proportions of the "rustic", vaguely South American–accented room, which makes "reservations obligatory"; P.S. cash only.

Emporio Armani Caffè ● *Italian*   19 | 19 | 17 | €59

6ᵉ | Emporio Armani | 149, bd St-Germain (St-Germain-des-Prés) | 01-45-48-62-15

There's "lots of finesse" in the "delicious pasta" and other designer Northern Italian fare at this well-tailored Saint-Germain spot, where the "trendy" minimalist decor "conforms to what one expects of Armani"; service can border on "indifferent", and some stomachs growl that it's "too expensive for so little food" (the portions "make you think we're all models"), but there's "some added value from watching the crowd."

Enfants Terribles (Les) ☒ *Classic French*   20 | 21 | 19 | €58

8ᵉ | 8, rue Lord Byron (George V/Etoile) | 01-53-89-90-91 | www.enfantsterribles-paris.com

Run by the Sibuet group, known for its chic Alpine hotels, this 8th-arrondissement Second Empire dining room with a contemporary, shelter-magazine gloss is appreciated for its figure-preserving Classic cooking (think Escoffier goes to the spa) as well as the "updated elegance" of its decor (parquet floors, contemporary art, velvet chairs), which flatters the "VIPs" who complete the "trendy" ambiance; as at the best inns, service is "attentive", and it all comes at predictably high-altitude prices.

Enoteca (L') ● *Italian/Wine Bar*   22 | 18 | 19 | €48

4ᵉ | 25, rue Charles V (St-Paul/Sully Morland) | 01-42-78-91-44 | www.enoteca.fr

"The real Italy" is "on your plate and in your glass" at this Marais wine bar, where "colorful, appetizing" antipasti and pastas are matched by an "exceptional" vino list that satisfies "all tastes and all wallets"; servers offer "good advice", and the old-fashioned room with its exposed beams is a "warm" respite – in sum, a "*bonne* table" when "you need a change."

Entêtée (L') ☒Ⓜ *Bistro*   ▽ 20 | 16 | 22 | €39

14ᵉ | 4, rue Danville (Denfert-Rochereau) | 01-40-47-56-81

A warm welcome awaits at this contemporary bistro in the 14th, where the chalkboard menu shows off the "adventurous" cooking of a chef-owner whose "explorations of flavors" change with the seasons; the simple, wood-floored space is "tiny", but locals nonetheless declare it an "enjoyable experience" and a real "value."

Entredgeu (L') *Bistro* 21 | 14 | 17 | €48

17e | 83, rue Laugier (Porte de Champerret) | 01-40-54-97-24

"If you want to eat with Parisians", not tourists, consider this "casual" bistro in "the great north" of the 17th, offering "flavorful" fare that hits the spot on "a cold and blustery" day; "too bad it's so noisy" carp claustrophobes who feel "crammed" into the red banquettes, but fans say it's "worth the jaunt" for its "reasonable" tabs and "old bistro atmosphere."

NEW Entrée des Artistes (L') *Wine Bar/Bistro* - | - | - | I

11e | 8, rue du Crussol (Oberkampf) | 09-50-99-67-11

Artisan cocktails and natural wines are the draw at this hipster harbor in the 11th, a *bar à vins* serving simple nosh like charcuterie and cheeses alongside a heartier *plat* or two to soak up the sips, in a speakeasy-style, barely decorated sliver of a space that bulges at the seams at prime time; the servers are also the owners - one an experienced barman, the other a wine wonk - and they know their stuff.

Z Epicure (L') *Haute Cuisine* 27 | 27 | 28 | €187

(fka Le Bristol)

8e | Hôtel Le Bristol | 112, rue du Faubourg St-Honoré (Miromesnil) | 01-53-43-43-40 | www.lebristolparis.com

Chef Eric Frechon remains at the helm of this "gastronomic paradise" in the Hôtel Le Bristol, ensuring that the "phenomenal" Haute Cuisine remains as "imaginative" as ever, even while the name has changed and the former 'summer' dining room went year-round with the addition of a fireplace and an airy new design by Pierre-Yves Rochon (not fully reflected in the Decor rating; the 'winter' room is now a private-event space, to the regret of many); the "solicitous" service remains intact too, as do the "once-in-a-lifetime" prices; P.S. reservations and jackets required.

Epi d'Or (L') *Bistro* ▽ 19 | 18 | 19 | €56

1er | 25, rue Jean-Jacques Rousseau (Louvre-Rivoli) | 01-42-36-38-12 | www.faget-benard.com/jojo/epidor

Once upon a time this bistro fed Les Halles workers late into the night, and it continues to serve "dependable" classics like frisée aux lardons and steak tartare in a 1930s-era setting that retains its "old-fashioned" "character" (prices, however, are thoroughly modern); the staff is "very friendly", though the tight tables mean "you'd better be friendly with your neighbor" too.

Epi Dupin (L') *Bistro* 24 | 17 | 20 | €53

6e | 11, rue Dupin (Sèvres-Babylone) | 01-42-22-64-56 | www.epidupin.com

"Wonderful", "original" dishes feed a perpetually "packed" house at this "polished" bistro in the 6th, a "perennial favorite" known for its "great value"; surveyors like the redone "contemporary" digs, but unfortunately it's still "crowded beyond belief" ("Americans abound"), and the early seating may be "the fastest dinner service in Paris" warn those who feel "rushed", so "if you want to linger" arrive later; P.S. closed weekends.

Epigramme (L') *Bistro* 23 | 18 | 19 | €50

6e | 9, rue de l'Eperon (Odéon/St-Michel) | 01-44-41-00-09

The menu is "modest" at this little "gem" of a bistro, but the food is quite "fine" - and it's French, which is "rather a rare thing" in Saint-Germain; prices are moderate and the "familial" service makes diners feel at home in the "comfortable" room done up like a country inn, though its diminutive size means you'll "need a reservation."

Escargot Montorgueil (L') *Bistro* 22 | 22 | 19 | €69

1er | 38, rue Montorgueil (Etienne Marcel/Les Halles) | 01-42-36-83-51 | www.escargot-montorgueil.com

"Yes, you really can make a dinner of escargots" at this Les Halles classic (around since 1832), where the "delicious critters" get gussied up with a variety of sauces and the rest of the "traditional" French menu is also "very good" and served by an "efficient" crew amid "magnificent", historic decor; true, you'll shell out a lot to settle the bill, but "everyone should go here once", even if it is a little "touristy"; P.S. takeout is available for gastropods only.

Etc. *New French* ▽ 25 | 21 | 26 | €89

16e | 2, rue La Pérouse (Kléber) | 01-49-52-10-10

This haute (i.e. "expensive") bistro in the "upscale" 16th caters to the area's working professionals with a "superb", "continuously changing menu" of New French cuisine that offers "some surprises with every dish"; "impeccable" service is a plus, and the "chic", black-and-gray setting matches the suits that fill many of the seats.

Eugène *Eclectic* ▽ 18 | 17 | 18 | €45

8e | 166, bd Haussmann (Miromesnil/St-Philippe-du-Roule) | 01-42-89-00-13

Eclectic, cosmopolitan cooking is on the midpriced menu at this 8th-arrondissement local, in a swanky dining room adorned by crushed velvet and orange chandeliers, and given a little historicity by a massive Eiffel-designed picture window; service is solid enough, but it's the "fun and hip" scene that unfolds around the long pewter bar that truly "marks this place."

Européen (L') ◐ *Brasserie* 20 | 19 | 19 | €42

12e | 21 bis, bd Diderot (Gare de Lyon) | 01-43-43-99-70 | www.brasserie-leuropeen.fr

With "efficient" service as "fast" "as the TGV" (France's high-speed rail), this "incredibly large" "classic brasserie" across from the Gare de Lyon is a "practical" pit stop between trains; the 1970s Slavik look is kinda "retro" but the Chesterfield banquettes are comfy enough, and besides, those just traveling through are more interested in the "very correct oysters", "good beer" and "fair prices."

FOOD | DECOR | SERVICE | COST

Fables de La Fontaine (Les) *Seafood* — 25 | 21 | 23 | €67

7e | 131, rue St-Dominique (Ecole Militaire) | 01-44-18-37-55 | www.lesfablesdelafontaine.net

"From the amuse-bouche to dessert, don't skip a thing" at this "inventive", "fabulous fish" place overlooking a quiet square with a fountain in the 7th that's helmed by a pair of cooks who apprenticed with founding chef Christian Constant; a "deft" staff navigates the "contemporary" but "cozy" "vest pocket" of a space, making it all the more "worth the splurge."

Fakhr el Dine ◐ *Lebanese* — 25 | 20 | 22 | €56

16e | 30, rue de Longchamp (Trocadéro) | 01-47-27-90-00 | www.fakhreldine.com

"Refined" Lebanese cooking marked by "quality ingredients and expert preparation" has kept this Middle Eastern on a quiet corner of the 16th a destination for over 30 years; it's "rather expensive", but long-time fans appreciate its professional service (up four points this year), traditional if "faded" decor and live music nightly except Monday.

Famille (La) ☒ ☒ *New French* — ▽ 23 | 19 | 19 | €47

18e | 41, rue des Trois-Frères (Abbesses/Anvers) | 01-42-52-11-12

This "hip" Montmartre table with a "rotating menu" of "original" New French food elicits a "trendy New York" resto-lounge, with the difference, perhaps, that the staff is "really nice"; a "young crowd" out for a good time is relatively heedless of the moderate tabs as they down "incredible" cocktails in the "dark", "intimate" digs.

Ferdi ◐ *Eclectic* — ▽ 21 | 18 | 20 | €44

1er | 32, rue du Mont-Thabor (Madeleine/Tuileries/Concorde) | 01-42-60-82-52

At this "chic sliver" of a place in the 1st, there's a "well-prepared" Eclectic mix of items - everything from "Venezuelan tapas" to what some tout as the "best cheeseburger" in Paris; cosmopolitan types appreciate reasonably moderate prices for the 'hood and groove on its "casual" atmosphere, created by a "friendly" staff and whimsical gewgaws like a Playmobil toy collection.

Ferme St-Simon (La) ☒ *Classic French* — 21 | 21 | 22 | €69

7e | 6, rue de St-Simon (Rue du Bac/Solférino) | 01-45-48-35-74 | www.fermestsimon.com

The kind of "old-fashioned" restaurant that's "becoming scarcer in Paris every year", this "reliable" stalwart in the 7th still puts "heart" into its "quality" French classics; pricey, *oui,* but it's a fine place to treat "*grand-mère*" to a meal in the "warm" "country-style" dining room graced by "attentive" servers.

Fermette Marbeuf 1900 (La) ◐ *Classic French* — 19 | 25 | 19 | €63

8e | 5, rue Marbeuf (Alma Marceau/George V) | 01-53-23-08-00 | www.fermettemarbeuf.com

"Return to the belle epoque" via the "sumptuous" art nouveau interior (stunning stained-glass ceiling, ornately mirrored walls) of this "touristy" yet "good" Classic French on a corner just off the Champs-Elysées; service varies between "lovely" and "overwhelmed", and "you pay for the setting" - but how "glorious" it is.

Ferrandaise (La) ☒ *Bistro* 20 | 16 | 19 | €54

6e | 8, rue de Vaugirard (Odéon/Cluny-La Sorbonne) | 01-43-26-36-36 | www.laferrandaise.com

Specializing in "rich French stews" and Ferrandaise beef from the Auvergne, this "inviting" bistro across from the popular Luxembourg Gardens is surprisingly "not loaded with tourists"; a "welcoming staff" patrols three "compact" levels that include a "medieval"-looking stone-vaulted cellar, and though it's not cheap it remains "a good buy" thanks in part to the prix fixe; P.S. "don't miss" the "divine cheese course."

Findi ◐ *Italian* 21 | 21 | 19 | €58

8e | 24, av George V (Alma Marceau/George V) | 01-47-20-14-78 | www.findi.net

"Enjoyable", "consistent" Italian cuisine in "understated" living-room-like digs draws a following to this homemade-pasta palace - even if "prices are a bit inflated" (hardly a surprise in this Golden Triangle area heavy with luxe shopping and hotels); down-to-earth folks appreciate dining "without the hype" typical of so many places in the area, and say the "friendly" staff "has the right idea."

Fines Gueules (Les) *Wine Bar/Bistro* 20 | 16 | 20 | €51

1er | 43, rue Croix-des-Petits-Champs (Bourse/Palais Royal-Musée du Louvre) | 01-42-61-35-41 | www.lesfinesgueules.fr

With a "great location" just off the Places des Victoires in the 1st, this "swell neighborhood" wine bar-cum-bistro serves a "limited menu" of "simple but delicious" edibles including "amazing charcuterie"; the staff is "adorable" and the small space is exceedingly "cozy" and always "bustling" upstairs (via a winding staircase) and down in the bar area, and though bills add up fast, the wines are "reasonable."

Fins Gourmets (Aux) ☒ *Southwest* ▽ 18 | 18 | 15 | €54

7e | 213, bd St-Germain (Rue du Bac) | 01-42-22-06-57

The "look hasn't changed" much at this "quintessential Paris bistro" in Saint-Germain since it opened over a century ago, giving it an ambered charm suited to the "basic" Southwestern victuals; it's not as popular with the locals as it once was, perhaps because the service could use some fine tuning and prices remain high.

Finzi ☒ *Italian* 19 | 17 | 17 | €67

8e | 182, bd Haussmann (St-Philippe-du-Roule) | 01-45-62-88-68

"Good Italian cooking", including "marvelous salads", explains a smart bounce in the Food score at this "refined" and "amiable" eatery near the Musée Jacquemart-André in an office-heavy corner of the 8th; the "dining room hasn't changed for a long time", but most habitués are *molto contento* anyway - at least until the check comes.

	FOOD	DECOR	SERVICE	COST

Firmin le Barbier Ⓜ *Bistro* ▽ 21 | 15 | 21 | €53

7e | 20, rue de Monttessuy (Ecole Militaire) | 01-45-51-21-55 | www.firminlebarbier.fr

An owner who was once a surgeon before succumbing to his love of food animates this "charming little" storefront in the 7th serving solid bistro standards; a "warm" staff operates in the exposed-brick and tiled room, anesthetizing diners to the somewhat large bills.

Fish La Boissonnerie *New French* 21 | 16 | 21 | €45

6e | 69, rue de Seine (Mabillon/Odéon) | 01-43-54-34-69

"A haven for English speakers" owing to its "enthusiastic", "mostly Anglophone" staff and "friendly" owners (a New Zealander and a Miami native), this "inventive" fish-focused Modern French in Saint-Germain is expat and "tourist" central; the simple, rustic room echoes with "spirited vibes" courtesy of "outstanding" wines (these gents also own a nearby *boutique de vins*) whose moderate markup contributes to the overall "value."

Flandrin (Le) ◐ *Brasserie* 15 | 16 | 18 | €63

16e | 80, av Henri Martin (Rue de la Pompe) | 01-45-04-34-69

The "golden people" of this "well-to-do" corner of the 16th love to "see and be seen" at this "fashionable" brasserie housed in a former train station, which boasts a "pleasant" atmosphere and large sunny terrace; others find the standard fare "not that interesting" and too expensive, saying you're mostly "paying for the real estate and the face time."

Flora Danica *Classic French/Danish* 21 | 19 | 20 | €65

8e | 142, av des Champs-Elysées (Charles de Gaulle-Etoile/George V) | 01-44-13-86-26 | www.floradanica-paris.com

The Scandinavian fare at this popular Nordic enclave on the Champs-Elysées is "appealing", "especially if you love salmon", which is famously cooked here "*à l'unilatéral*" or skin-side down (it also serves some Classic French dishes); it's "expensive", but the staff is "attentive" and diners can choose between a "pretty", "IKEA catalog"-like modern dining room and a large, "beautiful interior courtyard garden"; P.S. spendier sibling Copenhague is upstairs.

NEW Floréal (Le) ◐ *Brasserie* - | - | - | M

10e | 73, rue du Faubourg du Temple (Goncourt) | 01-40-18-46-79 | www.lefloreal.fr

With its Mondrian-ish red-white-black-and-yellow facade, it's hard to miss this new *branché* brasserie near the Canal Saint-Martin, where hip locals make themselves seen if not heard (the jukebox blares) over victuals that vary from eggs Benedict at brunch to oysters, Caesar salad and burgers (plus deftly mixed cocktails) later in the day; moderate prices suit the casual, retro-diner setting.

Flore en l'Ile (Le) ◐ *Classic French* 17 | 19 | 18 | €37

4e | 42, quai d'Orléans (Cité/Pont-Marie) | 01-43-29-88-27

You "can't beat the view" of Notre Dame from this "touristy" Classic French with an "idyllic location" at the tip of Ile Saint-Louis, and most find that it's "still good after all these years" for breakfast, lunch, tea, dinner or a Berthillon ice cream "fix"; the old-school brasserie look resonates with out-of-towners who also note solid service, midrange prices and a 2 AM closing bell.

Florimond (Le) 🅂 *Classic French* — 25 | 20 | 26 | €58

7e | 19, av de La Motte-Picquet (Ecole Militaire/La Tour-Maubourg) | 01-45-55-40-38 | www.leflorimond.com

"You walk in a stranger and leave a friend" at this bistro in the 7th whose "tremendous" Classic French food with "modern flair" (try the "stuffed cabbage! oh my!") is served with a "side of exceptional service"; the "small, intimate" room is "bright and warm", and although the tabs are high, most deem them "reasonable"; P.S. closed the first and third Saturday of each month.

Flottes O. Trement 🅂 🄼 *New French* — 21 | 18 | 20 | €59

1er | 2, rue Cambon (Concorde/Tuileries) | 01-42-61-31-15 | www.brasserie-flottes.fr

Up a flight of stairs from sibling brasserie Les Flottes in the 1st, this "serene", low-lit New French has an in-the-know supper club vibe that's made it a hideaway for fashion executives, bankers and government types looking to let their hair down; it's "pricey" but a "great find" thanks to dishes with the signature "modern touch" of food stylist and consultant Frédérick Grasser-Hermé, served by a "discreet" staff.

Fogón ◐ 🄼 *Spanish* — 23 | 18 | 21 | €71

6e | 45, quai des Grands-Augustins (Odéon/St-Michel) | 01-43-54-31-33 | www.fogon.fr

The "best Spanish restaurant in Paris" is this "paella paradise" (also dishing up "creative", "refined" tapas) perched on the banks of the Seine in Saint-Germain; it's "expensive" and the handsome, modern space is often "crowded", but with solid service it's your best bet "if you can't get to Spain."

🅉 **Fontaine de Mars (La)** *Southwest* — 22 | 21 | 22 | €60

7e | 129, rue St-Dominique (Ecole Militaire) | 01-47-05-46-44 | www.fontainedemars.com

"It's like being in a movie about Paris" murmur those charmed by the "prototypic" bistro look – "red-checked tablecloths and all" – of this "satisfying" Southwestern French in the 7th dishing up standouts like "ethereal foie gras" and "don't-miss" cassoulet; proximity to the Eiffel Tower and an Obama visit several years ago make reservations "a must" and it's "a bit expensive", but tourists and locals alike enjoy being "treated with respect" by the "tried-and-true" staff.

Fontaine Gaillon (La) ◐ 🅂 *Classic French* — 21 | 22 | 21 | €76

2e | 1, pl Gaillon (Opéra/Quatre-Septembre) | 01-42-65-87-04 | www.la-fontaine-gaillon.com

Owned by actor Gérard Depardieu ("*vive* Cyrano"!) and appreciated for its "delightful" greenery-bordered terrace overlooking a small square with the namesake fountain, this Classic French in the 2nd makes a splash, particularly with its "excellent fish" preparations;

although they don't come cheap, "practiced, professional" service and, oftentimes, "celebrity-spotting" are included amenities.

Fontaines (Les) *Bistro* 19 | 13 | 20 | €34

5e | 9, rue Soufflot (Cluny/Luxembourg) | 01-43-26-42-80

Midway between the Panthéon and the Luxembourg Gardens in the Latin Quarter, this corner bistro with "gentle tabs" offers "good value" in its "Rabelaisian" portions of "classic" fare ferried by a "welcoming" staff (the Service score is up five points); the "drab" interior could use a redo, so many prefer to watch the "passing parade" of Parisians from the sidewalk tables.

Fougères (Les) *New French* ▽ 27 | 19 | 22 | €66

17e | 10, rue du Villebois-Mareuil (Ternes) | 01-40-68-78-66 | www.restaurant-les-fougeres.com

Not far from the Place des Ternes in the 17th, chef Stéphane Duchiron's contemporary French remains an insider's address, but those in the know extol his "creative", "high-quality" cooking using "the very best produce"; it's a "bit expensive", as befits the professional service and formal decor, which includes a green cut-velvet banquette with a *fougère* (fern) pattern.

Foujita *Japanese* 25 | 14 | 20 | €38

1er | 41, rue St-Roch (Pyramides) | 01-42-61-42-93

1er | 7, rue du 29 Juillet (Tuileries) | 01-49-26-07-70

"Ultrafresh sashimi and sushi" is the name of the game at these Japanese twins near the Tuileries; sure, the digs "could use some updating" and the "service is sometimes almost too fast", but no one's complaining about the "great value for money."

Fouquet's (Le) *Classic French* 20 | 22 | 19 | €87

8e | 99, av des Champs-Elysées (George V) | 01-40-69-60-50 | www.lucienbarriere.com

This circa-1899 "landmark" may be an "expensive", "touristy" place to chow down on "solid" Classic French fare, but an "outstanding" location on the Champs-Elysées offering the "perfect vantage" to watch "Paris roll by" explains its enduring popularity; besides, the service is "fine" and there's plenty of "history" in the dining room's "old world glamour."

Fourchette du Printemps (La) *Bistro* 23 | 23 | 22 | €48

17e | 30, rue du Printemps (Wagram) | 01-42-27-26-97

"A smiling welcome" awaits those who trek to this bistro in a remote northern corner of the 17th to sample "original and refined" dishes at moderate prices that offer "great bang for the buck", er, euro; be sure to book, though, because the "calm", "cozy" simple red-and-white setting "doesn't have many tables."

Frédéric Simonin *Haute/New French* - | - | - | E

17e | 25, rue Bayen (Ternes) | 01-45-74-74-74 | www.fredericsimonin.com

After working with Ghislaine Arabian and Joël Robuchon ("the Robuchon connection is apparent"), chef Frédéric Simonin made "an excellent debut" with his own New French/Haute table in the

17th in 2010; his "elegant" cuisine, the "appealing" black-and-white mod-deco setting and almost-"perfect service" come with an "expensive" price tag, but most feel it's worth it as this place just "continues to improve."

Z Frenchie *Bistro* 26 | 19 | 21 | €57

2e | 5, rue du Nil (Sentier) | 01-40-39-96-19 | www.frenchie-restaurant.com

Chef Gregory Marchand lives up to the "hype" with the "intriguingly deep and delicious flavors" he brings out in his contemporary French creations at this "tiny" bistro in the 2nd that's pricey but considered a "deal" by "foodies"; "cool" exposed brick and industrial illumination plus an "approachable" staff add to the "wow" factor, and though scoring reservations "is an Olympic event", you can "kill time" and nosh at Marchand's new wine bar across the alley; P.S. closed weekends.

Fumoir (Le) *Eclectic* 18 | 22 | 17 | €44

1er | 6, rue de l'Amiral de Coligny (Louvre-Rivoli) | 01-42-92-00-24 | www.lefumoir.com

Inhale the "Paris vibe" at this "trendy classic" across from the Louvre that pulls a "very 'in'" "local" crowd for "people-watching" in an "agreeable" setting with a bar up front and a spacious dining room that has a "British library" feel (except for the "noise"); the Eclectic "comfort food" may be "unsurprising" and the staff can have "a bit of an attitude", but "prices are reasonable" given that it's prix fixe-only for dinner (it's also "perfect for a relaxed lunch" *après l'art*).

Gaigne (Le) *New French* 24 | 17 | 23 | €57

4e | 12, rue Pecquay (Hôtel-de-Ville/Rambuteau) | 01-44-59-86-72 | www.restaurantlegaigne.fr

"What a team" gush fans of chef Mickaël Gaignon and his wife, Aurélie, whose "endearing" New French "gem in the Marais" is "well worth seeking out" for "creative" and "intricately fashioned dishes that are both hearty and delicate" albeit "expensive"; it's kind of "plain" and "very tiny" but "excellent for a tête-à-tête."

Gallopin *Brasserie* 20 | 21 | 20 | €51

2e | 40, rue Notre-Dame-des-Victoires (Bourse/Grands Boulevards) | 01-42-36-45-38 | www.brasseriegallopin.com

Across from the Bourse, this "pretty", "old-fashioned" brasserie can be "noisy" at noontime but quiets down in the evening when locals come for "traditional", "honest cooking" (the Food score is up four points under new ownership) served by a "professional" staff (Service improved by three); some charm may have rubbed off during a "recent renovation", but the original belle epoque ornamentation remains and tabs are still "easy on" the "wallet."

NEW Galopin (Le) *Bistro* - | - | - | M

10e | 34, rue Ste-Marthe (Colonel Fabien) | 01-42-06-05-03

Well-informed foodies are galloping to this modern bistro in the deep 10th for a go at *Top Chef* winner (and Ze Kitchen Galerie vet) Romain Tischenko's creative, market-driven dishes, served in a mandatory seven-course cavalcade at night, or one-, two- or three-step sets at lunch; scruff-sporting servers match the room's boho cool, and the palatable prices prove you're far from central Paris.

Gare (La) ◐ *Classic French* 18 | 24 | 17 | €53

16e | 19, chaussée de la Muette (La Muette) | 01-42-15-15-31 | www.restaurantlagare.com

This "super-hip" Classic French housed in a "beautifully restored" former train station in the 16th boasts an "immense", often "noisy" dining room whose "brilliant design" includes plasma screens (there's an equally large and "lovely" terrace for warm-weather dining); the staff is "diligent but slow" and the moderate prices are perhaps "a little high" for the "small portions", but that doesn't derail trainloads of folks who call it a "favorite."

Garnier ◐ *Brasserie* 22 | 17 | 19 | €71

8e | 111, rue St-Lazare (St-Lazare) | 01-43-87-50-40

Everyone loves the "little oyster bar" just inside the front door, the "fresh, well-cooked shellfish" and "superb" fin fare at this "time-honored" brasserie across the street from the Gare Saint-Lazare in the 8th, but the mishmash decor of Lalique lamps and mirrors plus aquariums comes off as "faded grandeur" to some, while service can be uneven and it sure isn't cheap.

Gauloise (La) *Bistro* 18 | 19 | 20 | €61

15e | 59, av de La Motte-Picquet (La Motte-Picquet-Grenelle) | 01-47-34-11-64

A bit "out of the way" in the 15th, this "comfortable", "old-time Paris" bistro is "always good without being exceptional"; "friendly service" earns accolades, while relatively "reasonable prices" explain its continuing popularity with "French politicians" and others for whom it remains a "reliable" "old favorite."

Gavroche (Le) ◐ ☒ *Bistro* 24 | 20 | 23 | €61

2e | 19, rue St-Marc (Bourse/Richelieu-Drouot) | 01-42-96-89-70

"You want meat, this is the place to go" crow carnivores about this open-late bistro in the 2nd with a "retro" WWII-era dining room and a "convivial" atmosphere that lures the locals; with improved scores across the board and a "nice-guy" owner, it's no surprise that it's "often packed and noisy", and though it's "a bit pricey", most consider it "worth it."

Gaya ☒ *Seafood* 24 | 18 | 22 | €89

7e | 44, rue du Bac (Rue du Bac) | 01-45-44-73-73 | www.pierre-gagnaire.com

Pierre Gagnaire's modern maritime "gem" on the Left Bank may be "way too expensive" according to some, but "it's a real treat" for "eclectically prepared" seafood and other "inventive" New French dishes; the bi-level space's "minimalist" decor is either "relaxed" or of "questionable taste", but most agree that the staff is "attentive", and if the food is "not as good as Gagnaire's" eponymous effort, it's still a "wonderful evening" out.

	FOOD	DECOR	SERVICE	COST

Gazzetta (La) ⓢⓜ *New French* — 24 | 22 | 22 | €57

12e | 29, rue de Cotte (Ledru-Rollin) | 01-43-47-47-05 | www.lagazzetta.fr
Swedish-born chef Petter Nilsson's "imaginative" daily changing tasting menus ("think French omakase") tempt adventurous types to this "in" spot in the 12th; the "easygoing" staff fits right in with the "stylish", low-lit "New York" look (tiled floors, flea-market finds) and tabs that are on the "reasonable" end of pricey.

Georges ◐ *Eclectic* — 17 | 25 | 14 | €68

4e | Centre Georges Pompidou | 19, rue Beaubourg (Hôtel-de-Ville/Rambuteau) | 01-44-78-47-99 | www.maisonthierrycostes.com
All of "Paris at your feet" via an "incredible" panoramic vista is why folks flock to this Costes brothers Eclectic set in a glass-encased, "avant-garde" aerie atop the Pompidou Center; "supermodel" waitresses provide additional eye candy, but "don't expect much" in the way of service or from the "safe", "ok" menu – and since the prices are "high", "insist on a table near the window" or on the "beautiful" terrace and "linger to get your money's worth"; P.S. closed Tuesday.

Georgette ⓢⓜ *Bistro* — ▽ 17 | 16 | 19 | €41

9e | 29, rue St-Georges (Notre-Dame-de-Lorette) | 01-42-80-39-13
Penny-wise epicures flock to this midpriced neighborhood bistro in the 9th for "real family-style" French chow served in a "funky" "'60s"-esque "diner" environment; the "nice" owner presides and ensures a "great atmosphere"; open Tuesday-Friday only.

Gitane (La) *Classic French* — ▽ 18 | 17 | 19 | €55

15e | 53 bis, av de La Motte-Picquet (La Motte-Picquet-Grenelle) | 01-47-34-62-92 | www.la-gitane.com
"Warm and welcoming", this "old-fashioned" Classic French in the 15th is run by Condé Nast vets Olivier and Corinne Mayeras, and it sates the locals with "traditional basics that never disappoint"; service is "discreet and efficient" in the dining room decked out with tile floors, oil paintings and linens, and tabs are reasonable.

Gli Angeli ⓢ *Italian* — 20 | 17 | 18 | €42

3e | 5, rue St-Gilles (St-Paul) | 01-42-71-05-80
"Dependable", authentic Italian fare lures *paesani* to this "delightful" joint in the Marais; service is "friendly", though "a little rough around the edges", but most are happy to come to this "lively" "little" spot for a reasonably priced plate of scratch-made pasta.

Glou *Bistro* — 20 | 17 | 17 | €47

3e | 101, rue Vieille-du-Temple (Filles du Calvaire/Rambuteau) | 01-42-74-44-32 | www.glou-resto.com
"Fresh organic takes" on "uncomplicated" standards please the crowd at this northern Marais bistro from Julien Fouin (former editor of French food mag *Régal*), occupying a "pretty", apartmentlike space whose second floor overlooks part of the Picasso Museum; the staff can be a bit "clueless" at times, and some snipe that it's "trendy run amok" and "lacks that little something extra to justify the prices", which nonetheless are moderate.

	FOOD	DECOR	SERVICE	COST
Goumard ◐ *Seafood*	23	21	21	€72

1er | 9, rue Duphot (Madeleine) | 01-42-60-36-07 | www.goumard.com

Seafood "so fresh it was probably swimming that morning" lures waves of diners to this "inventive" fish house anchored near the Madeleine; a "chic", modern look with whimsical maritime flourishes plus vestiges of the original belle epoque trappings (including "notable" toilets) distract most from service that's "knowledgeable" but occasionally "uptight" and "expensive" prices.

	FOOD	DECOR	SERVICE	COST
Gourmand (Au) ☒ *Classic/New French*	25	18	24	€57

1er | 17, rue Molière (Palais Royal-Musée du Louvre/Pyramides) | 01-42-96-22-19 | www.augourmand.fr

The "superb" Classic and New French menu "follows the seasons" but remains consistently "original" and "creative", with "lots of vegetable dishes", at this "perennial favorite" just off the Avenue de l'Opéra in the 1st; it's "small" but "charming" (the food "arrives magically" by dumbwaiter), the owner-maitre d' and his staff "serve exquisitely" and it's considered a relatively "good buy" – especially the lunch and dinner prix fixe.

	FOOD	DECOR	SERVICE	COST
Gourmets des Ternes (Les) ☒ *Bistro*	23	15	18	€57

8e | 87, bd de Courcelles (Ternes) | 01-42-27-43-04 | www.lesgourmetsdesternes.com

It's "the real McCoy" say fans of this "genuine French bistro" near the Place des Ternes serving up some of the "best meat in Paris" polished off with a baba au rhum that "makes grown men weep"; some beef that "regulars get better service" and say "it's time to change" the "typical", "retro" decor, but on the plus side the "owner is adorable" and it's always "buzzing", even though it's hardly cheap; P.S. closed weekends.

	FOOD	DECOR	SERVICE	COST
Graindorge ☒ *Belgian/Northern French*	▽ 23	19	19	€61

17e | 15, rue de l'Arc-de-Triomphe (Charles de Gaulle-Etoile) | 01-47-54-00-28

Specializing in "authentic" Northern French and Belgian cuisine (and "great beers"), this long-running but relatively confidential table near the Etoile is "cozy" and "comfortable" like a good *estaminet* (northern French cafe); it's expensive and service could use the occasional tune-up, but it's appreciated as one of the few places in Paris that plows this "regional" turf.

	FOOD	DECOR	SERVICE	COST
Grand Café (Le) ◐ *Brasserie*	19	22	18	€49

9e | 4, bd des Capucines (Opéra) | 01-43-12-19-00 | www.legrandcafe.com

With a "great location" near the Opéra and "wonderful" art nouveau decor, this "big", "loud" Frères Blanc brasserie is a fine place "to end a night at the theater", but while many deem the kitchen "reliable" (with "extraordinary shellfish" as a standout), service gets mixed marks and some find the place "touristy"; still, tabs are generally midrange and it's "lively and exciting" 24/7.

	FOOD	DECOR	SERVICE	COST

Grand Colbert (Le) ◐ *Brasserie* 19 | 25 | 20 | €58

2e | 2, rue Vivienne (Bourse/Palais Royal-Musée du Louvre) | 01-42-86-87-88 | www.legrandcolbert.fr

The "stunning" belle epoque decor and "quality" "traditional" eats at this brasserie next to the Bibliothèque Nationale "still deliver" "years after its free commercial" in the Nicholson-Keaton rom-com *Something's Got to Give* – even if some feel it's taken on a "bus tour" vibe; fame aside, it's fun to have the staff "fawn over you", and the prix fixe lunch is an especially "good value."

Grande Armée (La) ◐ *Classic French* 16 | 18 | 16 | €54

16e | 3, av de la Grande-Armée (Charles de Gaulle-Etoile) | 01-45-00-24-77

"Typical Costes brothers" (i.e. a "trendy" "place to be seen"), this Classic French near the Arc de Triomphe wins praise for its "neo-Directoire" design by Jacques Grange, but takes a few hits for "middling" cooking and "erratic" service; rebels also open fire on the prices, which although moderate, are deemed "high for what you get."

Grande Cascade (La) *Haute Cuisine* 24 | 27 | 25 | €125

16e | Bois de Boulogne | Allée de Longchamp (Porte Maillot) | 01-45-27-33-51 | www.grandecascade.com

"Unbeatable in good weather" thanks to its "breathtaking" setting that includes an "awesome terrace" overlooking the Bois de Boulogne, this "romantic" Second Empire glass pavilion also delivers "exceptional", "soignée" Haute Cuisine; "irreproachable" service makes a big splash too, so "go for a celebration" – "if someone else is paying"; P.S. reservations required.

Grand Louvre (Le) *Classic French* 20 | 22 | 19 | €56

1er | Musée du Louvre | below the Pyramide (Palais Royal-Musée du Louvre) | 01-40-20-53-41 | www.eliancemusee.com

"Not your typical museum restaurant", this "ultraminimalist" "oasis of calm" beneath I.M. Pei's glass pyramid in the courtyard of the Louvre is "convenient" for grabbing "light" Classic French fare; the staff is "pleasant", and while it's not cheap it maintains a "good price/quality ratio"; P.S. open from lunch till 6 PM daily except Friday (when it's also open for dinner) and Tuesday (closed).

Grand Pan (Le) ⊠ *Bistro* ▽ 23 | 14 | 21 | €58

15e | 20, rue Rosenwald (Convention/Plaisance) | 01-42-50-02-50 | www.legrandpan.fr

"Unpretentious and tiny", this "meat-lover's" bistro in the 15th remains undiscovered by many carnivores, but those in the know laud its "excellent steak frites" along with the "unobtrusive service"; centime-counters warn that "prices have been creeping up", but a "pleasurable" wine list argues for making "the trek"; P.S. closed weekends.

Z Grand Véfour (Le) ⊠ *Haute Cuisine* 28 | 28 | 28 | €159

1er | Palais-Royal | 17, rue de Beaujolais (Palais Royal-Musée du Louvre) | 01-42-96-56-27 | www.grand-vefour.com

Over "200 years of history" are on display in this Haute Cuisine "jewel box" tucked away in the Palais-Royal, whose neoclassical murals, gilt-framed mirrors and Directoire chairs are "evocative" of the legendary "literary figures" who have dined here - although the likes of Balzac, Colette and Hugo never tasted chef Guy Martin's "complex", "breakthrough" dishes; service is "formal" but the staff is "congenial" and "adaptable", making every diner "feel like a visiting duke" or duchess, so just "close your eyes and pay the check" (or try the "'bargain' lunch"); P.S. jacket suggested; closed weekends.

Z Grand Venise (Le) S M *Italian* 26 | 22 | 24 | €96

15e | 171, rue de la Convention (Convention) | 01-45-32-49-71

"It's a bit of a trek to this truly grand" spot in the 15th, but an "excellent welcome" awaits in the "flower-filled" dining room, along with "incredible" Italian fare, including "amazing" antipasti and a "do-not-miss" caramel ice-cream log; it's *très* "expensive", but "gargantuan" portions compensate; P.S. jackets suggested at dinner.

Grille (La) S *Bistro* ∇ 21 | 16 | 20 | €65

10e | 80, rue du Faubourg Poissonnière (Poissonnière) | 01-47-70-89-73

Though a few find that this "kitschy"-looking bistro in the 10th is "not the same" since an ownership change, the majority thinks it's on the right track with its "perfectly prepared" entrecôte and "gold-standard" turbot with beurre blanc; a "super-friendly" staff makes it "good for a romantic dinner", even if "quality comes at a price" here; P.S. closed weekends.

Grille St-Germain (La) ● *Bistro* 21 | 20 | 20 | €43

6e | 14, rue Mabillon (Mabillon) | 01-43-54-16-87

There's "nothing fancy" about this cozy bistro in Saint-Germain with heavy red-velvet curtains at the door and celeb pix on the walls, but it's generally "reliable" for "traditional" bistro dishes (e.g. "the best" beef *daube*); if it's a bit of a "tourist trap", the service is still "good" and it's "reasonably priced."

Z Guilo-Guilo M *Asian* 27 | 21 | 24 | €68

18e | 8, rue Garreau (Abbesses) | 01-42-54-23-92 | www.guiloguilo.com

A "succession" of "creative" small plates on a daily changing tasting menu takes diners on a culinary "journey" at star chef Eiichi Edakuni's Japanese-inspired Asian fusion laboratory in Montmartre; tabs are high and the black box of a space is "microscopic", but the staff is "friendly" and the circular counter is continuously "crammed" with devotees watching the chefs at work - so "book now for the 22nd century."

Guinguette de Neuilly (La) *Classic French* 18 | 19 | 17 | €49

Neuilly-sur-Seine | 12, bd Georges Seurat (Pont-de-Levallois) | 01-46-24-25-04 | www.laguinguette.net

"A warm if bourgeois" ambiance prevails at this old-fashioned *guinguette* (restaurant on a barge) on the Ile de la Jatte in Neuilly where a crowd of "advertising execs" and locals appreciates the "grandmotherly" Classic French cookery ("blanquette de veau, pot-au-feu"); lulled by the "tranquil atmosphere" overlooking the Seine, most judge the service fine and the prices "fair."

	FOOD	DECOR	SERVICE	COST
Z Guy Savoy, Restaurant *Haute Cuisine*	28	26	28	€194

17e | 18, rue Troyon (Charles de Gaulle-Etoile) | 01-43-80-40-61 | www.guysavoy.com

"Imaginative works of contemporary art" by "brilliant" chef Guy Savoy grace the plates at his Haute Cuisine home base near the Arc de Triomphe (he has outposts in Vegas and Singapore); fans also swoon over "personalized", nearly "perfect" service and a "beautiful", "modern" space, so although you'll need to "bring a wheelbarrow full of euros", almost everyone says it's "worth" it; P.S. reservations (and jackets for gents) required; a move to the Hôtel de la Monnaie is planned for late 2012.

NEW Gyoza Bar *Japanese*	-	-	-	I

2e | 56, passage des Panoramas (Grands Boulevards/Richelieu-Drouot) | 01-44-82-00-62

The name says it all: well-priced pan-fried dumplings filled with Desnoyer pork are easily washed down with Kirin at the counter bar of this sleek new wood-and-stone-clad Japanese joint in the 2nd's Passage des Panoramas, run by Guillaume Guedj and Shinichi Sato of neighboring Passage 53.

Hangar (Le) *Classic French*	23	17	19	€40

3e | 12, impasse Berthaud (Rambuteau) | 01-42-74-55-44

"Simple", "well-prepared" Classic French dishes (e.g. "superb" foie gras) shine at this "cute, intimate" and very "Parisian" spot "hidden away" down a quiet lane in the 3rd; with a "warm welcome" and "reasonable" prices, it's also a "convenient" lunch stop for visitors to the nearby Pompidou and surrounding museums; P.S. no credit cards accepted.

Hédoniste (L') *Bistro*	∇ 22	18	24	€48

2e | 14, rue Léopold Bellan (Sentier/Les Halles) | 01-40-26-87-33 | www.lhedoniste.com

This bistro near Les Halles lives up to its name with a full slate of *vins naturels*, cocktails and whiskies matching the reasonably priced "quality dishes" that skew modern in style; a "pleasant" staff patrols the cozy storefront space enhanced by mirrors and comfortably spaced wooden tables.

Z Hélène Darroze *New French/Southwest*	26	22	22	€131

6e | 4, rue d'Assas (Rennes/Sèvres-Babylone) | 01-42-22-00-11 | www.helenedarroze.com

"Hélène Darroze is a real pro" and "brings Gascony to Paris" (even if she's often at the Connaught in London) with "triumphant" Southwestern French dishes feathered into the "innovative" New French menu at her eponymous table near Sèvres-Babylone; not quite equal to the food is the service ("affable" vs. "disappointing"), but the majority maintains the wallet-walloping cost is well "worth it"; P.S. insiders declare the "lower-priced" ground-floor tapas bar "just as good" as the "modern" main dining room.

	FOOD	DECOR	SERVICE	COST

Hide (Le) ☒ *Bistro* ▽ 24 | 12 | 21 | €41

17e | 10, rue du Général Lanrezac (Charles de Gaulle-Etoile) | 01-45-74-15-81 | www.lehide.fr

"How does Koba do it?" wonder fans of chef Hide 'Koba' Kobayashi as he heaps up "fantastic" bistro fare from the "fabulous-value" prix fixe menus at this "find" near L'Etoile; window dressing is "minimal" in the "small" "simple" joint, but at least the staff is "amiable."

Higuma *Japanese* 20 | 10 | 15 | €20

1er | 163, rue St-Honoré (Palais Royal-Musée du Louvre) | 01-58-62-49-22
1er | 32 bis, rue Ste-Anne (Pyramides) | 01-47-03-38-59 ☒
www.higuma.fr

"Everyday Japanese" food (noodles and gyoza, not sushi) at "accessible prices" brings crowds to this pair of "no-frills" "canteens" in the 1st; not to worry: the "line out the door" at the Rue Ste-Anne location "goes fast" thanks to "quick" service.

Z Hiramatsu ☒ *Haute Cuisine/New French* 27 | 21 | 26 | €107

16e | 52, rue de Longchamp (Boissière/Trocadéro) | 01-56-81-08-80 | www.hiramatsu.co.jp

Chef-owner Hiroyuki Hiramatsu pays "attention to every detail" and achieves "the perfect melding of Japanese subtlety and French culinary depth" on a New French–Haute Cuisine menu that's "innovative without being too much of a science experiment" at this "understated", flower-filled dining room near the Trocadéro; a "warm welcome" previews "irreproachable service", leaving only one complaint: "it's too expensive to go every day"; P.S. closed weekends.

Hôtel Amour ● *New French* 15 | 22 | 14 | €39

9e | Hôtel Amour | 8, rue de Navarin (St-Georges) | 01-48-78-31-80 | www.hotelamourparis.fr

Very "bobo chic", this "trendy" hotel resto-lounge in the 9th is owned by the son of one of the Costes brothers and slings New York–inspired New French fare; its "hipster" habitués don't care that the food's "average" or the service forgettable, finding it a "romantic" rendezvous (particularly the "beautiful" back garden) that won't break the bank.

Hotel du Nord ● *Bistro* - | - | - | M

10e | 102, quai de Jemmapes (Jacques Bonsergent) | 01-40-40-78-78 | www.hoteldunord.org

Made famous by a 1938 film of the same name, this legendary locale is a polestar of the Canal Saint-Martin scene, serving moderately priced bistro fare in a dark, deliberately shabby room chockablock with antiques, tiles and an old zinc bar; it serves lunch and dinner but remains open all day till late for coffee and drinks, best sipped on the terrace with the international hipster crowd.

Z Huîtrerie Régis M *Shellfish* 26 | 15 | 19 | €48

6e | 3, rue de Montfaucon (Mabillon) | 01-44-41-10-07 | www.huitrerieregis.com

There's "simple perfection" in what connoisseurs claim are "the best oysters in Paris" at this "pristine", white-and-gold-painted raw bar in

Saint-Germain, which represents some folks' "idea of heaven" – and since it's positively pearl-sized, there's "no room for non-believers"; you "often have to wait", but the "smiling" staff and moderate tabs help make it "worth it."

Huîtrier (L') [M] *Seafood* 22 | 15 | 20 | €64

17e | 16, rue Saussier-Leroy (Ternes) | 01-40-54-83-44 | www.huitrier.fr
"Oysters, oysters and oysters" ("and maybe some other things") are the pride of this stalwart seafooder in the 17th; it's "a shame" the "minimalist" decor is so "uninteresting", but "attentive" service and Neptune's bounty, though it comes at a price, make up for it.

I Golosi [S] *Italian* ▽ 23 | 18 | 18 | €45

9e | 6, rue de la Grange-Batelière (Grands Boulevards/Richelieu-Drouot) | 01-48-24-18-63 | www.igolosi.com
This "treat" of a trattoria tucked in a passage in the 9th serves mid-priced "real Italian" fare that's popular with hungry bankers at noon, pasta-loving locals after hours and "gourmet antique-hunters" bidding at the nearby Drouot auction house; the staff can be "laconic" and surveyors are equally tight-lipped about the decor, but *i golosi*, 'the greedy ones', keep returning for more of its "succulent" fare.

Il Barone ◐ [S] *Italian* 22 | 14 | 20 | €51

14e | 5, rue Léopold Robert (Raspail/Vavin) | 01-43-20-87-14
"Reliable and refined", this Italian stalwart in Montparnasse pleases regulars with "great homemade pasta" and other "good-value" Transalpine treats; those in the know sit in back to "avoid the boring-to-death" front room and advise: "don't miss the zabaglione."

Ile (L') *Classic/New French* 19 | 25 | 17 | €52

Issy-les-Moulineaux | Parc de l'Ile St-Germain | 170, quai de Stalingrad (Issy-Val de Seine RER) | 01-41-09-99-99 | www.restaurant-lile.com
"Time slows down" on the Ile Saint-Germain and "you'd almost think you were in the country" when dining at this "beautiful" Classic-New French that "charms" year-round with a breezy terrace in summer and "romantic" fireside tables during the cold months; most like the sprawling setting better than the "hectic" service, but the food is "pleasant" enough and a relatively "good buy."

Ilot Vache (L') *Classic French* 20 | 22 | 21 | €59

4e | 35, rue St-Louis-en-l'Ile (Pont-Marie) | 01-46-33-55-16 | www.restaurant-ilotvache.com
This "old-style romantic" destination on the "lovely" Ile Saint-Louis serves "well-prepared" French classics in a "warm", "charming" interior stuffed with "floral displays" and cow figurines; "discreet" service adds to the pleasure of a meal in this "quiet" spot – even if "the prices match the exclusive location."

Il Vino ◐ [S] *New French* 22 | 20 | 24 | €99

7e | 13, bd de la Tour-Maubourg (Invalides) | 01-44-11-72-00 | www.ilvinobyenricobernardo.com
"Wine-lovers" cellarbrate this "slick and professional" New French in the 7th run by Italian-born sommelier Enrico Bernardo and featur-

ing a "wonderful, fun concept": you "select your wine and they make you a meal" to match; you'll blow your wad, but it's "worth" a visit to the "pretty" contemporary space to put yourself in the hands of the "genial, knowledgeable staff", which makes the "discovery of fantastic off-the-beaten track" wine producers "enlightening and entertaining."

NEW Instant d'Or (L') *New French* — | — | — | VE

8e | 36, av George V (George V) | 01-47-23-46-78 | www.instantdor.com

Chef Frédéric Duca attempts to spin products of privileged provenance (e.g. Wagyu beef, wild turbot) into modern French gold at this luxe Champs-Elysées newcomer, outfitted with pearly-white walls, high-design furniture and glowing lights worthy of a set from *2001: A Space Odyssey*; there's a sub-50-euro lunch formula, but otherwise you might have to melt down a ring to pay the bill; P.S. oenophiles, note the cellarful of red Bordeaux gems.

Isami *Japanese* 25 | 15 | 18 | €63

4e | 4, quai d'Orléans (Pont-Marie) | 01-40-46-06-97

Sushi and sashimi of "unquestionable quality" brings afishionados to this svelte, "scantily clad" Japanese on the banks of the Ile Saint-Louis "for what many consider the best" raw fish in town; an "interesting sake menu" doubtless adds to the "calm and discreet atmosphere", and even if it's "not cheap" and the staff is sometimes "squirrely", reservations are in short supply.

Itinéraires *New French* 23 | 19 | 20 | €57

5e | 5, rue de Pontoise (Maubert-Mutualité) | 01-46-33-60-11 | www.restaurant-itineraires.com

Chef Sylvain Sendra demonstrates "youthful verve" in the "cutting-edge" New French dishes that have become more "sophisticated" over time, pairing perfectly with the "sleek and modern" look of his Latin Quarter space; other pluses are the "friendly" staff and prices that are "reasonable" given the "quality"; P.S. closed weekends.

Izakaya Issé *Japanese* 23 | 17 | 19 | €57
(fka Issé)

1er | 45, rue de Richelieu (Palais Royal-Musée du Louvre/Pyramides) | 01-42-96-26-60 | www.isse-et-cie.fr

"Original" yet "authentic" Japanese small plates (and a name tweak) signal a change in the menu's format at this sake specialist in the 1st; it's pricey and not everyone will like sitting on stools in the small, "design"-forward dining room, but the staff is "welcoming" and the kitchen makes "no concessions on the quality of their ingredients."

Jadis *Bistro* 23 | 17 | 22 | €62

15e | 208, rue de la Croix Nivert (Boucicaut) | 01-45-57-73-20 | www.bistrot-jadis.com

"It's worth the schlep" to this "gastro-bistro" in a residential part of the 15th for Guillaume Delage's "creative" "classics done with a twist" say surveyors, who insist that even if it's slightly expensive, the "quality/price ratio is very good"; the "very French clientele" that seeks out this small corner spot with its "unassuming" decor of framed vintage prints appreciates being "treated with the utmost sincerity and kindness"; P.S. closed weekends.

NEW Jaja *Bistro* 17 | 20 | 20 | €41

4e | 3, rue Ste-Croix de la Bretonnerie (Hôtel de Ville) | 01-42-74-71-52 | www.jaja-resto.com

"In a lively corner of the Marais", this latest address from ex-food-mag editor Julien Fouin (he owns Glou in the 3rd) is a wine-oriented bistro with a relaxing terrace and friendly, young staff; the menu runs from casual favorites at midday to more elaborate food (e.g. "very good pot-au-feu") at dinner, and if the kitchen works with mostly "organic" produce, a happy surprise is the "not-so-organic" (i.e. moderate) price point.

Jamin *New French* 23 | 23 | 24 | €96

16e | 32, rue de Longchamp (Iéna/Trocadéro) | 01-45-53-00-07 | www.restaurant-jamin.com

The "inventive" French cuisine is "exquisitely presented" (even if it's "not what it once was" when Joël Robuchon ran the kitchen) at this "cozy", "romantic" respite owned by restaurateur Alain Pras in an "upscale" quarter of the 16th; it's still considered "chic" by a monied, "older crowd of Parisians", and big-spending tourists appreciate the "knowledgeable", "English-speaking staff."

Jardins de Bagatelle (Les) *Classic French* 20 | 24 | 18 | €70

16e | Parc de Bagatelle | Route de Sèvres (Pont-de-Neuilly) | 01-40-67-98-29 | www.bagatellelerestaurant.com

It "looks like a Monet with a colorful crowd of every age" "under white umbrellas" enthuse those impressed by the "magnificent" scenery at this largely alfresco repose in the verdant Parc de Bagatelle, where horticulturalists relax after a "stroll among the roses"; service can be "a bit spotty" and the Classic French fare is "honest" but "expensive for the quality" - no matter, the setting is "magical."

Jean *New French* ▽ 26 | 21 | 24 | €74

9e | 8, rue St-Lazare (Notre-Dame-de-Lorette/St-Georges) | 01-48-78-62-73 | www.restaurantjean.fr

It's "a well-kept secret", which suits fans of this "gem in the 9th", where "amiable" owner Jean-Frédéric Guidoni metes out "charming" service and young chef Anthony Boucher dreams up "sophisticated" "modern French" dishes that "just get better every year"; it's mainly for fat wallets, but the catalog-pretty "French country-style" dining room is "as good for business as pleasure"; P.S. closed weekends.

Jean-François Piège *Haute/New French* 27 | 24 | 24 | €107

7e | Hôtel Thoumieux | 79, rue St-Dominique (Invalides/ La Tour-Maubourg) | 01-47-05-49-75 | www.jeanfrancoispiege.com

After launching the redone Thoumieux in the 7th, "superb" young chef Jean-François Piège created this plush, exclusive-feeling lounge with a retro '50s Rat Pack design by India Mahdavi upstairs, and this is where he holds forth, cooking in a small windowed kitchen behind the dining room and often delivering the "delicate, creative" Haute-New French dishes to the table himself (the rest of the staff is "efficient" too); it's "nearly impossible" to reserve any of the 20 seats, but it's "worth the effort and cost"; P.S. closed weekends.

Jeanne A *Bistro* — | - | - | M

11e | 42, rue Jean-Pierre Timbaud (Oberkampf/Parmentier) | 01-43-55-09-49

Few surveyors have found their way to this tiny hybrid market/cafe serving "excellent" French comfort food (from the kitchen of Astier next door) in the 11th, but those who have are impressed: "hard to find, but glad we did"; "darling service" and easygoing prices are among the rewards, along with shelves full of the makings for gourmet picnic lunches (wine, cheese, bread, etc.).

Jeu de Quilles (Le) ☒ ☒ *Wine Bar/Bistro* — | - | - | M

14e | 45, rue Boulard (Mouton-Duvernet) | 01-53-90-76-22

"Superb produce", plus meat from boldface butcher Hugo Desnoyer next door, is "remarkably well cooked" at this "friendly" *bistrot à vins* in the 14th; not many surveyors have ventured into the small space that's simply furnished with white walls and wood floors, but those who have say it's "excellent" and a "good value."

Joséphine "Chez Dumonet" ☒ *Bistro* 25 | 19 | 22 | €68

6e | 117, rue du Cherche-Midi (Duroc) | 01-45-48-52-40

One of the last "old-style Paris bistros" on the Left Bank, this belle epoque beauty with beveled glass dividers and gas lamp fixtures is a true "classic serving the classics", like "outstanding duck confit", "rich" boeuf bourguignon and other "fabulous" favorites; the "very French service adds to the charm", and if the prices appear daunting, know that you can keep the bill down if you "order the half portions" – though even then you'll still "waddle out"; P.S. closed weekends.

Z Jules Verne (Le) *Haute Cuisine* 23 | 27 | 24 | €142

7e | Tour Eiffel | Av Gustave Eiffel, Champ de Mars, 2nd level (Ecole Militaire/Varenne) | 01-45-55-61-44 | www.lejulesverne-paris.com

Gastronauts are "whisked" via private elevator 125 meters up to this "dream"-like "special-occasion" destination high in the Eiffel Tower, where "incomparable" views of "the most beautiful city in the world" serve as backdrop to "sophisticated" Haute Cuisine from a kitchen under the aegis of Alain Ducasse; an "exemplary" staff and designer Patrick Jouin's "ingenious" low-lit, noir-and-taupe interior add to its charms, so despite concerns about "astronomical" prices and a "touristy" rep, most find the experience as "enchanting" as it is "unforgettable"; P.S. "make sure to book months in advance."

Juveniles ☒ *Wine Bar/Bistro* 15 | 11 | 17 | €39

1er | 47, rue de Richelieu (Bourse/Palais Royal-Musée du Louvre) | 01-42-97-46-49 | www.juveniles.winebar.com

This "narrow", "hole-in-the-wall" wine bar near the Palais-Royal is a real corker thanks to the "exceptional depth" of its wine list (the bottles line the walls) and "fine casual nibbles"; the Scottish owner "will make you feel at home and perhaps keep you laughing", and the experience won't cost you much – another reason to lift a glass.

	FOOD	DECOR	SERVICE	COST

Kai Ⓢ Ⓜ *Japanese* ▽ 25 | 20 | 19 | €63

1er | 18, rue du Louvre (Louvre-Rivoli) | 01-40-15-01-99

Near the Louvre, this "excellent" Japanese is a "refined" place boasting "creative" sushi, beautiful bento boxes and other "haute"-style dishes, including Pierre Hermé desserts; its "sleek" decor, including a bamboo ceiling, is another reason why it's popular with fashion mavens who book ahead and don't seem to mind its couture price tag.

Kaïten ◐ Ⓢ *Japanese* 22 | 14 | 18 | €54

8e | 63, rue Pierre Charron (Franklin D. Roosevelt) | 01-43-59-78-78 | www.kaiten.fr

Close to the Champs-Elysées, this conveyor-belt sushi salon is good for a "quick meal" since you "serve yourself", and most find the moveable feast "varied and original"; it's not cheap, however, and no one much notices the anonymous decor, but folks go anyway because it's "consistent", "fresh" and "tasty."

NEW Kei Ⓢ Ⓜ *New French* ▽ 28 | 25 | 26 | €103

1er | 5, rue Coq-Héron (Louvre-Rivoli) | 01-42-33-14-74 | www.restaurant-kei.fr

Installed in the former premises of Gérard Besson, young Japanese chef-owner Kei Kobayashi gets raves from the few surveyors who've discovered his "remarkable", "refined" New French cooking; the silver-and-gray dining room is suitably elegant and the "impeccable" staff maintains a "discreet presence", so all in all it's a stellar performer with accordingly celestial prices; P.S. jacket suggested.

KGB Ⓢ Ⓜ *Asian/New French* 23 | 18 | 21 | €59

6e | 25, rue des Grands-Augustins (Odéon) | 01-46-33-00-85 | www.kitchengaleriebis.com

"Decor that's like a modern-art gallery" frames the "artistry on the plate" at chef William Ledeuil's annex to Ze Kitchen Galerie in Saint-Germain-des-Prés, where a "creative" menu of Asian fusion-New French tasting-portion appetizers and "fascinating" mains are served up by a "friendly" crew; it's not cheap and can be "noisy", but even so fans advise "don't miss it."

Khun Akorn Ⓜ *Thai* 21 | 19 | 18 | €46

11e | 8, av de Taillebourg (Nation) | 01-43-56-20-03

"Smiling service" from the "family who owns it" awaits at this "quality" Thai in a distant corner of the 11th that's deemed "a great buy for the money"; the Eastern-accented dining room is "pleasant" enough, but insiders say the "little terrace" upstairs is "tops."

Kifune Ⓢ Ⓜ *Japanese* ▽ 23 | 15 | 18 | €54

17e | 44, rue St-Ferdinand (Porte Maillot) | 01-45-72-11-19

"Far from the touristy places in the center of Paris", this "small" "Japanese-run" spot in the 17th is "like the taverns you find in Tokyo" (so "bring your pocket translator if you're not fluent"), attracting lots of Japanese salarymen and other fans of the "authentic" sushi and sashimi; moderate tabs are a nice ending after the "warm welcome" and "fast, smiling service."

	FOOD	DECOR	SERVICE	COST

Kiku [S] *Japanese* — - | - | - | M

9ᵉ | 56, rue Richer (Cadet/Grands Boulevards) | 01-44-83-02-30

Still not widely known, perhaps because it's "well hidden" on a small street in the 9th, this "inventive" Japanese is worth tracking down for its "original" and "delicious" Franco-Japanese cooking; area office workers and theatergoers appreciate its "good value", and if the minimalist look isn't for everyone, there's always takeout and delivery.

Kim Anh [M] *Vietnamese* — ▽ 23 | 18 | 22 | €41

15ᵉ | 51, av Emile Zola (Charles Michel) | 01-45-79-40-96 | www.kimanh-restaurant.com

Count on the kitchen at this venerable Vietnamese in the 15th to deliver "a mixture of flavors from the highest levels of Saigonese cooking" on its midpriced menu; the staff delivers a "warm welcome", complete with a hot towel and a smile, and the contemporary space is also relaxing in a Zen kind of way.

Kinugawa [S] *Japanese* — 24 | 18 | 21 | €75

1ᵉʳ | 9, rue du Mont-Thabor (Tuileries) | 01-42-60-65-07 | www.kinugawa.free.fr

Fresh-fish fiends nibble "excellent" sushi and tuck into tempura at this "refined", "authentic" place near the Tuileries, one of the "grande dames of Japanese restaurants in Paris"; service is professional if occasionally "impersonal", and prices are as lofty as the quality; P.S. the "somber" minimalist space will get a "revamp" as new post-Survey owners have planned a major renovation for spring 2012.

Kong ◐ *Eclectic* — 16 | 24 | 13 | €60

1ᵉʳ | Pont Neuf Bldg. | 1, rue du Pont-Neuf (Pont-Neuf) | 01-40-39-09-00 | www.kong.fr

This "ultracool" aerie atop the Pont Neuf in the 1st occupies a "flashy" Tokyoesque space designed by Philippe Starck, set under a glass dome offering "killer" views of the Seine and "the fabled rooftops of Paris"; service is not king at Kong, and tabs can seem "too high" for the "fair" Eclectic eats, but with its "loud music" and "glam" scene, it's really more "nightclub than restaurant."

Lac-Hong [S] *Vietnamese* — ▽ 21 | 10 | 14 | €52

16ᵉ | 67, rue Lauriston (Boissière/Victor Hugo) | 01-47-55-87-17

"Authentic" Vietnamese "home cooking" that's "faithful" to the homeland makes this "efficient" but no-frills hole-in-the-wall in the 16th "worth a visit"; a few find it "too expensive" for its milieu, but fans insist the prices are "fair."

Languedoc (Le) *Southwest* — ▽ 21 | 17 | 21 | €48

5ᵉ | 64, bd de Port-Royal (Les Gobelins) | 01-47-07-24-47

Since 1974, this "traditional", family-run restaurant in the 5th has been serving "hefty portions" of "typical French bistro food", with an accent on its namesake region in the Southwest; with red-gingham curtains and a "typewritten, mimeographed menu", it has a "timeless", country feel, and "reasonable prices" make it a "family-friendly" option; P.S. closed Tuesday and Wednesday.

	FOOD	DECOR	SERVICE	COST
Lao Lane Xang *Asian*	22	15	16	€27

13ᵉ | 102, av d'Ivry (Tolbiac) | 01-58-89-00-00
"Excellent Laotian" specialties highlight the "authentic", "quality" Asian menu at this popular, "affordable" spot in the "Paris Chinatown of the 13th"; service is "efficient" ("too much so" for some), and while the "modern" decor is "pleasant", some find the seating a bit "tight", especially since the place is "always packed."

	FOOD	DECOR	SERVICE	COST
Lao Siam ◐ *Thai*	22	10	15	€31

19ᵉ | 49, rue de Belleville (Belleville/Pyrénées) | 01-40-40-09-68
"Go early, or spend 45 minutes in line" since they don't take reservations at this "unpretentious", affordable Lao-Thai table in Belleville serving surprisingly "refined" fare in a simple, Asian-accented setting; some say it's become a "victim of its own success", evident in service that "leaves much to be desired."

	FOOD	DECOR	SERVICE	COST
Lapérouse [S] *Haute Cuisine*	23	25	24	€107

6ᵉ | 51, quai des Grands-Augustins (Pont-Neuf/St-Michel) | 01-43-26-90-14 | www.laperouse.com
Once frequented by "Voltaire and other 18th-century writers", this Saint-Germain landmark is set in a "magnificent" space featuring a "romantic" "old-world" main dining room (that recently underwent a "caring restoration", which may outdate the Decor score) and a bevy of private dining rooms "seething" in the "juicy histories of politicians and their mistresses"; the chef (ex Le Bristol) creates "inventive" Haute Cuisine dishes "based on time-honored classics", and service is suitably "discreet", making an assignation with this "grand lady" "worth its weight in gold"; P.S. jackets required.

	FOOD	DECOR	SERVICE	COST
[Z] **Lasserre** [S][M] *Haute Cuisine*	27	28	27	€163

8ᵉ | 17, av Franklin D. Roosevelt (Franklin D. Roosevelt) | 01-43-59-02-13 | www.restaurant-lasserre.com
This "timeless classic" in the 8th is "total theater", starring chef Christophe Moret's "excellent" Haute Cuisine, supported by service that runs like a "well-orchestrated symphony" and a "sumptuous", orchid-filled setting featuring "enough silver and linen to make Versailles proud" plus a "famous" retractable roof that opens to the "star-lit" sky; it's "wonderful for special occasions", but the bill, "like everything else" here, is "extraordinary"; P.S. jackets required.

	FOOD	DECOR	SERVICE	COST
Laurent [S] *Haute Cuisine*	25	24	25	€146

8ᵉ | 41, av Gabriel (Champs-Elysées-Clémenceau) | 01-42-25-00-39 | www.le-laurent.com
"The perfect venue for a special celebration", this "dreamy pavilion" surrounded by gardens just off the Champs-Elysées is "especially magical in summer" when you can dine outside, although the "refined" Haute Cuisine by chef Alain Pégouret plus "top-notch" service make its "formal" dining rooms a year-round destination for a Paris power crowd; sure, it's "expensive", but most consider it a "lovely blow-the-budget" experience; P.S. jacket suggested.

	FOOD	DECOR	SERVICE	COST

Legrand Filles et Fils [S] *Wine Bar/Bistro* 21 | 22 | 19 | €63

2e | Galerie Vivienne | 1, rue de la Banque (Bourse/Palais Royal-Musée du Louvre) | 01-42-60-07-12 | www.caves-legrand.com

Tucked away in the "gorgeous" Galerie Vivienne arcade in the 2nd is this "world-class wine shop" sporting a *bar à vins* that serves "delicious, simple" bites and by-the-glass pours from the "famous cellar" in a "secluded", old-fashioned Paris setting; it's not cheap, but it's a "must-visit for wine lovers" who are "charmed" by the approachable sommeliers.

Lescure [S] *Southwest* 19 | 16 | 21 | €40

1er | 7, rue de Mondovi (Concorde) | 01-42-60-18-91

Open since 1919, this "institution" near the Place de la Concorde is a "quintessential Parisian bistro" where "country-style" Southwestern French dishes are served by a "friendly" team at affordable prices; the "tight quarters" of the rustic dining room are usually "filled with locals", who would no doubt agree that this "memorable" "gem" is "one of the last of its kind"; P.S. closed weekends; no reservations.

Lilane [S] [M] *New French* ▽ 25 | 19 | 23 | €44

5e | 8, rue Gracieuse (Place Monge) | 01-45-87-90-68

Tucked away behind the Place Monge in the 5th, this New French attracts a professional (and professorial) Latin Quarter crowd with "inventive", "well-presented" dishes by chef Stéphane Guilçou, which are served in a dimly lit room with widely spaced tables; cognoscenti consider it an "outstanding value."

Liza *Lebanese* 24 | 20 | 21 | €47

2e | 14, rue de la Banque (Bourse) | 01-55-35-00-66 | www.restaurant-liza.com

An "unexpected treasure" in the 2nd, Liza Soughayar's love letter to modern Beirut offers "tasteful", "excellent updates" of Lebanese cuisine and "pleasant" service in a stylish, contemporary space bathed in natural light; though some find the wines "expensive", most consider it "reasonably priced" overall.

Lozère (La) [S] [M] *Auvergne* 21 | 17 | 19 | €37

6e | 4, rue Hautefeuille (St-Michel) | 01-43-54-26-64 | www.lozere-a-paris.com

This "charming", "affordable" eatery in the Latin Quarter dishes up "simple", "authentic" fare from the Lozère region, including "excellent cheeses", charcuterie and lamb, as well as the Thursday night *aligot* (potatoes whipped with cheese curds and garlic); "welcoming" service makes up for "noisy" conditions in the "tiny", rustic space.

Luna (La) [S] *Seafood* ▽ 26 | 20 | 24 | €104

8e | 69, rue du Rocher (Europe/Villiers) | 01-42-93-77-61 | www.restaurantlaluna.com

"Simplicity" and "refinement" are the hallmarks of the seafood dishes at this "outstanding" *poissonnerie* in an "offbeat location" near the Gare Saint-Lazare; "beautiful service" and "chic, sober" decor are further pluses, leading those with deep pockets to confirm that "escalating prices do not detract from the wonderful quality" of everything here; P.S. its rhum baba may be "the best in Paris."

Lyonnais (Aux) *Lyon* 22 | 19 | 20 | €61

2e | 32, rue St-Marc (Opera/Richelieu-Drouot) | 01-42-96-65-04 | www.auxlyonnais.com

"There is a lot to like" about Alain Ducasse's bistro in the 2nd: its "unfussy" "traditional" Lyonnais-style cuisine, "authentic" circa-1900 "belle epoque" dining room and an aproned staff that runs like a "well-oiled machine" (though some diners feel pressured to "hurry up and eat"); prices are a tad high, but most say it's "worth the splurge."

Ma Bourgogne *Burgundy* 19 | 18 | 19 | €51

4e | 19, pl des Vosges (Bastille/St-Paul) | 01-42-78-44-64 | www.ma-bourgogne.fr

"Touristy, yes", but this "stereotypical Parisian cafe" offers "grand-motherly" Burgundian fare and "well-intentioned" service that "would please even if" it didn't also boast "just about the best location in Paris": most of the tables are under the arches of the Place des Vosges; it's "moderately priced" to boot, making it a "must-stop"; P.S. one quibble: "it's time for a credit card machine."

Macéo *Classic/New French* 23 | 21 | 20 | €61

1er | 15, rue des Petits-Champs (Palais Royal-Musée du Louvre/ Pyramides) | 01-42-97-53-85 | www.maceorestaurant.com

Near the Palais-Royal, this "light, airy" place from Englishman Mark Williamson (Willi's Wine Bar) sports a look that "marries modernity with British tradition" and a menu, by newly installed Korean chef Maitre Park, that melds contemporary and Classic French fare in "inventive and refined" ways (there's also a "splendid vegetarian" roster); "impeccable service" adds to the prevailing aura of "calm", which even the "expensive" tabs don't disturb.

Maharajah (Le) *Indian* 23 | 19 | 21 | €33

5e | 72, bd St-Germain (Maubert-Mutualité/St-Michel) | 01-43-54-26-07 | www.maharajah.fr

"A beautiful Indian escapade" awaits at one of the oldest curry houses in the Latin Quarter, boasting "refined, original cooking" presented by a "friendly" staff in a space that's decorated with subcontinental *objets d'art*; best of all: "it's a great buy."

Mai Do *Vietnamese* - | - | - | M

6e | 23, bd du Montparnasse (Duroc) | 01-45-48-54-60

Eaters in the know recommend the "delicious Vietnamese cooking for reasonable prices" at this long-standing joint sporting a stylish, modern look not far from the Gare Montparnasse; with "ma-and-pa" management going back three generations, it's a "real" keeper.

Main d'Or (La) *Corsica* ▽ 22 | 16 | 17 | €37

11e | 133, rue du Faubourg St-Antoine (Ledru-Rollin) | 01-44-68-04-68

"It's like being in Corsica" at this Mediterranean maestro near the Bastille, where "most of the produce" used in the "seasonal", "traditional cooking" originates on the island, attracting lots of guests who do too; the rustic interior can get "crowded", but on the bright side prices are downright Bonaparte-esque (i.e. small).

Maison Blanche *New French* 23 | 26 | 22 | €103

8e | 15, av Montaigne (Alma Marceau) | 01-47-23-55-99 | www.maison-blanche.fr

A "panoramic Parisian view" that includes the Eiffel Tower, the Seine and Les Invalides is the high point of this "trendy" duplex atop the Théâtre des Champs Elysèes, though its "superbly prepared" New French cooking, "extensive" wine list and "professional" service are similarly tip-top; tabs are vertiginous too, but the "*très* chic" types who can afford to breathe the rarified air in the "sophisticated" black-and-white interior or out on the new summer terrace find the experience "romantic" and "enchanting"; P.S. jacket suggested.

Maison Courtine (La) *New French* 20 | 18 | 20 | €54

14e | 157, av du Maine (Denfert-Rochereau/Mouton-Duvernet) | 01-45-43-08-04 | www.lamaisoncourtine.com

Since an ownership change, the previously Southwestern menu at this "refined" Montparnasse mainstay has "modernized" to New French, leading some to judge it as "solid" but no longer anything "out of the ordinary"; the vaguely whimsical, orange-accented decor redo is "pleasant" enough, the "good values" remain and most still find the servers quite "friendly."

Maison de l'Amérique Latine *Classic French* 21 | 26 | 21 | €68

7e | 217, bd St-Germain (Solférino) | 01-49-54-75-10 | www.mal217.org

"One of the most beautiful settings in Paris" – the "fantastic" garden hidden behind a limestone mansion housing the Latin American cultural institute – offers a "moment of grace" in "the heart" of the 7th; everything else plays a supporting role, from the "tasty" Classic French fare to the "correct" service and the "very reasonable" prices; P.S. closed weekends; outside seating available May–September only.

Maison du Caviar (La) ◐ *Russian* 25 | 19 | 23 | €112

8e | 21, rue Quentin-Bauchart (George V) | 01-47-23-53-43 | www.caviar-volga.com

"Vodka, vodka, vodka!" plus the "best blini and caviar" fuel an "outrageous scene" full of "beautiful people" at this '30s-style "hedonistic outpost" just off the Champs-Elysées, where the namesake specialty is professionally "served in abundance" and in "various styles" along with other indulgent Russian comestibles; "astronomic" prices are part of the package, but "what a way to go."

Maison du Jardin (La) *Bistro* 25 | 19 | 23 | €48

6e | 27, rue de Vaugirard (Rennes/St-Placide) | 01-45-48-22-31

"A perfect neighborhood restaurant in a perfect neighborhood" near the Luxembourg Gardens, this "tiny" New French bistro with a "comfortable atmosphere" wins raves for its "skillfully prepared" dishes, "warm, welcoming" service (even for "bumbling tourists")

and "reasonable prices"; though the "understated" decor falls short of the food, few seem to mind at this "little treasure."

NEW Maison Mère (La) *American/Bistro* | - | - | - | M |

9e | 4, rue de Navarin (St-Georges) | 01-42-81-11-00 | www.lamaisonmere.fr

It's Brooklyn-sur-Seine at this new midpriced bar and bistro in the 9th, where Gallic goods like leeks vinaigrette and steak tartare share menu space with American eats like burgers and Cobb salad; the self-consciously retro room (Formica tables, kitschy paper place mats, white subway tiles) suits the au courant media and music biz bunch who crowd in for cocktails and Sunday brunch.

Mama Shelter *Brasserie* | 16 | 23 | 16 | €49 |

20e | Mama Shelter | 109, rue de Bagnolet (Gambetta/Porte de Bagnolet) | 01-43-48-45-45 | www.mamashelter.com

With a "trendy" "lounge" design by Philippe Starck, this late-night brasserie in a boutique hotel in the "remote" 20th offers a "fashionable" ambiance for sampling chef Alain Senderens' midpriced, "updated traditional" French dishes; not everyone's convinced - some cite "untrained" service and say the cuisine was "dialed in from an old cell phone over coffee" - but nonetheless it's "quite a scene any night of the week" due to its main "asset": the "large" bar; P.S. an adjoining pizzeria expands the options.

Mansouria *Moroccan* | 21 | 18 | 17 | €51 |

11e | 11, rue Faidherbe (Faidherbe-Chaligny) | 01-43-71-00-16 | www.mansouria.fr

"Take a magic carpet ride to Morocco" via the "high-quality" cuisine that "goes beyond couscous (though that in itself is excellent)" at this "low-key" eatery in the 11th with multiple rooms, each done up with North African motifs; service is "fair" and tabs are "reasonable" for this part of town, furthering its appeal to "families" and "groups."

Marée (La) *Seafood* | 23 | 19 | 22 | €73 |

8e | 1, rue Daru (Etoile/Ternes) | 01-43-80-20-00 | www.lamaree.fr

This "super" seafooder in the 8th has been hauling in a Paris power crowd for almost 50 years with its "fine fish" and other "outstanding" *fruits de mer* served amid "old-fashioned" decor that has a certain "charm" (plus a new terrace opening in 2012); service is "fast and attentive", and even though it's far from cheap, it's "more affordable" than in the past; P.S. "beware of being seated in the 'penalty box' reserved for Americans."

Marée Passy (La) *Seafood* | 22 | 17 | 18 | €60 |

16e | 71, av Paul Doumer (La Muette/Trocadéro) | 01-45-04-12-81 | www.lamareepassy.com

"An affluent local clientele" casts their nets at this "busy" but "efficient" favorite in the 16th, hauling in simply prepared, "always very fresh" fish; the "pleasantly decorated" interior is awash in maritime trimmings (wood, brass, pictures of sailboats), and the "quality" of the catch easily compensates for somewhat "expensive" tabs.

	FOOD	DECOR	SERVICE	COST

Marius ☒ *Provence/Seafood* 25 | 18 | 21 | €67

16e | 82, bd Murat (Porte de St-Cloud) | 01-46-51-67-80

A "very 16*ème*" crowd flocks to this "first-class" Provençal seafooder for "incredible" dishes at relatively decent prices given their "remarkable" "gastronomic" quality; with "welcoming" service in the comfortably elegant, light-filled interior and on the breezy terrace, it's the kind of place surveyors "return to again and again."

Marius et Janette *Seafood* 23 | 19 | 21 | €82

8e | 4, av George V (Alma Marceau) | 01-47-23-41-88 | www.mariusetjanette.com

In the swanky 8th, this longtime "fish mecca" known for its "pristine", "classically prepared" seafood and "attentive" crew remains as popular with "businesspeople" and "French old money" as it is with tourists; it's "not for the faint of wallet", but it's an "unforgettable" meal, whether sitting in the "boat cabin" interior (wood paneling, portholes, captain's chairs, rods and tackle) or the "marvelous" outdoor area with a "charming view of the Eiffel Tower"; P.S. its next-door sibling, Petit Marius, is "cheaper."

Market ◐ *Eclectic* 22 | 21 | 20 | €71

8e | 15, av Matignon (Champs-Elysées-Clémenceau/ Franklin D. Roosevelt) | 01-56-43-40-90 | www.jean-georges.com

"Popular with the fashion crowd", this "trendy" Jean-Georges Vongerichten vehicle off the Champs serves up "creative" Eclectic dishes ("truffle pizza", etc.) that please most comers; the "sleek", "contemporary" decor, "efficient" (if "not always pleasant") service and "sky-high prices" give it a "New York City" vibe.

Marlotte (La) *Bistro* 18 | 16 | 18 | €42

6e | 55, rue du Cherche-Midi (Sèvres-Babylone/St-Placide) | 01-45-48-86-79 | www.lamarlotte.com

This "quiet, little" Left Bank bistro around the corner from the Bon Marché department store is ideal for a "solid, no-nonsense" feast of French classics after a day of shopping; the "friendly" service and "reasonable" prices are well suited to the rustic dining room's "low-key", "old-fashioned" ambiance.

Martel (Le) ◐☒ *Classic French/Moroccan* ▽ 21 | 16 | 21 | €35

10e | 3, rue Martel (Château d'Eau) | 01-47-70-67-56

You might spy the "occasional *Vogue* editor" at this "relaxed" eatery in the increasingly trendy "artists' neighborhood" of the 10th, where the menu features Moroccan and French classics "of excellent quality"; the turn-of-the-last-century decor isn't exactly fashion-mag material, but the "accommodating" service and wallet-friendly prices will never go out of style.

Marty *Brasserie* 20 | 21 | 22 | €57

5e | 20, av des Gobelins (Les Gobelins) | 01-43-31-39-51 | www.martyrestaurant.com

A family affair since it opened in 1913, this brasserie in the 5th with a "pretty" art deco dining room is now run by the original founder's granddaughter, who continues its heritage of providing "very good", "traditional" cuisine, with particularly "excellent" seafood; the "speedy" service is up to date, as are the "high" prices (though the prix fixe is a good deal).

Mascotte (La) ◐ *Auvergne* | 20 | 17 | 17 | €48

18e | 52, rue des Abbesses (Abbesses/Blanche) | 01-46-06-28-15 | www.la-mascotte-montmartre.com

Popular with Montmartre locals, "tourists" and the occasional "French celebrity", this "old-style" Auvergnat brasserie in the "cool" Rue des Abbesses is "recommended for shellfish" above all else; the staff can seem "harried" at times but remains "competent" even during the rush, and with such moderate prices, it's a good bet in the area.

Mauzac (Le) Ⓢ *Wine Bar/Bistro* | ▽ 15 | 15 | 14 | €37

5e | 7, rue de l'Abbé de l'Epée (Luxembourg) | 01-46-33-75-22 | www.lemauzac.net

Located on a Latin Quarter street "bordered with large trees", this carnivores' bistro and wine bar is not well known, but habitués consider it "friendly" and a good value in the neighborhood; the "shaded terrace" is a sweet summer hang.

Mavrommatis Ⓜ *Greek* | 22 | 18 | 20 | €50

5e | 42, rue Daubenton (Censier-Daubenton) | 01-43-31-17-17 | www.mavrommatis.fr

It's worth an odyssey to the Latin Quarter for what a chorus of fans calls "the best Greek table west of Corfu", offering a midpriced slate of "top-quality" Hellenic and Cypriot dishes made with a "touch of refinement"; service holds it own, and surveyors also appreciate the Greek music in the rustic dining room and the "superb" terrace surrounded by olive trees.

Maxan (Le) Ⓢ *New French* | ▽ 20 | 15 | 19 | €70

8e | 3, rue Quentin-Bauchart (Miromesnil) | 01-42-65-78-60 | www.rest-maxan.com

Since moving to new quarters in the 8th - a dove-gray dining room with widely spaced tables and convex mirrors dappling the wall - this New French is more popular for "business lunches" than it was before, and also pulls a cosmopolitan crowd in the evening from neighboring hotels; the cuisine remains "imaginative" and the service "formal but friendly", making it "a great value" despite high tabs.

Maxim's ⓈⓂ *Classic French* | 20 | 24 | 21 | €109

8e | 3, rue Royale (Concorde/Madeleine) | 01-42-65-27-94 | www.maxims-de-paris.com

It may be "touristy", but this "legendary" grandest of grande dames on the Rue Royale still pleases "hopeless romantics" with its lavish, "step-back-in-time" art nouveau interior, even if the Classic French cooking is "not at the same level" and comes at maximal prices; service can be "courtly" or less so and the entire package strikes modernists as "passé", but supporters say "old is still gold" and insist it's worth a visit "at least once"; P.S. reservations (and jackets) required.

	FOOD	DECOR	SERVICE	COST

MBC ☒ *New French* | - | - | - | M |

17ᵉ | 4, rue du Débarcadère (Argentine/Porte Maillot) | 01-45-72-22-55 | www.gilleschoukroun.com

Chef Gilles Choukroun's New French near the Porte Maillot remains largely under the radar, but it attracts an international business clientele and young locals who appreciate the inventive herb-accented cooking (the name is short for '*menthe, basilique, coriandre*'), mid-range prices and trendy loungelike look with graffiti artwork and metal mesh room dividers.

Méditerranée (La) *Seafood* | 22 | 22 | 19 | €66 |

6ᵉ | 2, pl de l'Odéon (Odéon) | 01-43-26-02-30 | www.la-mediterranee.com

Dressed up with Cocteau murals, this "elegant" antique "gem" across from the Théâtre de l'Odéon in the 6th is applauded for its "excellent seafood", including "superb bouillabaisse"; service can be "spotty" ("charming" vs. "a challenge"), but most dub it a "special night out" and consider the expense "justified."

Mémère Paulette ☒ *Bistro* | ▽ 23 | 19 | 20 | €34 |

2ᵉ | 5, rue Paul Lelong (Bourse) | 01-40-26-12-36

"Welcome to the real Paris" say fans of this "perfect little" bistro with a "friendly owner" hidden away in the 2nd that boasts "no frills, no hype and almost no tourists!"; the rustic digs are leavened by knowing touches (e.g. 'mémère's' baking tins form a modern art piece on the wall), and there are "affordable", "interesting wines to discover."

Mesturet (Le) *Southwest* | 16 | 13 | 17 | €44 |

2ᵉ | 77, rue de Richelieu (Bourse) | 01-42-97-40-68 | www.lemesturet.com

Run by "charming" owner Alain Fontaine, this all-day "neighborhood spot" near the old Bourse may have its ups and downs in the kitchen, with some finding the Southwestern bistro dishes "good and copious", others "mediocre", but no matter: it's swarmed by "locals" during lunch, when it's often "noisy", and is a solid choice for a "post-opera" meal as it's "quieter at dinner"; a "warm" staff and "easy-on-the-wallet" prices give it appeal.

Z Meurice (Le) ☒ *Haute Cuisine* | 28 | 28 | 28 | €173 |

1ᵉʳ | Le Meurice | 228, rue de Rivoli (Concorde/Tuileries) | 01-44-58-10-55 | www.meuricehotel.com

"This is what heaven must be" enthuse the many admirers of chef Yannick Alléno's "sublime", "highly exciting" Haute Cuisine dishes, which are fittingly showcased in an "exquisite", faux-gilded setting designed by Philippe Starck at the Le Meurice Hotel in the 1st; add in "remarkable" service that strikes "a perfect balance between formal tradition and a relaxed modern feeling", and most conclude it's "worth the once-in-a-lifetime splurge"; P.S. closed weekends.

Z Michel Rostang ☒ *Classic French* | 27 | 23 | 26 | €156 |

17ᵉ | 20, rue Rennequin (Pereire/Ternes) | 01-47-63-40-77 | www.michelrostang.com

"Still great after all these years", chef-owner Michel Rostang's "lovely" table in the 17th is eminently "dependable" for "exquisite", "artfully presented" French classics, including an "incredible" truffle menu in season; "certainly the price is high", but with "superior" service throughout its four "intimate" dining rooms, each "carefully decorated" with a different theme (e.g. art nouveau, Lalique), it's perfect for "special occasions"; P.S. jacket required.

Minipalais ◐ *New French* — 21 | 26 | 18 | €60

8e | Grand Palais | 3, av Winston Churchill (Champs-Elysées-Clémenceau) | 01-42-56-42-42 | www.minipalais.com

"After viewing art at the Grand Palais", connoisseurs can refuel at this "trendy" New French inside the exhibition hall, where chef Eric Frechon's portfolio of "inventive", "precise" culinary pieces (e.g. an "outstanding" duck burger) are served by a "courteous" staff; with a "cool", high-ceilinged setting that calls to mind an artist's studio plus a "stunning" colonnaded terrace, it draws a "chic Parisian crowd" that takes the museum-quality price tags in stride; P.S. a formal tea service is available.

Mirama *Chinese* — 22 | 10 | 14 | €45

5e | 17, rue St-Jacques (Maubert-Mutualité/St-Michel) | 01-43-54-71-77

The "queues are warranted" outside this "dumpy storefront" Chinese in the Latin Quarter complete with ducks dangling in the front window – despite the "simple" decor, it dishes up "excellent", "authentic" Cantonese fare, including "lacquered pork like you won't find elsewhere", noodle soups and dumplings; service isn't always up to snuff, but it's ideal "if you just care about [good] food" at good prices.

Miroir Ⓢ Ⓜ *Bistro* — ▽ 21 | 18 | 22 | €42

18e | 94, rue des Martyrs (Abbesses) | 01-46-06-50-73

At this "hip" bistro in Montmartre's Abbesses quarter, a "Ducasse grad" delights with "inventive interpretations of bistro classics", with bonus points for a "tailor-made wine experience" and "overall great prices for the quality"; the "clean-lined, comfortable room with flattering lighting" and mirrors (*mais oui*) gets a thumbs-up too, but be sure to make a reservation since "everyone's talking about it"; P.S. if it's too crowded, check out their wine bar opposite in a former butcher shop.

Moissonnier Ⓢ Ⓜ *Lyon* — ▽ 24 | 19 | 21 | €54

5e | 28, rue des Fossés St-Bernard (Cardinal Lemoine/Jussieu) | 01-43-29-87-65

Not many surveyors know this "bona fide bistro" in the Latin Quarter, but those who do call it a "don't-miss" for "fantastic", "homestyle Lyonnais" cooking "served without frills or fanfare by people who care about food"; further appeals include moderate prices for "gargantuan" portions, "cordial" service and "simple", old-fashioned decor.

Montagnards (Les) Ⓢ *Alpine* — ▽ 23 | 20 | 21 | €24

1er | 58, rue Jean-Jacques Rousseau (Les Halles) | 01-40-26-68-75 | www.lesmontagnardsparis.fr

Though set in a former Les Halles butcher shop, this family-run place has a "mountain"-style look that evokes a "Savoyard chalet", and the kitchen follows suit, turning out "tasty" Alpine eats like fondue and raclette; with a "charming" staff and can't-go-wrong prices, it's popular with plenty of young, citybound snowbirds.

Montalembert (Le) *New French* 19 | 21 | 21 | €76

7e | Hôtel Montalembert | 3, rue de Montalembert (Rue du Bac) | 01-45-49-68-03 | www.montalembert.com

With "plush" *Mad Men*-esque decor by Christian Liaigre, this "sexy" Saint-Germain New French "almost makes you forget you're in a hotel restaurant", so it's popular with Left Bank editors and art dealers as well as international business travelers who can swing the "pricey" tabs; expect "light, refined" dishes discreetly delivered by a professional staff.

Mon Vieil Ami M *Bistro* 23 | 19 | 21 | €60

4e | 69, rue St-Louis-en-l'Ile (Pont-Marie) | 01-40-46-01-35 | www.mon-vieil-ami.com

"Modern Alsatian" fare highlighting "marvelous fresh vegetables" (there's a vegetarian menu too) distinguishes chef-owner Antoine Westermann's bistro "ideally located" on the Ile Saint-Louis, making for a "happy" cliéntele (including "many American tourists"); doubters deem the "minimalist" space "crammed" and service "rushed", but most 'old friends' "love the vibe"; P.S. closed Monday and Tuesday.

Mori Venice Bar *Italian* 21 | 20 | 20 | €86

2e | 2, rue du Quatre Septembre (Bourse) | 01-44-55-51-55 | www.mori-venicebar.com

Just across the street from the Bourse (the old stock exchange), this "stylish" Italian lures in "lots of local bankers" with its "inventive", Venetian-influenced cuisine and glitzy, "modern" surroundings via Philippe Starck; if non-financiers feel the fees are "too expensive for simple pasta", at least the gondoliers are "friendly" when pocketing your money.

Moulin à Vent (Au) S M *Bistro* 20 | 16 | 20 | €59

5e | 20, rue des Fossés St-Bernard (Cardinal Lemoine/Jussieu) | 01-43-54-99-37 | www.au-moulinavent.com

"Huge portions" of "great meat" (including "excellent Châteaubriand") deftly served amid "extremely tight" tables in a lively, old-school bistro setting explain the enduring popularity of this "busy" carnivore's crib with a Beaujolais-centric wine list in the Latin Quarter; indeed, "it's just what you want to find in Paris", even if it's not cheap anymore.

Moulin de la Galette (Le) M *Classic French* 20 | 23 | 19 | €54

18e | 83, rue Lepic (Abbesses/Lamarck-Caulaincourt) | 01-46-06-84-77 | www.moulindelagalette.fr

Ok, it's a bit "touristy", but chef Antoine Heerah is also pulling Parisians with his "refined" Classic French dishes (reflected by a jump in the Food score) at this "awesome" former Montmartre dance hall, made famous in Renoir's paintings; enhancing the "exceptional" setting are "amiable" service and a "garden terrace in summer."

	FOOD	DECOR	SERVICE	COST

Mousson (La) ☒ *Cambodian* | - | - | - | M

1er | 9, rue Thérèse (Pyramides) | 01-42-60-59-46 | www.lamousson.fr
"Cheerful" servers usher guests through "splendid" Cambodian meals at this "little corner of Asia" not far from the Louvre and the Palais-Royal; quarters are "tiny" and a bit on the "kitschy" side, but strong "value for the money" seals the deal.

Moustache ☒ M *Bistro* | ▽ 19 | 16 | 18 | €54

6e | 33, rue Ste-Beuve (Vavin) | 01-42-22-56-65 | www.moustache-restaurant.com
Left Bank bobos get into a New York state of mind in the loftlike setting (wood plank floors, exposed-brick walls) of this "neighborhood gem" in the 6th with an "inventive" menu that offers bistro standards spiked "with an Asian twist"; "friendly" service and middling prices make it worth a "return" visit in most people's books.

Murat (Le) ◐ *Brasserie* | 17 | 18 | 17 | €60

16e | 1, bd Murat (Porte d'Auteuil) | 01-46-51-33-17
"You pay for the trendiness" at this Costes brasserie near the Porte d'Auteuil, but the "light" fare is generally "well executed"; the "well-heeled locals" who frequent it may pooh-pooh the "pretty" but sometimes "indifferent" staff, but they still "come back because it's reliable" and the Napoleon-meets-log-cabin-look is "cozy."

Muscade M *Eclectic/Tearoom* | - | - | - | M

1er | 36, rue Montpensier (Palais Royal-Musée du Louvre/Pyramides) | 01-42-97-51-36 | www.muscade-palais-royal.com
Even if the Eclectic fare "isn't always as tasty as expected", this "lovely" tearoom with a covered terrace in the Palais-Royal gardens provide "amazing people-watching" to enhance menu offerings that includes some "delicious salads" and pastries; it's also not the most expensive option around, so you'll have to book way ahead to secure a spot on the terrace, which is open March-October.

Nanashi *Eclectic* | - | - | - | I

NEW **3e** | 57, rue Charlot (Filles du Calvaire) | (33-1) 44-61-45-49
10e | 31, rue du Paradis (Poissonnière) | 01-40-22-05-55
Bento boxes go bobo at this pair of cool, airy canteens in the 10th and 3rd, where Rose Bakery alum Kaori Endo's colorful, Japanese-influenced Eclectic fare appeals to vegetarians and creative types (and their kids on the weekends, especially the sweets); easy-to-swallow prices don't dim the healthy glow.

Nemrod (Le) ◐ *Brasserie* | 17 | 15 | 16 | €35

6e | 51, rue du Cherche-Midi (Sèvres-Babylone/St-Placide) | 01-45-48-17-05 | www.lenemrod.com
This "great standby" near the Bon Marché bags shoppers all day long for "excellent croque monsieurs", "superb salads" and other "light" fare in typical brasserie surroundings (there's also a large, "sunny" terrace); "don't expect to get in and out" easily since it's always "mobbed", but the price is right, and fans contend the "waiters are nicer here than elsewhere" in the 6th.

	FOOD	DECOR	SERVICE	COST

NEW Neva ☒ *New French* | - | - | - | M |

8e | 2, rue de Berne (Europe/St-Lazare) | 01-45-22-18-91

Occupying an old corner cafe with gorgeous 1930s chandeliers behind the Gare Saint-Lazare, this "nifty" newcomer gets a "wow" from the few who've found it, winning praise for its "inventive" New French dishes and "delicious desserts"; boasting a "youthful" atmosphere to boot, it's earning praise as "one of the best values in Paris."

Nos Ancêtres les Gaulois ◐ *Classic French* | 13 | 19 | 14 | €43 |

4e | 39, rue St-Louis-en-l'Ile (Pont-Marie) | 01-46-33-66-07 | www.nosancetreslesgaulois.com

Surveyors wrestle over the merits of this sprawling, "boisterous" Ancient Gaul–themed Classic French "feast" on the Ile Saint-Louis sporting a "folkloric" decorative motif that pits Roman helmets and stone walls against taxidermy and animal pelts; to be sure, the "touristy" trappings won't win over foodies, but it's a "total hoot" that's particularly suited to "students and groups" thanks to the civilized cost and "free-flowing" wine that makes the "bland", "far-from gourmet" grub "palatable."

Nouveau Village Tao-Tao ◐ *Chinese/Thai* | 19 | 14 | 16 | €29 |

13e | 159, bd Vincent Auriol (Nationale) | 01-45-86-40-08

A "loyal clientele" appreciates the "diverse" Chinese and Thai offerings at this sizable, "value"-priced survivor in the 13th; the "traditional" decor (fish tank, Chinoiserie, carpeting) is perhaps a bit "tired", but at least the service is "fast."

Office (L') ☒ *New French* | - | - | - | M |

9e | 3, rue Richer (Bonne Nouvelle/Cadet) | 01-47-70-67-31

The recent arrival of new chef Kevin O'Donnell (ex NYC's Del Posto) has made this small, loftlike bistro in the 9th a hot address; his Italian-influenced New French cooking, on a prix fixe menu that changes weekly, is "original", the prices are accessible and the staff is "warm" and engaged, so hit it *tout de suite* before it's hard to book.

Ogre (L') ☒ *Bistro* | - | - | - | M |

16e | 1, av de Versailles (Av du Pdt Kennedy RER/Mirabeau) | 01-45-27-93-40

Kitted out in urban-chic style (industrial lighting, exposed pipes), this bobo bistro in the 16th on the banks of the Seine (affording a view of the Eiffel Tower from a couple of tables) is a carnivores' crib serving "remarkable" beef, such as "hand-chopped steak tartare" and other deftly "revisited" Parisian favorites; its "cool" young owners have assembled a "terrific" wine list too, all while keeping the prices down-to-earth.

Ombres (Les) *New French* | 21 | 25 | 19 | €80 |

7e | Musée du Quai Branly | 27, quai Branly, Portail Debilly (Alma Marceau) | 01-47-53-68-00 | www.lesombres-restaurant.com

A "magical", all-glass design by architect Jean Nouvel gives diners the "incredible sensation of being outdoors" (actual outdoor seating

is available on the terrace) at this "chic" New Fr
du Quai Branly boasting an "unbelievable", "ey
Eiffel Tower; many find the "modern" French fa
vice "attentive" if rather "average" compare
most feel it's worth a "high" sum for the "roma

NEW Opéra Restaurant (L') [S] [M] *New French*

9e | Palais Garnier | Place Jacques Rouché (Opéra) | 01-42-68-86-80 | www.opera-restaurant.fr

Flaunting a "futuristic" red-and-white design by architect Odile Decq that juxtaposes "classical and modern" lines, this spacious New French arrival strikes a "unique" profile inside the venerable Palais Garnier; chef Christophe Aribert's menu is "creative", and though some find prices a tad "excessive", it's a "convenient" stop for operagoers, especially those who love to "see and be seen."

Opportun (L') ◐ [S] *Lyon* ∇ 22 | 16 | 19 | €52

14e | 64, bd Edgar Quinet (Edgar Quinet) | 01-43-20-26-89 | www.lopportun.com

Carnivores vaunt *la viande* (meat) at this Montparnasse bistro that rounds out its "quality" steaks with "traditional" dishes from Lyon (aka "the gastronomic capital of France"); the faux-vintage look doesn't please all comers and the bill is "not cheap", but most savor the opportun-ity to enjoy the "hearty" "*cuisine de terroir*" and "warm welcome" from the "always smiling" owner.

Orient-Extrême [S] *Japanese* 23 | 19 | 20 | €55

6e | 4, rue Bernard Palissy (St-Germain-des-Prés) | 01-45-48-92-27

"Honest" sushi crafted by an "excellent" chef stands out at this stylish, low-lit Japanese haunt in Saint-Germain, catering to an "attractive" clientele; while service falls a tad short of the food, the occasional celeb sighting helps distract.

Ostéria (L') [S] *Italian* 24 | 17 | 20 | €43

4e | 10, rue de Sévigné (St-Paul) | 01-42-71-37-08

Regulars at this "tiny" terra-cotta-toned Italian "gem" in the Marais note a few changes since a new owner arrived, the most obvious being the presence of a sign out front, so a "great secret" has been "given away"; still, with "perfect" risotto and gnocchi to "dream about", along with "cordial" service and fairly reasonable prices, it draws a "cool crowd" nonetheless.

Oth Sombath [S] *Asian* 23 | 20 | 23 | €71

8e | 184, rue du Faubourg St-Honoré (St-Philippe-du-Roule) | 01-42-56-55-55 | www.othsombath.com

Celebrity chef Oth Sombath's "innovative", Thai-oriented Asian fusion eatery in the 8th is "a long way from the streets of Bangkok", but the "refined" fare fits in with the "modern" surroundings, a streamlined study in red, white and gold leaf; reviewers report "top-quality" service too, though you do "pay for" it all.

	FOOD	DECOR	SERVICE	COST

Oto ☒ *Japanese* | - | - | - | M |

, 6, rue du Sabot (Mabillon/St-Germain-des-Prés) | 01-42-22-21-56 | www.otooto-paris.com

"Connoisseurs" of fine Japanese fare adore this Saint-Germain spot whose "genius" chef earns acclaim with his deft little rolls, as well as tasty udon, tempura and other cooked dishes; a snug set of rooms with 18th-century beamed ceilings is tended by a "friendly" staff, and there are are reasonable prix fixe deals for lunch and dinner.

Oulette (L') ☒ *New French/Southwest* | 26 | 17 | 24 | €62 |

12e | 15, pl Lachambeaudie (Cour St-Emilion/Dugommier) | 01-40-02-02-12 | www.l-oulette.com

It's "a little isolated" in the 12th, but "terrific", "cutting-edge" food by chef-owner Marcel Baudis, backed by "caring" service, makes this Southwestern-influenced New French "worth the trip" to Bercy (and it's "not prohibitively expensive", either); the upscale environs (blond-wood paneling, white-linen tablecoths) make it "ideal for business meals", and it pulls in plenty of arty locals too; P.S. closed weekends.

Oum el Banine *Moroccan* | ▽ 22 | 19 | 21 | €54 |

16e | 16 bis, rue Dufrenoy (Porte Dauphine/Rue de la Pompe) | 01-45-04-91-22 | www.oumelbanine.com

An oasis of sorts in the 16th, this Moroccan tantalizes with "lovely tajines", couscous and other "tasty" North African dishes, all doled out in generous portions; the Fez-inspired surroundings are "warmed" by an engaging staff, so while it's not cheap, most are happy here; P.S. be sure to book in advance.

Ourcine (L') ☒ M *Classic/New French* | 25 | 16 | 22 | €48 |

13e | 92, rue Broca (Glacière/Les Gobelins) | 01-47-07-13-65

This "unpretentious" "neighborhood" "wonder" may be "a bit out of the way" in the 13th, but fans of chef-owner Sylvain Danière's "constantly changing" menus of "innovative" contemporary and classic cuisine boldly proclaim "comparable meals in the 8th" might "cost triple and not satisfy you" nearly half as much as the "great deals" here; besides, the servers in the small, rustic dining room are "as sweet as the chocolate quenelles."

Palanquin (Le) ☒ *Vietnamese* | ▽ 24 | 14 | 21 | €46 |

6e | 12, rue Princesse (Mabillon/St-Germain-des-Prés) | 01-43-29-77-66

The Vietnamese "home cooking" – including *banh cuon* (steamed ravioli) that zealots declare "one of the world's supreme dishes" – is "still excellent after all these years" at this Saint-Germain survivor in a setting distinguished by old stone walls and rough-hewn beams; it draws a mix of French locals and English-speaking visitors, all of whom appreciate the "friendly service" and everyday tabs.

NEW Pantruche (Le) ☒ *Bistro* | ▽ 24 | 17 | 22 | €49 |

9e | 3, rue Victor-Massé (Pigalle/St-Georges) | 01-48-78-55-60 | www.lepantruche.com

A new arrival in "a charming area" below Sacré Coeur, this "delightful" contemporary French bistro has been "embraced" by "young"

	FOOD	DECOR	SERVICE	COST

"locals" who dig its "astounding" eats from a "talented" chef (ex Le Bristol); the former storefront cafe space has been given a retro, glam makeover that's perhaps outshone by the pleasant, "handsome guys" who own it - all in all, it's "a terrific buy for the money."

Papilles (Les) Ⓢ Ⓜ *Classic French* — 25 | 20 | 24 | €47

5e | 30, rue Gay-Lussac (Luxembourg) | 01-43-25-20-79 | www.lespapillesparis.fr

Booking is "mandatory" at this "funky" Latin Quarter wine store/bistro that's one of the most popular spots on the Left Bank thanks to its "excellent" market-driven French classics, "amiable" owner and "courteous" staff; diners choose a bottle from the "amazing" open-shelf selection, and everyone eats the same "good-value" prix fixe menu.

Parc aux Cerfs (Le) *Bistro* — 20 | 17 | 19 | €45

6e | 50, rue Vavin (Notre-Dame-des-Champs/Vavin) | 01-43-54-87-83

Like "an old pair of loafers", this "neighborhood" fixture in Montparnasse provides "comfort" in the form of dependable "traditional" bistro eats and "obliging service" in a "quaint", slightly down-at-the-heels '30s-style setting; prices are reasonable for the area, and it's "romantic" to boot, especially on the little terrace in back.

NEW Passage (Au) Ⓢ *Wine Bar/Bistro* — - | - | - | M

11e | 1 bis, passage St-Sébastien (St-Sébastien-Froissart) | 01-43-55-07-52

Stellar ingredients and natural wines are the stars, but the cost stays terrestrial at this new *bistrot à vins,* where you can graze on small plates - classic charcuterie, trendy burrata - or go big with items like an XL-sized lamb shoulder; located down a passage (*bien sûr*) in the 11th, the mismatched space really comes together once filled by cool eastern Parisians - and it does fill up, so consider booking.

Z Passage 53 Ⓢ Ⓜ *Haute Cuisine* — 27 | 19 | 24 | €108

2e | 53, passage des Panoramas (Bourse/Grands Boulevards) | 01-42-33-04-35

"A wonderful find", this Haute "gem" "hidden" in a 19th-century covered arcade in the 2nd is a "gastronomic revelation" thanks to chef Shinichi Sato's "hyper-inventive" Japanese-accented creations, served by an "attentive" staff in a "tiny" loungelike space with a "luxuriously" "spare" look; expect to "leave with a large hole in your pocket, but a smile on your face"; P.S. "climb the ancient circular staircase for a peek at the chefs laboring above" (just take care if you've been sampling the "nice wine list").

Passiflore Ⓢ Ⓜ *Asian/Classic French* — 23 | 20 | 21 | €74

16e | 33, rue de Longchamp (Boissière/Trocadéro) | 01-47-04-96-81 | www.restaurantpassiflore.com

At Roland Durand's "delightful" place near the Trocadéro, you get "all you want in a fine restaurant": "attentive" service, a deep wine list and "refined", "serious food" that's "imaginatively spiced" (the chef loves to wake up Classic French dishes with Asian ingredients); the violet-and-gold-accented interior glimmers with a sort of "serene" glitz, leaving most happy here despite the hefty tabs.

	FOOD	DECOR	SERVICE	COST
Paul Chêne	23	19	23	€84
Pavillon du Lac (Le)	19	24	20	€58
Pavillon Ledoyen	25	26	24	€181
Pavillon Montsouris	22	25	22	€74
Père Claude (Le)	21	15	18	€60

Paul Chêne ☒ *Classic French*

16^e^ | 123, rue Lauriston (Trocadéro) | 01-47-27-63-17 | www.paulchene.com

A "warm" atmosphere pervades this "simple", "old-fashioned" dining room "off the beaten path" in the 16th, "*un vrai classique*" with a menu that transports diners "back to a time when sauces were a work of art", and "fat content never an issue"; it's "very pricey", but "you should visit at least once", especially to sample its "to-die-for" selection of "cognacs and Armagnacs."

Pavillon du Lac (Le) *Classic/New French*

19^e^ | Parc des Buttes-Chaumont | Entrée pl Armand Carrel (Laumiere) | 01-42-00-07-21 | www.lepavillondulac.fr

This somewhat secret spot in the 19th's Parc des Buttes-Chaumont is an alfresco address par excellence thanks to its "pleasant terrace" and sylvan setting; the Classic and New French dishes exhibit "quality" but are a bit expensive and the staff can get "overwhelmed" when it's busy, but fans find it worth it for a breath of fresh air in the city, especially on summer evenings when there's live music or DJs.

Pavillon Ledoyen ☒ *Haute Cuisine*

8^e^ | Parc Montsouris | 1, av Dutuit (Champs-Elysées-Clemenceau/Concorde) | 01-53-05-10-01

"Remarkably situated" in a "historic" Napoleon III pavilion in the gardens at the lower end of the Champs-Elysées, this standout wows with chef Christian Le Squer's "exceptional" Haute Cuisine enhanced by "beautiful views" of the foliage just outside the Jacques Grange-designed dining room (and "what a room!"); a "formal" staff that "doesn't miss a thing" adds to the "unforgettable" "old-world" experience - just "bring your bond portfolio" for this "ultimate splurge"; P.S. reservations required; jackets suggested; closed weekends.

Pavillon Montsouris *Classic French*

14^e^ | 20, rue Gazan (Porte d'Orléans) | 01-43-13-29-00 | www.pavillon-montsouris.fr

"The setting is magical" - a glass-roofed dining room with a terrace overlooking the greenery in the "magnificent" Parc Montsouris - and most diners appreciate this Classic French kitchen's "precise flavors and cooking" too; the "attentive" staff helps make it work equally well whether it's a "romantic meal for two or a family" dinner, so even though "you'll pay a pretty penny", it's "worth it."

Père Claude (Le) *Classic French*

15^e^ | 51, av de La Motte-Picquet (La Motte-Picquet-Grenelle) | 01-47-34-03-05 | www.lepereclaude.com

Head for this mostly "tourist-free" "meat-lover's paradise" in the 15th - a beau monde address that's "a favorite of [former French president] Jacques Chirac" - for "good traditional French cooking", including grilled and rotisseried *viandes* worth vaunting, plus "fantastic frogs' legs"; it's pricey, and the look hasn't changed much since the '60s, but "it's a sure bet" with "well-done service."

	FOOD	DECOR	SERVICE	COST

Pères et Filles *Bistro* 17 | 16 | 17 | €39

6e | 81, rue de Seine (Mabillon/Odéon) | 01-43-25-00-28
It's located in the heart of Saint-Germain, so it's no surprise that this "trendy" "little bistro" with a "convivial" atmosphere attracts a mix of tourists looking to let their hair down and locals looking to "meet up with friends"; consequently, the classic, old-school digs can get "sooo noisy", but at least the classic, old-school fare is "generously served", especially for such moderate prices; P.S. book ahead, especially for the terrace.

Perraudin *Bistro* 18 | 19 | 19 | €34

5e | 157, rue St-Jacques (Cluny La Sorbonne/Luxembourg) | 01-46-33-15-75 | www.restaurant-perraudin.com
The "old-fashioned" decor (think checked tablecloths) at this "charming" Left Bank bistro is almost as much of a crowd-pleaser as the "unpretentious" traditional French cooking; a "relaxing atmosphere" and "friendly waiters" are additional draws, but it's the easy-on-the-wallet prices that seal the deal for students from the nearby Sorbonne.

Perron (Le) *Italian* - | - | - | M

7e | 6, rue Perronet (Rue du Bac/St-Germain-des-Prés) | 01-45-44-71-51 | www.restaurantleperron.fr
"Since a lot of Italians go here, you can be sure it's a good address" if you're after pasta or risotto on the Left Bank; it's also popular with editors, antique and art dealers and a few famous faces, all of whom like the midrange tabs and "warm atmosphere" created by exposed beams and stone walls.

Petit Châtelet (Le) *Classic French* ▽ 22 | 22 | 24 | €35

5e | 39, rue de la Bûcherie (St-Michel) | 01-46-33-53-40
With a "highly touristy" location just across the Seine from Notre Dame, this little old house with a pitched roof pleases with its "spectacular views" of the cathedral as well as its "delicious", "reasonably" priced French classics; naturally, it can get "a little tight on the terrace", but the "attentive, friendly staff" keeps everything running smoothly.

NEW Petit Cheval de Manège (Le) *Bistro* - | - | - | I

11e | 5, rue Froment (Bréguet-Sabin) | 09-82-37-18-52
The menu is limited but so are the prices at this new bistro turning out thoughtful, market-based comestibles in the 11th; a kaleidoscopic tiled floor and carmine walls complete the package, making it another *belle adresse* in this bistro-blessed 'hood.

Petite Chaise (A la) *Classic French* 18 | 18 | 20 | €44

7e | 36, rue de Grenelle (Rue du Bac) | 01-42-22-13-35 | www.alapetitechaise.fr
"Charming and perfectly located" in the 7th just off the Boulevard Raspail, this historic spot (it claims to be the oldest restaurant in Paris, dating to the 1600s) is "quaint" and "cute" enough to appeal

to the "many Americans" who dine here; most are happy enough with the "honestly prepared" Classic French fare, especially given the "kind and efficient" service and easygoing prices.

Petite Cour (La) *New French* 20 | 22 | 21 | €71

6e | 8, rue Mabillon (Mabillon/St-Germain-des-Prés) | 01-43-26-52-26 | www.lapetitecour.fr

Though the sunken garden terrace – "an island of greenery and tranquility" – makes this "inventive" New French near the Saint-Sulpice church especially popular in summer, its fans aren't fair-weather friends, since they also find the interior "romantic" and "charming"; prices are not petite, but folks are big on the "attentive but relaxed service."

Petite Sirène de Copenhague (La) [S] [M] *Danish* ▽ 25 | 18 | 24 | €60

9e | 47, rue Notre-Dame-de-Lorette (St-Georges) | 01-45-26-66-66

The "wonderful" Danish chef-owner really "cares about his diners", ensuring that they're always provided with "excellent" service and "fabulous" food at his "intimate", little white-walled Nordic seafood spot in the 9th; tabs are slightly "expensive", but it's "perfect" for a "romantic dinner", all of which makes it more of a 'great Dane' than a 'little mermaid.'

Petites Sorcières de Ghislaine Arabian (Les) [S] [M] *Northern French* 25 | 16 | 19 | €55

14e | 12, rue Liancourt (Denfert-Rochereau) | 01-43-21-95-68

Riding a new wave of popularity thanks to chef-owner Ghislaine Arabian's appearances on TV's *Top Chef,* this "packed" and "noisy" bistro in the 14th lives up to the hype with a menu that features "always inspired" Northern French and Belgian dishes; the basic, white-walled space is nothing fancy, but the staff treats diners "with grace and kindness" and the prices are right, so most dub it "a real treat."

Petit Lutetia (Le) *Brasserie* 17 | 19 | 18 | €46

6e | 107, rue de Sèvres (Notre-Dame-des-Champs/Vaneau) | 01-45-48-33-53 | www.lepetitlutetia.com

Adjacent to the Hotel Lutetia on the Left Bank, this "upscale" neighborhood brasserie charms with its "smiling service" and "lovely", "authentic" belle epoque decor; besides the shellfish trays from the stand out front, the "simple" fare is "just like at mom's", although the prices are slightly higher.

Petit Marché (Le) ◐ *New French* 23 | 18 | 21 | €37

3e | 9, rue de Béarn (Chemin-Vert) | 01-42-72-06-67

This "chic neighborhood spot in the Marais" stands out for its "excellent" Asian-accented contemporary French cuisine (it also serves some bistro standards) and its "hip" but "no attitude" staff, which lends it a "warm corner-cafe atmosphere"; it's "a great buy", so "reservations are recommended" for a berth in the "tight", "noisy", stone-walled and wood-beamed digs.

	FOOD	DECOR	SERVICE	COST

Petit Marguery (Au) *Bistro* 23 | 19 | 21 | €55

13e | 9, bd de Port-Royal (Les Gobelins) | 01-43-31-58-59 | www.petitmarguery.com

This "real Parisian" bistro "like they don't make anymore" is "a must" for "fine bourgeois" fare (particularly "game" and other "rib-sticking meats") and also wins kudos for its "sincere" service and "retro" digs; it's "not cheap, but worth the experience", which is why it's always "brimming with locals and tourists alike" despite its location in the 13th.

Petit Marius (Le) ◐ *Seafood* 20 | 16 | 18 | €59
(fka Le Bistrot de Marius)

8e | 6, av George V (Alma Marceau) | 01-40-70-11-76 | www.lepetitmarius.com

Under a bright-orange awning just off the Champs-Elysées in the 8th, this small-fry annex to big fish Marius et Janette next door strikes fans as a comparatively "great buy" for "really fresh" fish served with aplomb (though given the fact that it's hardly cheap, some say "go next door and pay the extra price for better food"); a "relaxed" atmosphere flows on the pleasant terrace and in the "unpretentious" interior, dressed simply with wooden floors and paneling, fish sculptures and a large ovoid mirror.

Petit Niçois (Le) *Provence* ▽ 20 | 18 | 19 | €46

7e | 10, rue Amélie (La Tour-Maubourg) | 01-45-51-83-65 | www.lepetitnicois.com

The signature bouillabaisse "is a meal for two" at this contemporary-looking touch of Nice in the 7th; "friendly" service and prices that are reasonable for the area are appreciated by those looking to spend a night in Provence without leaving Paris.

Petit Pergolèse (Le) ⊠ *Bistro* 25 | 19 | 21 | €63

16e | 38, rue Pergolèse (Argentine/Porte Maillot) | 01-45-00-23-66

"You'll feel at home" at "friendly" owner Albert Corre's "gem" in the Porte Maillot section of the 16th, where a "warm welcome" is followed by an "excellent" (albeit "expensive") mix of bistro favorites and contemporary dishes served in "trendy", pop-art digs; insiders call it a place "to divulge only to your closest friends", or else tables will be even harder to book; P.S. closed weekends.

Petit Pontoise (Le) *Bistro* 25 | 18 | 23 | €50

5e | 9, rue de Pontoise (Maubert-Mutualité) | 01-43-29-25-20

"Everything one dreams about" in a "Parisian bistro" is reality at this "warm" and "welcoming" Latin Quarter "neighborhood" place serving "spectacular" French "comfort food"; relatively "reasonable" rates mean it's beloved by locals, tourists and students from the nearby Sorbonne, ergo "reservations are a must."

Petit Rétro (Le) ⊠ *Bistro* ▽ 18 | 20 | 20 | €51

16e | 5, rue Mesnil (Victor Hugo) | 01-44-05-06-05 | www.petitretro.fr

Oui, this bistro in the 16th is both small and retro, with an "authentic turn-of-the-century" feel enhanced by floral belle epoque tiles and an "antique copper coffeemaker"; while most love the "charming" decor, opinions on the traditional French fare are more nuanced, with some saying quite "decent" and others "mediocre", but "unobtrusive" service and digestible tabs in a pricey part of town help tilt the balance in its favor; P.S. closed weekends.

Petit Riche (Au) ◐ *Bistro* 22 | 21 | 21 | €55

9e | 25, rue le Peletier (Le Peletier/Richelieu-Drouot) | 01-47-70-68-68 | www.restaurant-aupetitriche.com

"Bravo" say theatergoers and other "regulars" charmed by the 19th-century decor (brass, banquettes, mirrors) at this "authentic-looking bistro" not far from Opéra Garnier and the Drouot auction house – and the "well-prepared French classics" get another round of applause; "speedy service" and moderate prices also make it "suitable for a quick business lunch."

Petit St. Benoît (Le) ≠ *Classic French* 16 | 17 | 18 | €31

6e | 4, rue St-Benoît (St-Germain-des-Prés) | 01-42-60-27-92 | www.petit-st-benoit.fr

"Seemingly unchanged from the dawn of time" (i.e. 1901), this "classic"-looking bistro provides "basic chow" that "won't bust the budget" in the heart of "expensive" Saint-Germain; "incredibly close quarters" and "utilitarian" service don't disappoint fans who "don't expect anything fancy" here – like, say, a credit card machine.

Petit Victor Hugo (Le) ◐ *Classic French* 19 | 19 | 18 | €46

16e | 143, av Victor Hugo (Rue de la Pompe/Victor Hugo) | 01-45-53-02-68 | www.petitvictorhugo.com

"With a wonderful atmosphere for a rainy day (or a sunny day)" – on account of the fireplace and tree-covered terrace, respectively – this big "neighborhood" "meeting place" in the "bustling" 16th offers a "diverse" menu of French classics in a "'70s-vintage", "borderline-kitsch" setting; a "friendly" staff and "reasonable" rates complete the groovy picture.

Petit Zinc (Le) ◐ *Bistro* 19 | 20 | 18 | €54

6e | 11, rue St-Benoît (St-Germain-des-Prés) | 01-42-86-61-00 | www.petitzinc.com

"Touristy, yes", but this "classic" bistro in Saint-Germain (owned by the Flo group) is a "friendly" go-to "standby" serving a "solid", mid-priced menu whose standout is the "fabulous seafood platter"; also "notable" is the "glorious", colorful art nouveau decor (just try to find a straight line in the place).

Petrelle ⊠ M *New French* ▽ 25 | 23 | 20 | €83

9e | 34, rue Pétrelle (Anvers) | 01-42-82-11-02 | www.petrelle.fr

The "gorgeous, romantic setting" – a "cozy" storefront "off the beaten path" in the 9th "smartly" decorated with plants, flowers and curios – combined with "scrumptious" New French fare, discreetly served, make this enclave popular with visiting celebs and the local beau monde; ok, it's "expensive" and there are "not many menu choices", but "don't worry: they're all good."

	FOOD	DECOR	SERVICE	COST

Pétrus ◐ *Brasserie* | 23 | 21 | 22 | €101 |

17ᵉ | 12, pl du Maréchal Juin (Pereire) | 01-43-80-15-95
"Very French" and "high end", this "classy" brasserie in the 17th flatters the mix of celebrities and corporate high rollers that can afford it with "pleasantly" plush, softly lit environs as a backdrop for "excellent" "traditional" eats that run to "great seafood" and upmarket comfort food; the staff is "attentive", and bonus: it's open on Sundays.

Pharamond ⊠ Ⓜ *Classic French* | 18 | 20 | 17 | €59 |

1ᵉʳ | 24, rue de la Grande Truanderie (Etienne Marcel/Les Halles) | 01-40-28-45-18
"Inspiring" belle epoque decor featuring beautiful tiled walls is the highlight of this long-running (since 1832) Classic French standby in Les Halles, best known for its "excellent tripe" *à la mode de Caen* and other Norman dishes (great "if you love cream"); although prices are anything but old-fashioned, it's "always a pleasure" to put yourself in the hands of the "gracious" staff at this "old-style classic."

Philou ⊠ *Bistro* | ▽ 21 | 16 | 19 | €43 |

10ᵉ | 12, av Richerand (Goncourt) | 01-42-38-00-13
A "young and lively" crowd "fires up" their "smartphones" to track down this "out-of-the-way" "hot spot" near the Canal Saint-Martin in the 10th, offering bistro eats of "quality" and "creativity" from a chalkboard menu; the storefront space is "warm" and contemporary, service is solid and it's a "good buy" too; P.S. closed weekends.

Pichet de Paris (Le) ⊠ *Seafood* | ▽ 22 | 16 | 20 | €82 |

8ᵉ | 68, rue Pierre Charron (Franklin D. Roosevelt) | 01-43-59-50-34
Once a favorite of late French president François Mitterrand, this "gem of a place" near the Champs in the 8th offers "quality" seafood and professional service in a "neighborhood brasserie atmosphere"; so even if it's "not as frequented by the jet set" as it once was, it's still worth going if you "have the means" to afford it.

Z Pied de Cochon (Au) ◐ *Brasserie* | 19 | 20 | 18 | €54 |

1ᵉʳ | 6, rue Coquillière (Châtelet-Les Halles) | 01-40-13-77-00 | www.pieddecochon.com
"Bring on the pig's feet!" (and other "body parts") cry "daring diners" who tuck their "napkins in their collars" and "pig out" on pork plus "elaborate seafood platters" and the "best onion soup in Paris" – "preferably washed down with a bottle of Beaujolais" – at this "big, loud", "old-school" Les Halles brasserie owned by the Frères Blanc group; despite "tourists", it retains a "very Parisian atmosphere", with a "speedy" staff, moderate tabs and 24/7 hours as pluses.

Pierre au Palais Royal ⊠ *Classic French* | 22 | 19 | 19 | €69 |

1ᵉʳ | 10, rue Richelieu (Palais Royal-Musée du Louvre) | 01-42-96-09-17 | www.pierreaupalaisroyal.fr
Boasting a "fantastic location" right next to the Palais-Royal in the heart of Paris, this good "business-meal" table also pulls stylish, deep-pocketed locals with its "savory" Classic French cuisine, "amiable" service and comfy, contemporary setup.

	FOOD	DECOR	SERVICE	COST
Pierre Gagnaire	28	24	28	€208
Pinxo	23	22	23	€66
Pizza Chic	21	18	17	€37
Polidor	15	18	16	€35
Pomponette (A la)	▽ 23	21	17	€38

Z Pierre Gagnaire *Haute Cuisine*

8e | 6, rue Balzac (Charles de Gaulle-Etoile/George V) | 01-58-36-12-50 | www.pierre-gagnaire.com

"Pierre has no peer" assert admirers of the talented toque who's as "gracious" a host as he is a "genius" in the kitchen, whipping up "explosions of flavor" that make "each bite memorable" at his Haute Cuisine showcase in the 8th arrondissement, just off the Champs-Elysées; the staff is as "extraordinary" as the dishes it ferries to the "well-spaced" tables in the "romantic", "contemporary", earth-toned interior, so "sell the baby and dine here" for a truly "life-changing" experience.

Pinxo ☒ *New French*

1er | Renaissance Paris Vendôme | 9, rue d'Alger (Tuileries) | 01-40-20-72-00 | www.pinxo.fr

An "adventurous", "modern take on Southwestern French cuisine" served "tapas-style" (i.e. small plates) with "extremely interesting wines" sets apart this pricey New French hotel restaurant near the Tuileries owned by chef Alain Dutournier; the staff is "polished" yet a "casual vibe" prevails in the "stylish" minimalist dining room; P.S. "if you like to see chefs at work, sit at the counter."

Pizza Chic *Pizza*

6e | 13, rue de Mézières (St-Sulpice) | 01-45-48-30-38 | www.pizzachic.fr

Living up to its name – with "perfectly fired" pizzas and a chic "ultramodern" look – this Saint-Germain spot provides a "casual, relaxed" transalpine "break from the three- and four-course routine" typical of most Parisian restaurants; it may be "quite expensive" for pizza, but the "accommodating" service and take-out option are additional selling points.

Polidor ◐ *Bistro*

6e | 41, rue Monsieur-le-Prince (Luxembourg/Odéon) | 01-43-26-95-34 | www.polidor.com

"Imagine Paris of 100 years ago" and this "historic", "old-world" Left Bank bistro comes to mind, which may be why Woody Allen filmed a scene from *Midnight in Paris* here; the bill of fare is similarly "classic", if often "less than lovingly prepared", and delivered by a staff that ranges from "friendly" to "surly", but hindrances like its cash-only policy don't deter "aging Sorbonners" and "tourists" from packing the communal tables for the "cheap" eats.

Pomponette (A la) ◐ ☒ *Bistro*

18e | 42, rue Lepic (Abbesses/Blanche) | 01-46-06-08-36 | www.pomponnette-montmartre.com

It's "not slick or chic" but that's just fine with fans of this antique checked-tablecloth Montmartre bistro that's been run by the same family since 1909; "serious eaters and drinkers" deem it eminently "reliable" for "generously portioned", "succulent long-simmered French dishes" (e.g. "terrine de lapin") at "fair prices" served by a gruffly friendly staff.

FOOD	DECOR	SERVICE	COST

NEW Pottoka 🅂 *Bistro* | - | - | - | E |

7e | 4, rue de l'Exposition (Ecole Militaire) | 01-45-51-88-38
The Basque bent of this casual bistro newly arrived in the 7th (from the pair behind Les Fables de la Fontaine) packs a meaty punch; wooden tables are squeezed into a cool, green-and-gray-accented space that's about as slim as the lunch tabs (dinner requires a fatter wallet).

Poule au Pot (La) ◐ 🄼 *Bistro* | 22 | 18 | 21 | €50 |

1er | 9, rue Vauvilliers (Châtelet-Les Halles/Louvre-Rivoli) | 01-42-36-32-96 | www.lapouleaupot.fr
"Yes, it's a cliché, but clichés can be based on things that are true and good", like the "homey", old-fashioned fare ("enormous" poule au pot, "outstanding" confit de canard) served by the "motherly" staff in the "country-style" dining room of this "charming", "old" bistro in Les Halles; fair prices sweeten the deal, and night owls appreciate that it's open 7 PM–5 AM.

Z Pramil 🄼 *Bistro* | 28 | 19 | 26 | €47 |

3e | 9, rue du Vertbois (Arts et Metiers/Temple) | 01-42-72-03-60 | www.pramilrestaurant.fr
"Stylish, small" and "an excellent deal considering the quality", this New French bistro near the Place de la République in the 3rd wins raves for its "delicate and imaginative" cuisine and "relaxed, yet upscale atmosphere"; "definitely the best restaurant in the area", it also charms with its "wonderful" staff – in sum, "highly recommended."

Z Pré Catelan (Le) 🅂 *Haute Cuisine* | 26 | 27 | 26 | €155 |

16e | Bois de Boulogne | Route de Suresnes (Pont-de-Neuilly/Porte Maillot) | 01-44-14-41-14 | www.precatelanparis.com
It's "like eating in your own private palace" say fans of this "breathtaking" "beauty" smack in the middle of the Bois de Boulogne (an expensive cab ride from central Paris); chef Frédéric Anton's "creatively classic" Haute Cuisine is "superb", the environs are "elegant", "dressy and romantic" and service is "impeccable", but "extravagant" prices mean it's strictly "for a special occasion"; P.S. "too bad they no longer serve outside on the garden terrace"; reservations required.

Pré Verre (Le) 🅂 🄼 *New French* | 23 | 14 | 19 | €39 |

5e | 8, rue Thénard (Maubert-Mutualité) | 01-43-54-59-47 | www.lepreverre.com
"Wonderfully crafted spicy surprises" lend a "world beat" accent to this New French in the Latin Quarter that, "unfortunately, has been found by everyone"; it's always "noisy" and "crowded" in the "minimalist" ground-floor digs ("avoid the basement"), but the staff is "attentive" if "overworked" and it's "one of the best values in Paris."

Z Procope (Le) ◐ *Classic French* | 17 | 24 | 18 | €55 |

6e | 13, rue de l'Ancienne Comédie (Odéon) | 01-40-46-79-00 | www.procope.com
It's "like traveling back in time and dining with de Tocqueville", "Rousseau" and "Benjamin Franklin" at this gilded Saint-Germain

"tourist destination" where you come as much "to get your oldest-cafe-in-the-world ticket punched" as for the Classic French menu, which is "traditional" and somewhat "ordinary"; service has its ups and downs, but prices are fair and ultimately it's "really about sightseeing" ("Napoleon's hat, Voltaire's desk!").

Prunier ☒ *Seafood* 24 | 23 | 23 | €101

16e | 16, av Victor Hugo (Charles de Gaulle-Etoile) | 01-44-17-35-85

Café Prunier ☒ *Seafood*

8e | 15, pl de la Madeleine (Madeleine) | 01-47-42-98-91
www.prunier.com

As if the "amazing" *fruits de mer,* smoked salmon and caviar weren't enough, this chic and "expensive" ("*c'est le* 16*ème*" after all) "seafood extravaganza" near the Etoile also boasts "professional" service and a "gorgeous" art deco dining room (plus smaller private salons upstairs), with a big raw bar and gold mosaics picked out in black stone; there's also a more casual offspring in the 8th, splashed with a contemporary blue-and-gold-hued maritime look.

P'tit Troquet (Le) ☒ *Bistro* 22 | 19 | 23 | €43

7e | 28, rue de l'Exposition (Ecole Militaire) | 01-47-05-80-39

"Great eats" for relative "bargain" prices served by the "friendly" and "gracious" family who run it mean that this "quiet" bistro near the Eiffel Tower is quite popular, especially with visiting "Americans"; however, the "quaint" bric-a-brac-filled space is *très "petit"*, so it's "recommended to book" ahead.

Pur' *New French* 24 | 23 | 22 | €131

2e | Park Hyatt Paris-Vendôme | 5, rue de la Paix (Opéra) | 01-58-71-12-34 | www.paris-restaurant-pur.fr

A "beautiful" circular design (by Ed Tuttle, who's also put his stamp on several Aman resorts) gives this low-lit dining room at the Park Hyatt an "intimate", "romantic" feel, while the open kitchen provides a window on all the work that goes into the "amazing" New French cooking by chef Jean-François Rouquette; most find the service "cordial" but wish they'd "make an effort with the prices", which are sky high.

Quai (Le) Ⓜ *New French* 19 | 24 | 19 | €50

7e | Quai Anatole France - Port de Solférino (Solférino) | 01-44-18-04-39 | www.restaurantlequai.com

All aboard this barge moored in front of the Musée d'Orsay with a "pretty" deck offering fine views of the Seine in summer, and an indoor fireplace enhancing the "boathouse atmosphere" in colder weather; you pay for the setting, of course, but the service is shipshape and the New French offerings "pleasant" for lunch (no dinner served); P.S. it also serves an "excellent Sunday brunch" buffet.

Quai-Quai ☒Ⓜ *Bistro* 18 | 20 | 18 | €50

1er | 74, quai des Orfèvres (Pont Neuf) | 01-46-33-69-75 | www.quaiquai-restaurant.com

In the heart of Paris but "away from urban stress" on the Ile de la Cité, this "cute", "cozy" bistro decked out with old reclaimed wood offers a "warm welcome" plus eats that are "unpretentious but well made"; "good value" seals the deal.

404 (Le) ◐ *Moroccan* | 20 | 23 | 17 | €45

3e | 69, rue des Gravilliers (Arts et Métiers) | 01-42-74-57-81 | www.404-resto.com

It "feels like the Kasbah" at this Arts et Métiers Moroccan thanks to the "transporting" "riad"-like decor and "deliciously perfumed" couscous and tagines; even if it's "a little tight" and the pace occasionally feels "rushed" - especially during the first service - the "chic" chowhounds who pack the place say the "moderate" tabs and "incredible" ambiance make for a good "night out with friends."

Quedubon Ⓢ *Wine Bar/Bistro* | ▽ 18 | 15 | 19 | €47

19e | 22, rue du Plateau (Buttes Chaumont) | 01-42-38-18-65

"Wine is king" at this "spectacular wine bar" in the "back of beyond" 19th that's "worth the trip" for its grape collection that's easily parsed with the help of the "knowledgeable" staff; it also offers a chalkboard menu of "simple", reasonably priced eats, making the sunny, wood-floored storefront a culinary bright spot in a "gastronomically impoverished" neighborhood.

Z **Quincy (Le)** Ⓢ Ⓜ ≠ *Bistro* | 26 | 20 | 23 | €55

12e | 28, av Ledru-Rollin (Gare de Lyon/Quai de la Rapée) | 01-46-28-46-76 | www.lequincy.fr

"You're transported to the country" as soon as you walk through the door of this red-checked-tablecloth bistro near the Gare de Lyon, run by a "true character" who gives the small, "old-fashioned" room a "genial atmosphere"; but it's the "copious amounts of hearty, delicious fare" made with "incomparable *produits de terroir*" that really "warm the heart", so no one minds if it's not cheap; P.S. cash only; closed Saturday-Monday.

Z **Quinzième (Le)** Ⓢ Ⓜ *New French* | 26 | 22 | 24 | €104

15e | 14, rue Cauchy (Javel) | 01-45-54-43-43 | www.restaurantlequinzieme.com

"Talented" TV chef Cyril Lignac "reconciles the richness of tradition with inventiveness" at his "fabulous" New French table deep in the 15th near the Parc André Citroën; service in the "*soignée*", "contemporary" dining room is "impeccable", and even though it's "pricey", most agree that it's a place you can go "again and again."

NEW **Qui Plume la Lune** Ⓢ Ⓜ *New French* | - | - | - | E

11e | 50, rue Amelot (Chemin Vert) | 01-48-07-45-48

This new narrow nook with exposed-stone walls, housed in a former 16th-century convent not far from the Place de la République, isn't well known yet, but its "creative", "original" Asian-inflected New French fare has been getting good word of mouth, even if it's a bit expensive.

Racines Ⓢ *Wine Bar/Bistro* | 20 | 15 | 20 | €56

2e | 8, passage des Panoramas (Grands Boulevards) | 01-40-13-06-41

"Serious French wines" by contemporary producers attract "hip" cork dorks to this pricey *bistrot à vins* run by "nice" folks in the

Passage des Panoramas, a covered 19th-century arcade in the 2nd; a new chef arrived post-Survey (possibly outdating the Food score), but it still serves "old favorites and cutting-edge" plates made from "locally sourced" ingredients in an "unassuming" nook decorated with antique furniture and an intricate tiled floor; P.S. check out its new spin-off, Racines 2, in a Philippe Starck–designed space in the 1st.

NEW Racines 2 ☒ *Bistro* — | — | — | E

1er | 39, rue de l'Arbre Sec (Louvre-Rivoli) | 01-42-60-77-34

The well-known Passage des Panoramas bistro Racines recently added this offshoot in the 1st, cooking well-sourced seasonal products in its characteristic direct style, paired with natural wines – which may help you swallow the considerable tabs; no mere reboot of the original, it boasts a slick downtown loft design by Philippe Starck, with a view onto the gleaming all-stainless kitchen, and a crowd that's definitely more bourgeois than bohème.

Ralph's *American* 17 | 26 | 20 | €60

6e | Ralph Lauren | 173, bd St-Germain (St-Germain-des-Prés) | 01-44-77-76-00

It's like "dining inside a magazine spread" say admirers of the "stunningly beautiful" courtyard and "very New England" interior of the in-store eatery at Ralph Lauren's clothing boutique in Saint-Germain, where the "courteous" staff is dressed in RL, natch; fans of "the horse guy" split on the pricey American fare ("best burgers in Paris" vs. just "ok"), but it's still "harder to get a seat here than it is for Christmas services at Notre Dame."

Ravi ◐ *Indian* — | — | — | M

7e | 50, rue de Verneuil (Rue du Bac) | 01-42-61-17-28 | www.restaurant-ravi.com

"Lovely traditional dishes" are the draw at this Indian spot with "discreet and efficient" service, known mainly to denizens of the 7th; it may be teeny-tiny, but at least the tabs aren't much bigger than that, and besides, its subcontinental decor (intricately carved wood screens, etc.) is rather "picturesque."

Rech (Le) ☒ Ⓜ *Seafood* 22 | 16 | 19 | €83

17e | 62, av des Ternes (Charles de Gaulle-Etoile/Ternes) | 01-45-72-29-47 | www.restaurant-rech.fr

Run by gastropreneur Alain Ducasse, this "legendary" seafooder just off the Place des Ternes nets kudos for its "excellent fish and shellfish"; service in the "refined", 1920s-era dining rooms is "amiable", and though it's "expensive", it's a solid bet for "special occasions."

Régalade (La) ☒ *Bistro* 25 | 16 | 21 | €52

14e | 49, av Jean Moulin (Alésia) | 01-45-45-68-58

Gourmands find themselves in good company, surrounded by other "serious eaters who've come to the edge of the 14th for something special", namely, the "outstanding" "French country cooking" of chef-owner Bruno Doucet at this old-fashioned "Parisian" bistro near the Porte d'Orléans; it's "one of the best values in Paris", which is why service can be "hectic" when it gets filled up – and it always does; P.S. closed weekends.

Régalade Saint-Honoré (La) Ⓢ *Bistro* | 23 | 16 | 20 | €50

1er | 123, rue St-Honoré (Louvre-Rivoli) | 01-42-21-92-40

"Much easier to access" than its older country cousin, La Régalade in the 14th, Bruno Doucet's "fabulous modern bistro" centrally located in the 1st near Les Halles serves the same "wonderful" fare – the complimentary pâté alone is "worth the visit"; there are "no bells and whistles" in the contemporary red-and-white dining room, but a "quality" staff and one of "the best 'low cost' deals in Paris" keep it "crowded"; P.S. closed weekends.

Relais d'Auteuil "Patrick Pignol" Ⓜ *Haute Cuisine* | 25 | 19 | 23 | €133

16e | 31, bd Murat (Michel-Ange-Molitor/Porte d'Auteuil) | 01-46-51-09-54 | www.relaisdauteuil-pignol.com

It's "seriously expensive", but so is the upmarket neighborhood near the Porte d'Auteuil, and as long as you're willing to cough up the euros for Patrick Pignol's "inventive" Haute Cuisine, you're in for a "great culinary moment"; stainless-steel accents in the contemporary dining room make it "less formal" than others of a similar ilk, but the service is suitably "soigné"; P.S. make sure to book for weekend dates.

Ⓩ **Relais de l'Entrecôte (Le)** *Steak* | 22 | 16 | 19 | €44

6e | 101, bd du Montparnasse (Vavin) | 01-46-33-82-82
6e | 20, rue St-Benoît (St-Germain-des-Prés) | 01-45-49-16-00 ◐
8e | 15, rue Marbeuf (Franklin D. Roosevelt) | 01-49-52-07-17 ◐
www.relaisentrecote.fr

The "only decision to make" is how well done "you want your steak cooked" at this mini-chain in rather "banal" brasserielike digs serving a "simple" set menu: "melt-in-your-mouth" beef enhanced by a "magical" sauce, plus "tasty" frites and a "fresh green salad"; they don't take reservations, but at least you "meet nice people while waiting" in line, and if the uniformed waitresses are "curt", they're also über-"efficient", adding up to an "extraordinary value."

Relais de Venise (Le) ◐ *Steak* | 23 | 16 | 20 | €42

17e | 271, bd Pereire (Porte Maillot) | 01-45-74-27-97 | www.relaisdevenise.com

"The best frites in *le monde*" ride shotgun to "succulent" steaks covered with a "mouthwatering secret sauce" at this "venerable" (since 1959) monument to meat and potatoes near the Porte Maillot, with further outposts in London and NYC; its no-choices prix fixe menu is well known as "one of the best buys in town", so "be prepared to wait" (outside) for a seat in the utilitarian interior – also know that the line "moves quickly" on account of the "professional" waitresses.

Ⓩ **Relais Louis XIII** ⓈⓂ *Haute Cuisine* | 26 | 25 | 24 | €114

6e | 8, rue des Grands-Augustins (Odéon/St-Michel) | 01-43-26-75-96 | www.relaislouis13.com

"Elegant and fabulous", this Haute Cuisine table in an old stone building in Saint-Germain occupies the site of the convent where the titular king was crowned in 1610, and its "half-timbered decor from a bygone era" serves as a "romantic" setting in which to enjoy chef-owner Manuel Martinez's "wonderful" creations; it's "not for the faint of wallet", but the service is nearly "perfect", making for a "peaceful and dignified" repast; P.S. jacket required.

Relais Plaza (Le) ◐ *Brasserie/Eclectic* 25 | 24 | 25 | €94

8e | Plaza Athénée | 25, av Montaigne (Alma Marceau/ Franklin D. Roosevelt) | 01-53-67-64-00 | www.plaza-athenee-paris.com

"Alain Ducasse at a lesser price" (but still quite "pricey") is one of the main selling points of this "classy" brasserie at the Plaza Athénée, boasting an "excellent" Eclectic menu and a "beautiful" art deco interior presided over by an "impeccable" staff; the "chic, hip" clientele finds it a "nice traditional place for lunch", perfect "for dinner after the theater" and terrific for "people-watching" at all times.

Réminet (Le) *New French* 23 | 22 | 23 | €61

5e | 3, rue des Grands-Degrés (Maubert-Mutualité/St-Michel) | 01-44-07-04-24 | www.lereminet.com

Behind an aubergine-hued facade on a "quiet little street" just south of the Seine and the Ile de la Cité lies this somewhat pricey "Left Bank delight" frequented by "locals" who laud its "fabulous", "hearty" New French fare; "candlelight" casts a "romantic" glow that's reflected in antique mirrors that dot the small space, much like the "genial" owner's "charm" is reflected in that of his "caring" staff.

Repaire de Cartouche (Le) ⊠ *Bistro* ▽ 17 | 16 | 19 | €60

11e | 8, bd des Filles du Calvaire (St-Sébastien Froissart) | 01-47-00-25-86

A "favorite old standby" for "*cuisine de terroir*", aka rustic regional cooking, is this bistro in the 11th with shopworn wood-paneled trim; service remains solid even as prices have crept up, so for most it remains "a great place to go when you can't think of a place to dine", especially when game is in season.

Restaurant de la Tour ⊠ *Classic French* 24 | 23 | 23 | €74

15e | 6, rue Desaix (Dupleix/La Motte-Picquet-Grenelle) | 01-43-06-04-24 | www.restaurant-delatour.fr

Not far from the Eiffel Tower but surprisingly "not touristy", this upscale address pleases with its "elegant" setting ("real tableware and linens"), "inventive" updates of French classics and "friendly" ambiance; the only sticking point is the high price, though that's largely overlooked by deep-pocketed "regulars"; P.S. closed weekends.

Restaurant du Marché ⊠Ⓜ *Bistro* ▽ 21 | 18 | 19 | €51

15e | 59, rue de Dantzig (Porte de Versailles) | 01-48-28-31-55 | www.restaurantdumarche.fr

"Worth the detour" "off the beaten track", this longtimer in the 15th is "down to earth and authentic" in both its "classic" bistro eats and "back-in-time" look (think bare-wood tables, Bordeaux-painted moldings, zinc-clad service bar); fans would "go more often" if they could, given the moderate prices and a staff that makes everyone feel "very welcome."

	FOOD	DECOR	SERVICE	COST

Restaurant du Palais Royal 🅂 *Classic French* | 20 | 21 | 19 | €64

1er | 110, galerie de Valois (Bourse/Palais Royal-Musée du Louvre) | 01-40-20-00-27 | www.restaurantdupalaisroyal.com

Perhaps "the most romantic table in Paris" – at least in summer thanks to a "sublime" terrace overlooking the gardens of the Palais-Royal – this Classic French plays the location card big time but backs it up with "good though unremarkable" fare; servers are "pleasant" but have no qualms making you pony up for the "splendid setting."

Restaurant Le Pergolèse 🅂 *Haute Cuisine* ▽ | 25 | 20 | 25 | €83

16e | 40, rue Pergolèse (Argentine) | 01-45-00-21-40 | www.lepergolese.com

For evidence that Stéphane Gaborieau "loves his job", look no further than the "excellent", "modern" plates he artfully composes at his long-running Haute Cuisine table in the 16th; true professionals cater to the well-heeled clients who appreciate the calm, earth-toned dining room, conservatively decorated with oil paintings, red-velvet armchairs and crisp white tablecloths, leading its champions to insist it's definitely a place "to be tried."

Restaurant Manufacture 🅂 *New French* | 22 | 20 | 22 | €58

Issy-les-Moulineaux | 20, esplanade de la Manufacture (Corentin-Celton) | 01-40-93-08-98 | www.restaurantmanufacture.com

Occupying an old tobacco factory in suburban Issy-les-Moulineaux, this "chic", white-beamed loft attracts ad execs at noon and bobos in the evening for "honest", "original" New French food by chef-owner Jean-Christophe Lebascle, who cooks almost exclusively with organic produce; "amiable" service and a lush terrace add "value for money" spent; P.S. closed weekends.

Restaurant Paul 🄼 *Bistro* | 18 | 17 | 15 | €42

1er | 15, pl Dauphine (Pont-Neuf) | 01-43-54-21-48

With a "picturesque setting away from the hustle and bustle of the city" on the Ile de la Cité, this "lovely bistro" straight outta "yesteryear" offers "competent" bistro classics that are best enjoyed when sitting outside overlooking the cobbled street and park; service gets mixed marks ("polite" vs. "glacial"), but it nonetheless draws a "big lunch crowd from the nearby courthouse" and advocates judge the cost "ok."

Reuan Thai ◐ *Thai* | - | - | - | I

11e | 36, rue de l'Orillon (Belleville) | 01-43-55-15-82 | www.reuanthai.com

Maybe its distant location in Belleville explains why this "almost-like-in-Bangkok" Thai isn't as well known as its ardent admirers think such a "real keeper" should be; the wood-paneled setting may not be much to look at, but "cheap" prices (especially for the lunch buffet) and "service with a smile" are reasons to visit.

Ribouldingue 🅂🄼 *Classic French* | 22 | 15 | 20 | €46

5e | 10, rue St-Julien-le-Pauvre (St-Michel) | 01-46-33-98-80 | www.restaurant-ribouldingue.com

"If you have the guts to eat guts", head for this Latin Quarter hide-away where the Classic French fare is just "offal" – that is, it's "a marvelous introduction to body parts" (lily-livered types take heart: they also serve more mainstream choices); the "small" setting is "cute" and "convivial", and prices are easy to stomach.

Rino 🅢🅜 *New French* 25 | 14 | 23 | €56

11e | 46, rue Trousseau (Ledru-Rollin) | 01-48-06-95-85 | www.rino-restaurant.com

"Rino rocks" roar fans who have horned in on this "hip" little bistro behind the Bastille where Italian-born chef Giovanni Passerini composes "inventive" contemporary French dishes in a setting that might make you wonder "am I in the wrong place?" since it's about as basic as a "dorm room"; doubts disappear once diners receive the attentions of the "gracious" staff and tuck into the pricey but "fabulous" fare – in short, "a must-try experience."

Robert et Louise 🅜 *Bistro* 20 | 17 | 20 | €42

3e | 64, rue Vieille-du-Temple (Rambuteau) | 01-42-78-55-89 | www.robertetlouise.com

Carnivores covet this "charming little" bistro in the Marais where "incredible", "well-marbled" steaks are "sizzled" on the hearth over a wood fire and "friendliness is guaranteed"; the "sure value" means it's always "packed to the gills with tourists and locals" who enjoy making "new friends" at the shared wooden tables in the ultra-"rustic" space.

Roi du Pot-au-Feu (Le) 🅢 *Bistro* ▽ 19 | 15 | 19 | €40

9e | 34, rue Vignon (Havre-Caumartin/Madeleine) | 01-47-42-37-10

Stewing "in its own juices" since the 1930s, this vintage bistro near the Grands Boulevards bowls folks over with its "soul-saving pot-au-feu", which comes with "lively broth, tangy gherkins and sinus-clearing mustard", "essential to surviving" "chilly winter nights" in Paris; there's "nothing fussy" about the place, including the solid service, but most agree that for a "simple", affordable meal it's "a good place to go."

Romantica (La) 🅢 *Italian* 22 | 21 | 20 | €55

Clichy | 73, bd Jean Jaurès (Mairie-de-Clichy) | 01-47-37-29-71 | www.laromantica.fr

Fans of this "excellent" Italian in suburban Clichy never say *basta* to the pasta, especially when it's served with "a light sage-seasoned cream sauce and flambéed" tableside in a hollowed-out round of Parmesan; prices are within reason, the staff is "attentive" and, yes, it's "romantic" – whether in the "warm", cozy interior with a working fireplace or out on the "magnificent terrace."

Rosa Bonheur 🅜 *Southwest* 16 | 24 | 16 | €26

19e | Parc des Buttes Chaumont | 2, allée de la Cascade (Botzaris) | 01-42-00-00-45 | www.rosabonheur.fr

A "hip rainbow crowd" flocks to this pavilion in the Parc des Buttes Chaumont perhaps "more for the atmosphere" than the "basic" Southwestern fare, because the "enchanting" setting transports city dwellers from "urban Paris to an old-time lake resort"; it gets "crazy" in summer with long waits and can feel more like a "snack bar" since there's "no service" to speak of – but "who cares" since this place delivers pure "happiness"; P.S. closed Monday and Tuesday.

Rose Bakery *Bakery/British* 22 | 16 | 18 | €26

3e | 30, rue Debelleyme (Filles du Calvaire) | 01-49-96-54-01
9e | 46, rue des Martyrs (Notre-Dame-de-Lorette) | 01-42-82-12-80 M
12e | La Maison Rouge | 10, bd de la Bastille (Bastille) | 01-46-28-21-14 M

"Homesick" Anglos are soothed by the "luscious carrot cake", scones and teas at this cafe mini-chain, a "bobo beachhead" that also offers organic salads and soups that are "so worth the wait in line"; the tight spaces are "far from fantastic", but the prices are right, and the polyglot staffs are "friendly" to fashionable foodies who've made this British bakery a Parisian "institution"; P.S. days and times vary by branch.

Rôtisserie d'en Face (La) ⊠ *Bistro* 20 | 18 | 20 | €55

6e | 2, rue Christine (Odéon/St-Michel) | 01-43-26-40-98 | www.jacques-cagna.com

Originally founded by chef Jacques Cagna (now retired), this popular Left Bank bistro/rotisserie attracts "lots of Americans" among others seduced by the scent of "amazingly good roast chicken" served by "sweet and attentive waiters" in a cozy farmhouse-style room; it's not quite the bargain it once was, but that in no way keeps the crowds away from this "steady standby."

Rôtisserie du Beaujolais (La) *Bistro* 22 | 19 | 22 | €53

5e | 19, quai de la Tournelle (Cardinal Lemoine/Pont-Marie) | 01-43-54-17-47 | www.larotisseriedubeaujolais.com

"An homage to the joys of rural French cooking" sums up this "cozy", "informal" bistro dishing up plates "overflowing" with "hearty comfort food" (with an "emphasis on rotisserie" items) and located Seine-side in the 5th just a few doors down from big sister La Tour d'Argent; prices are "reasonable", service is "friendly" and since it's open daily, it's a "favorite Sunday night spot."

Rotonde (La) ◐ *Brasserie* 19 | 20 | 19 | €54

6e | 105, bd du Montparnasse (Vavin) | 01-43-26-48-26 | www.rotondemontparnasse.com

A "throwback" to the days when Montparnasse eateries were "frequented by artists", this "typical Parisian brasserie" with "historical" ruby-red decor has survived for over a century by serving "consistently good", if "unoriginal", standards like shellfish trays and entrecôte; the staff is "quick" and "professional", so even though it's "a bit pricey" for what you get, "on balance" it's "a reasonable outing."

Royal Madeleine *Classic French* ▽ 23 | 19 | 23 | €58

8e | 11, rue du Chevalier St-Georges (Madeleine) | 01-42-60-14-36 | www.royalmadeleine.com

Conveniently located near the Madeleine in a neighborhood where rising rents have made restaurants scarce, this Classic French fills the void with its "excellent" menu (e.g. "superb" frogs' legs and veal) and "reasonable prices" - at least for the 8th; the staff sets a "warm" tone in the "nice" classic setting (think velvet banquettes, zinc bar), so all told, it's "a 'Royal' treat!"

Rubis (Le) ☒ *Wine Bar/Bistro* ▽ 19 | 15 | 19 | €28

1er | 10, rue du Marché St-Honoré (Pyramides/Tuileries) | 01-42-61-03-34

Long a local "favorite", this "delightful", "old-school" wine bar just off the Place du Marché Saint-Honoré comes recommended for "one of the best lunches in Paris: a ham-and-butter baguette sandwich eaten at the [zinc] bar with a glass of white Sancerre"; "casual" service, along with the fact that it's mostly "tourist-free" and easy on the wallet, makes for a "relaxed" time.

Rughetta (La) ◐ Ⓜ *Italian* ▽ 21 | 13 | 14 | €33

18e | 41, rue Lepic (Abbesses/Blanche) | 01-42-23-41-70

"Some of the best Neapolitan" pizza in Paris and "antipasti worth crossing" town for are high points at this trendy little Italian in Montmartre where it's fun to sit outside on the terrace; downsides are the red-and-zebra-striped interior (always "a bit of a squash") and service that can "stray", but the local bobos just keep on coming.

Sale e Pepe ◐ ☒ Ⓜ *Italian* 21 | 16 | 18 | €34

18e | 30, rue Ramey (Château Rouge/Jules Joffrin) | 01-46-06-08-01

Located in the northern part of the 18th ("the *other* side of Montmartre"), this unassuming Italian slings "really good" pizza as well as other standards from The Boot to a mostly local crowd; the small room is wrapped in marble and exposed brick, creating a "quaint", "cozy" vibe, which carries through to the easygoing tabs.

Saotico (Le) ◐ *New French* - | - | - | M

2e | 96, rue de Richelieu (Bourse/Richelieu-Drouot) | 01-42-96-03-20 | www.saotico.com

Run by the nice couple who previously made Le Réminet such a success, this "terrific" New French in the 2nd isn't well known yet, but wins major laurels from insiders for its "fresh, flavorful" fare, "delightful", airy duplex setting and "helpful" attitude ("Anne and Hugues make you feel at home"); overall, it "aims to please and mostly hits the mark", leading some to dub it one of the "best values in Paris"; P.S. it offers gluten-free items.

Sarladais (Le) ☒ *Southwest* 23 | 17 | 20 | €58

8e | 2, rue de Vienne (St-Augustin) | 01-45-22-23-62 | www.lesarladais.com

"Excellent" Southwestern French cooking that's strong on seafood plus "old-fashioned" hospitality reward those who've discovered this vintage locale behind the Gare Saint-Lazare; though the unchanging faux-auberge decor "doesn't have a lot of cachet", the combo of "intimacy and quality" keeps it reliable for business lunches and other (somewhat expensive) tête-à-têtes; P.S. jackets encouraged, closed Saturday lunch.

	FOOD	DECOR	SERVICE	COST

NEW Sassotondo *Italian* | - | - | - | M

11e | 40, rue Jean-Pierre Timbaud (Parmentier) | 01-43-55-57-00
Creating a sort of one-man Restaurant Row, Frédéric Hubig recently hung up another shingle – this one in Italian – next to his two French spots, Astier and Jeanne A, on this cute little stretch in the 11th; Tuscany is on *la tavola* here, courtesy of an Italian-born chef in the *cucina* turning out authentic fare at moderate prices that has kept the sleek, slim earth-toned storefront full from day one.

Saturne *New French* | 22 | 22 | 20 | €70

2e | 17, rue Notre-Dame des Victoires (Bourse) | 01-42-60-31-90
The "innovative", "ingredient-driven" cuisine of chef/co-owner Sven Chartier exhibits "flashes of brilliance", so even if it's "not quite there yet", it "screams purity and beauty", in concert with the "clean, crisp" setting featuring a small forest of raw wood and a huge glass roof at this "hip" New French near the old Bourse; the "no-decisions", prix fixe-only dinner ("remarkable" for the price) and "informed" staff further sells it; P.S. reservations required; closed weekends.

Saudade *Portuguese* | ▽ 16 | 14 | 16 | €46

1er | 34, rue des Bourdonnais (Châtelet-Les Halles) | 01-42-36-30-71 | www.restaurantsaudade.com
"Typical" Portuguese dishes, including cod "cooked half a dozen" ways, and a "very good cellar of port" are the draws at this midpriced place decorated with azulejo-tiled walls in Les Halles; critics carp everything's "better in Lisbon", but fado music the first Tuesday of each month may assuage their *saudade* (nostalgic longing).

Saut du Loup (Le) *New French* | 13 | 23 | 14 | €52

1er | Musée des Arts Décoratifs | 107, rue de Rivoli (Palais Royal-Musée du Louvre/Tuileries) | 01-42-25-49-55 | www.lesautduloup.com
The "matchless" location in the Musée des Arts Décoratifs offering "superb views" of the Louvre's I.M. Pei pyramid and the Tuileries lures "beautiful people" to the "sublime" terrace of this all-day New French (the "sleek", gray interior is somewhat "less glamorous"); *hélas*, the "average", "overpriced" eats are "disappointing", as is the "pretentious" service, but "who cares when you can sit outside?"

Scheffer (Le) *Bistro* | 19 | 15 | 18 | €46

16e | 22, rue Scheffer (Trocadéro) | 01-47-27-81-11
With a "classic kitchen" turning out crowd favorites for reasonable prices, no wonder this "old-fashioned" bistro exuding "19th-century charm" in the 16th is "always crowded"; though some *amis* admit "it's my friendly neighborhood joint, but I wouldn't travel to eat" here, others praise it as the "perfect spot on a cold night."

Schmidt – L'Os à Moëlle *Classic French* | 23 | 17 | 20 | €51
(fka L'Os à Moëlle)

15e | 3, rue Vasco de Gama (Lourmel) | 01-45-57-27-27 | www.paris-restaurant-osamoelle.com
A mid-Survey change of chef-owners (not fully reflected in our scores) – founder Thierry Faucher sold to Stéphane Schmidt (ex Le

Violon d'Ingres) – has brought new energy to this popular, "out-of-the-way" "foodie" favorite in the 15th, with Schmidt adding a number of dishes from his native Alsace to the Classic French menu; after minor renovations, the "tight" bistro's exposed beams and mirrors remain, as do the "attentive" service and "remarkable" value; P.S. "book in advance."

Sébillon ◐ *Brasserie* 22 | 19 | 20 | €60

Neuilly-sur-Seine | 20, av Charles de Gaulle (Les Sablons/Porte Maillot) | 01-46-24-71-31 | www.sebillon-neuilly.com

It's worth traveling to Neuilly to tuck into the "best" roast leg of lamb in town ("sliced on the shank in front of you") among other rib-sticking "traditional" eats at this "elegant but not daunting" brasserie that's been around since WWI; true, it's "not revolutionary" or cheap, but given the "honest" cooking and "delicious" desserts, it's ideal for a "family" meal.

Z Senderens *New French* 26 | 23 | 23 | €122

8e | 9, pl de la Madeleine (Madeleine) | 01-42-65-22-90 | www.senderens.fr

"No one does it like [Alain] Senderens" coo the many fans of his "marvelous" New French fare accompanied by an "unbeatable" wine list ("what a cellar!") and "refined" service at this "top-drawer" place in the 8th; though some still "miss" the old belle epoque dining room, most appreciate the "less formal", "modern" redesign, insisting the experience is "worth every centime"; P.S. if you forget to make reservations or are "on a tight budget, try the bar."

Sensing ☒ *New French* 23 | 20 | 22 | €88

6e | 19, rue Brea (Notre-Dame-des-Champs/Vavin) | 01-43-27-08-80 | www.restaurant-sensing.com

Chef Guy Martin's "ultrachic" New French in Montparnasse scores with "sensational" dishes served with "kindness" in a "cool" low-lit, plum-and-earth-toned space; the gorgeous 'in' crowd ("I'm not sure what's more beautiful, the food or the other patrons") gravitates to the coveted back room, but no matter where you sit you must steel yourself for a major bill.

NEW Septime ☒ *Bistro* 25 | 21 | 24 | €57

11e | 80, rue de Charonne (Charonne) | 01-43-67-38-29 | www.septime-charonne.fr

Living up to "the hype", this "brilliant" New French bistro by "dynamic" young chef Bertrand Grébaut (ex L'Arpège) is the "real thing", delivering "stellar", often "surprising" dishes in a "stylish" yet relaxed "minimalist" space sporting communal seating in the deep 11th; with "helpful" service and relatively "reasonable" prices, it's the "place to be"; P.S. "you definitely need a reservation"; closed weekends.

Z Severo (Le) ☒ *Steak* 26 | 14 | 17 | €57

14e | 8, rue des Plantes (Mouton-Duvernet) | 01-45-40-40-91

"If you think you've had great steaks, wait until you try these from an ex-butcher" dare devotees of this "beef-lover's delight" in

Montparnasse, serving "fantastic wines" from organic producers (listed on a blackboard filling one whole wall) to go with the "expertly prepared" aged cuts; it has a "simple" bistro setup and average service, but remember: "you come for the steaks."

Shan Gout Ⓜ *Chinese* | - | - | - | M

12e | 22, rue Hector-Malot (Gare de Lyon) | 01-43-40-62-14

"Exquisite", "cooked-to-order" Chinese dishes with a Sichuan emphasis on a regularly changing menu draw fans to this midpriced eatery near the Gare de Lyon, whose humble looks (simple wooden tables, a few Chinese art prints on the white walls) barely hint at the "refinement" of the food.

NEW Shang Palace *Chinese* | ▽ 24 | 20 | 23 | €93

16e | Shangri-La Hotel | 10, av d'Iéna (Iéna) | www.shangri-la.com

More evidence that the Chinese Century has officially begun: the arrival of this outpost of the Shangri-La group's luxe Sino restaurant chain in the basement of its hotel in the 16th, and some are already calling it the "best Cantonese cooking in Paris"; the contemporary, ornately decorated space displays high-level Asian opulence, and the gracious staff makes the experience smooth as silk (once you nab reservations), but oh, "the prices you pay"; P.S. closed Tuesday and Wednesday.

Shu Ⓢ *Japanese* | ▽ 25 | 23 | 25 | €57

6e | 8, rue Suger (Odéon/St-Michel) | 01-46-34-25-88 | www.restaurant-shu.com

"After the lesson in humility of the low door", which forces most to bow upon entering this Japanese in Saint-Germain, "the enchantment begins" as you dine on one of three set menus consisting mainly of kushiage (skewers) "like you've never imagined", crafted by chef-owner Osamu Ukai; the stone-walled subterranean space is "simple" yet "beautiful", and the service is "friendly", complementing the "refined", omakase-style meal.

6 New York Ⓢ *New French* | 23 | 22 | 22 | €71

16e | 6, av de New York (Alma Marceau) | 01-40-70-03-30 | www.6newyork.fr

An improved Food score makes this contemporary French in the 16th one "to rediscover" for its "creative" cooking based on "sublime", "market-fresh products", garnished with Eiffel Tower views; it's "expensive", but the chef himself works the "smart", "modern" room – "a nice touch" that adds to the already "warm", "convivial" welcome.

Société (La) ◐ *Classic French* | 17 | 23 | 17 | €93

6e | 4, pl St-Germain-des-Prés (St-Germain-des-Prés) | 01-53-63-60-60 | www.societe-restaurant.com

"Well-dressed, beautiful" people can't get enough of what is perhaps the "most glamorous of all the Costes brothers restaurants": this Classic French sporting a "sophisticated" 1930s Shanghai-esque interior by star designer Christian Liaigre, fabulously located in the heart of Saint-Germain; the eats are only "ok" and served by a staff that's "the same as at all Costes venues" (good-looking but rather "amateur"), yet it remains "*très cher,* my dear"; P.S. jacket suggested.

Sola *Japanese/New French* ▽ 27 | 25 | 24 | €83

5ᵉ | 12, rue de l'Hôtel Colbert (Maubert-Mutualité) | 01-43-29-59-04 | www.restaurant-sola.com

"Delicate" and "inventive", the New French-Japanese fusion cuisine "by a young Japanese chef" is a "revelation" for admirers of this well-run Latin Quarter venue with a thoughtful East-meets-West design that's respectful of the centuries-old building housing it; praising the "light" presentations of the dishes, fans recommend it as a "top" pick; P.S. jacket suggested.

Sormani *Italian* 24 | 22 | 23 | €97

17ᵉ | 4, rue du Général Lanrezac (Charles de Gaulle-Etoile) | 01-43-80-13-91

"The waiters take care of you" as they serve "high-class" Italian fare (e.g. "lovely truffle dishes") at this pricey pasta palace near the Etoile; "beautiful" red-and-white Venetian-style decor completes the postcard-perfect scene, leading most to return to this outpost of Italy in Paris with "pleasure"; P.S. reservations required.

Sot l'y Laisse (Le) *Bistro* ▽ 22 | 14 | 20 | €49

11ᵉ | 70, rue Alexandre Dumas (Alexandre Dumas) | 01-40-09-79-20

The post-Survey arrival of talented, French-trained Japanese chef Eiji Doihara, who previously ran one of Paul Bocuse's Japanese restaurants, has suddenly given this bistro south of Père Lachaise a lot of buzz, as well as a new menu that stars impeccably made Classic French dishes with an Asian touch or two (not reflected in the Food score); the decor doesn't amount to much - it's a simple storefront with chalkboards, mirrors and various doodads on the walls - but then, neither does the bill.

Soufflé (Le) *Classic French* 22 | 18 | 21 | €51

1ᵉʳ | 36, rue du Mont-Thabor (Concorde) | 01-42-60-27-19 | www.lesouffle.fr

As its name indicates, this "quaint gem" with a "charming tearoom atmosphere" in the 1st is "heaven" for fetishists of the puffed-up classic, since you "can get an appetizer, main course and dessert all as soufflés" (including an "unreal" chocolate version); a "kind" staff lends extra appeal to the "bright and sunny" setting, so customers are "still crazy" about it "after all these years."

Z Spring *New French* 27 | 21 | 24 | €88

1ᵉʳ | 6, rue Bailleul (Louvre-Rivoli) | 01-45-96-05-72 | www.springparis.fr

"Enthralled" eaters hail the "incredible" New French offerings of native Chicagoan Daniel Rose at his "don't-miss" table in Les Halles, "one of the hottest reservations in town", where the "open kitchen provides entertainment" to accompany the "beautifully harmonized" multicourse menus (no à la carte); the townhouse setting with exposed-brick walls is "gorgeous", service is "charming and relaxed" and the wine selection "brilliant" (oenophiles: check out the separate basement wine bar), so it's "worth every shekel" for an "experience that you won't soon forget."

NEW Square Gardette (Le) M *Bistro* | - | - | - | M |

11e | 24, rue St-Ambroise (Rue St-Maur) | 01-43-55-63-07 | www.squaregardette.fr

This new shabby-chic bistro/cafe in the 11th could be your eccentric aunt's parlor, if she drank caipirinhas, collected taxidermy and had a roster of hip east Paris pals; the stroller set descends for brunch on le weekend (there's a kids' menu), and a vet of Chez L'Ami Jean and Bistrot Paul Bert in the kitchen gives the reasonably priced menu some cred.

Square Marcadet S M *Classic/New French* | - | - | - | M |

18e | 227 bis, rue Marcadet (Guy Môquet) | 01-53-11-08-41

A "secret garden" beckons a bobo crowd to this indoor/outdoor bistro serving "inventive" Classic and New French fare in a distant corner of the 18th, though the interior, with its cozy bar area and chalkboard-lined dining room decked out with pewlike benches, is inviting too; "welcoming" service and decent prices seal the deal, making it a natural destination for meeting up "with a partner or friends."

Square Trousseau (Le) ◐ *Bistro* | 19 | 22 | 19 | €43 |

12e | 1, rue Antoine Vollon (Bastille/Ledru-Rollin) | 01-43-43-06-00 | www.squaretrousseau.com

A "romantic getaway" that's "off the beaten tourist track", this "pretty" perch with belle epoque decor (zinc bar, banquettes, etc.) overlooks a leafy square in the 12th; "decent" bistro fare, a "youthful" atmosphere, "pleasant" sidewalk seating and late hours (till 2 AM) all help keep it "bustling."

Stella (Le) *Brasserie* | 21 | 18 | 19 | €53 |

16e | 133, av Victor Hugo (Rue de la Pompe/Victor Hugo) | 01-56-90-56-00

"Dine with the locals" at this "true brasserie" with typical "old-fashioned" decor in the silk-stocking 16th that "merits its reputation", delivering "simple but well-prepared" favorites (including "standout" seafood dishes) at "breakneck speed"; open all day till late and always "noisy", it's perhaps a touch "high-end" for the genre, but most feel prices are "fair."

Stella Maris S *Classic French* | 25 | 19 | 24 | €103 |

8e | 4, rue Arsène Houssaye (Charles de Gaulle-Etoile) | 01-42-89-16-22 | www.stellamaris-paris.com

Japanese chef-owner Tateru Yoshino trained with some of the "best", including Joël Robuchon, and his Classic French dishes, updated with a "slight Asian flair", are duly "ambitious" and matched by "superlative" wines at this "bright", "spacious" contemporary dining room filled with "beautiful flowers and art" near Etoile; "exquisite courtesy" appears to be the staff's motto, which makes it a fine choice for "celebrating", if a bit of a splurge; P.S. jacket suggested.

	FOOD	DECOR	SERVICE	COST

Stéphane Martin *Classic French* ▽ 23 | 16 | 19 | €45

15e | 67, rue des Entrepreneurs (Charles Michels/Commerce) | 01-45-79-03-31 | www.stephanemartin.com

"You won't see many tourists" since "it's a bit of a trip" to get to this "local jewel" in the 15th owned by chef Stéphane Martin, offering "refined" French "classics and the chef's own marvels"; regulars also dig the "calm" ambiance and "warm" service that pervades the "cozy" if nondescript room, adding it's a "good value for the money" too.

Stresa (Le) *Italian* 22 | 18 | 22 | €92

8e | 7, rue Chambiges (Alma Marceau) | 01-47-23-51-62 | www.lestresa.com

"If you can get a table", there's prime "people-watching" (amid "mirrors to beat Versailles") at this "chic", "tiny" trattoria near the Champs-Elysées where you're likely to rub shoulders with "film people" or "executives from LVMH"; the "creative" Italian fare is "served impeccably by a wise staff" that caters to the caprices of its older, jet-set clientele that's straight outta "Botoxland" - just "be ready" for sticker-shock; P.S. closed weekends.

Suave *Vietnamese* - | - | - | M

13e | 20, rue de la Providence (Corvisart/Tolbiac) | 01-45-89-99-27

"Very different from traditional Asian restaurants", this Vietnamese near the Buttes aux Cailles surprises with its "sophisticated", "refined" cuisine; the "pretty" teak-wood room has a "nice ambiance" though limited space, and service that's as gentle as the prices.

NEW Sur Mesure *Haute Cuisine* - | - | - | VE

1er | Mandarin Oriental | 251, rue St-Honoré (Concorde) | 01-70-98-73-00 | www.mandarinoriental.com/paris

Avant-garde chef Thierry Marx recently arrived in Paris, checking into the Mandarin Oriental with this Haute Cuisine table serving "beautifully" composed plates (he also debuted the New French Camélia at the hotel); the dining room, with its futuristic white waveform walls by Patrick Jouin, "may surprise" traditionalists, but most "soon feel at ease" in the hands of the "impeccable" staff; premium prices aside, the "sublime" food is "enough to make any good capitalist a Marxist."

Z Table d'Eugène (La) *New French* 26 | 17 | 22 | €41

18e | 18, rue Eugène Sue (Jules Joffrin) | 01-42-55-61-64

Some of "the best food for the money in Paris today" can be found in a remote corner of the 18th at Geoffroy Maillard's "hip and trendy" New French table, judged a "revelation" by early adopters of his "creative" cooking that's priced quite "reasonably"; it's become "popular" and the "modest" willow-green digs are "small", making it tough to book; P.S. lunch is a real "steal."

Table d'Hédiard (La) *New French* 22 | 20 | 22 | €72

8e | Hédiard | 21, pl de la Madeleine (Madeleine) | 01-43-12-88-99 | www.hediard.fr

Amid the epicurean "temptations" of the renowned namesake boutique grocer in the 8th is this "chic" in-store eatery that attracts "ladies who lunch" and evening dates for "consistently surprising" New French dishes and "wonderful", "beautifully decorated" desserts; with "careful" service and tables "sufficiently spread apart to have a decent discussion" in the "subdued" earth-toned room, the experience is "expensive" but highly civilized.

Table du Lancaster (La) *Haute Cuisine* 25 | 21 | 26 | €127

8e | Hôtel Lancaster | 7, rue de Berri (Franklin D. Roosevelt/George V) | 01-40-76-40-18 | www.hotel-lancaster.fr

"Charming and intelligent", this Haute Cuisine table at the Hôtel Lancaster serves an "inventive" menu by chef Michel Troisgros in an elegant, "softly lit" dining room or a "pleasant" garden courtyard that's "ideal" on a summer evening; service is just about "perfect", but while the overall atmosphere is "calm", the bill sure is a stunner; P.S. jacket suggested.

Tablettes de Jean-Louis Nomicos (Les) *Haute Cuisine* ∇ 28 | 22 | 23 | €115

16e | 16, av Bugeaud (Victor Hugo) | 01-56-28-16-16 | www.lestablettesjeanlouisnomicos.com

A "sparkling" arrival in the 16th, this Haute French owned by chef Jean-Louis Nomicos (ex Lasserre) delivers "exquisite", Mediterranean-inspired creations in a "light and bright" space designed with a gray basket-weave ceiling and walls accented by burnt-orange banquettes; "informed" and "helpful" service is another reason why those willing to reach deep into their pockets agree it's "one of the best new finds in Paris."

Z Taillevent ⊠ *Haute Cuisine* 29 | 28 | 28 | €178

8e | 15, rue Lamennais (Charles de Gaulle-Etoile/George V) | 01-44-95-15-01 | www.taillevent.com

Rated tops for Food and Service in Paris, this "high court of Haute Cuisine" in the 8th still reigns as one of the "best restaurants in the world", despite the loss of the "incomparable" Jean-Claude Vrinat and a subsequent change of ownership (the first since its founding in 1946); "no detail is overlooked", from the "sublime" creations of longtime chef Alain Solivérès, who "remains true" to French traditions "while finding ways to enhance" them, to the "luxurious" townhouse setting, to the "wonderful staff" - still overseen by maître d' Jean-Marie Ancher - that provides "personal attention from start to finish"; if one puckish soul suggests "the Euro debt crisis was caused by expense-account dinners here", most would agree it's a worthy place to "break the bank"; P.S. closed weekends; jackets suggested.

Tan Dinh ⊠⊭ *Vietnamese* 22 | 16 | 21 | €65

7e | 60, rue de Verneuil (Rue du Bac/Solférino) | 01-45-44-04-84

"Exceptional" Vietnamese food, "terrific" service and a "world-class" wine list featuring "wonderful" Burgundies keep the local beau monde loyal to this "elegant", family-run old-timer in the 7th; on the downside, you must "bring your own atmosphere" to the rather "sedate" room, along with plenty of cash to foot the "expensive" bill (they don't take cards).

	FOOD	DECOR	SERVICE	COST

Tang ☒ *Chinese* | 22 | 15 | 21 | €57

16e | 125, rue de la Tour (Rue de la Pompe) | 01-45-04-35-35

Diners "delight" in the "quality" cooking (overlooking "kitschy '70s" decor) at this "upscale" Chinese in the 16th; expect a "charming welcome" from the owner and his "amiable" staff, plus a "pricey" check.

Tante Louise ☒ *Burgundy/Classic French* | 23 | 20 | 22 | €74

8e | 41, rue Boissy-d'Anglas (Concorde/Madeleine) | 01-42-65-06-85 | www.bernard-loiseau.com

"Spot-on" Classic French fare and Burgundian specialties are matched by well-chosen wines at this destination for "business lunches" and post-sightseeing and -shopping meals, thanks in part to its location in a chic corner of the 8th near the American Embassy, the Madeleine and Hermès; the staff "makes you feel special" as does the quiet, "sophisticated" art deco interior, though it's perhaps best for an "older", monied crowd; P.S. closed weekends.

Tante Marguerite ☒ *Classic French* | 22 | 18 | 21 | €74

7e | 5, rue de Bourgogne (Assemblée Nationale) | 01-45-51-79-42 | www.bernard-loiseau.com

"Mingle with politicians and the affluent" denizens of the 7th at this "old-style" spot serving "safe", "quality" Classic French in a "comfortable" wood-paneled room behind the Assemblée Nationale; the "unfussy" service and "good but not overwhelming" wine list are also appreciated, supporting the "expensive" tabs; P.S. closed weekends.

Taverne du Sergent Recruteur (La) ◐ ☒ Ⓜ *Classic French* | 17 | 17 | 17 | €54

4e | 41, rue St-Louis-en-l'Ile (Pont-Marie) | 01-43-54-75-42 | www.lesergentrecruteur.com

"Rowdy" and "tacky", this "Disneyesque" faux-medieval "tavern of yore" with communal tables and exposed-stone walls on the Ile Saint-Louis offers "big hunks" of "basic country food" (the "French version of an all-you-can-eat") and maybe a "good laugh" after lots of the house wine ("more than drinkable" slur the sloshed); there's "no polish" and prices have gone up, but if you don't mind the "touristy" crowd, it's the "perfect formula for groups with a large appetite."

Temps au Temps (Le) ☒ Ⓜ *Bistro* | 23 | 15 | 20 | €46

11e | 13, rue Paul Bert (Faidherbe-Chaligny) | 01-43-79-63-40

On one of the most gastronomically gifted little streets in the 11th is this "gem" "hidden" away in a "hole-in-the-wall", providing "outstanding", "refreshing" market-driven bistro dishes "served with care"; the "tiny", clock-adorned room is "cute" to some, "spartan" to others, but most agree the tabs are a real "bargain" ("spent more on the taxi"); P.S. you're advised to book at least four days in advance.

Temps des Cerises (Le) ◐ ☒ *Bistro* | 18 | 17 | 18 | €30

13e | 18, rue de la Butte aux Cailles (Tolbiac/Place d'Italie) | 01-45-89-69-48 | www.cooperativetempsdescerises.eu

The "revolution" lives on at this employee-owned-and-run cooperative in the pleasantly pastoral Butte aux Cailles neighborhood, where a "local crowd" gathers at communal tables to partake of "plain and unassuming but honest" bistro fare in a "warm, convivial" atmosphere; with "welcoming" service and "low" tabs, it's a "truly great French joint" for all.

Terminus Nord ◐ *Brasserie* 18 | 21 | 19 | €53

10e | 23, rue de Dunkerque (Gare du Nord) | 01-42-85-05-15 | www.terminusnord.com

"Always a standby", this "old-fashioned brasserie with an art deco interior" across the street from the Gare du Nord is just the ticket for "*très bons*" seafood platters, choucroute and other "typical" dishes at fairly "reasonable" prices before hopping the Eurostar or a north-bound train; the waiters are "constantly on the go", tending to a "huge, always busy" room where the "people-watching" is a "joy."

Terrasse Mirabeau (La) Ⓢ *Bistro* ▽ 26 | 17 | 19 | €50

16e | 5, pl de Barcelone (Javel/Mirabeau) | 01-42-24-41-51 | www.terrasse-mirabeau.com

One of the "best bets" in the 16th, this "pleasant" spot draws a stylish clientele for "well-presented", "classic" bistro fare shot through with "creative" streaks; some find the brown-and-red decor a bit "lacking in personality", but most agree the "lovely" terrace is "the perfect place for a fine summer evening"; P.S. closed weekends.

Thoumieux ◐ *New French* 20 | 21 | 18 | €65

7e | Hôtel Thoumieux | 79, rue St-Dominique (Invalides/La Tour-Maubourg) | 01-47-05-49-75 | www.thoumieux.com

Reminiscent of "Paris in the 1920s" – the Roaring Twenties, that is, since it's always "abuzz with activity" – this dark and "handsome" supper club in the 7th, whose mirrored, "red-plush" space was recently glammed up, slings "well-presented" "modern" French fare from a menu designed by Jean-François Piège (who cooks upstairs at his eponymous 20-seater); it's "noisy" and would benefit from prices being "revised down", but service is "satisfactory" and it adds up to a "lovely", "lively" time.

Timbre (Le) Ⓢ Ⓜ *Bistro* 25 | 17 | 22 | €52

6e | 3, rue Ste-Beuve (Notre-Dame-des-Champs/Vavin) | 01-45-49-10-40 | www.restaurantletimbre.com

"About as big as a walk-in closet", or a *timbre* (postage stamp), this "awesome" bistro near the Luxembourg Gardens feels "more like a dinner party" than a restaurant, with a "casual, comfortable" atmosphere for savoring "fantastic" dishes by English chef-owner Chris Wright; while "tight seating" is part of the package, the "accommodating" service really delivers, and "prices are honest given the quality."

Timgad (Le) ◐ *Moroccan* 22 | 23 | 22 | €67

17e | 21, rue Brunel (Argentine) | 01-45-74-23-70

"Delicious, copious" Moroccan fare and a "nice selection of North African wines" are "graciously served" in a "beautiful" "traditional" interior (think intricately hand-carved plaster) at this time-honored enclave in the 17th; though "pricey", there's no doubt it's "one of the best Moroccans in Paris."

NEW Tintilou (Le) ☒ *New French* | - | - | - | M |

11ᵉ | 37 bis, rue de Montreuil (Faidherbe-Chaligny) | 01-43-72-42-32 | www.tintilou.fr

While few surveyors have visited this New French in the 11th since chef-owner Jean-François Renard launched it in the old L'Aiguière space, those who have describe his cooking as "extremely imaginative"; redecorated in vivid colors, this onetime watering hole of Louis XIII's musketeers has a "friendly" feel, enhancing its strong "value."

Tong Yen ◐ *Chinese* | 22 | 15 | 21 | €58 |

8ᵉ | 1 bis, rue Jean Mermoz (Franklin D. Roosevelt) | 01-42-25-04-23

Still a firm favorite of former French president Jacques Chirac and other pols and celebs, this "classy" Chinese in the heart of the posh Golden Triangle serves "excellent Cantonese cuisine", along with upscale Thai and Vietnamese dishes; under the direction of proprietress Thérèse Luong, service is generally "very nice", which makes up for the "aging" '60s decor and "expensive" tabs.

Tourbillon (Le) ☒ *Bistro* ▽ | 24 | 21 | 22 | €48 |

5ᵉ | 45, rue Claude Bernard (Censier-Daubenton) | 01-47-07-86-32 | www.letourbillon.com

Run by a winning couple – "talented chef" Cédric Tessier and "charming" hostess Rebecca Tessier – this "small, nicely decorated" bistro in the Latin Quarter offers a "short but good" menu that's "excellent" "for the price"; with a "warm" "neighborhood" feeling, it's a keeper for "lots of French patrons", like profs and students.

Z Tour d'Argent (La) ☒ M *Haute Cuisine* | 25 | 27 | 26 | €156 |

5ᵉ | 15-17, quai de la Tournelle (Cardinal Lemoine/Pont-Marie) | 01-43-54-23-31 | www.latourdargent.com

"What history, what a location, what a view, what they do with a duck" sigh fans of this "stately and elegant" Haute Cuisine "landmark" perched six stories above the banks of the Seine overlooking Notre Dame; young chef Laurent Delarbre composes "fantastic" dishes that are brilliantly illuminated by selections from a truly "biblical" wine list and it's all enhanced by "exquisitely" "old-school" service, so while the whole package is "spendy" indeed, it's "worth it" for an "unforgettable" experience; P.S. reservations and jacket required.

Z Train Bleu (Le) *Classic French* | 19 | 27 | 20 | €67 |

12ᵉ | Gare de Lyon | Place Louis Armand (Gare de Lyon) | 01-43-43-09-06 | www.le-train-bleu.com

Like something "out of a film set", what must be one of "the world's finest restaurants in a train station" boasts a "magnificent" turn-of-the-last-century setting featuring ornate, vaulted ceilings and dreamy frescoes of southern locales accessible via the Gare de Lyon; the "pricey" Classic French fare is hardly the star, but it's "reliably good" and "skillfully" served to a "pleasant mix of locals, businessmen and a few tourists" – "all aboard!"

	FOOD	DECOR	SERVICE	COST
35° Ouest [S][M] *Seafood*	22	19	23	€67

7ᵉ | 35, rue de Verneuil (Rue du Bac) | 01-42-86-98-88
"Warm", "cordial" service tips the scales in favor of this "contemporary" "jewel box" near the Rue du Bac, where suits descend midday for "pristine seafood" that displays "classicism with a touch of originality"; prices are up there but are deemed "reasonable" for the area, especially the "stunning-value set lunch."

39V (Le) [S] *New French*	23	22	21	€99

8ᵉ | 39, av George V (George V) | 01-56-62-30-05 | www.le39v.com
Ducasse alum Frédéric Vardon's "heavenly" New French cuisine is showcased in this George V address' "magnificent", ultramodern circular space (accessed by private elevator), whose windows face a leafy terrace where diners can enjoy apéritifs and partial Eiffel Tower views; it's all "very Golden Triangle", from the suits who favor it for "discreet conversations", to the super-steep prices, which, "considering the neighborhood, seem reasonable"; P.S. closed weekends.

Tricotin ◐ *Asian*	19	9	13	€21

13ᵉ | 15, av de Choisy (Porte de Choisy) | 01-45-84-74-44
"No-frills" yet "respectable", this "big", "cafeteria"-like eatery serves a "wide selection" of "quality" Chinese, Vietnamese and Thai eats for "cheap", making it one of the "best values" in the 13th; while it's "noisy", with "fast", "impersonal" service, diners' main focus is wolfing down dim sum and other dishes "similar to what you'd find in Asia."

Troquet (Le) [S][M] *Basque/New French*	24	17	20	€47

15ᵉ | 21, rue François Bonvin (Cambronne/Sèvres-Lecourbe) | 01-45-66-89-00
"Foodies" flock to this "always-crowded little restaurant deep in the 15th" for its "delicious take" on "traditional Basque" and New French dishes on a frequently changing menu (it transitioned to a new chef post-Survey, not reflected in the Food score); despite its humble appearance, the "warm welcome", "convivial" atmosphere and "reasonable" prices win out.

Trou Gascon (Au) [S] *Southwest*	25	18	23	€81

12ᵉ | 40, rue Taine (Daumesnil) | 01-43-44-34-26 | www.autrougascon.fr
With its "out-of-the-way" location in the 12th, this "timeless classic" "always feels like a find", especially for anyone who loves its "specialties of the Southwest" (e.g. "the most delicious cassoulet") and doesn't mind the considerable "expense"; "it was redecorated a few years ago" in a more contemporary style, but the pretty belle epoque wedding-cake moldings survive, as does the "attentive", "old-school service" and "fine collection of old Armagnacs."

[Z] **Truffière (La)** [S][M] *Classic French*	26	23	24	€105

5ᵉ | 4, rue Blainville (Cardinal Lemoine/Place Monge) | 01-46-33-29-82 | www.latruffiere.com
"One of the most romantic restaurants in Paris", this "quaint" Classic French "just off the Place de la Contrescarpe" presents near-"flawless" cuisine in a "beautiful old-world" dining room complete

with exposed-stone walls, beamed ceilings and a working fireplace (there's also a candlelit wine cellar); though the truffle supplements can "sneak up on you pricewise", most deem dinner here an "absolute pleasure" that's "worth every euro", so relax and enjoy the "obliging" service; P.S. the lunch prix fixe is a "more affordable" option.

Trumilou (Le) *Bistro* 20 | 14 | 20 | €35

4e | 84, quai de l'Hôtel de Ville (Hôtel-de-Ville/Pont-Marie) | 01-42-77-63-98 | www.letrumilou.fr

Overlooking the Seine in the 4th arrondissement, this "old-timer" is known for its "honest" bistro eats, "smiling" staff and "unpretentious", "provincial" atmosphere; aside from pulling Parisian professionals and foreign backpackers, it works as a "casual, great-value family dining spot."

Tsé-Yang ◐ *Chinese* 22 | 21 | 21 | €71

16e | 25, av Pierre 1er de Serbie (Alma Marceau/Iéna) | 01-47-20-70-22

A "*véritable voyage asiatique*" awaits at this "opulent" black-and-gold Chinese dining room in the 16th, with "impeccable" service and an ample bar to suit the affluent clientele; "everything's good" on the menu, with "excellent Peking duck" a standout, though stiff prices lead many to save it for a "festive occasion."

Tsukizi Ⓜ *Japanese* ▽ 22 | 14 | 19 | €39

6e | 2 bis, rue des Ciseaux (Mabillon/St-Germain-des-Prés) | 01-43-54-65-19

"Sit at the bar and watch the masters at work" at this Japanese "favorite" in Saint-Germain-des-Prés, offering some of the "best (for the price) sushi in Paris"; the "minimalist" decor doesn't get much notice, but most appreciate its consistent quality "throughout the years."

Vagenende ◐ *Brasserie* 17 | 25 | 19 | €63

6e | 142, bd St-Germain (Mabillon/Odéon) | 01-43-26-68-18 | www.vagenende.fr

Sought out for its "sumptuous" landmarked interior, this century-old Saint-Germain brasserie boasts a "gorgeous" stained-glass ceiling and other well-preserved period art nouveau details, but a recent makeover updated some of the soft furnishings with jazzier colors and added South Beach–style furniture to the expanded sidewalk terrace; service is generally "ok", but the "retro" food strikes many as "unpredictable" and "overpriced."

Vaudeville (Le) ◐ *Brasserie* 20 | 23 | 20 | €53

2e | 29, rue Vivienne (Bourse) | 01-40-20-04-62 | www.vaudevilleparis.com

A "beautiful art deco interior" of marble and mosaics "transports diners back" in time at this brasserie by the old Bourse owned by Groupe Flo, serving a "traditional" midpriced menu (including "fantastic seafood platters on ice") that "rarely fails to satisfy"; if the staff's "a bit hurried", that's just part of the real "Parisian" "hustle and bustle."

	FOOD	DECOR	SERVICE	COST

NEW Verjus Ⓢ *American/Wine Bar* | - | - | - | E |

1er | 52, rue Richelieu (Pyramides) | 01-42-97-54-40 | www.verjusparis.com

The two young Yanks behind the much-lauded Hidden Kitchen supper club have unveiled a real restaurant in a warmly aglow duplex space nestled next to the Palais-Royal, offering small plates at small prices, biodynamic wine and Japanese whiskey in the cellar *bar à vins,* and higher-priced tasting menus of boldly flavored, creative American cuisine upstairs, winning raves from loyal expat clients and French foodies; service is bilingual, *bien sûr;* P.S. closed weekends.

Vernet (Le) Ⓢ *Haute Cuisine* ▽ | 24 | 25 | 25 | €86 |

(aka Les Elysees)

8e | Hôtel Vernet | 25, rue Vernet (Charles de Gaulle-Etoile/George V) | 01-44-31-98-98 | www.hotelvernet.com

Though few surveyors are acquainted with this "elegant" dining room in the Hôtel Vernet off the Champs-Elysées, those in the know love the "glass ceiling designed by Gustave Eiffel" and praise the "excellent" Haute Cuisine of chef Laurent Poitevin (ex Taillevent); prices are commensurate with the prestige of the setting, but "charming service" and a relative prix fixe bargain at lunch make this hideaway a smart choice for business dining.

Verre Bouteille (Le) ◐ Ⓢ Ⓜ *Wine Bar/Bistro* | 19 | 16 | 21 | €38 |

17e | 85, av des Ternes (Ternes) | 01-45-74-01-02 | www.leverrebouteille.com

Meat eaters maintain you'll find the "best hand-chopped steak tartare in Paris", among other "well-done" dishes and "new wines to discover", at this long-running night owls' perch (open till 4 AM most nights) in the 17th; even if the "narrow" *bistrot à vins* is slim on decor, the "affable" staff, "relaxing" atmosphere and modest prices easily make up for it.

Verre Volé (Le) *Wine Bar/Bistro* | 20 | 15 | 18 | €38 |

10e | 67, rue de Lancry (République/Jacques Bonsergent) | 01-48-03-17-34 | www.leverrevole.fr

This "hip", "friendly" wine bar near the Canal Saint-Martin is "always a madhouse, but that's half the fun" claim "foodies" savoring "inventive", "tasty" fare bolstered by the "intelligently" chosen bottles that line the open shelves; it seems to be "getting more popular every day", so book ahead.

Versance (Le) Ⓢ Ⓜ *Classic/New French* | - | - | - | E |

2e | 16, rue Feydeau (Bourse/Grands Boulevards) | 01-45-08-00-08 | www.leversance.fr

Still not well known, this "delightful" duplex by chef Samuel Cavagnis near the old Bourse pleases those in the know with "extraordinary" Classic and New French dishes, true "hospitality" and "elegant" white-and-gray decor incorporating the building's original belle epoque moldings and stained glass; it's expensive, but so "charming" that it's perfect for a special occasion or a "quiet" rendezvous.

	FOOD	DECOR	SERVICE	COST

Z Villa Corse (La) *Corsica* — 21 | 20 | 19 | €55

15e | 164, bd de Grenelle (Cambronne/La Motte-Picquet-Grenelle) | 01-53-86-70-81 ◐
16e | 141, av de Malakoff (Porte Maillot) | 01-40-67-18-44
www.lavillacorse.com

For a "little trip to Corsica" without leaving Paris, nothing beats these "havens of calm and taste" in the 15th and 16th, showcasing the Mediterranean island's "simple" but "delicious" cuisine and native wine in "warm" and "classy", "library"-like settings; service is Corsican-style too – "pro and without any fuss" – though many say the prices are a bit "daunting."

Villaret (Le) ◐ ☒ *Bistro* — 23 | 17 | 21 | €58

11e | 13, rue Ternaux (Oberkampf/Parmentier) | 01-43-57-89-76

"Off the beaten track" but "well worth the search", this "bistro extraordinaire" in the 11th features a menu that brings together "very good traditional dishes" with "cutting-edge" contemporary flair; "enthusiastic" service helps make up for the somewhat "cramped" dining room with its exposed beams and bricks, and if regulars regret rising prices, this is one they'd still rather keep to themselves, so "shhh!"

Vin Chai Moi ☒ M *Wine Bar/Bistro* — - | - | - | M

1er | 18, rue Duphot (Madeleine) | 01-40-15-06-69 | www.vin-chai-moi.fr

A boon for bacchanalians near the Madeleine, this upscale but moderately priced wine bar/bistro by Luc Menier (former sommelier at Guy Savoy) offers a "simple, tasty" modern French menu complemented by a "flawless" wine list and "lovely" service; the spacious, wood-accented upstairs dining room is inviting for quiet tête-à-têtes, but grape apes may want to swing by the street-level wine shop or the brightly lit tasting cellar.

Vin et Marée *Seafood* — 21 | 17 | 20 | €50

1er | 165, rue St-Honoré (Palais Royal-Musée du Louvre) | 01-42-86-06-96
7e | 71, av de Suffren (La Motte-Picquet-Grenelle) | 01-47-83-27-12 | www.vin-et-maree.com
11e | 276, bd Voltaire (Nation) | 01-43-72-31-23 | www.vin-et-maree.com
14e | 108, av du Maine (Gaîté) | 01-43-20-29-50 | www.vin-et-maree.com
16e | 183, bd Murat (Porte de St-Cloud) | 01-46-47-91-39 | www.vin-et-maree.com

Fin fans find "seafood paradise" at this mini-chain offering "generous", "quality" "feasts", complete with "well-chosen" wines and a "marvel" of a baba au rhum, for "reasonable" tabs; thanks to the "attentive" deckhands, all goes swimmingly in the spacious, ocean-blue-accented dining rooms, though a few wags contend the fish is much "fresher than the tired surroundings"; P.S. the location in the 1st is separately owned.

20 de Bellechasse (Le) ◐ ☒ *Bistro* — 20 | 18 | 19 | €55

7e | 20, rue de Bellechasse (Solférino) | 01-47-05-11-11

"French comfort food" plus standout burgers are the "simple" pleasures at this "trendy" bistro on a chic street near the Musée d'Orsay that's moderately priced for the 'hood; a "friendly welcome" greets the "beautiful" locals who pack into the "hip, hopping sardine-can" digs that benefit from mirrors on most all surfaces.

21 Ⓢ Ⓜ *Seafood* 23 | 20 | 20 | €66

6e | 21, rue Mazarine (Odéon) | 01-46-33-76-90

Chef Paul Minchelli uses "only the freshest" fish in his "ultrarefined" preparations at this "hard-to-find" Saint-Germain spot; reservations are suggested for the "intimate", mostly black dining room populated by chic Left Bank regulars who dig the "club"-like atmosphere that "welcoming" host Didier Granier cultivates and who can pay the "eye-wateringly expensive" tabs.

Vins des Pyrénées *Classic French* 17 | 17 | 18 | €35

4e | 25, rue Beautreillis (Bastille/St-Paul) | 01-42-72-64-94

An "international crowd" cleaves to this "noisy" wine bar in the Marais, known for its "friendly atmosphere", "no-fuss" service and art nouveau looks; the Gallic classics are "basic" but budget-friendly, so most focus on the cellar's offerings and enjoy a "delightful" "wine-soaked evening."

Vin sur Vin Ⓢ *New French* 21 | 18 | 18 | €95

7e | 20, rue de Monttessuy (Alma Marceau/Ecole Militaire) | 01-47-05-14-20

A "wonderful", "extensive" wine list comprising about 800 different labels complements "lovely" food presentations at this New French "treat" in the 7th; "expensive" tabs are unavoidable given the "fancy", art-filled room and "correct" service; P.S. jacket suggested.

Violon d'Ingres (Le) *Bistro* 25 | 20 | 22 | €86

7e | 135, rue St-Dominique (Ecole Militaire) | 01-45-55-15-05 | www.leviolondingres.com

As "sophisticated" as its 7th arrondissement surroundings, chef-owner Christian Constant's "elegant" bistro impresses with "very polished cuisine" and "fabulous" treatment by servers who are "always checking" on the tables; while a few say "the check is too heavy", most simply "adore" the whole package; P.S. reservations required.

NEW Vivant ◐ *Wine Bar/Bistro* ▽ 24 | 22 | 19 | €49

10e | 43, rue des Petites Ecuries (Bonne Nouvelle/Château d'Eau) | 01-42-46-43-55

Decorated with art nouveau tiles depicting the exotic birds sold here in the 19th century when the snug space was a pet shop, this "unpretentious" new wine bar by Pierre Jancou (founder of Racines) in a "gentrifying" corner of the 10th provides a "short" but upscale menu of "incredibly sourced and prepared" food and "top-notch natural wines"; it's quite a "happening bar scene" at night.

Voltaire (Le) Ⓢ Ⓜ *Classic French* 22 | 21 | 21 | €79

7e | 27, quai Voltaire (Rue du Bac) | 01-42-61-17-49

"Clubby, expensive and fun", this "elegant hideaway" on the Quai Voltaire in the 7th pulls in a "chic French and American crowd" for "tasty", "simple" French classics and bistro fare, including its famous "oeufs mayonnaise", "heavenly" frites and lots of "red meat"; though critics contend the prices continue "to rise beyond reason", for loyalists it "remains a lovely old Parisian standard" where one goes "to see and be seen"; P.S. jacket suggested.

Wepler ◐ *Brasserie* | 20 | 19 | 19 | €47

18e | 14, pl de Clichy (Place de Clichy) | 01-45-22-53-24 | www.wepler.com

Still independently owned, this "historic" brasserie overlooking the Place de Clichy finds fans with its "super" platters of *fruits de mers* and other "traditional" seafood offerings, as well as "fantastic" vintage decor that "takes you back to Old Paris"; the "charming" servers seem to "have been here forever" too, and prices are generally fair.

Willi's Wine Bar Ⓢ *Wine Bar/Bistro* | 20 | 18 | 20 | €49

1er | 13, rue des Petits-Champs (Palais Royal-Musée du Louvre/ Pyramides) | 01-42-61-05-09 | www.williswinebar.com

"Kick back" and soak in the "bustling" yet "relaxing" vibe at this "Parisian institution" in the 1st, run by British owner Mark Williamson, who proffers an "unbelievable wine list at reasonable prices", along with "creative" contemporary bites and bistro classics; the narrow, artwork-lined space is always packed with "interesting people at the bar", upping the "awesome" ambiance, so go "enjoy yourself" – the staff makes everyone "feel like a regular."

Z **Yam'Tcha** Ⓜ *Asian/New French* | 26 | 17 | 22 | €83

1er | 4, rue Sauval (Louvre-Rivoli) | 01-40-26-08-07 | www.yamtcha.com

"Just trust 'em and you won't be disappointed" at this petite powerhouse off Les Halles where "extraordinarily gifted" chef-owner Adeline Grattard turns "premium" ingredients into "completely new and original" French-Asian prix fixes (no à la carte) in a "microscopic" space with exposed-stone walls and a beamed ceiling; Grattard's husband, Chi Wah Chan, steers the "inspired" tea pairings, and service has a "gentle touch", so while prices are steep, they're "justified" for the "out-of-this-world" meals; P.S. closed Monday and Tuesday.

Yen Ⓢ *Japanese* | ▽ 22 | 19 | 19 | €45

6e | 22, rue St-Benoît (St-Germain-des-Prés) | 01-45-44-11-18

On par with the noodle houses of "Tokyo", this "spartan" but "stylish" standout in the heart of Saint-Germain excels with "extremely tasty, delicate" soba noodles and other "well-prepared" Japanese dishes (though not sushi) served in an "efficient" yet "reserved" style; while a few wonder "how can a bowl of buckwheat noodles be this expensive?", it's touted as one of the "best" to be had in Paris.

NEW **Yoom** Ⓢ *Asian* | - | - | - | I

6e | 5, rue Grégoire de Tours (Mabillon) | 01-43-54-94-56
9e | 20, rue des Martyrs (St-Georges) | 01-56-92-19-10 Ⓜ
www.yoom.fr

After a stint in Hong Kong, a couple of repatriated Parisians opened this pair of affordable dim sum spots, serving designer dumplings with a Pan-Asian flavor profile; the stylish digs (exposed brick and paper lanterns in the 9th, sky-blue walls in the 6th) are considerably cooler than the average Chinatown table, not to mention more centrally located.

Yugaraj 🅼 *Indian* 20 | 16 | 20 | €52

6e | 14, rue Dauphine (Odéon/Pont-Neuf) | 01-43-26-44-91

"Skillfully prepared" Indian cuisine highlighting "fresh", "local" produce excites the palate at this "fine Indian" in Saint-Germain, staffed by an "efficient, amiable" crew; decorated with colonial touches, the "subdued" surroundings strike diners as either "pleasant" or "somewhat dowdy", though the upscale tabs seem on target to most.

Zébra Square *Classic French/Italian* 16 | 19 | 15 | €55

16e | Hotel Square | 3, pl Clément-Ader (Av du Pdt Kennedy RER/Passy) | 01-44-14-91-91 | www.hotelsquare.com

Across the street from La Maison de la Radio in the 16th, this "modern" hangout appeals more for the "glitz" and "good music" by late-night DJs than for its Classic French and Italian eats, which seem like an "afterthought" (and fairly "expensive for not much on the plate"); indeed, some conclude it's best for "the young", while others lament a "lack of heat" these days, huffing it's "a little tired."

🅩 **Ze Kitchen Galerie** 🅢 *Eclectic* 25 | 21 | 21 | €72

6e | 4, rue des Grands-Augustins (Odéon/St-Michel) | 01-44-32-00-32 | www.zekitchengalerie.fr

"Imaginative" fusion dishes "flow from the open kitchen" of chef-owner William Ledeuil, who "successfully" uses Asian herbs, spices and jus on the fish and meat he prepares on a specially designed grill, making this Saint-Germain Eclectic "one of the few Parisian restaurants where non-European flavors are truly integrated into the cooking, not just sprinkled on like salt and pepper"; with a "lively" atmosphere and "unpretentious" service amid gallerylike surroundings, it's "a pleasure" that's "worth the splurge."

Zeyer (Le) ◐ *Brasserie* 19 | 18 | 19 | €47

14e | 62, rue d'Alésia (Alésia) | 01-45-40-43-88 | www.lezeyer.com

One advantage of being "out of the way" in the deep 14th at this nearly century-old "favorite" is that "you can have the experience of a brasserie as it was before the flood of tourists overwhelmed more fashionable places"; regulars recommend the decently priced "*très bonne* choucroute" and must-have seafood platters served by an "attentive" staff.

INDEXES

LOCATION MAPS

French Cuisines

Includes names, locations and Food ratings.

BISTRO

Restaurant	Location	Food
Absinthe	1er	21
Accolade	17e	20
NEW Affable	7e	–
NEW Affranchis	9e	–
Affriolé	7e	23
Allard	6e	21
Z Ami Louis	3e	24
Antoine	16e	22
AOC	5e	23
Ardoise	1er	23
Assiette	14e	19
Astier	11e	21
Atelier Maître Albert	5e	23
Bar/Théâtres	8e	17
Bastide Odéon	6e	20
NEW Bélisaire	15e	23
Z Benoît	4e	23
Beurre Noisette	15e	25
Biche/Bois	12e	22
Bistral	17e	22
Bistro/Vieux Chêne	11e	23
Bistro 121	15e	22
Bistro/Breteuil	7e	18
Bistro/Deux Théâtres	9e	21
NEW Bistro/Gastronomes	5e	23
Bistro du 17ème	17e	19
NEW Bistronomes	1er	–
Bistro Poulbot	18e	23
Bistro St. Ferdinand	17e	19
Bistrot/Côté Flaubert	17e	21
Bistrot/Côté La Boutarde	Neuilly	21
Bistrot d'André	15e	20
Bistrot/l'Oulette	4e	22
Bistrot de Paris	7e	19
Bistrot des Dames	17e	18
Bistrot des Vignes	16e	20
Bistrot d'Henri	6e	22
Bistrot du Dôme	multi.	22
Bistrot du Passage	17e	23
Bistrot du Peintre	11e	18
Bistrot Paul Bert	11e	21
Bistrot Vivienne	2e	19
Bistro Volnay	2e	21
Bon Accueil	7e	23
Bonne Franquette	18e	–
Botanistes	7e	19
Boucherie Roulière	6e	26
Bouchon/L'Assiette	17e	22
Boulangerie	20e	22
NEW Bourgogne Sud	9e	–
Buisson Ardent	5e	22
Café Cartouche	12e	–
Café Constant	7e	24
Café des Musées	3e	20
Café du Commerce	15e	17
Café Le Moderne	2e	22
Café Ruc	1er	15
Cantine/Troquet	14e	25
Casse-Noix	15e	–
Cerisaie	14e	23
Chardenoux	11e	23
NEW Chardenoux/Prés	6e	21
Charpentiers	6e	20
Chéri Bibi	18e	20
Chez André	8e	22
Chez Denise	1er	23
Chez Fred	17e	19
Z Chez Georges	2e	23
Chez Grenouille	9e	21
Chez Julien	4e	21
Z Chez L'Ami Jean	7e	25
Chez la Vieille	1er	23
Chez Léna et Mimile	5e	21
Chez Marie-Louise	10e	–
Chez Paul	11e	22
Chez Paul	13e	22
Chez Ramulaud	11e	–
Chez René	5e	19
Chez Savy	8e	20
Christophe	5e	24
Cinq Mars	7e	21

NEW Clocher/Montmartre | 18e –
Comme/Savonnières | 6e –
Z Comptoir/Relais | 6e 27
Comptoir Marguery | 13e 21
NEW Coq Rico | 18e –
NEW Cornichon | 14e –
Cotte Rôti | 12e –
Coulisses | 9e –
Coupe Gorge | 4e –
Crus/Bourgogne | 2e 20
Cuizine | 11e –
Cul de Poule | 9e 20
D'Chez Eux | 7e 24
Desvouges | 5e –
Deux Amis | 11e 21
Duc de Richelieu | 12e 22
Ebauchoir | 12e 24
Entêtée | 14e 20
Entredgeu | 17e 21
Epi d'Or | 1er 19
Epi Dupin | 6e 24
Epigramme | 6e 23
Escargot Montorgueil | 1er 22
Ferrandaise | 6e 20
Fins Gourmets | 7e 18
Firmin le Barbier | 7e 21
NEW Floréal | 10e –
Z Fontaine de Mars | 7e 22
Fontaines | 5e 19
Fourchette | 17e 23
Z Frenchie | 2e 26
NEW Galopin | 10e –
Gauloise | 15e 18
Gavroche | 2e 24
Georgette | 9e 17
Glou | 3e 20
Gourmets/Ternes | 8e 23
Grand Pan | 15e 23
Grille | 10e 21
Grille St-Germain | 6e 21
Hangar | 3e 23
Hédoniste | 2e 22
Hide | 17e 24
Hôtel Amour | 9e 15
Hotel du Nord | 10e –
Jadis | 15e 23
NEW Jaja | 4e 17
Jeanne A | 11e –
Joséphine/Dumonet | 6e 25
Lescure | 1er 19
Lyonnais | 2e 22
Maison du Jardin | 6e 25
NEW Maison Mère | 9e –
Marlotte | 6e 18
Mauzac | 5e 15
Mémère Paulette | 2e 23
Mesturet | 2e 16
Miroir | 18e 21
Moissonnier | 5e 24
Mon Vieil Ami | 4e 23
Moulin à Vent | 5e 20
Moustache | 6e 19
NEW Neva | 8e –
Ogre | 16e –
Opportun | 14e 22
NEW Pantruche | 9e 24
Parc aux Cerfs | 6e 20
Pères et Filles | 6e 17
Perraudin | 5e 18
NEW Petit Cheval/Manège | 11e –
Petit Marché | 3e 23
Petit Marguery | 13e 23
Petit Pergolèse | 16e 25
Petit Pontoise | 5e 25
Petit Rétro | 16e 18
Petit Riche | 9e 22
Petit Zinc | 6e 19
Philou | 10e 21
Polidor | 6e 15
Pomponette | 18e 23
NEW Pottoka | 7e –
Poule au Pot | 1er 22
Z Pramil | 3e 28
P'tit Troquet | 7e 22
Quai-Quai | 1er 18
Quedubon | 19e 18
Z Quincy | 12e 26
NEW Racines 2 | 1er –

Régalade | 14e	25
Régalade St-Honoré | 1er	23
Repaire/Cartouche | 11e	17
Rest. du Marché | 15e	21
Rest. Paul | 1er	18
Robert et Louise | 3e	20
Roi/Pot-au-Feu | 9e	19
Rôtiss. d'en Face | 6e	20
Rôtiss. du Beaujolais | 5e	22
Scheffer | 16e	19
NEW Septime | 11e	25
Sot l'y Laisse | 11e	22
Square Trousseau | 12e	19
Temps au Temps | 11e	23
Temps des Cerises | 13e	18
Terrasse Mirabeau | 16e	26
Timbre | 6e	25
Tourbillon | 5e	24
Trumilou | 4e	20
Villaret | 11e	23
20 de Bellechasse | 7e	20
Violon d'Ingres | 7e	25

BRASSERIE

Aub. Dab | 16e	20
Ballon des Ternes | 17e	19
Boeuf/le Toit | 8e	18
Bofinger | 4e	19
Brass./l'Ile St-Louis | 4e	19
Brass. Balzar | 5e	18
Brass. de la Poste | 16e	22
Brass. du Louvre | 1er	19
Brass. Flo | 10e	19
Brass. Julien | 10e	19
Brass. La Lorraine | 8e	18
Brass. Lipp | 6e	18
Brass. Lutetia | 6e	19
Brass. Mollard | 8e	18
Café de la Musique | 19e	17
Café Terminus | 8e	19
Charlot - Roi/Coquillages | 9e	21
NEW Chez Flottes | 1er	-
Chez Francis | 8e	18
Chez Georges | 17e	22
Chez Jenny | 3e	19
Chez Les Anges | 7e	24
Closerie/Lilas | 6e	20
Comptoir/Relais | 6e	27
Congrès Maillot | 17e	20
Coupole | 14e	18
Dessirier | 17e	24
Dôme | 14e	22
Editeurs | 6e	14
Européen | 12e	20
Flandrin | 16e	15
Gallopin | 2e	20
Garnier | 8e	22
Grand Café | 9e	19
Grand Colbert | 2e	19
Mama Shelter | 20e	16
Marty | 5e	20
Mascotte | 18e	20
Murat | 16e	17
Nemrod | 6e	17
Petit Lutetia | 6e	17
Pétrus | 17e	23
Pied de Cochon | 1er	19
Relais Plaza | 8e	25
Rosa Bonheur | 19e	16
Rotonde | 6e	19
Sébillon | Neuilly	22
Stella | 16e	21
Terminus Nord | 10e	18
Vagenende | 6e	17
Vaudeville | 2e	20
Wepler | 18e	20
Zeyer | 14e	19

CLASSIC

A et M | 16e	21
Aimant du Sud | 13e	21
Allard | 6e	21
Allobroges | 20e	22
Ami Louis | 3e	24
Astor | 8e	24
Aub. Bressane | 7e	22
NEW Auberge du 15 | 13e	24
Aub. du Champ/Mars | 7e	23
Aub. Nicolas Flamel | 3e	21
Auguste | 7e	24

Bacchantes | **9e** 21
Beaujolais/Auteuil | **16e** 19
Biche/Bois | **12e** 22
Bistro/Breteuil | **7e** 18
Bistro Poulbot | **18e** 23
Bistro St. Ferdinand | **17e** 19
Bistrot/Côté Flaubert | **17e** 21
Bistrot/Côté La Boutarde | **Neuilly** 21
Bistrot d'André | **15e** 20
Bistrot d'Henri | **6e** 22
Boeuf Couronné | **19e** 23
Bon Accueil | **7e** 23
Bon Saint Pourçain | **6e** 19
Bouillon Racine | **6e** 18
Brass. Printemps | **9e** 15
Buisson Ardent | **5e** 22
Café Cartouche | **12e** -
Z Café de Flore | **6e** 16
Café de la Paix | **9e** 19
Café/l'Esplanade | **7e** 18
Café Marly | **1er** 17
Café Rouge | **3e** 19
Café Terminus | **8e** 19
Cantine/Tontons | **15e** 17
Caves Pétrissans | **17e** 23
Céladon | **2e** 23
Chalet | **Neuilly** 21
Chalet des Iles | **16e** 18
Chartier | **9e** 15
Chéri Bibi | **18e** 20
Chez Cécile | **8e** 25
Chez Denise | **1er** 23
Chez Françoise | **7e** 20
Chez Gégène | **Joinville** 16
Chez Géraud | **16e** 20
Chez Léna et Mimile | **5e** 21
Chez Nénesse | **3e** 21
Christine | **6e** 21
Cigale Récamier | **7e** 22
Citrus Etoile | **8e** 24
Closerie/Lilas | **6e** 20
Comédiens | **9e** 19
Comme/Savonnières | **6e** -
Coupe-Chou | **5e** 20
Dali | **1er** -
Da Rosa | **6e** 21
Derrière | **3e** 15
Z Deux Magots | **6e** 17
Drouant | **2e** 23
Ebouillanté | **4e** 22
Ecluse | **multi.** 17
Enfants Terribles | **8e** 20
Ferme St-Simon | **7e** 21
Fermette Marbeuf | **8e** 19
Firmin le Barbier | **7e** 21
Flora Danica | **8e** 21
Flore en l'Ile | **4e** 17
Fontaine Gaillon | **2e** 21
Fouquet's | **8e** 20
Gare | **16e** 18
Gitane | **15e** 18
Gourmand | **1er** 25
Grande Armée | **16e** 16
Grand Louvre | **1er** 20
Grille | **10e** 21
Gourmand | **Neuilly** 18
Hangar | **3e** 23
Hide | **17e** 24
Ile | **Issy-les-Moul.** 19
Ilot Vache | **4e** 20
Jadis | **15e** 23
Jardins de Bagatelle | **16e** 20
Jeanne A | **11e** -
Joséphine/Dumonet | **6e** 25
Z Jules Verne | **7e** 23
Macéo | **1er** 23
Maison/Amér. Latine | **7e** 21
Marlotte | **6e** 18
Martel | **10e** 21
Maxim's | **8e** 20
Méditerranée | **6e** 22
Mémère Paulette | **2e** 23
Z Michel Rostang | **17e** 27
Miroir | **18e** 21
Moulin/Galette | **18e** 20
Nos Ancêtres les Gaulois | **4e** 13
Ourcine | **13e** 25
Papilles | **5e** 25

Passiflore | **16e**	23
Paul Chêne | **16e**	23
Pavillon/Lac | **19e**	19
Pavillon Montsouris | **14e**	22
Père Claude | **15e**	21
Pères et Filles | **6e**	17
Petit Châtelet | **5e**	22
Petite Chaise | **7e**	18
Petit Rétro | **16e**	18
Petit Riche | **9e**	22
Petit St. Benoît | **6e**	16
Petit Victor Hugo | **16e**	19
Petit Zinc | **6e**	19
Pharamond | **1er**	18
Philou | **10e**	21
Pierre/Palais Royal | **1er**	22
Z Procope | **6e**	17
Quai-Quai | **1er**	18
Quedubon | **19e**	18
Rest. de la Tour | **15e**	24
Rest. du Palais Royal | **1er**	20
Rest. Paul | **1er**	18
Ribouldingue | **5e**	22
Royal Madeleine | **8e**	23
Rubis | **1er**	19
Schmidt - L'Os/Moëlle | **15e**	23
Sébillon | **Neuilly**	22
Société | **6e**	17
Soufflé | **1er**	22
Square Marcadet | **18e**	-
Stéphane Martin | **15e**	23
Tante Louise | **8e**	23
Tante Marguerite | **7e**	22
Taverne/Sgt. Recruteur | **4e**	17
Temps des Cerises | **13e**	18
Z Train Bleu | **12e**	19
Versance | **2e**	-
Villaret | **11e**	23
Vins/Pyrénées | **4e**	17
Voltaire | **7e**	22
Zébra Square | **16e**	16

CONTEMPORARY

Accolade | **17e**	20
Afaria | **15e**	23
Agapé | **17e**	24
NEW Agapé Substance | **6e**	25
Agrume | **5e**	24
NEW Akrame | **16e**	23
Alcazar | **6e**	18
Arc | **16e**	16
Aromatik | **9e**	18
Avant Goût | **13e**	23
Avenue | **8e**	16
Z Bigarrade | **17e**	27
Bouquinistes | **6e**	23
Café de la Musique | **19e**	17
Café/l'Esplanade | **7e**	18
Café Lenôtre | **8e**	23
Café Marly | **1er**	17
Café Salle Pleyel | **8e**	16
Caïus | **17e**	24
NEW Camélia | **1er**	-
Camélia | **Bougival**	21
Cartes Postales | **1er**	-
Casa Olympe | **9e**	23
Z Chamarré Mont. | **18e**	26
Chateaubriand | **11e**	23
Chiberta | **8e**	24
Citrus Etoile | **8e**	24
Claude Colliot | **4e**	23
Clocher Péreire | **17e**	24
Clos/Gourmets | **7e**	25
NEW Cobéa | **14e**	-
Cocottes | **7e**	24
NEW Comptoir/Brice | **10e**	-
Concert/Cuisine | **15e**	-
Cottage Marcadet | **18e**	-
Cou de la Girafe | **8e**	13
Cristal de Sel | **15e**	27
Z Cristal Room | **16e**	20
1728 | **8e**	21
NEW Dodin/Mark Singer | **17e**	-
Dôme du Marais | **4e**	19
Etc. | **16e**	25
Famille | **18e**	23
Fish La Boiss. | **6e**	21
Florimond | **7e**	25
Flottes O. Trement | **1er**	21

Fougères | **17e**	27
Frédéric Simonin | **17e**	-
Gaigne | **4e**	24
Gazzetta | **12e**	24
Gourmand | **1er**	25
Z Hélène Darroze | **6e**	26
Z Hiramatsu | **16e**	27
Ile | **Issy-les-Moul.**	19
Il Vino | **7e**	22
NEW Instant d'Or | **8e**	-
Itinéraires | **5e**	23
Jadis | **15e**	23
Jamin | **16e**	23
Jean | **9e**	26
Jean-François Piège | **7e**	27
NEW Kei | **1er**	28
Lilane | **5e**	25
Macéo | **1er**	23
Maison Blanche | **8e**	23
Maison Courtine | **14e**	20
Mama Shelter | **20e**	16
Maxan | **8e**	20
MBC | **17e**	-
Minipalais | **8e**	21
Montalembert | **7e**	19
Office | **9e**	-
Ombres | **7e**	21
NEW Opéra Rest. | **9e**	19
Z Oulette | **12e**	26
Ourcine | **13e**	25
Pavillon/Lac | **19e**	19
Petite Cour | **6e**	20
Petit Marché | **3e**	23
Petit Pergolèse | **16e**	25
Petrelle | **9e**	25
Pinxo | **1er**	23
Z Pramil | **3e**	28
Pré Verre | **5e**	23
Pur' | **2e**	24
Quai | **7e**	19
Z Quinzième | **15e**	26
NEW Qui Plume/Lune | **11e**	-
Réminet | **5e**	23
Rest. Manufacture | **Issy-les-Moul.**	22
Rino | **11e**	25
Saotico | **2e**	-
Saturne | **2e**	22
Saut du Loup | **1er**	13
Z Senderens | **8e**	26
Sensing | **6e**	23
NEW Septime | **11e**	25
6 New York | **16e**	23
Sola | **5e**	27
Z Spring | **1er**	27
Square Marcadet | **18e**	-
Stella Maris | **8e**	25
Z Table d'Eugène | **18e**	26
Table d'Hédiard | **8e**	22
Thoumieux | **7e**	20
NEW Tintilou | **11e**	-
39V | **8e**	23
Troquet | **15e**	24
Versance | **2e**	-
Vin sur Vin | **7e**	21
Z Yam'Tcha | **1er**	26

HAUTE CUISINE

NEW Abeille | **16e**	23
Z Alain Ducasse | **8e**	28
Z Ambassadeurs | **8e**	27
Z Ambroisie | **4e**	27
Z Apicius | **8e**	27
Z Arpège | **7e**	27
Z Astrance | **16e**	28
Z Atelier/Joël Robuchon | **multi.**	27
Z Carré/Feuillants | **1er**	27
Z Cinq | **8e**	28
Cuisine | **8e**	22
Dominique Bouchet | **8e**	25
Z Epicure (Le Bristol) | **8e**	27
Frédéric Simonin | **17e**	-
Grande Cascade | **16e**	24
Z Grand Véfour | **1er**	28
Z Guy Savoy | **17e**	28
Z Hiramatsu | **16e**	27
Jean-François Piège | **7e**	27
Lapérouse | **6e**	23
Z Lasserre | **8e**	27
Laurent | **8e**	25

Z Meurice | **1er** 28

Z Passage 53 | **2e** 27

Pavillon Ledoyen | **8e** 25

Z Pierre Gagnaire | **8e** 28

Z Pré Catelan | **16e** 26

Relais d'Auteuil | **16e** 25

Z Relais Louis XIII | **6e** 26

Rest./Pergolèse | **16e** 25

NEW Sur Mesure | **1er** -

Table/Lancaster | **8e** 25

NEW Tablettes/Nomicos | **16e** 28

Z Taillevent | **8e** 29

Z Tour d'Argent | **5e** 25

Z Truffière | **5e** 26

Vernet | **8e** 24

REGIONAL

ALPINE

Chalet | **Neuilly** 21

Montagnards | **1er** 23

ALSACE/JURA

Z Bofinger | **4e** 19

Chez Jenny | **3e** 19

AUVERGNE

Ambassade/Auv. | **3e** 22

Bistrot/Vins Mélac | **11e** 18

Chantairelle | **5e** -

Lozère | **6e** 21

Mascotte | **18e** 20

AVEYRON

Ambassade/Auv. | **3e** 22

Chez Savy | **8e** 20

BASQUE

Afaria | **15e** 23

Bascou | **3e** 23

Cantine/Troquet | **14e** 25

Z Chez L'Ami Jean | **7e** 25

NEW Pottoka | **7e** -

Troquet | **15e** 24

BRITTANY

NEW Atao | **17e** -

Breizh Café | **3e** 22

Chez Michel | **10e** 24

NEW Compagnie/Bretagne | **6e** -

Crabe Marteau | **17e** 20

BURGUNDY

Comptoir Marguery | **13e** 21

Ma Bourgogne | **4e** 19

Tante Louise | **8e** 23

CORSICA

Main d'Or | **11e** 22

Z Villa Corse | **multi.** 21

LYON

Aub. Pyrénées | **11e** 24

Z Benoît | **4e** 23

Chez René | **5e** 19

Duc de Richelieu | **12e** 22

Lyonnais | **2e** 22

Moissonnier | **5e** 24

Opportun | **14e** 22

NORTHERN FRANCE

Graindorge | **17e** 23

Petites Sorcières | **14e** 25

PROVENCE

Bastide Odéon | **6e** 20

Casa Olympe | **9e** 23

Chez Janou | **3e** 21

Marius | **16e** 25

Petit Niçois | **7e** 20

SOUTHWEST

Afaria | **15e** 23

Assiette | **14e** 19

Aub. Pyrénées | **11e** 24

Bistrot/l'Oulette | **4e** 22

Cerisaie | **14e** 23

D'Chez Eux | **7e** 24

Domaine/Lintillac | **multi.** 20

Fins Gourmets | **7e** 18

Z Fontaine de Mars | **7e** 22

Z Hélène Darroze | **6e** 26

Languedoc | **5e** 21

Lescure | **1er** 19

Mesturet | **2e** 16

Z Oulette | **12e** 26

Rosa Bonheur | **19e** 16

Sarladais | **8e** 23

Trou Gascon | **12e** 25

SEAFOOD

Antoine | **16e**	22
NEW Atao | **17e**	–
Ballon/Coquillages | **17e**	–
Z Bar à Huîtres | **multi.**	21
Bistrot du Dôme | **multi.**	22
Brass. Lutetia | **6e**	19
Cagouille | **14e**	23
Z 144 Petrossian | **7e**	24
Comptoir/Mers | **4e**	23
Z Coupole | **14e**	18
Crabe Marteau | **17e**	20
Dessirier | **17e**	24
Z Divellec | **7e**	26
Dôme | **14e**	22
Z Duc | **14e**	28
Ecaille de Fontaine | **2e**	–
Ecailler du Bistrot | **11e**	25
Ecume St-Honoré | **1er**	23
Européen | **12e**	20
Fables/Fontaine | **7e**	25
Fish La Boiss. | **6e**	21
Fontaine Gaillon | **2e**	21
Garnier | **8e**	22
Gaya | **7e**	24
Goumard | **1er**	23
Grand Café | **9e**	19
Huîtrier | **17e**	22
Luna | **8e**	26
Marée | **8e**	23
Marée Passy | **16e**	22
Marius | **16e**	25
Marius et Janette | **8e**	23
Marty | **5e**	20
Mascotte | **18e**	20
Méditerranée | **6e**	22
Petit Marius | **8e**	20
Pétrus | **17e**	23
Pichet de Paris | **8e**	22
Prunier | **multi.**	24
Rech | **17e**	22
Sarladais | **8e**	23
Stella | **16e**	21
Terminus Nord | **10e**	18
35° Ouest | **7e**	22
Vin et Marée | **multi.**	21
21 | **6e**	23
Wepler | **18e**	20

SHELLFISH

Ballon des Ternes | **17e**	19
Ballon/Coquillages | **17e**	–
Z Bar à Huîtres | **multi.**	21
Charlot - Roi/Coquillages | **9e**	21
Dôme | **14e**	22
Z Duc | **14e**	28
Ecaille de Fontaine | **2e**	–
Ecailler du Bistrot | **11e**	25
Ecume St-Honoré | **1er**	23
Garnier | **8e**	22
Grand Café | **9e**	19
Z Huîtrerie Régis | **6e**	26
Huîtrier | **17e**	22
Marée | **8e**	23
Marius | **16e**	25
Marius et Janette | **8e**	23
Marty | **5e**	20
Mascotte | **18e**	20
Pichet de Paris | **8e**	22
Rech | **17e**	22
Stella | **16e**	21

STEAK

(See also Steakhouses in Other Cuisines)

Boeuf Couronné | **19e**	23
Boucherie Roulière | **6e**	26
Gourmets/Ternes | **8e**	23
Z Relais/l'Entrecôte | **multi.**	22
Relais de Venise | **17e**	23
Z Severo | **14e**	26

WINE BARS/BISTROS

NEW Albion | **10e**	–
Bacchantes | **9e**	21
Baratin | **20e**	24
Baron Rouge | **12e**	18
Bien Décidé | **6e**	–
Bistrot/Vins Mélac | **11e**	18
Bistrot/Sommelier | **8e**	22

Bons Crus | **1er**	21
Bourguignon/Marais | **4e**	25
Café Burq | **18e**	21
Café du Passage | **11e**	-
Cantine/Quentin | **10e**	-
Cave Schmidt | **15e**	23
Caves Pétrissans | **17e**	23
Cloche/Halles | **1er**	18
Clown Bar | **11e**	15
Couleurs/Vigne | **15e**	-
Crémerie | **6e**	21
Crudus | **1er**	-
NEW Dans les Landes | **5e**	23
Ecluse | **multi.**	17
Enoteca | **4e**	22
NEW Entrée/Artistes | **11e**	-
Fines Gueules | **1er**	20
NEW Jaja | **4e**	17
Jeu de Quilles | **14e**	-
Juveniles | **1er**	15
Legrand Filles/Fils | **2e**	21
Mauzac | **5e**	15
NEW Passage | **11e**	-
Quedubon | **19e**	18
Racines | **2e**	20
Rubis | **1er**	19
NEW Verjus | **1er**	-
Verre Bouteille | **17e**	19
Verre Volé | **10e**	20
Vin Chai Moi | **1er**	-
NEW Vivant | **10e**	24
Willi's Wine | **1er**	20

Other Cuisines

Includes names, locations and Food ratings.

AMERICAN

NEW Blend | 2e — -
NEW Camion Qui Fume | Location Varies — -
NEW Floréal | 10e — -
NEW Maison Mère | 9e — -
Ralph's | 6e — 17
NEW Verjus | 1er — -

ARGENTINEAN

Anahi | 3e — 19
El Palenque | 5e — 22

ASIAN

Z Guilo-Guilo | 18e — 27
Oth Sombath | 8e — 23
Passiflore | 16e — 23
Z Yam'Tcha | 1er — 26
NEW Yoom | 6e — -

BELGIAN

Graindorge | 17e — 23

BRITISH

Rose Bakery | multi. — 22

BURGERS

NEW Blend | 2e — -
NEW Camion Qui Fume | Location Varies — -
NEW Comptoir/Brice | 10e — -
NEW Maison Mère | 9e — -
Ralph's | 6e — 17

CAMBODIAN

Coin/Gourmets | multi. — 23
Mousson | 1er — -

CAVIAR

Z Caviar Kaspia | 8e — 26
Z 144 Petrossian | 7e — 24
Maison du Caviar | 8e — 25
Prunier | multi. — 24

CHINESE

(* dim sum specialist)

Chen Soleil d'Est | 15e — -
Chez Ly | 17e — 25
Chez Vong | 1er — 23
Davé | 1er — 17
Diep | 8e — 21
Mirama | 5e — 22
Nouveau Village | 13e — 19
Shan Gout | 12e — -
NEW Shang Palace | 16e — 24
Tang | 16e — 22
Tong Yen | 8e — 22
Tricotin | 13e — 19
Tsé-Yang | 16e — 22
NEW Yoom* | 9e — -

DANISH

Copenhague | 8e — 23
Flora Danica | 8e — 21
Petite Sirène | 9e — 25

DESSERT

Café Lenôtre | 8e — 23
Soufflé | 1er — 22

EASTERN EUROPEAN

Chez Marianne | 4e — 19

ECLECTIC

NEW Braisenville | 9e — -
Café Rouge | 3e — 19
Chez Prune | 10e — 15
Costes | 1er — 18
Eugène | 8e — 18
Ferdi | 1er — 21
Fumoir | 1er — 18
Georges | 4e — 17
KGB | 6e — 23
Kong | 1er — 16
Market | 8e — 22
Muscade | 1er — -
Nanashi | multi. — -

OTHER CUISINES

- Relais Plaza | 8e — 25
- Z Ze Kitchen Galerie | 6e — 25

GREEK

- Délices/Aphrodite | 5e — 20
- Mavrommatis | 5e — 22

INDIAN

- Annapurna | 8e — 23
- Z Chamarré Mont. | 18e — 26
- Maharajah | 5e — 23
- Ravi | 7e — –
- Yugaraj | 6e — 20

ISRAELI

- Z As/Fallafel | 4e — 23

ITALIAN

(N=Northern; S=Southern)

- Al Taglio | 11e — 22
- Assaggio | 1er — 22
- Bartolo | 6e — 20
- Bellini | 16e — 21
- Bistro Poulbot | 18e — 23
- Briciola | S | 3e — 19
- Café de la Jatte | **Neuilly** — 18
- NEW Caffe Burlot/Costes | 8e — –
- Caffé dei Cioppi | 11e — 25
- Caffé Toscano | 7e — 19
- Cailloux | 13e — 22
- Casa Bini | N | 6e — 23
- Cherche Midi | 6e — 22
- Chez Vincent | 19e — 23
- Cibus | 1er — –
- Corte | 1er — –
- Crudus | 1er — –
- Emporio Armani | N | 6e — 19
- Enoteca | 4e — 22
- Findi | 8e — 21
- Finzi | N | 8e — 19
- Gli Angeli | 3e — 20
- Z Grand Venise | 15e — 26
- I Golosi | 9e — 23
- Il Barone | 14e — 22
- Mori Venice | N | 2e — 21
- Ostéria | 4e — 24
- Perron | S | 7e — –
- Pizza Chic | 6e — 21
- Romantica | **Clichy** — 22
- Rughetta | 18e — 21
- Sale e Pepe | S | 18e — 21
- NEW Sassotondo | N | 11e — –
- Sormani | 17e — 24
- Stresa | 8e — 22
- Zébra Square | 16e — 16

JAPANESE

(* sushi specialist)

- Aida | 7e — 25
- Azabu | 6e — 24
- Benkay* | 15e — 25
- Bizan* | 2e — –
- Cartes Postales | 1er — –
- Concert/Cuisine | 15e — –
- Foujita* | 1er — 25
- Z Guilo-Guilo | 18e — 27
- Higuma | 1er — 20
- Isami* | 4e — 25
- Izakaya Issé* | 1er — 23
- Kai | 1er — 25
- Kaïten* | 8e — 22
- Kifune* | 17e — 23
- Kiku* | 9e — –
- Kinugawa/Hanawa* | 1er — 24
- Nanashi | **multi.** — –
- Orient-Extrême* | 6e — 23
- Oto-Oto* | 6e — –
- Shu | 6e — 25
- Sola | 5e — 27
- Tsukizi* | 6e — 22
- Yen | 6e — 22

LAOTIAN

- Lao Lane Xang | 13e — 22

LEBANESE

- Al Dar | **multi.** — 22
- Fakhr el Dine | 16e — 25
- Liza | 2e — 24

MAURITIAN

- Z Chamarré Mont. | 18e — 26

MEDITERRANEAN

Cuizine | 11e -

MEXICAN

Anahuacalli | 5e 23
NEW Candelaria | 3e -

MIDDLE EASTERN

Chez Marianne | 4e 19

MOROCCAN

Atlas | 5e 21
Chez Omar | 3e 19
El Mansour | 8e 21
Mansouria | 11e 21
Martel | 10e 21
Oum el Banine | 16e 22
404 | 3e 20
Timgad | 17e 22

NOODLE SHOPS

Higuma | 1er 20

NORTH AFRICAN

Boule Rouge | 9e 21

PIZZA

Al Taglio | 11e 22
Bartolo | 6e 20
Briciola | 3e 19
Mama Shelter | 20e 16
Pizza Chic | 6e 21
Rughetta | 18e 21
Sale e Pepe | 18e 21

PORTUGUESE

Saudade | 1er 16

RUSSIAN

Z Caviar Kaspia | 8e 26
Daru | 8e 19
Maison du Caviar | 8e 25

SEAFOOD

Copenhague | 8e 23

SMALL PLATES

(See also Spanish tapas specialist)
NEW Braisenville | Eclectic | 9e -
NEW Passage | French | 11e -

SPANISH

(* tapas specialist)
Fogón* | 6e 23

STEAKHOUSES

(See also Steak under French Cuisines)
Anahi | 3e 19
El Palenque | 5e 22

TEAROOMS

Muscade | 1er -

THAI

Chez Ly | 17e 25
Chieng Mai | 5e 22
Diep | 8e 21
Khun Akorn | 11e 21
Lao Lane Xang | 13e 22
Lao Siam | 19e 22
Nouveau Village | 13e 19
Oth Sombath | 8e 23
Reuan Thai | 11e -
Tricotin | 13e 19

TUNISIAN

Ebouillanté | 4e 22

VEGETARIAN

Mon Vieil Ami | 4e 23

VIETNAMESE

Coin/Gourmets | multi. 23
Davé | 1er 17
Diep | 8e 21
Kim Anh | 15e 23
Lac-Hong | 16e 21
Lao Lane Xang | 13e 22
Mai Do | 6e -
Palanquin | 6e 24
Suave | 13e -
Tan Dinh | 7e 22
Tricotin | 13e 19

1st Arrondissement

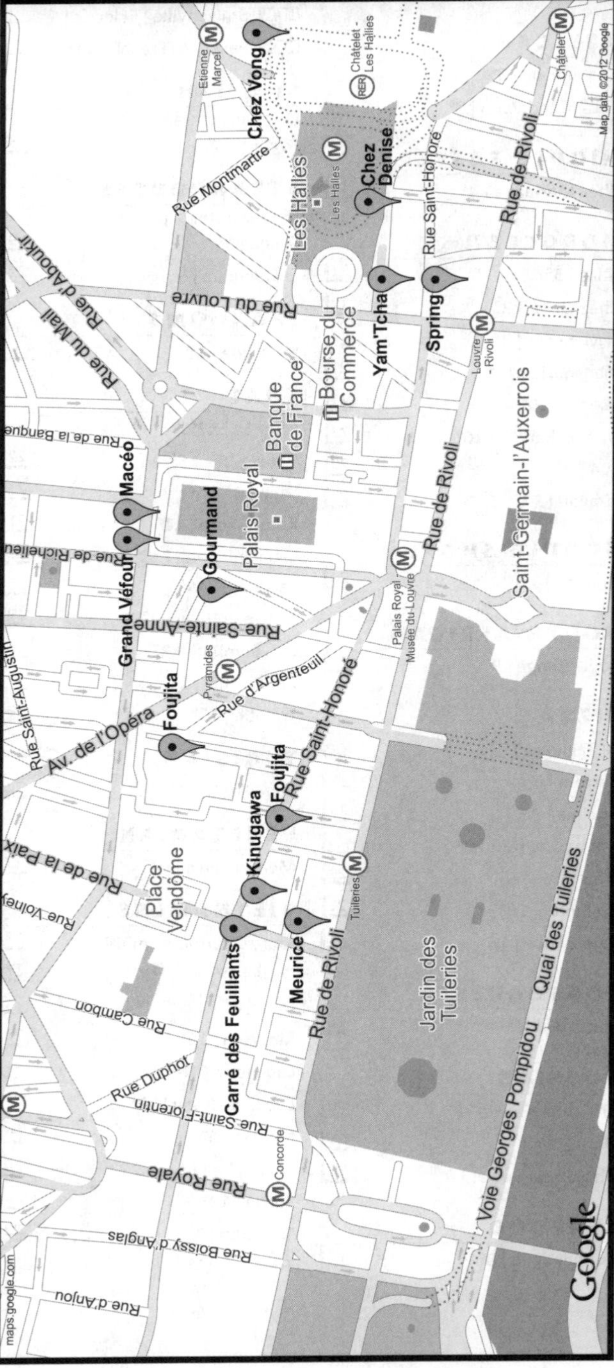

Chez Vong
Chez Denise
Yam'Tcha
Spring
Maceó
Grand Véfour
Gourmand
Foujita
Kinugawa
Carré des Feuillants
Meurice
Les Halles
Châtelet - Les Halles
Etienne Marcel
Châtelet
Rue Montmartre
Rue d'Aboukir
Rue du Mail
Rue du Louvre
Rue Saint-Honoré
Rue de Rivoli
Bourse du Commerce
Banque de France
Rue de la Banque
Palais Royal
Rue de Richelieu
Rue Sainte-Anne
Pyramides
Rue d'Argenteuil
Av. de l'Opéra
Rue Saint-Augustin
Palais Royal - Musée du Louvre
Louvre - Rivoli
Saint-Germain-l'Auxerrois
Rue de la Paix
Place Vendôme
Rue Volney
Rue Cambon
Rue Duphot
Rue Saint-Florentin
Tuileries
Jardin des Tuileries
Quai des Tuileries
Voie Georges Pompidou
Rue Royale
Concorde
Rue Boissy d'Anglas
Rue d'Anjou
maps.google.com
Map data ©2012 Google
Google

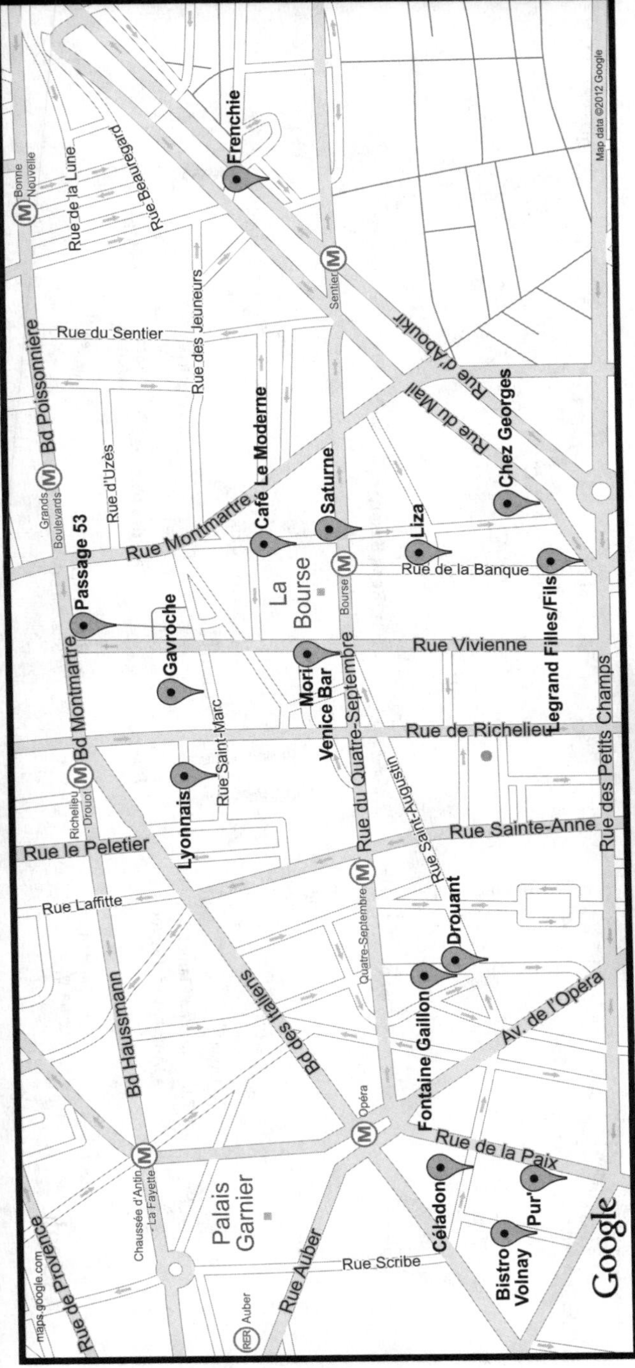

Frenchie
Café Le Moderne
Saturne
Liza
Chez Georges
Legrand Filles/Fils
Passage 53
Gavroche
Mori
Venice Bar
Lyonnais
Drouant
Fontaine Gaillon
Céladon
Pur'
Bistro Volnay
Rue de la Lune
Rue Beauregard
Rue du Sentier
Rue des Jeuneurs
Rue d'Aboukir
Rue du Mail
Rue Montmartre
Rue d'Uzès
Bd Poissonnière
Bonne Nouvelle
Grands Boulevards
Sentier
La Bourse
Bourse
Rue de la Banque
Rue Vivienne
Rue de Richelieu
Rue Saint-Marc
Bd Montmartre
Richelieu - Drouot
Rue le Peletier
Rue Laffitte
Rue du Quatre-Septembre
Rue Saint-Augustin
Rue Sainte-Anne
Rue des Petits Champs
Quatre-Septembre
Bd des Italiens
Av. de l'Opéra
Bd Haussmann
Opéra
Rue de la Paix
Chaussée d'Antin - La Fayette
Palais Garnier
Rue Scribe
Rue Auber
Auber
RER
Rue de Provence
maps.google.com
Map data ©2012 Google
Google

MAPS

3rd Arrondissement

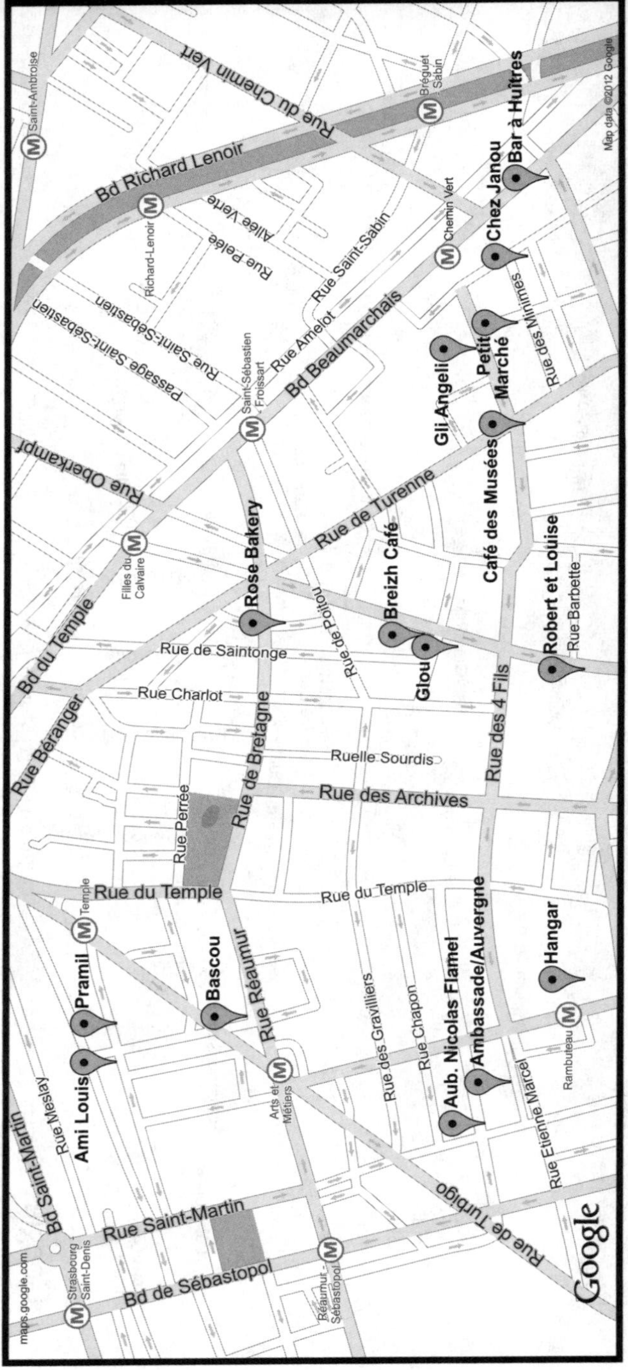

Bd Richard Lenoir
Rue du Chemin Vert
Saint-Ambroise
Bréguet Sabin
Map data ©2012 Google
Bar à Huîtres
Chez Janou
Chemin Vert
Richard-Lenoir
Allée Verte
Rue Pelée
Rue Saint-Sabin
Rue Saint-Sébastien
Passage Saint-Sébastien
Rue Amelot
Bd Beaumarchais
Saint-Sébastien Froissart
Rue des Minimes
Petit Marché
Gli Angeli
Café des Musées
Rue Oberkampf
Rue de Turenne
Rose Bakery
Breizh Café
Robert et Louise
Rue Barbette
Filles du Calvaire
Bd du Temple
Rue de Poitou
Rue de Saintonge
Glou
Rue Charlot
Rue Béranger
Rue de Bretagne
Rue des 4 Fils
Ruelle Sourdis
Rue des Archives
Rue Perrée
Rue du Temple
Rue du Temple
Temple
Rue Réaumur
Bascou
Pramil
Hangar
Ambassade/Auvergne
Aub. Nicolas Flamel
Rue Chapon
Rue des Gravilliers
Rambuteau
Ami Louis
Rue Meslay
Arts et Métiers
Rue Etienne Marcel
Bd Saint-Martin
Rue Saint-Martin
Rue de Turbigo
Strasbourg Saint-Denis
Bd de Sébastopol
Réaumur Sébastopol
maps.google.com
Google

4th Arrondissement

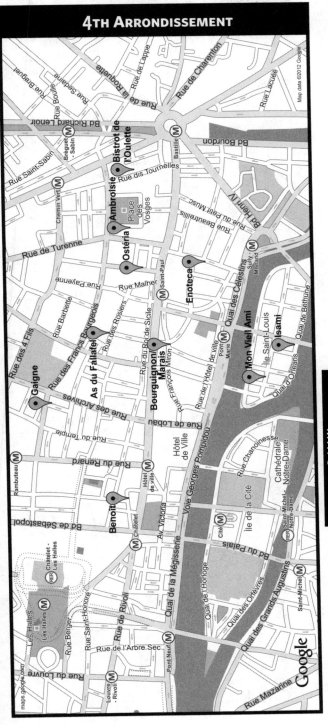

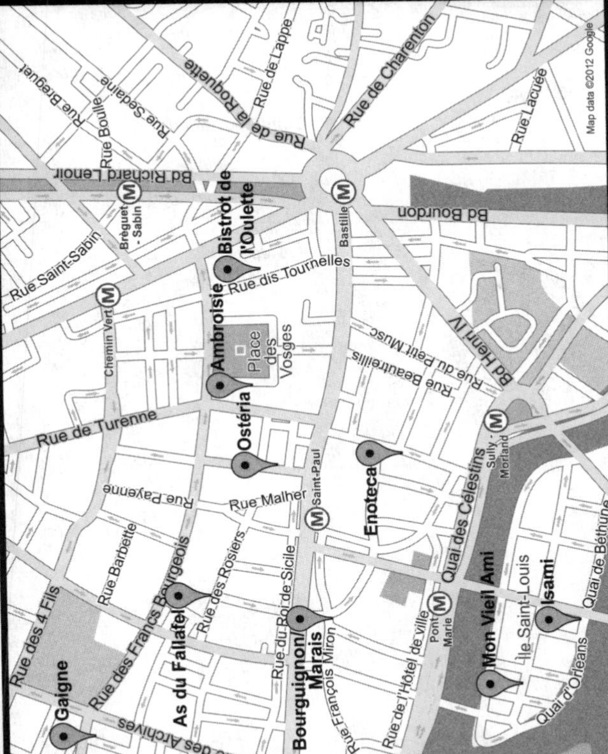
Rue de Charenton
Rue de la Roquette
Rue de Lappe
Rue Lacuée
Rue Breguet
Rue Sedaine
Rue Boulle
Bd Richard Lenoir
Bd Bourdon
Bastille
Breguet - Sabin
Bistrot de l'Oulette
Ambroisie
Rue dis Tournelles
Rue Saint-Sabin
Chemin Vert
Place des Vosges
Rue du Petit Musc
Rue Beautreillis
Bd Henri IV
Ostéria
Rue de Turenne
Sully - Morland
Enoteca
Rue Payenne
Rue Malher
Saint-Paul
Quai des Célestins
Rue Barbette
Rue des Francs Bourgeois
Rue des Rosiers
Rue du Roi de Sicile
Mon Vieil Ami
Ile Saint-Louis
Isami
Quai de Béthune
Rue des 4 Fils
As du Fallafel
Bourguignon/ Marais
Rue François Miron
Rue de l'Hôtel de ville
Pont Marie
Quai d'Orleans
Gaigne
Rue des Archives
Rue de Lobau
Rue du Temple
Hôtel de Ville
Voie Georges Pompidou
Rue Chanoinesse
Cathédrale Notre-Dame
Rambuteau
Rue du Renard
Hôtel de ville
Ile de la Cité
Benoît
Av. Victoria
Bd de Sébastopol
Châtelet
Cité
Saint-Michel - Notre-Dame
RER
Châtelet - Les Halles
Bd du Palais
Quai de la Mégisserie
Quai de l'Horloge
Quai des Orfèvres
Quai des Grands Augustins
Saint-Michel
Les Halles
Rue Berger
Rue Saint-Honoré
Rue de Rivoli
Rue de l'Arbre Sec
Pont-Neuf
Rue du Louvre
Louvre - Rivoli
Rue Mazarine
maps.google.com
Google
Map data ©2012 Google

MAPS

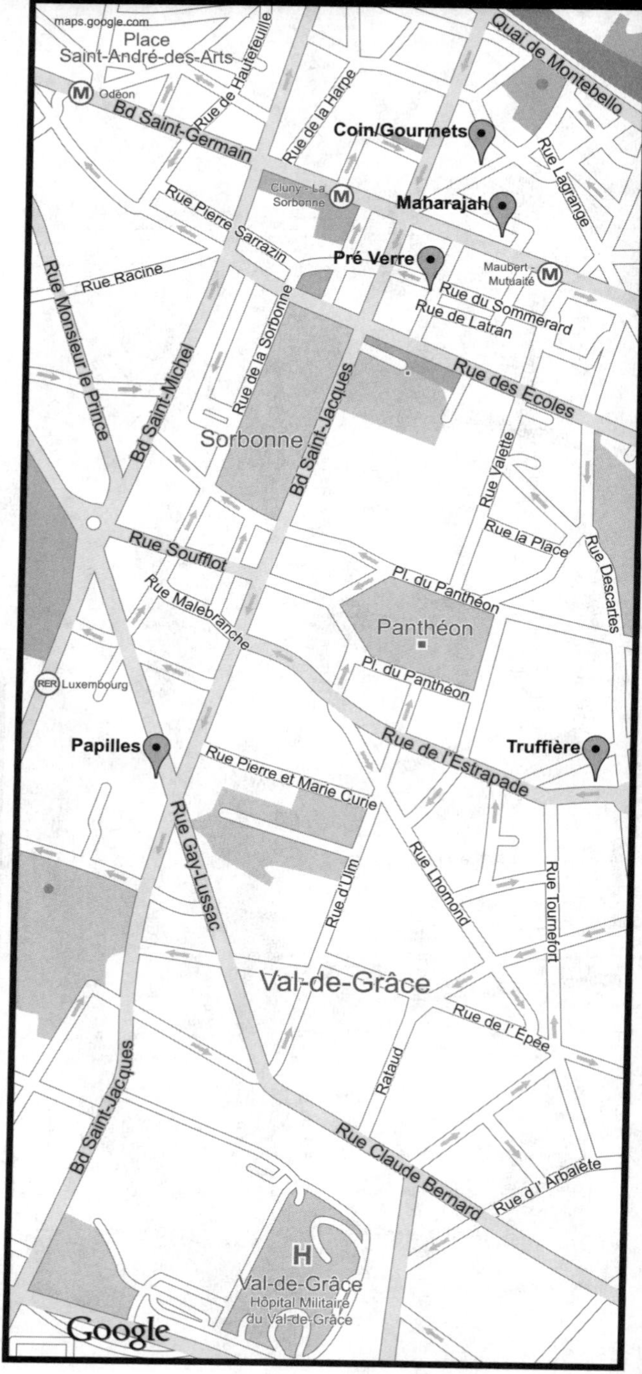
maps.google.com
Place Saint-André-des-Arts
Odéon
Bd Saint-Germain
Rue de Hautefeuille
Rue de la Harpe
Quai de Montebello
Coin/Gourmets
Rue Lagrange
Cluny - La Sorbonne
Maharajah
Rue Pierre Sarrazin
Pré Verre
Maubert - Mutualité
Rue Racine
Rue du Sommerard
Rue de Latran
Rue Monsieur le Prince
Rue de la Sorbonne
Bd Saint-Michel
Bd Saint-Jacques
Rue des Ecoles
Sorbonne
Rue Valette
Rue la Place
Rue Soufflot
Rue Descartes
Pl. du Panthéon
Rue Malebranche
Panthéon
Pl. du Panthéon
Luxembourg
Papilles
Truffière
Rue de l'Estrapade
Rue Pierre et Marie Curie
Rue Gay-Lussac
Rue Lhomond
Rue d'Ulm
Rue Tournefort
Val-de-Grâce
Rue de l' Epée
Rataud
Bd Saint-Jacques
Rue Claude Bernard
Rue d' Arbalète
Val-de-Grâce
Hôpital Militaire du Val-de-Grâce
Google

5th Arrondissement

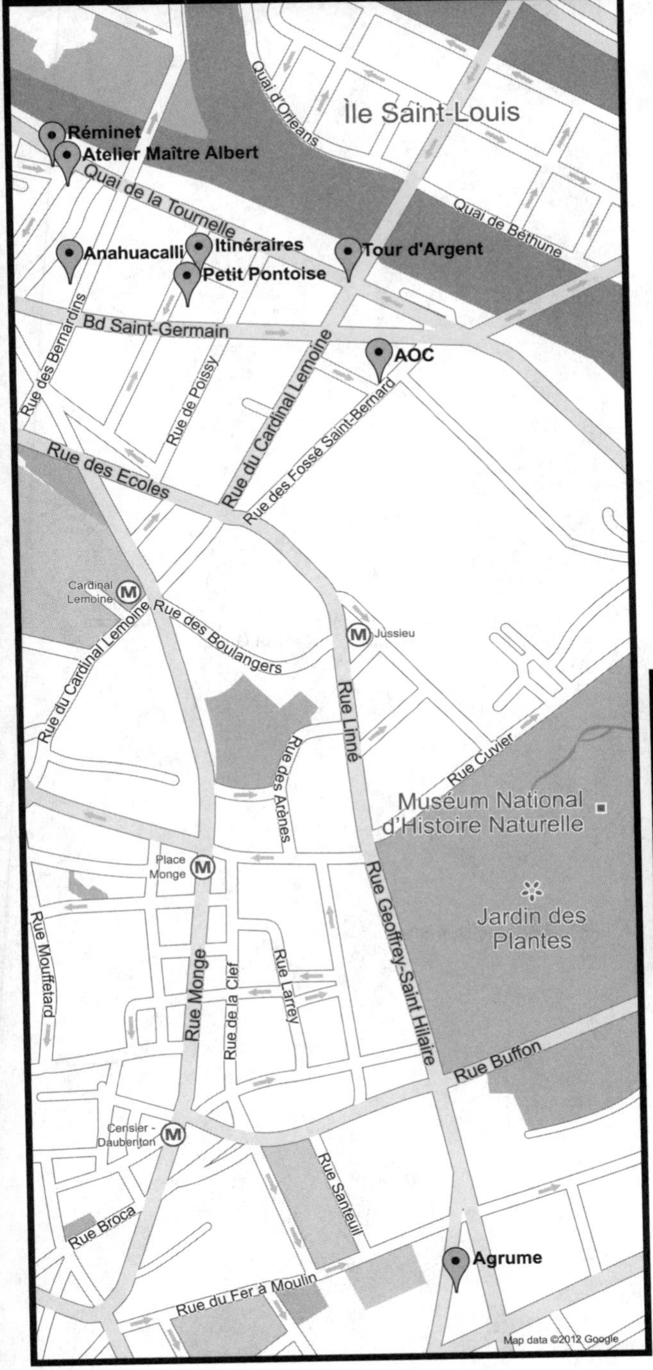

Île Saint-Louis
Quai d'Orléans
Quai de Béthune
Réminet
Atelier Maître Albert
Quai de la Tournelle
Anahuacalli
Itinéraires
Petit Pontoise
Tour d'Argent
Bd Saint-Germain
AOC
Rue des Bernardins
Rue de Poissy
Rue du Cardinal Lemoine
Rue des Fossé Saint-Bernard
Rue des Ecoles
Cardinal Lemoine
Rue des Boulangers
Jussieu
Rue Linné
Rue des Arènes
Rue Cuvier
Muséum National d'Histoire Naturelle
Place Monge
Jardin des Plantes
Rue Mouffetard
Rue Monge
Rue de la Clef
Rue Larrey
Rue Geoffrey-Saint Hilaire
Rue Buffon
Censier - Daubenton
Rue Santeuil
Rue Broca
Agrume
Rue du Fer à Moulin
Map data ©2012 Google

MAPS

6th Arrondissement

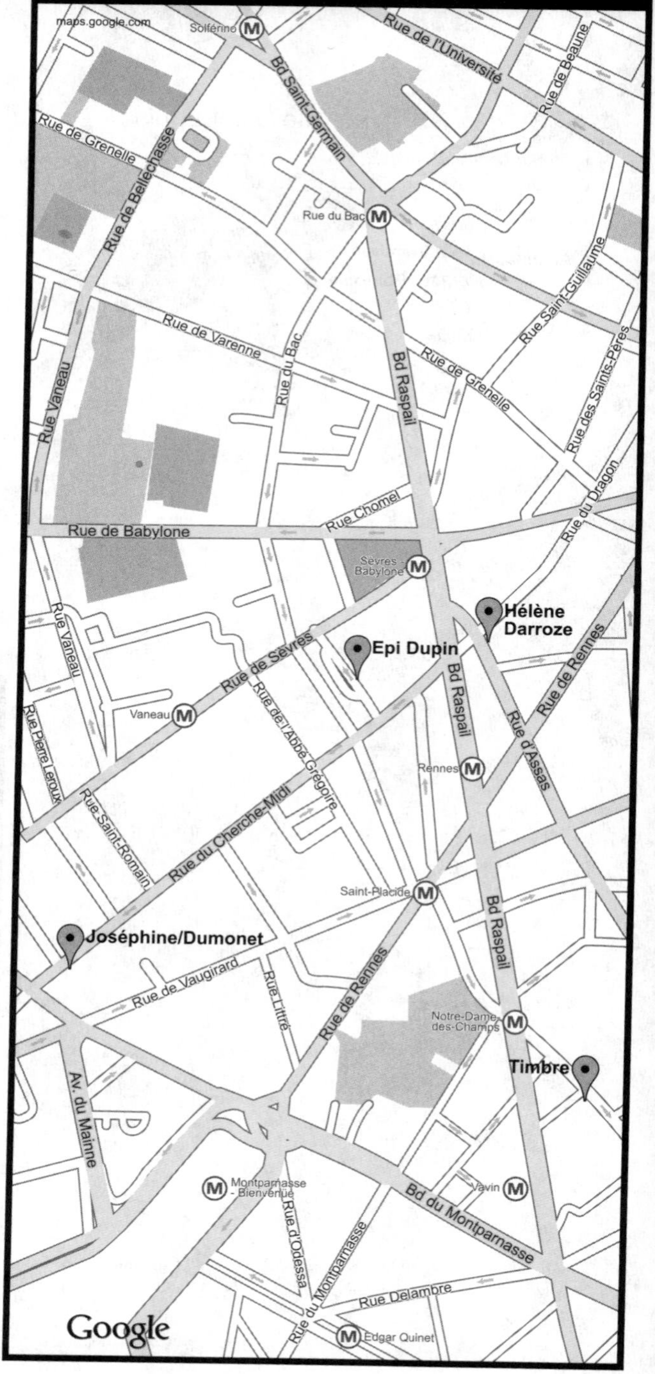
maps.google.com
Solférino
Rue de l'Université
Rue de Beaune
Bd Saint-Germain
Rue de Grenelle
Rue de Bellechasse
Rue du Bac
Rue Saint-Guillaume
Rue de Varenne
Rue de Grenelle
Rue des Saints-Pères
Rue Vaneau
Rue du Bac
Bd Raspail
Rue Chomel
Rue du Dragon
Rue de Babylone
Sèvres-Babylone
Hélène Darroze
Epi Dupin
Rue Vaneau
Rue de Sèvres
Rue de l'Abbé Grégoire
Bd Raspail
Rue de Rennes
Rue d'Assas
Vaneau
Rue Pierre Leroux
Rennes
Rue-Saint-Romain
Rue du Cherche-Midi
Saint-Placide
Bd Raspail
Joséphine/Dumonet
Rue de Vaugirard
Rue Littré
Rue de Rennes
Notre-Dame-des-Champs
Timbre
Av. du Mainne
Montparnasse - Bienvenüe
Rue d'Odessa
Vavin
Bd du Montparnasse
Rue du Montparnasse
Rue Delambre
Edgar Quinet
Google

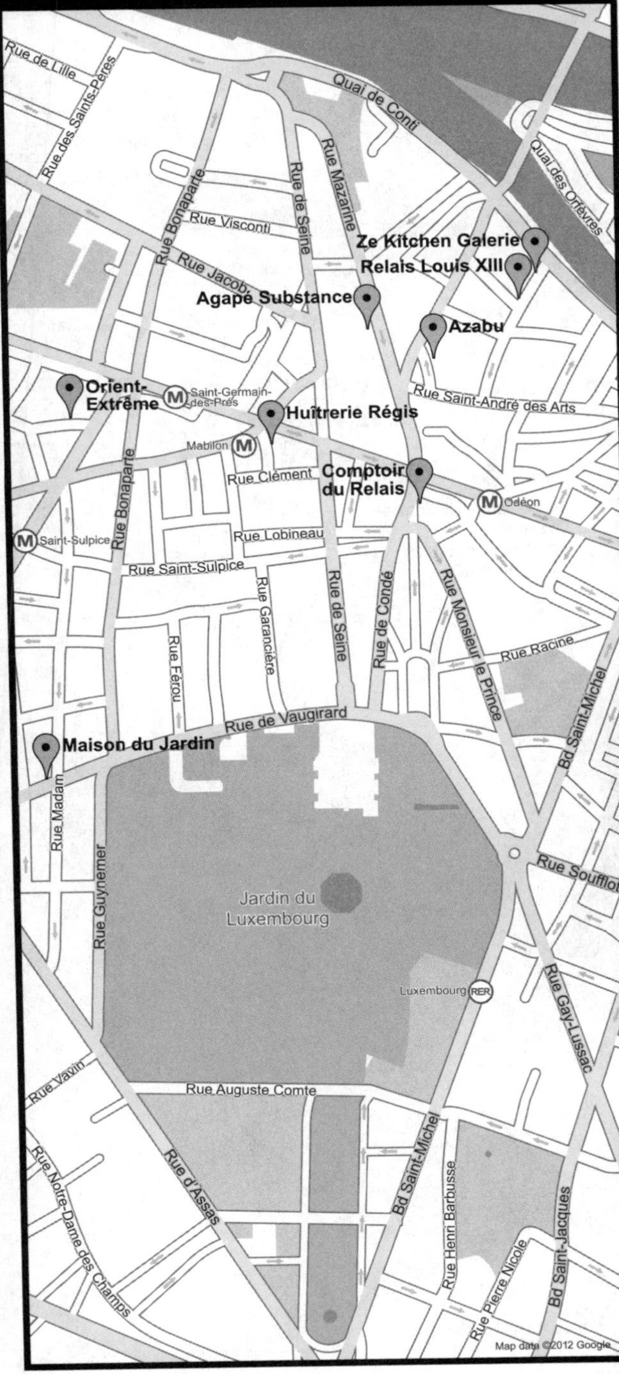
Rue de Lille
Rue des Saints-Pères
Quai de Conti
Quai des Orfèvres
Rue Mazarine
Rue de Seine
Rue Bonaparte
Rue Visconti
Rue Jacob
Ze Kitchen Galerie
Relais Louis XIII
Agapé Substance
Azabu
Rue Saint-André des Arts
Orient-Extrême
Saint-Germain-des-Prés
Huîtrerie Régis
Mabillon
Rue Clément
Comptoir du Relais
Odéon
Saint-Sulpice
Rue Lobineau
Rue Saint-Sulpice
Rue Garancière
Rue de Condé
Rue Monsieur le Prince
Rue Racine
Rue Férou
Rue de Vaugirard
Bd Saint-Michel
Maison du Jardin
Rue Madam
Rue Soufflot
Jardin du Luxembourg
Rue Guynemer
Luxembourg RER
Rue Gay-Lussac
Rue Vavin
Rue Auguste Comte
Rue d'Assas
Rue Notre-Dame des Champs
Rue Henri Barbusse
Rue Pierre Nicole
Bd Saint-Jacques
Map data ©2012 Google

7th Arrondissement

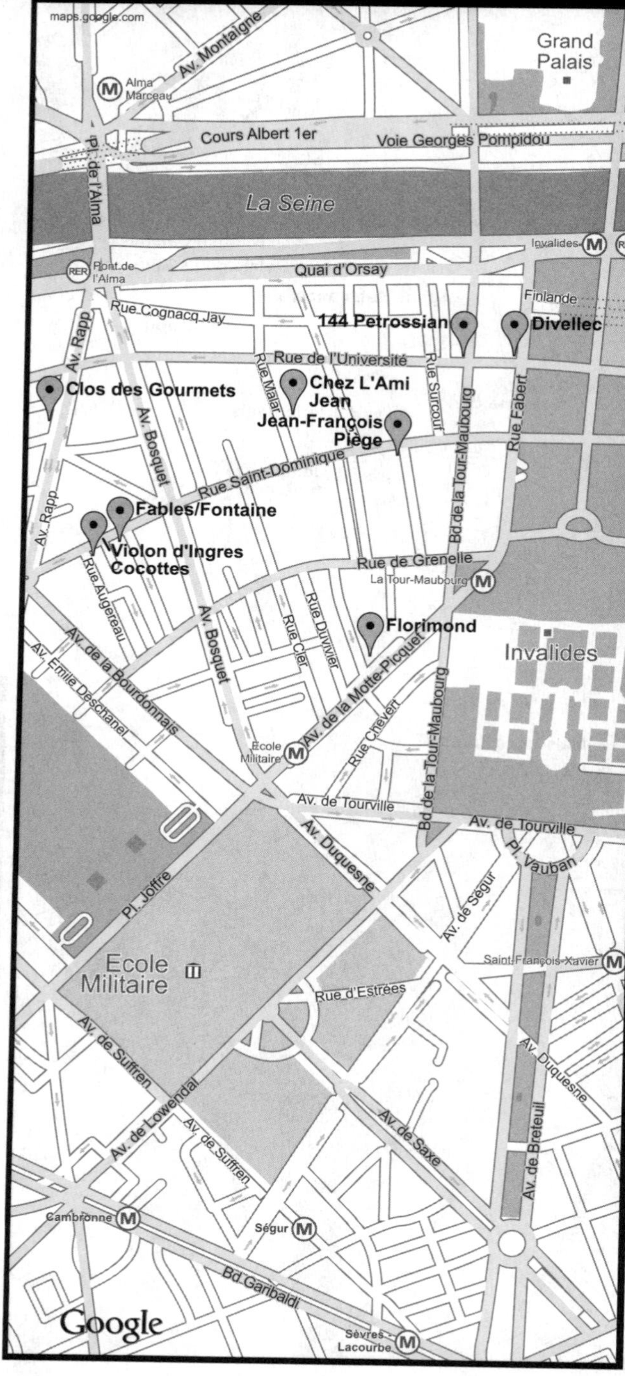
maps.google.com
Grand Palais
Av. Montaigne
Alma Marceau
Cours Albert 1er
Voie Georges Pompidou
Pl. de l'Alma
La Seine
Invalides
Pont de l'Alma
Quai d'Orsay
Finlande
Rue Cognacq Jay
144 Petrossian
Divellec
Av. Rapp
Rue de l'Université
Clos des Gourmets
Rue Malar
Chez L'Ami Jean
Rue Surcouf
Jean-François Piège
Av. Bosquet
Bd de la Tour-Maubourg
Rue Fabert
Rue Saint-Dominique
Fables/Fontaine
Violon d'Ingres
Cocottes
Rue Augereau
Rue de Grenelle
La Tour-Maubourg
Rue Cler
Rue Duvivier
Florimond
Invalides
Av. de la Bourdonnais
Av. Emile Deschanel
Av. de la Motte-Picquet
Rue Chevert
Ecole Militaire
Av. de Tourville
Av. Duquesne
Pl. Vauban
Pl. Joffre
Av. de Ségur
Saint-François-Xavier
Ecole Militaire
Rue d'Estrées
Av. de Suffren
Av. de Lowendal
Av. de Saxe
Av. de Breteuil
Cambronne
Ségur
Bd Garibaldi
Google
Sèvres Lacourbe

7th Arrondissement

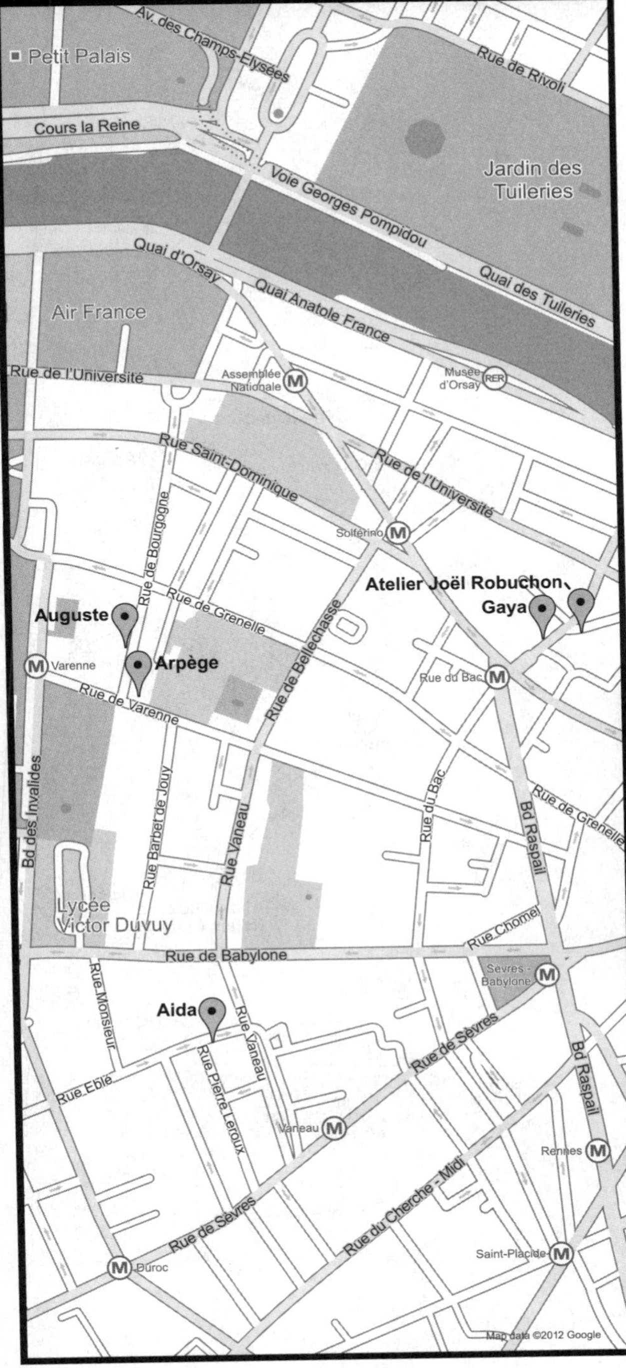

Petit Palais
Av. des Champs-Elysées
Rue de Rivoli
Cours la Reine
Jardin des Tuileries
Voie Georges Pompidou
Quai d'Orsay
Quai Anatole France
Quai des Tuileries
Air France
Rue de l'Université
Assemblée Nationale
Musée d'Orsay
RER
Rue Saint-Dominique
Rue de l'Université
Solférino
Rue de Bourgogne
Atelier Joël Robuchon
Gaya
Auguste
Rue de Grenelle
Rue de Bellechasse
Varenne
Arpège
Rue de Varenne
Rue du Bac
Bd des Invalides
Rue Barbet de Jouy
Rue Vaneau
Rue du Bac
Rue de Grenelle
Bd Raspail
Lycée Victor Duruy
Rue Chomel
Rue de Babylone
Sevres - Babylone
Rue Monsieur
Aida
Rue Vaneau
Rue de Sèvres
Rue Eblé
Rue Pierre Leroux
Bd Raspail
Vaneau
Rennes
Rue du Cherche - Midi
Rue de Sèvres
Saint-Placide
Duroc
Map data ©2012 Google

8th Arrondissement

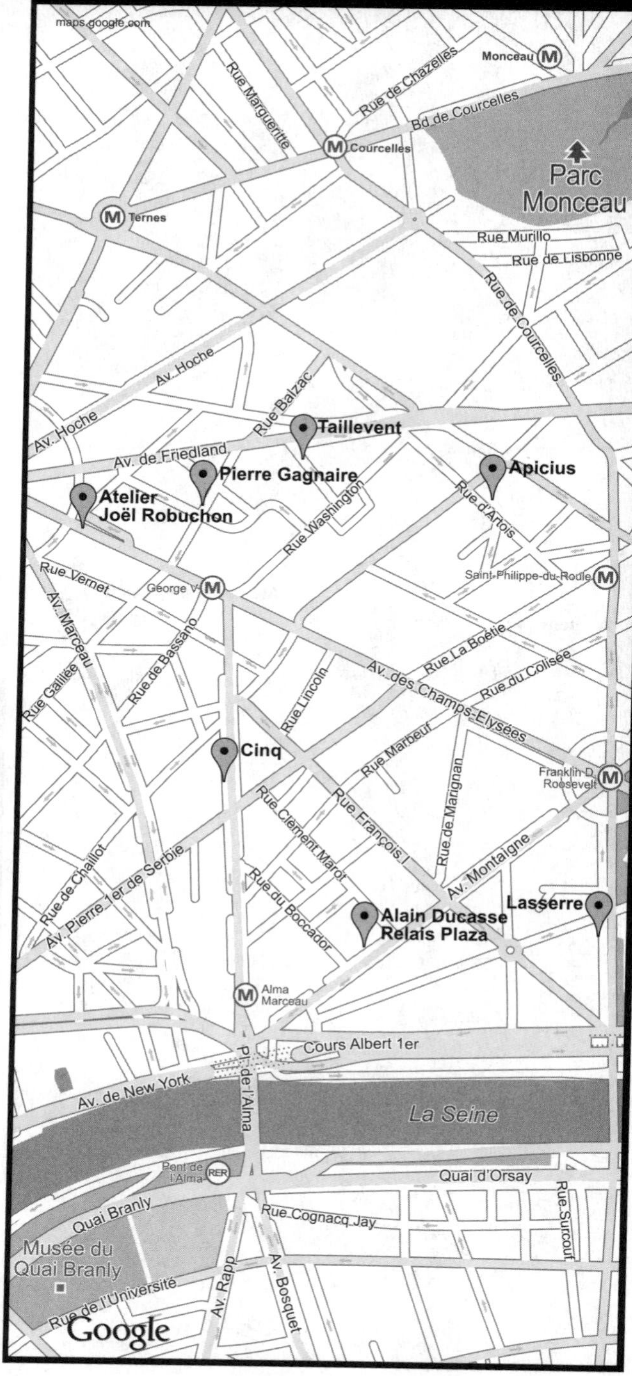

maps.google.com
Monceau
Rue de Chazelles
Bd de Courcelles
Rue Margueritte
Courcelles
Parc Monceau
Ternes
Rue Murillo
Rue de Lisbonne
Rue de Courcelles
Av. Hoche
Rue Balzac
Taillevent
Av. de Friedland
Pierre Gagnaire
Apicius
Atelier Joël Robuchon
Rue Washington
Rue d'Artois
Rue Vernet
George V
Saint-Philippe-du-Roule
Av. Marceau
Rue de Bassano
Rue La Boétie
Rue Galilée
Rue Lincoln
Av. des Champs-Elysées
Rue du Colisée
Cinq
Rue Marbeuf
Franklin D. Roosevelt
Rue Clément Marot
Rue François I
Rue de Marignan
Av. Montaigne
Rue de Chaillot
Av. Pierre 1er de Serbie
Rue du Boccador
Lasserre
Alain Ducasse Relais Plaza
Alma Marceau
Cours Albert 1er
Av. de New York
Pl. de l'Alma
La Seine
Pont de l'Alma
RER
Quai d'Orsay
Rue Surcouf
Quai Branly
Rue Cognacq Jay
Musée du Quai Branly
Rue de l'Université
Av. Rapp
Av. Bosquet
Google

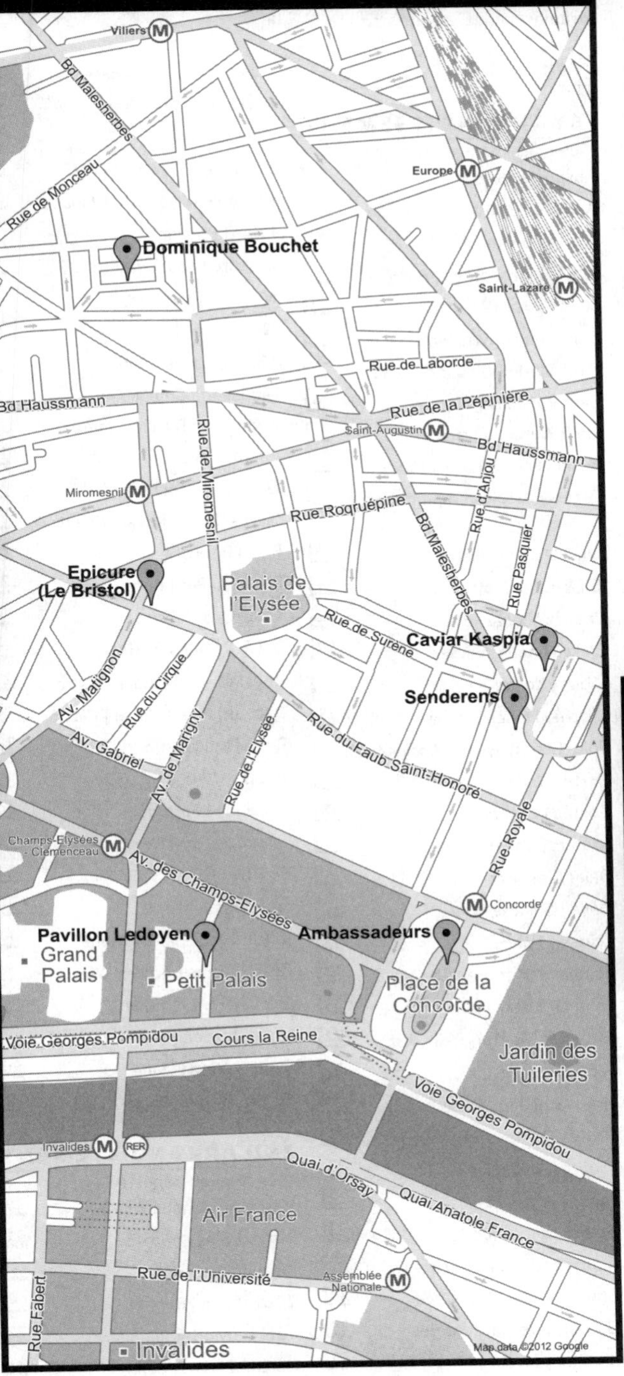
Villiers
Bd Malesherbes
Rue de Monceau
Europe
Dominique Bouchet
Saint-Lazare
Rue de Laborde
Bd Haussmann
Rue de la Pépinière
Saint-Augustin
Bd Haussmann
Rue de Miromesnil
Miromesnil
Rue Roqruépine
Bd Malesherbes
Rue d'Anjou
Rue Pasquier
Epicure
(Le Bristol)
Palais de
l'Elysée
Rue de Surène
Caviar Kaspia
Senderens
Av. Matignon
Rue du Cirque
Av. Gabriel
Av. de Marigny
Rue de l'Elysée
Rue du Faub Saint-Honoré
Rue Royale
Champs-Elysées - Clemenceau
Av. des Champs-Elysées
Concorde
Pavillon Ledoyen
Ambassadeurs
Grand
Palais
Petit Palais
Place de la
Concorde
Voie Georges Pompidou
Cours la Reine
Jardin des
Tuileries
Voie Georges Pompidou
Invalides
RER
Quai d'Orsay
Quai Anatole France
Air France
Rue de l'Université
Assemblée
Nationale
Rue Fabert
Invalides
Map data ©2012 Google

Locations

Includes names, cuisines and Food ratings.

Paris

1ST ARRONDISSEMENT

(See map on page 162)

Absinthe | *Bistro* 21
Ardoise | *Bistro* 23
Assaggio | *Italian* 22
NEW Bistronomes | *Bistro* -
Bons Crus | *Wine* 21
Brass. du Louvre | *Brass.* 19
Café Marly | *Classic/New Fr.* 17
Café Ruc | *Bistro* 15
NEW Camélia | *New Fr.* -
Z Carré/Feuillants | *Haute* 27
Cartes Postales | *Japanese/New Fr.* -
Chez Denise | *Bistro* 23
NEW Chez Flottes | *Brass.* -
Chez la Vieille | *Bistro* 23
Chez Vong | *Chinese* 23
Cibus | *Italian* -
Cloche/Halles | *Wine* 18
Coin/Gourmets | *Cambodian/Viet.* 23
Corte | *Italian* -
Costes | *Eclectic* 18
Crudus | *Italian/Wine* -
Dali | *Classic Fr.* -
Davé | *Chinese/Viet.* 17
Ecluse | *Wine* 17
Ecume St-Honoré | *Shellfish* 23
Epi d'Or | *Bistro* 19
Escargot Montorgueil | *Bistro* 22
Ferdi | *Eclectic* 21
Fines Gueules | *Wine* 20
Flottes O. Trement | *New Fr.* 21
Foujita | *Japanese* 25
Fumoir | *Eclectic* 18
Goumard | *Seafood* 23
Gourmand | *Classic/New Fr.* 25
Grand Louvre | *Classic Fr.* 20
Z Grand Véfour | *Haute* 28
Higuma | *Japanese* 20
Izakaya Issé | *Japanese* 23
Juveniles | *Wine Bar* 15
Kai | *Japanese* 25
NEW Kei | *New Fr.* 28
Kinugawa/Hanawa | *Japanese* 24
Kong | *Eclectic* 16
Lescure | *Southwest* 19
Macéo | *Classic Fr./New Fr.* 23
Z Meurice | *Haute* 28
Montagnards | *Alpine* 23
Mousson | *Cambodian* -
Muscade | *Eclectic/Tearoom* -
Pharamond | *Classic Fr.* 18
Z Pied de Cochon | *Brass.* 19
Pierre/Palais Royal | *Classic Fr.* 22
Pinxo | *New Fr.* 23
Poule au Pot | *Bistro* 22
Quai-Quai | *Bistro* 18
NEW Racines 2 | *Bistro* -
Régalade St-Honoré | *Bistro* 23
Rest. du Palais Royal | *Classic Fr.* 20
Rest. Paul | *Bistro* 18
Rubis | *Wine* 19
Saudade | *Portuguese* 16
Saut du Loup | *New Fr.* 13
Soufflé | *Classic Fr.* 22
Z Spring | *New Fr.* 27
NEW Sur Mesure | *Haute* -
NEW Verjus | *Amer./Wine* -
Vin Chai Moi | *Wine* -
Vin et Marée | *Seafood* 21
Willi's Wine | *Wine* 20
Z Yam'Tcha | *Asian/New Fr.* 26

2ND ARRONDISSEMENT

(See map on page 163)

Bistrot Vivienne | *Bistro* 19
Bistro Volnay | *Bistro* 21
Bizan | *Japanese* -
NEW Blend | *Burgers* -
Café Le Moderne | *Bistro* 22
Céladon | *Classic Fr.* 23

Z Chez Georges | *Bistro* 23
Crus/Bourgogne | *Bistro* 20
Domaine/Lintillac | *Southwest* 20
Drouant | *Classic Fr.* 23
Ecaille de Fontaine | *Shellfish* –
Fontaine Gaillon | *Classic Fr.* 21
Z Frenchie | *Bistro* 26
Gallopin | *Brass.* 20
Gavroche | *Bistro* 24
Grand Colbert | *Brass.* 19
NEW Gyoza Bar | *Japanese* –
Hédoniste | *Bistro* 22
Legrand Filles/Fils | *Wine* 21
Liza | *Lebanese* 24
Lyonnais | *Lyon* 22
Mémère Paulette | *Bistro* 23
Mesturet | *Southwest* 16
Mori Venice | *Italian* 21
Z Passage 53 | *Haute* 27
Pur' | *New Fr.* 24
Racines | *Wine* 20
Saotico | *New Fr.* –
Saturne | *New Fr.* 22
Vaudeville | *Brass.* 20
Versance | *Classic/New Fr.* –

3RD ARRONDISSEMENT

(See map on page 164)

Ambassade/Auv. | *Auvergne* 22
Z Ami Louis | *Bistro* 24
Anahi | *Argent./Steak* 19
Aub. Nicolas Flamel | *Classic Fr.* 21
Z Bar à Huîtres | *Seafood* 21
Bascou | *Basque* 23
Breizh Café | *Brittany* 22
Briciola | *Pizza* 19
Café des Musées | *Bistro* 20
Café Rouge | *Classic Fr./Eclectic* 19
NEW Candelaria | *Mex.* –
Chez Janou | *Provence* 21
Chez Jenny | *Alsace* 19
Chez Nénesse | *Classic Fr.* 21
Chez Omar | *Moroccan* 19
Derrière | *New Fr.* 15
Gli Angeli | *Italian* 20
Glou | *Bistro* 20
Hangar | *Classic Fr.* 23
Nanashi | *Eclectic* –
Petit Marché | *New Fr.* 23
Z Pramil | *Bistro* 28
404 | *Moroccan* 20
Robert et Louise | *Bistro* 20
Rose Bakery | *Bakery/British* 22

4TH ARRONDISSEMENT

(See map on page 165)

Z Ambroisie | *Haute* 27
Z As/Fallafel | *Israeli* 23
Z Benoît | *Lyon* 23
Bistrot/l'Oulette | *Southwest* 22
Bistrot du Dôme | *Seafood* 22
Z Bofinger | *Brass.* 19
Bourguignon/Marais | *Wine* 25
Brass./l'Ile St-Louis | *Brass.* 19
Chez Julien | *Bistro* 21
Chez Marianne | *Mideast.* 19
Claude Colliot | *New Fr.* 23
Comptoir/Mers | *Seafood* 23
Coupe Gorge | *Bistro* –
Dôme du Marais | *New Fr.* 19
Ebouillanté | *Classic Fr./Tea* 22
Enoteca | *Italian/Wine* 22
Flore en l'Ile | *Classic Fr.* 17
Gaigne | *New Fr.* 24
Georges | *Eclectic* 17
Ilot Vache | *Classic Fr.* 20
Isami | *Japanese* 25
NEW Jaja | *Bistro* 17
Ma Bourgogne | *Burgundy* 19
Mon Vieil Ami | *Bistro* 23
Nos Ancêtres les Gaulois | *Classic Fr.* 13
Ostéria | *Italian* 24
Taverne/Sgt. Recruteur | *Classic Fr.* 17
Trumilou | *Bistro* 20
Vins/Pyrénées | *Classic Fr.* 17

5TH ARRONDISSEMENT

(See map on page 166)

Agrume | *New Fr.* 24
Al Dar | *Lebanese* 22
Anahuacalli | *Mex.* 23
AOC | *Bistro* 23
Atelier Maître Albert | *Bistro* 23
Atlas | *Moroccan* 21
Z Bar à Huîtres | *Seafood* 21
NEW Bistro/Gastronomes | *Bistro* 23
Brass. Balzar | *Brass.* 18
Buisson Ardent | *Bistro* 22
Chantairelle | *Auvergne* –
Chez Léna et Mimile | *Bistro* 21
Chez René | *Lyon* 19
Chieng Mai | *Thai* 22
Christophe | *Bistro* 24
Coin/Gourmets | *Cambodian/Viet.* 23
Coupe-Chou | *Classic Fr.* 20
NEW Dans les Landes | *Southwest* 23
Délices/Aphrodite | *Greek* 20
Desvouges | *Bistro* –
El Palenque | *Argent./Steak* 22
Fontaines | *Bistro* 19
Itinéraires | *New Fr.* 23
Languedoc | *Southwest* 21
Lilane | *New Fr.* 25
Maharajah | *Indian* 23
Marty | *Brass.* 20
Mauzac | *Wine* 15
Mavrommatis | *Greek* 22
Mirama | *Chinese* 22
Moissonnier | *Lyon* 24
Moulin à Vent | *Bistro* 20
Papilles | *Classic Fr.* 25
Perraudin | *Bistro* 18
Petit Châtelet | *Classic Fr.* 22
Petit Pontoise | *Bistro* 25
Pré Verre | *New Fr.* 23
Réminet | *New Fr.* 23
Ribouldingue | *Classic Fr.* 22
Rôtiss. du Beaujolais | *Bistro* 22
Sola | *Japanese/New Fr.* 27
Tourbillon | *Bistro* 24
Z Tour d'Argent | *Haute* 25
Z Truffière | *Classic Fr.* 26

6TH ARRONDISSEMENT

(See map on page 168)

NEW Agapé Substance | *New Fr.* 25
Alcazar | *New Fr.* 18
Allard | *Bistro* 21
Azabu | *Japanese* 24
Bartolo | *Pizza* 20
Bastide Odéon | *Provence* 20
Bien Décidé | *Wine* –
Bistrot d'Henri | *Bistro* 22
Bon Saint Pourçain | *Classic Fr.* 19
Boucherie Roulière | *Bistro* 26
Bouillon Racine | *Classic Fr.* 18
Bouquinistes | *New Fr.* 23
Z Brass. Lipp | *Brass.* 18
Brass. Lutetia | *Brass.* 19
Z Café de Flore | *Classic Fr.* 16
Casa Bini | *Italian* 23
NEW Chardenoux/Prés | *Bistro* 21
Charpentiers | *Bistro* 20
Cherche Midi | *Italian* 22
Christine | *Classic Fr.* 21
Closerie/Lilas | *Classic Fr.* 20
Comme/Savonnières | *Bistro* –
NEW Compagnie/Bretagne | *Brittany* –
Z Comptoir/Relais | *Bistro/Brass.* 27
Crémerie | *Wine* 21
Da Rosa | *Eclectic/Wine* 21
Z Deux Magots | *Classic Fr.* 17
Ecluse | *Wine* 17
Editeurs | *Brass.* 14
Emporio Armani | *Italian* 19
Epi Dupin | *Bistro* 24
Epigramme | *Bistro* 23
Ferrandaise | *Bistro* 20
Fish La Boiss. | *New Fr.* 21
Fogón | *Spanish* 23
Grille St-Germain | *Bistro* 21
Z Hélène Darroze | *New Fr./Southwest* 26
Z Huîtrerie Régis | *Shellfish* 26

Joséphine/Dumonet | *Bistro*	25
KGB | *Asian/New Fr.*	23
Lapérouse | *Haute*	23
Lozère | *Auvergne*	21
Mai Do | *Viet.*	-
Maison du Jardin | *Bistro*	25
Marlotte | *Bistro*	18
Méditerranée | *Seafood*	22
Moustache | *Bistro*	19
Nemrod | *Brasserie*	17
Orient-Extrême | *Japanese*	23
Oto-Oto | *Japanese*	-
Palanquin | *Viet.*	24
Parc aux Cerfs | *Bistro*	20
Pères et Filles | *Bistro*	17
Petite Cour | *New Fr.*	20
Petit Lutetia | *Brass.*	17
Petit St. Benoît | *Classic Fr.*	16
Petit Zinc | *Bistro*	19
Pizza Chic | *Pizza*	21
Polidor | *Bistro*	15
Z Procope | *Classic Fr.*	17
Ralph's | *Amer.*	17
Z Relais/l'Entrecôte | *Steak*	22
Z Relais Louis XIII | *Haute*	26
Rôtiss. d'en Face | *Bistro*	20
Rotonde | *Brass.*	19
Sensing | *New Fr.*	23
Shu | *Japanese*	25
Société | *Classic Fr.*	17
Timbre | *Bistro*	25
Tsukizi | *Japanese*	22
Vagenende | *Brass.*	17
21 | *Seafood*	23
Yen | *Japanese*	22
NEW Yoom | *Asian*	-
Yugaraj | *Indian*	20
Z Ze Kitchen Galerie | *Eclectic*	25

7TH ARRONDISSEMENT

(See map on page 170)

NEW Affable | *Bistro*	-
Affriolé | *Bistro*	23
Aida | *Japanese*	25
Z Arpège | *Haute*	27
Z Atelier/Joël Robuchon | *Haute*	27
Aub. Bressane | *Classic Fr.*	22
Aub. du Champ/Mars | *Classic Fr.*	23
Auguste | *Classic Fr.*	24
Bistro/Breteuil | *Bistro*	18
Bistrot de Paris | *Bistro*	19
Bon Accueil | *Bistro*	23
Botanistes | *Bistro*	19
Café Constant | *Bistro*	24
Café/l'Esplanade | *Classic/New Fr.*	18
Caffé Toscano | *Italian*	19
Z 144 Petrossian | *Seafood*	24
Chez Françoise | *Classic Fr.*	20
Z Chez L'Ami Jean | *Basque*	25
Chez Les Anges | *Brass.*	24
Cigale Récamier | *Classic Fr.*	22
Cinq Mars | *Bistro*	21
Clos/Gourmets | *New Fr.*	25
Cocottes | *New Fr.*	24
D'Chez Eux | *Southwest*	24
Z Divellec | *Seafood*	26
Domaine/Lintillac | *Southwest*	20
Fables/Fontaine | *Seafood*	25
Ferme St-Simon | *Classic Fr.*	21
Fins Gourmets | *Southwest*	18
Firmin le Barbier | *Bistro*	21
Florimond | *Classic Fr.*	25
Z Fontaine de Mars | *Southwest*	22
Gaya | *Seafood*	24
Il Vino | *New Fr.*	22
Jean-François Piège | *Haute/New Fr.*	27
Z Jules Verne | *Haute*	23
Maison/Amér. Latine | *Classic Fr.*	21
Montalembert | *New Fr.*	19
Ombres | *New Fr.*	21
Perron | *Italian*	-
Petite Chaise | *Classic Fr.*	18
Petit Niçois | *Provence*	20
NEW Pottoka | *Bistro*	-
P'tit Troquet | *Bistro*	22
Quai | *New Fr.*	19
Ravi | *Indian*	-

Tan Dinh | *Viet.* 22
Tante Marguerite | *Classic Fr.* 22
Thoumieux | *New Fr.* 20
35° Ouest | *Seafood* 22
Vin et Marée | *Seafood* 21
20 de Bellechasse | *Bistro* 20
Vin sur Vin | *New Fr.* 21
Violon d'Ingres | *Bistro* 25
Voltaire | *Classic Fr.* 22

8TH ARRONDISSEMENT

(See map on page 172)

Z Alain Ducasse | *Haute* 28
Z Ambassadeurs | *Haute* 27
Annapurna | *Indian* 23
Z Apicius | *Haute* 27
Astor | *Classic Fr.* 24
Z Atelier/Joël Robuchon | *Haute* 27
Avenue | *New Fr.* 16
Bar/Théâtres | *Bistro* 17
Bistrot/Sommelier | *Wine* 22
Boeuf/le Toit | *Brass.* 18
Brass. La Lorraine | *Brass.* 18
Brass. Mollard | *Brass.* 18
Café Lenôtre | *New Fr.* 23
Café Salle Pleyel | *New Fr.* 16
Café Terminus | *Brass.* 19
NEW Caffe Burlot/Costes | *Italian* –
Z Caviar Kaspia | *Russian* 26
Chez André | *Bistro* 22
Chez Cécile | *Classic Fr.* 25
Chez Francis | *Brass.* 18
Chez Savy | *Aveyron* 20
Chiberta | *New Fr.* 24
Z Cinq | *Haute* 28
Citrus Etoile | *Classic/New Fr.* 24
Copenhague | *Danish* 23
Cou de la Girafe | *New Fr.* 13
Cuisine | *New Fr.* 22
Daru | *Russian* 19
Diep | *Asian* 21
1728 | *New Fr.* 21
Dominique Bouchet | *Haute* 25
Ecluse | *Wine* 17
El Mansour | *Moroccan* 21
Enfants Terribles | *Classic Fr.* 20
Z Epicure (Le Bristol) | *Haute* 27
Eugène | *Eclectic* 18
Fermette Marbeuf | *Classic Fr.* 19
Findi | *Italian* 21
Finzi | *Italian* 19
Flora Danica | *Classic Fr./Danish* 21
Fouquet's | *Classic Fr.* 20
Garnier | *Brass.* 22
Gourmets/Ternes | *Bistro* 23
NEW Instant d'Or | *New Fr.* –
Kaïten | *Japanese* 22
Z Lasserre | *Haute* 27
Laurent | *Haute* 25
Luna | *Seafood* 26
Maison Blanche | *New Fr.* 23
Maison du Caviar | *Russian* 25
Marée | *Seafood* 23
Marius et Janette | *Seafood* 23
Market | *Eclectic* 22
Maxan | *New Fr.* 20
Maxim's | *Classic Fr.* 20
Minipalais | *New Fr.* 21
NEW Neva | *New Fr.* –
Oth Sombath | *Asian* 23
Pavillon Ledoyen | *Haute* 25
Petit Marius | *Seafood* 20
Pichet de Paris | *Seafood* 22
Z Pierre Gagnaire | *Haute* 28
Prunier | *Seafood* 24
Z Relais/l'Entrecôte | *Steak* 22
Relais Plaza | *Brass./Eclectic* 25
Royal Madeleine | *Classic Fr.* 23
Sarladais | *Southwest* 23
Z Senderens | *New Fr.* 26
Stella Maris | *Classic Fr.* 25
Stresa | *Italian* 22
Table d'Hédiard | *New Fr.* 22
Table/Lancaster | *Haute* 25
Z Taillevent | *Haute* 29
Tante Louise | *Burgundy/Classic* 23
Tong Yen | *Chinese* 22
39V | *New Fr.* 23
Vernet | *Haute* 24

9TH ARRONDISSEMENT

NEW Affranchis | *Bistro* –
Aromatik | *New Fr.* 18
Bacchantes | *Wine* 21
NEW Big Fernand | *Burgers* –
Bistro/Deux Théâtres | *Bistro* 21
Boule Rouge | *N African* 21
NEW Bourgogne Sud | *Burgundy* –
NEW Braisenville | *Eclectic* –
Brass. Printemps | *Classic Fr.* 15
Café de la Paix | *Classic Fr.* 19
Casa Olympe | *New Fr./Provence* 23
Charlot - Roi/Coquillages | *Brass.* 21
Chartier | *Classic Fr.* 15
Chez Grenouille | *Bistro* 21
Comédiens | *Classic Fr.* 19
Coulisses | *Bistro* –
Cul de Poule | *Bistro* 20
Domaine/Lintillac | *Southwest* 20
Georgette | *Bistro* 17
Grand Café | *Brass.* 19
Hôtel Amour | *New Fr.* 15
I Golosi | *Italian* 23
Jean | *New Fr.* 26
Kiku | *Japanese* –
NEW Maison Mère | *Amer./Bistro* –
Office | *New Fr.* –
NEW Opéra Rest. | *New Fr.* 19
NEW Pantruche | *Bistro* 24
Petite Sirène | *Danish* 25
Petit Riche | *Bistro* 22
Petrelle | *New Fr.* 25
Roi/Pot-au-Feu | *Bistro* 19
Rose Bakery | *Bakery/British* 22
NEW Yoom | *Asian* –

10TH ARRONDISSEMENT

NEW Albion | *Wine/Bistro* –
Brass. Flo | *Brass.* 19
Brass. Julien | *Brass.* 19
Cantine/Quentin | *Wine* –
Chez Marie-Louise | *Bistro* –
Chez Michel | *Brittany* 24
Chez Prune | *Eclectic* 15
NEW Comptoir/Brice | *New Fr.* –
NEW Floréal | *Brass.* –
NEW Galopin | *Bistro* –
Grille | *Bistro* 21
Hotel du Nord | *Bistro* –
Martel | *Classic Fr./Moroccan* 21
Nanashi | *Eclectic* –
Philou | *Bistro* 21
Terminus Nord | *Brass.* 18
Verre Volé | *Wine* 20
NEW Vivant | *Wine* 24

11TH ARRONDISSEMENT

Al Taglio | *Pizza* 22
Astier | *Bistro* 21
Aub. Pyrénées | *Lyon/Southwest* 24
Bistro/Vieux Chêne | *Bistro* 23
Bistrot/Vins Mélac | *Wine* 18
Bistrot du Peintre | *Bistro* 18
Bistrot Paul Bert | *Bistro* 21
Café du Passage | *Wine* –
Caffé dei Cioppi | *Italian* 25
Chardenoux | *Bistro* 23
Chateaubriand | *New Fr.* 23
Chez Paul | *Bistro* 22
Chez Ramulaud | *Bistro* –
Clown Bar | *Wine* 15
Cuizine | *Bistro* –
NEW Dauphin | *New Fr.* 22
Deux Amis | *Wine/Bistro* 21
Ecailler du Bistrot | *Seafood* 25
NEW Entrée/Artistes | *Wine/Bistro* –
Jeanne A | *Bistro* –
Khun Akorn | *Thai* 21
Main d'Or | *Corsica* 22
Mansouria | *Moroccan* 21
NEW Passage | *Wine/Bistro* –
NEW Petit Cheval/Manège | *Bistro* –
NEW Qui Plume/Lune | *New Fr.* –
Repaire/Cartouche | *Bistro* 17
Reuan Thai | *Thai* –
Rino | *New Fr.* 25
NEW Sassotondo | *Italian* –
NEW Septime | *Bistro* 25

- Sot l'y Laisse | *Bistro* 22
- NEW Square Gardette | *Bistro* –
- Temps au Temps | *Bistro* 23
- NEW Tintilou | *New Fr.* –
- Villaret | *Bistro* 23
- Vin et Marée | *Seafood* 21

12TH ARRONDISSEMENT

- Baron Rouge | *Wine* 18
- Biche/Bois | *Bistro* 22
- Café Cartouche | *Bistro* –
- Cotte Rôti | *Bistro* –
- Duc de Richelieu | *Lyon* 22
- Ebauchoir | *Bistro* 24
- Européen | *Brass.* 20
- Gazzetta | *New Fr.* 24
- Z Oulette | *New Fr./Southwest* 26
- Z Quincy | *Bistro* 26
- Rose Bakery | *Bakery/British* 22
- Shan Gout | *Chinese* –
- Square Trousseau | *Bistro* 19
- Z Train Bleu | *Classic Fr.* 19
- Trou Gascon | *Southwest* 25

13TH ARRONDISSEMENT

- Aimant du Sud | *Classic Fr.* 21
- NEW Auberge du 15 | *Classic Fr.* 24
- Avant Goût | *New Fr.* 23
- Cailloux | *Italian* 22
- Chez Paul | *Bistro* 22
- Comptoir Marguery | *Burgundy* 21
- Lao Lane Xang | *Asian* 22
- Nouveau Village | *Chinese/Thai* 19
- Ourcine | *Classic/New Fr.* 25
- Petit Marguery | *Bistro* 23
- Suave | *Viet.* –
- Temps des Cerises | *Bistro* 18
- Tricotin | *Asian* 19

14TH ARRONDISSEMENT

- Assiette | *Bistro/Southwest* 19
- Z Bar à Huîtres | *Seafood* 21
- Bistrot du Dôme | *Seafood* 22
- Cagouille | *Seafood* 23
- Cantine/Troquet | *Basque* 25
- Cerisaie | *Southwest* 23
- NEW Cobéa | *New Fr.* –
- NEW Cornichon | *Bistro* –
- Z Coupole | *Brass.* 18
- Dôme | *Seafood* 22
- Z Duc | *Seafood* 28
- Entêtée | *Bistro* 20
- Il Barone | *Italian* 22
- Jeu de Quilles | *Wine* –
- Maison Courtine | *New Fr.* 20
- Opportun | *Lyon* 22
- Pavillon Montsouris | *Classic Fr.* 22
- Petites Sorcières | *Northern Fr.* 25
- Régalade | *Bistro* 25
- Z Severo | *Steak* 26
- Vin et Marée | *Seafood* 21
- Zeyer | *Brass.* 19

15TH ARRONDISSEMENT

- Afaria | *Basque/New Fr.* 23
- NEW Bélisaire | *Bistro* 23
- Benkay | *Japanese* 25
- Beurre Noisette | *Bistro* 25
- Bistro 121 | *Bistro* 22
- Bistrot d'André | *Bistro* 20
- Café du Commerce | *Bistro* 17
- Cantine/Tontons | *Classic Fr.* 17
- Cantine/Troquet | *Basque* 25
- Casse-Noix | *Bistro* –
- Cave Schmidt | *Wine* 23
- Chen Soleil d'Est | *Chinese* –
- Concert/Cuisine | *Japanese/New Fr.* –
- Couleurs/Vigne | *Wine* –
- Cristal de Sel | *New Fr.* 27
- Gauloise | *Bistro* 18
- Gitane | *Classic Fr.* 18
- Grand Pan | *Bistro* 23
- Z Grand Venise | *Italian* 26
- Jadis | *Bistro* 23
- Kim Anh | *Viet.* 23
- Père Claude | *Classic Fr.* 21
- Z Quinzième | *New Fr.* 26
- Rest. de la Tour | *Classic Fr.* 24
- Rest. du Marché | *Bistro* 21
- Schmidt - L'Os/Moëlle | *Classic Fr.* 23

Stéphane Martin | *Classic Fr.*	23
Troquet | *Basque/New Fr.*	24
Z Villa Corse | *Corsica*	21

16TH ARRONDISSEMENT

NEW Abeille | *Haute*	23
A et M | *Classic Fr.*	21
NEW Akrame | *New Fr.*	23
Al Dar | *Lebanese*	22
Antoine | *Bistro/Seafood*	22
Arc | *New Fr.*	16
Z Astrance | *Haute*	28
Aub. Dab | *Brass.*	20
Beaujolais/Auteuil | *Classic Fr.*	19
Bellini | *Italian*	21
Bistrot des Vignes | *Bistro*	20
Brass. de la Poste | *Brass.*	22
Chalet des Iles | *Classic Fr.*	18
Chez Géraud | *Classic Fr.*	20
Z Cristal Room | *New Fr.*	20
Domaine/Lintillac | *Southwest*	20
Etc. | *New Fr.*	25
Fakhr el Dine | *Lebanese*	25
Flandrin | *Brass.*	15
Gare | *Classic Fr.*	18
Grande Armée | *Classic Fr.*	16
Grande Cascade | *Haute*	24
Z Hiramatsu | *Haute/New Fr.*	27
Jamin | *New Fr.*	23
Jardins de Bagatelle | *Classic Fr.*	20
Lac-Hong | *Viet.*	21
Marée Passy | *Seafood*	22
Marius | *Seafood*	25
Murat | *Brass.*	17
Ogre | *Bistro*	-
Oum el Banine | *Moroccan*	22
Passiflore | *Asian/Classic Fr.*	23
Paul Chêne | *Classic Fr.*	23
Petit Pergolèse | *Bistro*	25
Petit Rétro | *Bistro*	18
Petit Victor Hugo | *Classic Fr.*	19
Z Pré Catelan | *Haute*	26
Prunier | *Seafood*	24
Relais d'Auteuil | *Haute*	25
Rest./Pergolèse | *Haute*	25
Scheffer | *Bistro*	19
NEW Shang Palace | *Chinese*	24
6 New York | *New Fr.*	23
Stella | *Brass.*	21
NEW Tablettes/Nomicos | *Haute*	28
Tang | *Chinese*	22
Terrasse Mirabeau | *Bistro*	26
Tsé-Yang | *Chinese*	22
Z Villa Corse | *Corsica*	21
Vin et Marée | *Seafood*	21
Zébra Square | *Classic Fr./Italian*	16

17TH ARRONDISSEMENT

Accolade | *Bistro*	20
Agapé | *New Fr.*	24
NEW Atao | *Brittany/Seafood*	-
Ballon des Ternes | *Brass.*	19
Ballon/Coquillages | *Seafood*	-
Z Bar à Huîtres | *Seafood*	21
Z Bigarrade | *New Fr.*	27
Bistral | *Bistro*	22
Bistro du 17ème | *Bistro*	19
Bistro St. Ferdinand | *Bistro*	19
Bistrot/Côté Flaubert | *Bistro*	21
Bistrot des Dames | *Bistro*	18
Bistrot du Passage | *Bistro*	23
Bouchon/L'Assiette | *Bistro*	22
Caïus | *New Fr.*	24
Caves Pétrissans | *Wine*	23
Chez Fred | *Bistro*	19
Chez Georges | *Brass.*	22
Chez Ly | *Chinese/Thai*	25
Clocher Péreire | *New Fr.*	24
Congrès Maillot | *Brass.*	20
Crabe Marteau | *Brittany/Seafood*	20
Dessirier | *Brass./Seafood*	24
NEW Dodin/Mark Singer | *New Fr.*	-
Ecluse | *Wine*	17
Entredgeu | *Bistro*	21
Fougères | *New Fr.*	27
Fourchette | *Bistro*	23
Frédéric Simonin | *Haute/New Fr.*	-
Graindorge | *Belgian/Northern Fr.*	23

- Z Guy Savoy | *Haute* 28
- Hide | *Bistro* 24
- Huîtrier | *Seafood* 22
- Kifune | *Japanese* 23
- MBC | *New Fr.* -
- Z Michel Rostang | *Classic Fr.* 27
- Pétrus | *Brass.* 23
- Rech | *Seafood* 22
- Relais de Venise | *Steak* 23
- Sormani | *Italian* 24
- Timgad | *Moroccan* 22
- Verre Bouteille | *Wine* 19

18TH ARRONDISSEMENT

- Bistro Poulbot | *Bistro* 23
- Bonne Franquette | *Bistro* -
- Café Burq | *Wine* 21
- Z Chamarré Mont. | *Mauritian/New Fr.* 26
- Chéri Bibi | *Bistro* 20
- NEW Clocher/Montmartre | *Bistro* -
- NEW Coq Rico | *Bistro* -
- Cottage Marcadet | *New Fr.* -
- Famille | *New French* 23
- Z Guilo-Guilo | *Asian* 27
- Mascotte | *Auvergne* 20
- Miroir | *Bistro* 21
- Moulin/Galette | *Classic Fr.* 20
- Pomponette | *Bistro* 23
- Rughetta | *Italian* 21
- Sale e Pepe | *Italian* 21
- Square Marcadet | *Classic/New Fr.* -
- Z Table d'Eugène | *New Fr.* 26
- Wepler | *Brass.* 20

19TH ARRONDISSEMENT

- Boeuf Couronné | *Classic Fr.* 23
- Café de la Musique | *Brass./New Fr.* 17
- Chez Vincent | *Italian* 23
- Lao Siam | *Thai* 22
- Pavillon/Lac | *Classic/New Fr.* 19
- Quedubon | *Wine/Bistro* 18
- Rosa Bonheur | *Southwest* 16

20TH ARRONDISSEMENT

- Allobroges | *Classic Fr.* 22
- Baratin | *Wine* 24
- Boulangerie | *Bistro* 22
- NEW Chatomat | *New Fr.* -
- Mama Shelter | *Brass.* 16

Outlying Areas

BOUGIVAL

- Camélia | *New Fr.* 21

CLICHY

- Romantica | *Italian* 22

ISSY-LES-MOULINEAUX

- Ile | *Classic/New Fr.* 19
- Rest. Manufacture | *New Fr.* 22

JOINVILLE-LE-PONT

- Chez Gégène | *Classic Fr.* 16

NEUILLY-SUR-SEINE

- Bistrot/Côté La Boutarde | *Bistro* 21
- Café de la Jatte | *Italian* 18
- Chalet | *Alpine/Classic Fr.* 21
- Gourmand | *Classic Fr.* 18
- Sébillon | *Brass.* 22

Special Features

Listings cover the best in each category and include names, locations and Food ratings. Multi-location restaurants' features may vary by branch.

BREAKFAST

(See also Hotel Dining)

Avenue | 8e	16
Bar/Théâtres | 8e	17
Brass. Balzar | 5e	18
Brass. La Lorraine | 8e	18
Brass. Printemps | 9e	15
Z Café de Flore | 6e	16
Café de la Musique | 19e	17
Café/l'Esplanade | 7e	18
Café Lenôtre | 8e	23
Café Marly | 1er	17
Café Ruc | 1er	15
Chez Prune | 10e	15
Cloche/Halles | 1er	18
Congrès Maillot | 17e	20
Z Coupole | 14e	18
Z Deux Magots | 6e	17
Dôme | 14e	22
Editeurs | 6e	14
Flandrin | 16e	15
Flore en l'Ile | 4e	17
Fontaines | 5e	19
Fouquet's | 8e	20
Grand Café | 9e	19
Grande Armée | 16e	16
Ma Bourgogne | 4e	19
Main d'Or | 11e	22
Mascotte | 18e	20
Murat | 16e	17
Nemrod | 6e	17
Rose Bakery | **multi.**	22
Rotonde | 6e	19
Terminus Nord | 10e	18
Tricotin | 13e	19
Zeyer | 14e	19
Chez Prune | 10e	15
Editeurs | 6e	14
Findi | 8e	21
Flora Danica | 8e	21
Flore en l'Ile | 4e	17
Fumoir | 1er	18
Mama Shelter | 20e	16
Market | 8e	22
Quai | 7e	19
404 | 3e	20
Rose Bakery | **multi.**	22
Wepler | 18e	20
Zébra Square | 16e	16

BRUNCH

Alcazar | 6e	18
Café de la Jatte | **Neuilly**	18
Café de la Musique | 19e	17

BUFFET

(Check availability)

Astor | 8e	24
Café de la Paix | 9e	19
Chéri Bibi | 18e	20
NEW Floréal | 10e	-
Gare | 16e	18
Mama Shelter | 20e	16
Quai | 7e	19
Reuan Thai | 11e	-
Rosa Bonheur | 19e	16

BUSINESS DINING

Agapé | 17e	24
Z Ami Louis | 3e	24
Z Astrance | 16e	28
Auguste | 7e	24
Bistro St. Ferdinand | 17e	19
Bistro Volnay | 2e	21
Boeuf Couronné | 19e	23
Boeuf/le Toit | 8e	18
Café/l'Esplanade | 7e	18
NEW Camélia | 1er	-
Caves Pétrissans | 17e	23
Céladon | 2e	23
Z 144 Petrossian | 7e	24
Z Chamarré Mont. | 18e	26
Chez André | 8e	22

Chez Les Anges | **7e** 24
Chez Savy | **8e** 20
Chiberta | **8e** 24
Clocher Péreire | **17e** 24
Clos/Gourmets | **7e** 25
Copenhague | **8e** 23
Costes | **1er** 18
Dali | **1er** -
Dessirier | **17e** 24
Z Divellec | **7e** 26
NEW Dodin/Mark Singer | **17e** -
Dôme | **14e** 22
Dôme du Marais | **4e** 19
Dominique Bouchet | **8e** 25
Drouant | **2e** 23
Z Duc | **14e** 28
Z Epicure (Le Bristol) | **8e** 27
Etc. | **16e** 25
Flora Danica | **8e** 21
Fougères | **17e** 27
Fouquet's | **8e** 20
Frédéric Simonin | **17e** -
Gaya | **7e** 24
Goumard | **1er** 23
Graindorge | **17e** 23
Z Guy Savoy | **17e** 28
Z Hélène Darroze | **6e** 26
Il Vino | **7e** 22
Itinéraires | **5e** 23
Izakaya Issé | **1er** 23
Jamin | **16e** 23
Z Jules Verne | **7e** 23
Lapérouse | **6e** 23
Macéo | **1er** 23
Maison Blanche | **8e** 23
Marée | **8e** 23
Marius | **16e** 25
Marius et Janette | **8e** 23
Marty | **5e** 20
Maxan | **8e** 20
Z Meurice | **1er** 28
Montalembert | **7e** 19
Mori Venice | **2e** 21
Oth Sombath | **8e** 23
Petit Marguery | **13e** 23
Petit Pergolèse | **16e** 25
Pétrus | **17e** 23
Pichet de Paris | **8e** 22
Pierre/Palais Royal | **1er** 22
Z Pierre Gagnaire | **8e** 28
Pur' | **2e** 24
Z Relais Louis XIII | **6e** 26
Sébillon | **Neuilly** 22
Sormani | **17e** 24
Stella Maris | **8e** 25
Stresa | **8e** 22
Table/Lancaster | **8e** 25
NEW Tablettes/Nomicos | **16e** 28
Tan Dinh | **7e** 22
Tante Louise | **8e** 23
Terrasse Mirabeau | **16e** 26
Z Train Bleu | **12e** 19
35° Ouest | **7e** 22
39V | **8e** 23
Trou Gascon | **12e** 25
Vagenende | **6e** 17
Vaudeville | **2e** 20
Versance | **2e** -
Vin et Marée | **multi.** 21
Voltaire | **7e** 22

CELEBRITY CHEFS

Yannick Alléno
Dali | **1er** -
Z Meurice | **1er** 28
Ghislaine Arabian
Petites Sorcières | **14e** 25
Pascal Barbot
Z Astrance | **16e** 28
Eric Briffard
Z Cinq | **8e** 28
Yves Camdeborde
Z Comptoir/Relais | **6e** 27
Sven Chartier
Saturne | **2e** 22
Christian Constant
Café Constant | **7e** 24
Cocottes | **7e** 24
Violon d'Ingres | **7e** 25

Hélène Darroze
- **Z** Hélène Darroze | **6e** 26
Bruno Doucet
- Régalade | **14e** 25
- Régalade St-Honoré | **1er** 23
Alain Ducasse
- **Z** Alain Ducasse | **8e** 28
- **Z** Benoît | **4e** 23
- **Z** Jules Verne | **7e** 23
- Lyonnais | **2e** 22
- Rech | **17e** 22
- Relais Plaza | **8e** 25
Alain Dutournier
- **Z** Carré/Feuillants | **1er** 27
- Pinxo | **1er** 23
- Trou Gascon | **12e** 25
Eric Frechon
- **Z** Epicure (Le Bristol) | **8e** 27
- Minipalais | **8e** 21
Pierre Gagnaire
- Gaya | **7e** 24
- **Z** Pierre Gagnaire | **8e** 28
Antoine Heerah
- **Z** Chamarré Mont. | **18e** 26
- **NEW** Clocher/Montmartre | **18e** -
- Moulin/Galette | **18e** 20
Hiroyuki Hiramatsu
- **Z** Hiramatsu | **16e** 27
William Ledeuil
- KGB | **6e** 23
- **Z** Ze Kitchen Galerie | **6e** 25
Cyril Lignac
- Chardenoux | **11e** 23
- **NEW** Chardenoux/Prés | **6e** 21
- **Z** Quinzième | **15e** 26
Guy Martin
- **Z** Grand Véfour | **1er** 28
- Sensing | **6e** 23
Thierry Marx
- **NEW** Sur Mesure | **1er** -
Paul Minchelli
- 21 | **6e** 23

Jean-Louis Nomicos
- **NEW** Tablettes/Nomicos | **16e** 28
Bernard Pacaud
- **Z** Ambroisie | **4e** 27
Alain Passard
- **Z** Arpège | **7e** 27
Jean-François Piège
- Jean-François Piège | **7e** 27
- Thoumieux | **7e** 20
Joël Robuchon
- **Z** Atelier/Joël Robuchon | **multi.** 27
Daniel Rose
- **Z** Spring | **1er** 27
Michel Rostang
- Bistrot/Côté Flaubert | **17e** 21
- Bistrot/Côté La Boutarde | **Neuilly** 21
- Dessirier | **17e** 24
- **Z** Michel Rostang | **17e** 27
Guy Savoy
- Atelier Maître Albert | **5e** 23
- Bouquinistes | **6e** 23
- Chiberta | **8e** 24
- **Z** Guy Savoy | **17e** 28
Alain Senderens
- Mama Shelter | **20e** 16
- **Z** Senderens | **8e** 26
Alain Solivérès
- **Z** Taillevent | **8e** 29
Oth Sombath
- Oth Sombath | **8e** 23
Christian Le Squer
- Pavillon Ledoyen | **8e** 25
Romain Tischenko
- **NEW** Galopin | **10e** -
Michel Troisgros
- Table/Lancaster | **8e** 25
Jean-Pierre Vigato
- **Z** Apicius | **8e** 27
Jean-Georges Vongerichten
- Market | **8e** 22
Antoine Westermann
- **NEW** Coq Rico | **18e** -
- Drouant | **2e** 23
- Mon Vieil Ami | **4e** 23

SPECIAL FEATURES

CHILD-FRIENDLY

(Alternatives to the usual fast-food places; * children's menu available)

Alcazar* | **6e** 18
Anahuacalli* | **5e** 23
Z Atelier/Joël Robuchon | **7e** 27
Atlas* | **5e** 21
Aub. Dab* | **16e** 20
Z Bar à Huîtres* | **multi.** 21
Bistro 121 | **15e** 22
Bistro/Breteuil* | **7e** 18
Bistrot d'André* | **15e** 20
Bistrot des Vignes* | **16e** 20
Bistrot du Dôme | **14e** 22
Boeuf/le Toit* | **8e** 18
Z Bofinger* | **4e** 19
Brass. de la Poste* | **16e** 22
Brass. du Louvre* | **1er** 19
Brass. Julien* | **10e** 19
Brass. Lutetia* | **6e** 19
Brass. Mollard* | **8e** 18
Café de la Musique | **19e** 17
Café de la Paix* | **9e** 19
Chalet* | **Neuilly** 21
Chalet des Iles* | **16e** 18
NEW Chez Flottes* | **1er** -
Chez Jenny* | **3e** 19
Congrès Maillot* | **17e** 20
Z Coupole* | **14e** 18
Drouant | **2e** 23
Fouquet's* | **8e** 20
Gare* | **16e** 18
Gauloise* | **15e** 18
Gitane | **15e** 18
Languedoc | **5e** 21
Pavillon Montsouris* | **14e** 22
Petite Cour | **6e** 20
Petite Sirène | **9e** 25
Z Pied de Cochon | **1er** 19
Z Procope | **6e** 17
Z Relais/l'Entrecôte | **6e** 22
Rest. du Palais Royal | **1er** 20
Rôtiss. d'en Face | **6e** 20
Rôtiss. du Beaujolais | **5e** 22
Rotonde* | **6e** 19
Sébillon* | **Neuilly** 22
NEW Square Gardette* | **11e** -
Tang | **16e** 22
Terminus Nord* | **10e** 18
Z Train Bleu* | **12e** 19
Trumilou | **4e** 20
Vagenende* | **6e** 17
Vaudeville* | **2e** 20
Wepler* | **18e** 20

CLOSED JULY/ AUGUST

(Varies; call ahead to confirm dates)

Accolade | **17e** 20
A et M | **16e** 21
NEW Affranchis | **9e** -
Affriolé | **7e** 23
Agapé | **17e** 24
Agrume | **5e** 24
Aida | **7e** 25
NEW Albion | **10e** -
Allobroges | **20e** 22
Al Taglio | **11e** 22
Z Ambassadeurs | **8e** 27
Z Ami Louis | **3e** 24
Anahi | **3e** 19
Antoine | **16e** 22
AOC | **5e** 23
Z Apicius | **8e** 27
Z Astrance | **16e** 28
NEW Atao | **17e** -
Aub. du Champ/Mars | **7e** 23
Aub. Pyrénées | **11e** 24
Auguste | **7e** 24
Baratin | **20e** 24
Bar/Théâtres | **8e** 17
Bascou | **3e** 23
Bellini | **16e** 21
Z Benoît | **4e** 23
Bien Décidé | **6e** -
Z Bigarrade | **17e** 27
Bistral | **17e** 22
Bistro Poulbot | **18e** 23
Bistrot/Vins Mélac | **11e** 18
Bistrot/Côté Flaubert | **17e** 21

Bistrot de Paris | 7e 19
Bistrot des Vignes | 16e 20
Bistrot du Dôme | 4e 22
Bistrot du Passage | 17e 23
Bistrot/Sommelier | 8e 22
Bistrot Paul Bert | 11e 21
Botanistes | 7e 19
Boucherie Roulière | 6e 26
Boulangerie | 20e 22
Boule Rouge | 9e 21
Bourguignon/Marais | 4e 25
Café des Musées | 3e 20
Café Le Moderne | 2e 22
Café Lenôtre | 8e 23
Caffé dei Cioppi | 11e 25
Caffé Toscano | 7e 19
Camélia | **Bougival** 21
Cantine/Quentin | 10e –
Z Carré/Feuillants | 1er 27
Casa Olympe | 9e 23
Caves Pétrissans | 17e 23
Z Caviar Kaspia | 8e 26
Chen Soleil d'Est | 15e –
Chez Géraud | 16e 20
Chez Grenouille | 9e 21
Z Chez L'Ami Jean | 7e 25
Chez Les Anges | 7e 24
Chez Marie-Louise | 10e –
Chez Michel | 10e 24
Chez Nénesse | 3e 21
Chez René | 5e 19
Chez Savy | 8e 20
Chieng Mai | 5e 22
Cibus | 1er –
Cinq Mars | 7e 21
Clocher Péreire | 17e 24
Clos/Gourmets | 7e 25
NEW Cobéa | 14e –
Comme/Savonnières | 6e –
Concert/Cuisine | 15e –
Copenhague | 8e 23
Corte | 1er –
Cottage Marcadet | 18e –
Cou de la Girafe | 8e 13
Crémerie | 6e 21
Crudus | 1er –
Cuizine | 11e –
Daru | 8e 19
Desvouges | 5e –
Deux Amis | 11e 21
1728 | 8e 21
NEW Dodin/Mark Singer | 17e –
Dominique Bouchet | 8e 25
Z Duc | 14e 28
Ecaille de Fontaine | 2e –
Ecailler du Bistrot | 11e 25
Ecume St-Honoré | 1er 23
Enfants Terribles | 8e 20
Enoteca | 4e 22
Entêtée | 14e 20
Entredgeu | 17e 21
Epi d'Or | 1er 19
Epi Dupin | 6e 24
Epigramme | 6e 23
Eugène | 8e 18
Ferrandaise | 6e 20
Finzi | 8e 19
Firmin le Barbier | 7e 21
Florimond | 7e 25
Flottes O. Trement | 1er 21
Fogón | 6e 23
Fontaine Gaillon | 2e 21
Fougères | 17e 27
Fourchette | 17e 23
Frédéric Simonin | 17e –
Gaigne | 4e 24
Gazzetta | 12e 24
Georgette | 9e 17
Gourmets/Ternes | 8e 23
Graindorge | 17e 23
Grand Pan | 15e 23
Z Grand Véfour | 1er 28
Z Grand Venise | 15e 26
Grille | 10e 21
Hangar | 3e 23
Z Hélène Darroze | 6e 26
Z Hiramatsu | 16e 27
Z Huîtrerie Régis | 6e 26

Huîtrier	**17e**	22
Il Barone	**14e**	22
Isami	**4e**	25
Itinéraires	**5e**	23
Jadis	**15e**	23
Jamin	**16e**	23
Jean	**9e**	26
Jeu de Quilles	**14e**	-
Kai	**1er**	25
Kim Anh	**15e**	23
Lapérouse	**6e**	23
Z Lasserre	**8e**	27
Lescure	**1er**	19
Lilane	**5e**	25
Luna	**8e**	26
Lyonnais	**2e**	22
Macéo	**1er**	23
Mai Do	**6e**	-
Maison Blanche	**8e**	23
Maison Courtine	**14e**	20
Maison du Jardin	**6e**	25
Marius	**16e**	25
Martel	**10e**	21
Marty	**5e**	20
MBC	**17e**	-
Z Meurice	**1er**	28
Miroir	**18e**	21
Montagnards	**1er**	23
Mon Vieil Ami	**4e**	23
Moulin à Vent	**5e**	20
Moustache	**6e**	19
Muscade	**1er**	-
Nos Ancêtres les Gaulois	**4e**	13
Office	**9e**	-
Ogre	**16e**	-
Opportun	**14e**	22
Ostéria	**4e**	24
Oth Sombath	**8e**	23
Z Oulette	**12e**	26
Palanquin	**6e**	24
Parc aux Cerfs	**6e**	20
Paul Chêne	**16e**	23
Pavillon Ledoyen	**8e**	25
Perron	**7e**	-
Petite Sirène	**9e**	25
Petit Pergolèse	**16e**	25
Petit Rétro	**16e**	18
Petit St. Benoît	**6e**	16
Petit Victor Hugo	**16e**	19
Pétrus	**17e**	23
Philou	**10e**	21
Pichet de Paris	**8e**	22
Pierre/Palais Royal	**1er**	22
Z Pierre Gagnaire	**8e**	28
Pinxo	**1er**	23
Pizza Chic	**6e**	21
Pomponette	**18e**	23
Z Pré Catelan	**16e**	26
Prunier	**16e**	24
P'tit Troquet	**7e**	22
Quai-Quai	**1er**	18
Racines	**2e**	20
Rech	**17e**	22
Régalade	**14e**	25
Régalade St-Honoré	**1er**	23
Relais d'Auteuil	**16e**	25
Relais de Venise	**17e**	23
Z Relais/l'Entrecôte	**multi.**	22
Z Relais Louis XIII	**6e**	26
Relais Plaza	**8e**	25
Rest. de la Tour	**15e**	24
Rest./Pergolèse	**16e**	25
Rest. Manufacture	**Issy-les-Moul.**	22
Ribouldingue	**5e**	22
Rino	**11e**	25
Rose Bakery	**9e**	22
Saotico	**2e**	-
Saturne	**2e**	22
Schmidt - L'Os/Moëlle	**15e**	23
Sensing	**6e**	23
Z Severo	**14e**	26
6 New York	**16e**	23
Sot l'y Laisse	**11e**	22
Soufflé	**1er**	22
Suave	**13e**	-
Z Table d'Eugène	**18e**	26
Table/Lancaster	**8e**	25
Tang	**16e**	22

Temps au Temps | **11e**	23
Tourbillon | **5e**	24
35° Ouest | **7e**	22
Trou Gascon | **12e**	25
NEW Verjus | **1er**	–
Vernet | **8e**	24
Versance | **2e**	–
21 | **6e**	23
Z Yam'Tcha | **1er**	26
Yugaraj | **6e**	20

DANCING

Brass. de la Poste | **16e**	22
Chez Gégène | **Joinville**	16
Z Coupole | **14e**	18

DELIVERY

Affriolé | **7e**	23
Al Taglio | **11e**	22
Anahuacalli | **5e**	23
NEW Atao | **17e**	–
Atlas | **5e**	21
Bistro 121 | **15e**	22
Caffé Toscano | **7e**	19
Chez Vincent | **19e**	23
Comptoir/Mers | **4e**	23
Diep | **8e**	21
Duc de Richelieu | **12e**	22
Fakhr el Dine | **16e**	25
Ferme St-Simon | **7e**	21
Findi | **8e**	21
Graindorge | **17e**	23
Huîtrier | **17e**	22
Kifune | **17e**	23
Kiku | **9e**	–
Kim Anh | **15e**	23
Legrand Filles/Fils | **2e**	21
Liza | **2e**	24
Maharajah | **5e**	23
Marée | **8e**	23
Mesturet | **2e**	16
Mousson | **1er**	–
Philou | **10e**	21
Ravi | **7e**	–
Vernet | **8e**	24

DESSERT SPECIALISTS

Ambassade/Auv. | **3e**	22
Assiette | **14e**	19
Café Lenôtre | **8e**	23
Chez Janou | **3e**	21
Ebouillanté | **4e**	22
Z Epicure (Le Bristol) | **8e**	27
Flore en l'Ile | **4e**	17
Jean | **9e**	26
Kai | **1er**	25
Z Lasserre | **8e**	27
Z Pré Catelan | **16e**	26
Soufflé | **1er**	22

DINING ALONE

(Other than hotels and places with counter service)

NEW Affranchis | **9e**	–
Aimant du Sud | **13e**	21
Alcazar | **6e**	18
Z As/Fallafel | **4e**	23
Assiette | **14e**	19
Azabu | **6e**	24
Ballon des Ternes | **17e**	19
Z Bar à Huîtres | **multi.**	21
Bar/Théâtres | **8e**	17
NEW Big Fernand | **9e**	–
Bistro/Vieux Chêne | **11e**	23
Bistrot/Vins Mélac | **11e**	18
Bistrot du Peintre | **11e**	18
Boeuf/le Toit | **8e**	18
Bouillon Racine | **6e**	18
Bourguignon/Marais | **4e**	25
Brass./l'Ile St-Louis | **4e**	19
Buisson Ardent | **5e**	22
Z Café de Flore | **6e**	16
Café du Commerce | **15e**	17
Café du Passage | **11e**	–
Café Lenôtre | **8e**	23
Café Marly | **1er**	17
Café Salle Pleyel | **8e**	16
Cantine/Troquet | **14e**	25
Charpentiers | **6e**	20
Chartier | **9e**	15
Z Chez Georges | **2e**	23

Chez Jenny | **3e** 19
Chez la Vieille | **1er** 23
Chez Marianne | **4e** 19
NEW Clocher/Montmartre | **18e** –
Closerie/Lilas | **6e** 20
Cocottes | **7e** 24
Congrès Maillot | **17e** 20
Corte | **1er** –
Cotte Rôti | **12e** –
Z Coupole | **14e** 18
Z Deux Magots | **6e** 17
Ecluse | **multi.** 17
Emporio Armani | **6e** 19
Epi d'Or | **1er** 19
Escargot Montorgueil | **1er** 22
Fakhr el Dine | **16e** 25
Ferdi | **1er** 21
Fines Gueules | **1er** 20
Fins Gourmets | **7e** 18
Fish La Boiss. | **6e** 21
Fumoir | **1er** 18
Gaigne | **4e** 24
Gauloise | **15e** 18
Georgette | **9e** 17
Gourmand | **1er** 25
NEW Gyoza Bar | **2e** –
Isami | **4e** 25
Itinéraires | **5e** 23
Jean | **9e** 26
Joséphine/Dumonet | **6e** 25
Languedoc | **5e** 21
Legrand Filles/Fils | **2e** 21
Ma Bourgogne | **4e** 19
Marty | **5e** 20
Mauzac | **5e** 15
Maxan | **8e** 20
Moulin à Vent | **5e** 20
Mousson | **1er** –
Nemrod | **6e** 17
Papilles | **5e** 25
Pères et Filles | **6e** 17
Perraudin | **5e** 18
Petite Chaise | **7e** 18
Petite Sirène | **9e** 25
Petites Sorcières | **14e** 25
Petit Lutetia | **6e** 17
Petit Marguery | **13e** 23
Petit Marius | **8e** 20
Petit Pergolèse | **16e** 25
Petit Rétro | **16e** 18
Petit Riche | **9e** 22
Polidor | **6e** 15
Poule au Pot | **1er** 22
P'tit Troquet | **7e** 22
Racines | **2e** 20
Roi/Pot-au-Feu | **9e** 19
Rose Bakery | **multi.** 22
Z Table d'Eugène | **18e** 26
Table d'Hédiard | **8e** 22
Tan Dinh | **7e** 22
Terminus Nord | **10e** 18
Vagenende | **6e** 17
Vin et Marée | **multi.** 21
Vin sur Vin | **7e** 21
NEW Vivant | **10e** 24
Wepler | **18e** 20

ENTERTAINMENT

(Call for days and times of performances)

Alcazar | varies | **6e** 18
Annapurna | sitar | **8e** 23
Avenue | DJ | **8e** 16
Boeuf/le Toit | jazz | **8e** 18
Chez Cécile | jazz | **8e** 25
Chez Françoise | live music | **7e** 20
Chez Gégène | dancing | **Joinville** 16
Fakhr el Dine | live music | **16e** 25
Z Lasserre | pianist | **8e** 27
Maxim's | piano/vocalist | **8e** 20
Nos Ancêtres les Gaulois | guitar/vocalist | **4e** 13
Saudade | fado | **1er** 16
Zébra Square | DJ | **16e** 16

FIREPLACES

Atelier Maître Albert | **5e** 23
Chalet des Iles | **16e** 18
Costes | **1er** 18
Coupe-Chou | **5e** 20

Z Cristal Room | 16e 20
1728 | 8e 21
NEW Dodin/Mark Singer | 17e –
Européen | 12e 20
Ferme St-Simon | 7e 21
Fermette Marbeuf | 8e 19
Flottes O. Trement | 1er 21
Fontaine Gaillon | 2e 21
Frédéric Simonin | 17e –
Gaya | 7e 24
Grande Cascade | 16e 24
Ile | **Issy-les-Moul.** 19
Maison/Amér. Latine | 7e 21
Maison Blanche | 8e 23
Miroir | 18e 21
Montalembert | 7e 19
Nos Ancêtres les Gaulois | 4e 13
Pavillon Montsouris | 14e 22
Petit Châtelet | 5e 22
Petit Victor Hugo | 16e 19
Petrelle | 9e 25
Z Pré Catelan | 16e 26
Ralph's | 6e 17
Robert et Louise | 3e 20
Romantica | **Clichy** 22
Z Truffière | 5e 26
Z Villa Corse | 16e 21
Yugaraj | 6e 20

HISTORIC PLACES

(Year opened; * building)

1407 | Aub. Nicolas Flamel* | 3e 21
1582 | Spring* | 1er 27
1582 | Tour d'Argent | 5e 25
1629 | Rest. du Palais Royal* | 1er 20
1680 | Petite Chaise | 7e 18
1686 | Procope | 6e 17
1728 | 1728* | 8e 21
1758 | Ambassadeurs* | 8e 27
1766 | Lapérouse | 6e 23
1784 | Grand Véfour | 1er 28
1792 | Pavillon Ledoyen | 8e 25
1800 | Chardenoux/Prés* | 6e 21
1807 | Ma Bourgogne | 4e 19
1832 | Escargot Montorgueil | 1er 22
1832 | Pharamond | 1er 18
1842 | Laurent* | 8e 25
1845 | Polidor | 6e 15
1850 | Akrame* | 16e 23
1854 | Arc* | 16e 16
1854 | Petit Riche | 9e 22
1856 | Charpentiers | 6e 20
1862 | Café de la Paix | 9e 19
1864 | Bofinger | 4e 19
1870 | Bistro/Gastronomes* | 5e 23
1870 | Perraudin | 5e 18
1872 | Goumard | 1er 23
1876 | Gallopin | 2e 20
1879 | Grand Café | 9e 19
1880 | Epi d'Or | 1er 19
1880 | Legrand Filles/Fils* | 2e 21
1880 | Macéo | 1er 23
1881 | Café Terminus | 8e 19
1885 | Deux Magots | 6e 17
1889 | Jules Verne* | 7e 23
1889 | Pavillon Montsouris | 14e 22
1890 | Languedoc* | 5e 21
1890 | Lyonnais* | 2e 22
1892 | Abeille* | 16e 23
1892 | Gavroche | 2e 24
1892 | Wepler | 18e 20
1893 | Maxim's | 8e 20
1899 | Fouquet's | 8e 20
1896 | Shang Palace* | 16e 24
1900 | Bistro/Vieux Chêne* | 11e 23
1900 | Café Lenôtre* | 8e 23
1900 | Fermette Marbeuf | 8e 19
1900 | Gauloise | 15e 18
1900 | Grande Cascade | 16e 24
1900 | Rest. Paul | 1er 18
1900 | Table d'Eugène* | 18e 26
1901 | Petit St. Benoît | 6e 16
1901 | Train Bleu | 12e 19
1904 | Petit Rétro | 16e 18
1904 | Rest. Manufacture* | **Issy-les-Moul.** 22
1904 | Vagenende | 6e 17
1905 | Pré Catelan | 16e 26
1908 | Fins Gourmets | 7e 18

1908 | Fontaine de Mars | **7e** 22
1909 | Pomponette | **18e** 23
1911 | Rotonde | **6e** 19
1913 | Marty | **5e** 20
1913 | Zeyer | **14e** 19
1914 | Sébillon | **Neuilly** 22
1915 | Petit Lutetia | **6e** 17
1918 | Petit Marguery | **13e** 23
1919 | Lescure | **1er** 19
1920 | Chez Julien | **4e** 21
1920 | Hôtel Amour* | **9e** 15
1920 | Mémère Paulette | **2e** 23
1920 | Petit Niçois | **7e** 20
1922 | Boeuf/le Toit | **8e** 18
1923 | Thoumieux | **7e** 20
1924 | Ami Louis | **3e** 24
1925 | Grand Venise | **15e** 26
1925 | Prunier | **16e** 24
1925 | Rech | **17e** 22
1925 | Terminus Nord | **10e** 18
1927 | Caviar Kaspia | **8e** 26
1929 | Tante Louise | **8e** 23
1930 | Allard | **6e** 21
1930 | Bélisaire* | **15e** 23
1930 | Garnier | **8e** 22
1930 | Trumilou | **4e** 20
1935 | Grand Colbert | **2e** 19
1935 | Poule au Pot | **1er** 22
1936 | Relais Plaza | **8e** 25
1939 | Voltaire | **7e** 22
1940 | Flandrin | **16e** 15
1942 | Lasserre | **8e** 27
1943 | Méditerranée | **6e** 22
1946 | Moulin à Vent | **5e** 20
1946 | Taillevent | **8e** 29
1947 | Pied de Cochon | **1er** 19
1948 | Marius et Janette | **8e** 23
1948 | Rubis | **1er** 19
1950 | Mascotte | **18e** 20
1950 | Terrasse Mirabeau* | **16e** 26
1951 | Petit Châtelet | **5e** 22
1955 | Flora Danica | **8e** 21
1956 | Maison du Caviar | **8e** 25
1956 | Robert et Louise | **3e** 20
1959 | Paul Chêne | **16e** 23
1959 | Relais de Venise | **17e** 23
1960 | Bonne Franquette | **18e** -
1960 | Flore en l'Ile | **4e** 17
1960 | Truffière | **5e** 26
1961 | Pierre/Palais Royal | **1er** 22
1961 | Relais Louis XIII | **6e** 26
1961 | Soufflé | **1er** 22
1962 | Gourmets/Ternes | **8e** 23
1962 | Moissonnier | **5e** 24
1962 | Taverne/Sgt. Recruteur | **4e** 17
1962 | Tong Yen | **8e** 22

HOTEL DINING

Amour
Hôtel Amour | **9e** 15
Astor
Astor | **8e** 24
Bristol
Epicure (Le Bristol) | **8e** 27
Castille
Assaggio | **1er** 22
Concorde St-Lazare
Café Terminus | **8e** 19
Costes
Costes | **1er** 18
Crillon
Ambassadeurs | **8e** 27
El Dorado
Bistrot des Dames | **17e** 18
Four Seasons George V
Cinq | **8e** 28
InterContinental Le Grand
Café de la Paix | **9e** 19
Lancaster
Table/Lancaster | **8e** 25
Louvre
Brass. du Louvre | **1er** 19
Lutetia
Brass. Lutetia | **6e** 19
Maison Rouge
Rose Bakery | **12e** 22
Mama Shelter
Mama Shelter | **20e** 16

Mandarin Oriental
- NEW Camélia | 1er — -
- NEW Sur Mesure | 1er — -

Meurice
- Dali | 1er — -
- Z Meurice | 1er — 28

Montalembert
- Montalembert | 7e — 19

Novotel Tour Eiffel
- Benkay | 15e — 25

Park Hyatt Paris-Vendôme
- Pur' | 2e — 24

Plaza Athénée
- Z Alain Ducasse | 8e — 28
- Relais Plaza | 8e — 25

Pont Royal
- Z Atelier/Joël Robuchon | 7e — 27

Relais Saint-Germain
- Z Comptoir/Relais | 6e — 27

Renaissance Paris Vendôme
- Pinxo | 1er — 23

Royal Monceau
- Cuisine | 8e — 22

Shangri-La
- NEW Abeille | 16e — 23
- NEW Shang Palace | 16e — 24

Square
- Zébra Square | 16e — 16

Thoumieux
- Jean-François Piège | 7e — 27
- Thoumieux | 7e — 20

Vernet
- Vernet | 8e — 24

Westminster
- Céladon | 2e — 23

JACKET REQUIRED

(* Tie also required)

- NEW Abeille | 16e — 23
- Z Alain Ducasse | 8e — 28
- Z Ambroisie* | 4e — 27
- Z Astrance | 16e — 28
- Z Carré/Feuillants* | 1er — 27
- Z Cinq | 8e — 28
- Z Epicure (Le Bristol) | 8e — 27
- Z Guy Savoy | 17e — 28
- Lapérouse | 6e — 23
- Z Lasserre | 8e — 27
- Maxim's | 8e — 20
- Z Meurice | 1er — 28
- Z Michel Rostang | 17e — 27
- Z Relais Louis XIII | 6e — 26
- Z Taillevent | 8e — 29
- Z Tour d'Argent | 5e — 25

LATE DINING

(Weekday closing hour)

- Al Dar | 12 AM | **multi.** — 22
- Anahi | 12 AM | 3e — 19
- Z Atelier/Joël Robuchon | 12 AM | **multi.** — 27
- Aub. Dab | 2 AM | 16e — 20
- Avenue | 1 AM | 8e — 16
- Bacchantes | 12:30 AM | 9e — 21
- Ballon des Ternes | 12 AM | 17e — 19
- Z Bar à Huîtres | varies | **multi.** — 21
- Bar/Théâtres | 1 AM | 8e — 17
- Bistro/Deux Théâtres | 12:30 AM | 9e — 21
- Bistrot des Dames | 2 AM | 17e — 18
- Bistrot du Peintre | 12 AM | 11e — 18
- Boeuf Couronné | 12 AM | 19e — 23
- Z Bofinger | 12:30 AM | 4e — 19
- Brass. Balzar | 12 AM | 5e — 18
- Brass. Flo | 12:30 AM | 10e — 19
- Brass. Julien | 1 AM | 10e — 19
- Brass. La Lorraine | 1 AM | 8e — 18
- Z Brass. Lipp | 1 AM | 6e — 18
- Brass. Mollard | 12:30 AM | 8e — 18
- Café Burq | 12 AM | 18e — 21
- Z Café de Flore | 1:30 AM | 6e — 16
- Café de la Musique | varies | 19e — 17
- Café/l'Esplanade | 12:45 AM | 7e — 18
- Café du Commerce | 12 AM | 15e — 17
- Café du Passage | 1 AM | 11e — -
- Café Marly | 2 AM | 1er — 17
- Café Ruc | 1 AM | 1er — 15
- Z Caviar Kaspia | 1 AM | 8e — 26
- Charlot - Roi/Coquillages | varies | 9e — 21

Chéri Bibi | 12 AM | **18e** 20
Chez André | 1 AM | **8e** 22
NEW Chez Flottes | 12:30 AM | **1er** -
Chez Francis | 12:30 AM | **8e** 18
Chez Françoise | 12 AM | **7e** 20
Chez Janou | 12 AM | **3e** 21
Chez Jenny | 12 AM | **3e** 19
Z Chez L'Ami Jean | 12 AM | **7e** 25
Chez Paul | 12 AM | **11e** 22
Chez Paul | 12 AM | **13e** 22
Chez Prune | 1 AM | **10e** 15
Chez Vincent | 12 AM | **19e** 23
Christine | 12 AM | **6e** 21
Comme/Savonnières | 12 AM | **6e** -
Congrès Maillot | 2 AM | **17e** 20
Costes | 24 hrs. | **1er** 18
Coupe Gorge | 12 AM | **4e** -
Z Coupole | 1:30 AM | **14e** 18
Z Deux Magots | 1 AM | **6e** 17
Diep | 12:30 AM | **8e** 21
Dôme du Marais | 2 AM | **4e** 19
Duc de Richelieu | 12 AM | **12e** 22
Ecluse | 1 AM | **multi.** 17
Editeurs | 2 AM | **6e** 14
Emporio Armani | 12 AM | **6e** 19
Européen | 1 AM | **12e** 20
NEW Floréal | 2 AM | **10e** -
Flore en l'Ile | 2 AM | **4e** 17
Fogón | 12 AM | **6e** 23
Gallopin | 12 AM | **2e** 20
Gavroche | 1 AM | **2e** 24
Goumard | 12 AM | **1er** 23
Grand Café | 24 hrs. | **9e** 19
Grand Colbert | 1 AM | **2e** 19
Grande Armée | 1 AM | **16e** 16
Grille St-Germain | 12:30 AM | **6e** 21
Hôtel Amour | 11:30 PM | **9e** 15
Hotel du Nord | 12 AM | **10e** -
Il Vino | 12 AM | **7e** 22
Kaïten | 12 AM | **8e** 22
Kong | 12:30 AM | **1er** 16
Ma Bourgogne | 1 AM | **4e** 19
Maison du Caviar | 1 AM | **8e** 25
Mama Shelter | 12 AM | **20e** 16
Mascotte | 12 AM | **18e** 20
Murat | 12 AM | **16e** 17
Petit Marché | 12 AM | **3e** 23
Petit Marius | 12 AM | **8e** 20
Petit Riche | 12:15 AM | **9e** 22
Petit Zinc | 12 AM | **6e** 19
Z Pied de Cochon | 24 hrs. | **1er** 19
Polidor | 12:30 AM | **6e** 15
Pomponette | 12 AM | **18e** 23
Poule au Pot | 5 AM | **1er** 22
Z Procope | 1 AM | **6e** 17
404 | 12 AM | **3e** 20
Rotonde | 1 AM | **6e** 19
Sébillon | 12 AM | **Neuilly** 22
Société | 2 AM | **6e** 17
Square Trousseau | 2 AM | **12e** 19
Terminus Nord | 1 AM | **10e** 18
Thoumieux | 12 AM | **7e** 20
Tong Yen | 12:15 AM | **8e** 22
Vagenende | 1 AM | **6e** 17
Vaudeville | 1 AM | **2e** 20
Verre Bouteille | 4 AM | **17e** 19
NEW Vivant | 12 AM | **10e** 24
Wepler | 1 AM | **18e** 20
Zeyer | 12:30 AM | **14e** 19

MEET FOR A DRINK

Alcazar | **6e** 18
Arc | **16e** 16
Bar/Théâtres | **8e** 17
Baron Rouge | **12e** 18
Bistrot/Vins Mélac | **11e** 18
Bistrot du Peintre | **11e** 18
Bistrot Paul Bert | **11e** 21
Bons Crus | **1er** 21
Bourguignon/Marais | **4e** 25
Brass. Balzar | **5e** 18
Café Burq | **18e** 21
Z Café de Flore | **6e** 16
Café de la Jatte | **Neuilly** 18
Café de la Musique | **19e** 17
Café/l'Esplanade | **7e** 18
Café du Passage | **11e** -
Café Lenôtre | **8e** 23
Café Marly | **1er** 17

Café Ruc | **1er**	15
Cave Schmidt | **15e**	23
Cloche/Halles | **1er**	18
Closerie/Lilas | **6e**	20
Clown Bar | **11e**	15
Z Coupole | **14e**	18
NEW Dauphin | **11e**	22
Deux Amis | **11e**	21
Z Deux Magots | **6e**	17
Dôme | **14e**	22
Ecluse | **multi.**	17
Enoteca | **4e**	22
Ferdi | **1er**	21
Fines Gueules | **1er**	20
Fish La Boiss. | **6e**	21
Flottes O. Trement | **1er**	21
Fontaines | **5e**	19
Fouquet's | **8e**	20
Z Frenchie | **2e**	26
Fumoir | **1er**	18
Gavroche | **2e**	24
Grande Armée | **16e**	16
Hotel du Nord | **10e**	-
Juveniles | **1er**	15
Legrand Filles/Fils | **2e**	21
Ma Bourgogne | **4e**	19
Mama Shelter | **20e**	16
Mauzac | **5e**	15
Minipalais | **8e**	21
Nemrod | **6e**	17
NEW Passage | **11e**	-
Racines | **2e**	20
Rest. du Palais Royal | **1er**	20
Rubis | **1er**	19
NEW Verjus | **1er**	-
Vin sur Vin | **7e**	21
NEW Vivant | **10e**	24
Wepler | **18e**	20
Willi's Wine | **1er**	20
Zébra Square | **16e**	16

NEWCOMERS

Abeille | **16e**	23
Affable | **7e**	-
Affranchis | **9e**	-
Agapé Substance | **6e**	25
Akrame | **16e**	23
Albion | **10e**	-
Atao | **17e**	-
Auberge du 15 | **13e**	24
Bélisaire | **15e**	23
Big Fernand | **9e**	-
Bistro/Gastronomes | **5e**	23
Bistronomes | **1er**	-
Blend | **2e**	-
Bourgogne Sud | **9e**	-
Braisenville | **9e**	-
Caffe Burlot/Costes | **8e**	-
Camélia | **1er**	-
Camion Qui Fume | **Location Varies**	-
Candelaria | **3e**	-
Chardenoux/Prés | **6e**	21
Chatomat | **20e**	-
Chez Flottes | **1er**	-
Clocher/Montmartre | **18e**	-
Cobéa | **14e**	-
Compagnie/Bretagne | **6e**	-
Comptoir/Brice | **10e**	-
Coq Rico | **18e**	-
Cornichon | **14e**	-
Dans les Landes | **5e**	23
Dauphin | **11e**	22
Dodin/Mark Singer | **17e**	-
Entrée/Artistes | **11e**	-
Floréal | **10e**	-
Galopin | **10e**	-
Gyoza Bar | **2e**	-
Instant d'Or | **8e**	-
Jaja | **4e**	17
Kei | **1er**	28
Maison Mère | **9e**	-
Neva | **8e**	-
Opéra Rest. | **9e**	19
Pantruche | **9e**	24
Passage | **11e**	-
Petit Cheval/Manège | **11e**	-
Pottoka | **7e**	-
Qui Plume/Lune | **11e**	-

Racines 2 | **1er** –
Sassotondo | **11e** –
Septime | **11e** 25
Shang Palace | **16e** 24
Square Gardette | **11e** –
Sur Mesure | **1er** –
Tintilou | **11e** –
Verjus | **1er** –
Vivant | **10e** 24
Yoom | **multi.** –

NO AIR-CONDITIONING

Accolade | **17e** 20
A et M | **16e** 21
Afaria | **15e** 23
Agrume | **5e** 24
Aimant du Sud | **13e** 21
Al Taglio | **11e** 22
Z Ami Louis | **3e** 24
Anahuacalli | **5e** 23
AOC | **5e** 23
Assiette | **14e** 19
Aub. du Champ/Mars | **7e** 23
Aub. Nicolas Flamel | **3e** 21
Z Bar à Huîtres | **17e** 21
Baratin | **20e** 24
Bascou | **3e** 23
Biche/Bois | **12e** 22
Bistro/Vieux Chêne | **11e** 23
Bistrot/Côté La Boutarde | **Neuilly** 21
Bistrot d'André | **15e** 20
Bistrot/l'Oulette | **4e** 22
Bistrot de Paris | **7e** 19
Bistrot des Dames | **17e** 18
Bistrot d'Henri | **6e** 22
Bistrot Vivienne | **2e** 19
Bon Saint Pourçain | **6e** 19
Botanistes | **7e** 19
Bouchon/L'Assiette | **17e** 22
Brass./l'Ile St-Louis | **4e** 19
Breizh Café | **3e** 22
Café Burq | **18e** 21
Café Cartouche | **12e** –
Caffé dei Cioppi | **11e** 25
Cagouille | **14e** 23
Cailloux | **13e** 22
Cantine/Tontons | **15e** 17
Cantine/Troquet | **14e** 25
Caves Pétrissans | **17e** 23
Cerisaie | **14e** 23
Chalet | **Neuilly** 21
Chalet des Iles | **16e** 18
Chantairelle | **5e** –
Chardenoux | **11e** 23
Chéri Bibi | **18e** 20
Chez Françoise | **7e** 20
Chez Georges | **17e** 22
Chez Géraud | **16e** 20
Chez Grenouille | **9e** 21
Chez Julien | **4e** 21
Chez Marianne | **4e** 19
Chez Marie-Louise | **10e** –
Chez Michel | **10e** 24
Chez Nénesse | **3e** 21
Chez Omar | **3e** 19
Chez Paul | **11e** 22
Chez Paul | **13e** 22
Chez Prune | **10e** 15
Chez René | **5e** 19
Christophe | **5e** 24
Cibus | **1er** –
Cloche/Halles | **1er** 18
Closerie/Lilas | **6e** 20
Clown Bar | **11e** 15
Coin/Gourmets | **5e** 23
Cotte Rôti | **12e** –
Coupe Gorge | **4e** –
Crémerie | **6e** 21
Cristal de Sel | **15e** 27
Crudus | **1er** –
Crus/Bourgogne | **2e** 20
Desvouges | **5e** –
Deux Amis | **11e** 21
Duc de Richelieu | **12e** 22
Ebouillanté | **4e** 22
Ecluse | **multi.** 17
Ecume St-Honoré | **1er** 23
El Palenque | **5e** 22

Epi d'Or | **1er**	19
Epi Dupin | **6e**	24
Epigramme | **6e**	23
Ferdi | **1er**	21
Fines Gueules | **1er**	20
Fins Gourmets | **7e**	18
Flandrin | **16e**	15
Flore en l'Ile | **4e**	17
Fontaines | **5e**	19
Fourchette | **17e**	23
Gauloise | **15e**	18
Georgette | **9e**	17
Gitane | **15e**	18
Gli Angeli | **3e**	20
Gourmets/Ternes | **8e**	23
Graindorge | **17e**	23
Grande Cascade | **16e**	24
Grand Pan | **15e**	23
Grille | **10e**	21
Gourmand | **Neuilly**	18
Hôtel Amour | **9e**	15
Z Huîtrerie Régis | **6e**	26
Il Barone | **14e**	22
Ile | **Issy-les-Moul.**	19
Jadis | **15e**	23
Jardins de Bagatelle | **16e**	20
Joséphine/Dumonet | **6e**	25
Juveniles | **1er**	15
Khun Akorn | **11e**	21
Lilane | **5e**	25
Ma Bourgogne | **4e**	19
Maison/Amér. Latine | **7e**	21
Marée Passy | **16e**	22
Marius | **16e**	25
Marlotte | **6e**	18
Martel | **10e**	21
Mascotte | **18e**	20
Mauzac | **5e**	15
Mémère Paulette | **2e**	23
Miroir | **18e**	21
Moissonnier | **5e**	24
Montalembert | **7e**	19
Mon Vieil Ami | **4e**	23
Moulin à Vent | **5e**	20
Mousson | **1er**	-
Moustache | **6e**	19
Oto-Oto | **6e**	-
Ourcine | **13e**	25
Pavillon/Lac | **19e**	19
Pavillon Montsouris | **14e**	22
Pères et Filles | **6e**	17
Petit Châtelet | **5e**	22
Petites Sorcières | **14e**	25
Petit Lutetia | **6e**	17
Petit Marché | **3e**	23
Petit Marius | **8e**	20
Petit Niçois | **7e**	20
Petit St. Benoît | **6e**	16
Petrelle | **9e**	25
Pharamond | **1er**	18
Philou | **10e**	21
Pizza Chic | **6e**	21
Pomponette | **18e**	23
P'tit Troquet | **7e**	22
Quai-Quai | **1er**	18
Quedubon | **19e**	18
Racines | **2e**	20
Relais de Venise | **17e**	23
Repaire/Cartouche | **11e**	17
Rest. du Marché | **15e**	21
Rest. du Palais Royal | **1er**	20
Rest. Paul | **1er**	18
Robert et Louise | **3e**	20
Roi/Pot-au-Feu | **9e**	19
Romantica | **Clichy**	22
Rose Bakery | **3e**	22
Rughetta | **18e**	21
Sale e Pepe | **18e**	21
Scheffer | **16e**	19
Schmidt - L'Os/Moëlle | **15e**	23
Sot l'y Laisse | **11e**	22
Square Marcadet | **18e**	-
Square Trousseau | **12e**	19
Temps au Temps | **11e**	23
Temps des Cerises | **13e**	18
Terrasse Mirabeau | **16e**	26
Timbre | **6e**	25
Tourbillon | **5e**	24

Z Train Bleu | **12e** 19
Troquet | **15e** 24
Tsukizi | **6e** 22
Vaudeville | **2e** 20
Verre Volé | **10e** 20
Vin et Marée | **16e** 21
Willi's Wine | **1er** 20
Z Yam'Tcha | **1er** 26

OPEN SUNDAY

NEW Abeille | **16e** 23
A et M | **16e** 21
Alcazar | **6e** 18
Al Dar | **multi.** 22
Allard | **6e** 21
Allobroges | **20e** 22
Al Taglio | **11e** 22
Ambassade/Auv. | **3e** 22
Z Ambassadeurs | **8e** 27
Z Ami Louis | **3e** 24
Anahi | **3e** 19
Anahuacalli | **5e** 23
Antoine | **16e** 22
Ardoise | **1er** 23
Aromatik | **9e** 18
Z As/Fallafel | **4e** 23
Assaggio | **1er** 22
Assiette | **14e** 19
Astier | **11e** 21
NEW Atao | **17e** -
Z Atelier/Joël Robuchon | **multi.** 27
Atelier Maître Albert | **5e** 23
Atlas | **5e** 21
Aub. Bressane | **7e** 22
Aub. Dab | **16e** 20
Aub. du Champ/Mars | **7e** 23
Aub. Nicolas Flamel | **3e** 21
Avenue | **8e** 16
Azabu | **6e** 24
Ballon des Ternes | **17e** 19
Ballon/Coquillages | **17e** -
Z Bar à Huîtres | **multi.** 21
Baratin | **20e** 24
Bar/Théâtres | **8e** 17
Baron Rouge | **12e** 18
Bartolo | **6e** 20
Bastide Odéon | **6e** 20
Beaujolais/Auteuil | **16e** 19
Bellini | **16e** 21
Benkay | **15e** 25
Z Benoît | **4e** 23
Bistro 121 | **15e** 22
Bistro/Breteuil | **7e** 18
Bistro/Deux Théâtres | **9e** 21
NEW Bistro/Gastronomes | **5e** 23
Bistro du 17ème | **17e** 19
Bistro St. Ferdinand | **17e** 19
Bistrot/Côté Flaubert | **17e** 21
Bistrot/Côté La Boutarde | **Neuilly** 21
Bistrot des Dames | **17e** 18
Bistrot des Vignes | **16e** 20
Bistrot d'Henri | **6e** 22
Bistrot du Dôme | **multi.** 22
Bistrot du Peintre | **11e** 18
Boeuf Couronné | **19e** 23
Boeuf/le Toit | **8e** 18
Z Bofinger | **4e** 19
Bonne Franquette | **18e** -
Botanistes | **7e** 19
Boucherie Roulière | **6e** 26
Bouillon Racine | **6e** 18
Brass./l'Ile St-Louis | **4e** 19
Brass. Balzar | **5e** 18
Brass. du Louvre | **1er** 19
Brass. Flo | **10e** 19
Brass. Julien | **10e** 19
Brass. La Lorraine | **8e** 18
Z Brass. Lipp | **6e** 18
Brass. Lutetia | **6e** 19
Brass. Mollard | **8e** 18
Breizh Café | **3e** 22
Café Constant | **7e** 24
Z Café de Flore | **6e** 16
Café de la Jatte | **Neuilly** 18
Café de la Musique | **19e** 17
Café de la Paix | **9e** 19
Café/l'Esplanade | **7e** 18
Café des Musées | **3e** 20
Café du Commerce | **15e** 17

Café Lenôtre | **8e**	23
Café Rouge | **3e**	19
Café Ruc | **1er**	15
NEW Caffe Burlot/Costes | **8e**	-
Caffé Toscano | **7e**	19
Cagouille | **14e**	23
Cailloux | **13e**	22
NEW Camélia | **1er**	-
NEW Camion Qui Fume | **Location Varies**	-
NEW Candelaria | **3e**	-
Cantine/Quentin | **10e**	-
Cantine/Troquet | **15e**	25
Casa Bini | **6e**	23
Céladon | **2e**	23
Chalet | **Neuilly**	21
Chalet des Iles | **16e**	18
Z Chamarré Mont. | **18e**	26
Chardenoux | **11e**	23
NEW Chardenoux/Prés | **6e**	21
Charlot - Roi/Coquillages | **9e**	21
Charpentiers | **6e**	20
Chartier | **9e**	15
NEW Chatomat | **20e**	-
Cherche Midi | **6e**	22
Chez André | **8e**	22
NEW Chez Flottes | **1er**	-
Chez Francis | **8e**	18
Chez Françoise | **7e**	20
Chez Gégène | **Joinville**	16
Chez Georges | **17e**	22
Chez Janou | **3e**	21
Chez Jenny | **3e**	19
Chez Julien | **4e**	21
Chez Ly | **17e**	25
Chez Marianne | **4e**	19
Chez Omar | **3e**	19
Chez Paul | **11e**	22
Chez Paul | **13e**	22
Chez Prune | **10e**	15
Christine | **6e**	21
Christophe | **5e**	24
Z Cinq | **8e**	28
NEW Clocher/Montmartre | **18e**	-
Closerie/Lilas | **6e**	20
Cocottes | **7e**	24
Coin/Gourmets | **5e**	23
NEW Compagnie/Bretagne | **6e**	-
NEW Comptoir/Brice | **10e**	-
Comptoir/Mers | **4e**	23
Z Comptoir/Relais | **6e**	27
Comptoir Marguery | **13e**	21
Congrès Maillot | **17e**	20
NEW Coq Rico | **18e**	-
Costes | **1er**	18
Coupe-Chou | **5e**	20
Coupe Gorge | **4e**	-
Z Coupole | **14e**	18
Cuisine | **8e**	22
Cul de Poule | **9e**	20
Dali | **1er**	-
NEW Dans les Landes | **5e**	23
Da Rosa | **6e**	21
Délices/Aphrodite | **5e**	20
Derrière | **3e**	15
Dessirier | **17e**	24
Z Deux Magots | **6e**	17
Diep | **8e**	21
Domaine/Lintillac | **multi.**	20
Dôme | **14e**	22
Dôme du Marais | **4e**	19
Drouant | **2e**	23
Ebouillanté | **4e**	22
Ecluse | **multi.**	17
Editeurs | **6e**	14
Emporio Armani | **6e**	19
Enoteca | **4e**	22
Z Epicure (Le Bristol) | **8e**	27
Escargot Montorgueil | **1er**	22
Européen | **12e**	20
Fables/Fontaine | **7e**	25
Fakhr el Dine | **16e**	25
Ferdi | **1er**	21
Fermette Marbeuf | **8e**	19
Findi | **8e**	21
Fines Gueules | **1er**	20
Firmin le Barbier | **7e**	21
Fish La Boiss. | **6e**	21

Flandrin | **16e**	15
Flora Danica | **8e**	21
NEW Floréal | **10e**	-
Flore en l'Ile | **4e**	17
Fogón | **6e**	23
Z Fontaine de Mars | **7e**	22
Fontaines | **5e**	19
Foujita | **1er**	25
Fouquet's | **8e**	20
Fumoir | **1er**	18
Gallopin | **2e**	20
Gare | **16e**	18
Garnier | **8e**	22
Gauloise | **15e**	18
Georges | **4e**	17
Gitane | **15e**	18
Glou | **3e**	20
Goumard | **1er**	23
Grand Café | **9e**	19
Grand Colbert | **2e**	19
Grande Armée | **16e**	16
Grande Cascade | **16e**	24
Grand Louvre | **1er**	20
Grille St-Germain | **6e**	21
Z Guilo-Guilo | **18e**	27
Gourmand | **Neuilly**	18
Higuma | **1er**	20
Hôtel Amour | **9e**	15
Hotel du Nord | **10e**	-
Z Huîtrerie Régis | **6e**	26
Huîtrier | **17e**	22
Ile | **Issy-les-Moul.**	19
Ilot Vache | **4e**	20
NEW Jaja | **4e**	17
Jardins de Bagatelle | **16e**	20
Jeanne A | **11e**	-
Z Jules Verne | **7e**	23
Khun Akorn | **11e**	21
Kim Anh | **15e**	23
Kong | **1er**	16
Languedoc | **5e**	21
Lao Lane Xang | **13e**	22
Lao Siam | **19e**	22
Liza | **2e**	24
Ma Bourgogne | **4e**	19
Maharajah | **5e**	23
Mai Do | **6e**	-
Maison Blanche | **8e**	23
Maison du Caviar | **8e**	25
NEW Maison Mère | **9e**	-
Mama Shelter | **20e**	16
Marée | **8e**	23
Marée Passy | **16e**	22
Marius et Janette | **8e**	23
Market | **8e**	22
Marlotte | **6e**	18
Marty | **5e**	20
Mascotte | **18e**	20
Mavrommatis | **5e**	22
Méditerranée | **6e**	22
Mesturet | **2e**	16
Minipalais | **8e**	21
Mirama | **5e**	22
Montalembert | **7e**	19
Mon Vieil Ami | **4e**	23
Mori Venice | **2e**	21
Moulin/Galette | **18e**	20
Murat | **16e**	17
Muscade | **1er**	-
Nanashi | **multi.**	-
Nemrod | **6e**	17
Nos Ancêtres les Gaulois | **4e**	13
Nouveau Village | **13e**	19
Ombres | **7e**	21
Oum el Banine | **16e**	22
Parc aux Cerfs | **6e**	20
Pavillon/Lac | **19e**	19
Pavillon Montsouris | **14e**	22
Père Claude | **15e**	21
Pères et Filles | **6e**	17
Perraudin | **5e**	18
Perron | **7e**	-
Petit Châtelet | **5e**	22
Petite Chaise | **7e**	18
Petite Cour | **6e**	20
Petit Lutetia | **6e**	17
Petit Marché | **3e**	23
Petit Marguery | **13e**	23

Petit Marius | **8e** 20
Petit Niçois | **7e** 20
Petit Pontoise | **5e** 25
Petit Riche | **9e** 22
Petit St. Benoît | **6e** 16
Petit Victor Hugo | **16e** 19
Petit Zinc | **6e** 19
Pétrus | **17e** 23
Z Pied de Cochon | **1er** 19
Z Pierre Gagnaire | **8e** 28
Pizza Chic | **6e** 21
Polidor | **6e** 15
Poule au Pot | **1er** 22
Z Pramil | **3e** 28
Z Procope | **6e** 17
Pur' | **2e** 24
Quai | **7e** 19
404 | **3e** 20
Ralph's | **6e** 17
Ravi | **7e** -
Relais d'Auteuil | **16e** 25
Z Relais/l'Entrecôte | **multi.** 22
Relais de Venise | **17e** 23
Relais Plaza | **8e** 25
Réminet | **5e** 23
Rest. Paul | **1er** 18
Reuan Thai | **11e** -
Robert et Louise | **3e** 20
Rosa Bonheur | **19e** 16
Rose Bakery | **multi.** 22
Rôtiss. du Beaujolais | **5e** 22
Rotonde | **6e** 19
Royal Madeleine | **8e** 23
Rughetta | **18e** 21
Saotico | **2e** -
NEW Sassotondo | **11e** -
Saut du Loup | **1er** 13
Sébillon | **Neuilly** 22
Z Senderens | **8e** 26
Shan Gout | **12e** -
NEW Shang Palace | **16e** 24
Société | **6e** 17
NEW Square Gardette | **11e** -
Square Trousseau | **12e** 19
Stella | **16e** 21
Table/Lancaster | **8e** 25
NEW Tablettes/Nomicos | **16e** 28
Terminus Nord | **10e** 18
Thoumieux | **7e** 20
Timgad | **17e** 22
Tong Yen | **8e** 22
Z Train Bleu | **12e** 19
Tricotin | **13e** 19
Trumilou | **4e** 20
Tsé-Yang | **16e** 22
Tsukizi | **6e** 22
Vagenende | **6e** 17
Vaudeville | **2e** 20
Verre Volé | **10e** 20
Z Villa Corse | **multi.** 21
Vin et Marée | **multi.** 21
Vins/Pyrénées | **4e** 17
Violon d'Ingres | **7e** 25
NEW Vivant | **10e** 24
Wepler | **18e** 20
Z Yam'Tcha | **1er** 26
Yugaraj | **6e** 20
Zébra Square | **16e** 16
Zeyer | **14e** 19

OUTDOOR DINING

(G=garden; P=patio; S=sidewalk; T=terrace)

Absinthe | S, T | **1er** 21
A et M | S | **16e** 21
Aimant du Sud | S, T | **13e** 21
Z Alain Ducasse | P | **8e** 28
Al Dar | S, T | **multi.** 22
Antoine | T | **16e** 22
AOC | T | **5e** 23
Arc | **16e** 16
Astier | S | **11e** 21
Atlas | S | **5e** 21
Aub. Dab | S | **16e** 20
Avenue | T | **8e** 16
Ballon des Ternes | S, T | **17e** 19
Bartolo | S, T | **6e** 20
Beaujolais/Auteuil | S | **16e** 19
Bistro/Vieux Chêne | S | **11e** 23

Bistro/Breteuil | T | **7e** 18
Bistro du 17ème | S | **17e** 19
Bistrot/Vins Mélac | S | **11e** 18
Bistrot/Côté Flaubert | S | **17e** 21
Bistrot/Côté La Boutarde | S | **Neuilly** 21
Bistrot des Dames | G | **17e** 18
Bistrot du Peintre | T | **11e** 18
Bistrot Vivienne | T | **2e** 19
Bon Accueil | S | **7e** 23
Bon Saint Pourçain | S | **6e** 19
Bourguignon/Marais | T | **4e** 25
Brass./l'Ile St-Louis | T | **4e** 19
Brass. du Louvre | T | **1er** 19
Buisson Ardent | S | **5e** 22
Z Café de Flore | S, T | **6e** 16
Café de la Jatte | G, T | **Neuilly** 18
Café de la Musique | T | **19e** 17
Café de la Paix | S | **9e** 19
Café/l'Esplanade | S | **7e** 18
Café du Passage | S | **11e** –
Café Lenôtre | G, P | **8e** 23
Café Marly | T | **1er** 17
Café Ruc | S | **1er** 15
Cagouille | T | **14e** 23
Cailloux | S | **13e** 22
NEW Camélia | G | **1er** –
Caves Pétrissans | T | **17e** 23
Chalet des Iles | G, T | **16e** 18
Chantairelle | G | **5e** –
Charpentiers | S | **6e** 20
Cherche Midi | S | **6e** 22
Chez André | S | **8e** 22
Chez Francis | S | **8e** 18
Chez Gégène | S, T | **Joinville** 16
Chez Janou | T | **3e** 21
Chez Léna et Mimile | T | **5e** 21
Chez Les Anges | S | **7e** 24
Chez Ly | S | **17e** 25
Chez Marianne | S, T | **4e** 19
Chez Michel | S | **10e** 24
Chez Omar | T | **3e** 19
Chez Paul | S | **11e** 22
Chez Paul | S | **13e** 22
Chez Prune | S | **10e** 15
Chez Ramulaud | S | **11e** –
Chez René | T | **5e** 19
Chez Savy | S | **8e** 20
Chez Vong | T | **1er** 23
Cigale Récamier | T | **7e** 22
Z Cinq | T | **8e** 28
Cloche/Halles | S, T | **1er** 18
Clos/Gourmets | T | **7e** 25
Closerie/Lilas | T | **6e** 20
Clown Bar | S | **11e** 15
Copenhague | T | **8e** 23
Costes | G, P | **1er** 18
Coupe-Chou | T | **5e** 20
Crus/Bourgogne | S | **2e** 20
Da Rosa | T | **6e** 21
Daru | S | **8e** 19
Délices/Aphrodite | S | **5e** 20
Z Deux Magots | G, T | **6e** 17
Ebauchoir | S | **12e** 24
Editeurs | S | **6e** 14
El Mansour | T | **8e** 21
Z Epicure (Le Bristol) | G | **8e** 27
Eugène | S | **8e** 18
Fables/Fontaine | T | **7e** 25
Findi | S | **8e** 21
Fins Gourmets | S | **7e** 18
Flandrin | S, T | **16e** 15
Flora Danica | G, S, T | **8e** 21
Flore en l'Ile | S | **4e** 17
Florimond | S | **7e** 25
Z Fontaine de Mars | S, T | **7e** 22
Fontaine Gaillon | T | **2e** 21
Fontaines | S | **5e** 19
Fouquet's | S, T | **8e** 20
Fumoir | S | **1er** 18
Gallopin | S | **2e** 20
Gare | G, T | **16e** 18
Gauloise | S, T | **15e** 18
Georges | T | **4e** 17
Gitane | S, T | **15e** 18
Gourmets/Ternes | S | **8e** 23
Grand Café | S | **9e** 19
Grande Armée | S | **16e** 16

Grande Cascade | G, T | **16e** 24
Grille St-Germain | S | **6e** 21
Gourmand | G, T | **Neuilly** 18
Hangar | S | **3e** 23
Ile | G, T | **Issy-les-Moul.** 19
Jardins de Bagatelle | G, T | **16e** 20
Kaïten | S, T | **8e** 22
Khun Akorn | T | **11e** 21
Laurent | G, T | **8e** 25
Legrand Filles/Fils | P | **2e** 21
Lescure | G, T | **1er** 19
Ma Bourgogne | G, S, T | **4e** 19
Main d'Or | S, T | **11e** 22
Maison/Amér. Latine | G | **7e** 21
Maison Blanche | T | **8e** 23
Mama Shelter | T | **20e** 16
Marius | S, T | **16e** 25
Marius et Janette | S, T | **8e** 23
Market | S | **8e** 22
Marlotte | S | **6e** 18
Martel | S | **10e** 21
Marty | S, T | **5e** 20
Mauzac | S | **5e** 15
Mavrommatis | S, T | **5e** 22
Méditerranée | S, T | **6e** 22
Montalembert | S, T | **7e** 19
Moulin à Vent | S | **5e** 20
Moulin/Galette | G, P | **18e** 20
Murat | S, T | **16e** 17
Muscade | G, T | **1er** -
Nemrod | S, T | **6e** 17
Opportun | S | **14e** 22
Parc aux Cerfs | P | **6e** 20
Pavillon Montsouris | G | **14e** 22
Père Claude | S | **15e** 21
Pères et Filles | S, T | **6e** 17
Petite Cour | T | **6e** 20
Petit Marché | S | **3e** 23
Petit Marguery | S, T | **13e** 23
Petit Marius | S | **8e** 20
Petit Pontoise | S | **5e** 25
Petit Victor Hugo | S, T | **16e** 19
Pharamond | S | **1er** 18
Pichet de Paris | S | **8e** 22
Z Pré Catelan | G, T | **16e** 26
Relais de Venise | S, T | **17e** 23
Réminet | S | **5e** 23
Rest. du Palais Royal | G | **1er** 20
Rest. Manufacture | S, T | **Issy-les-Moul.** 22
Romantica | P, T | **Clichy** 22
Rosa Bonheur | **19e** 16
Rotonde | S, T | **6e** 19
Rughetta | T | **18e** 21
Saut du Loup | T | **1er** 13
Square Marcadet | G | **18e** -
Square Trousseau | S | **12e** 19
Stella | S | **16e** 21
Stresa | S | **8e** 22
Temps au Temps | S, T | **11e** 23
Terrasse Mirabeau | T | **16e** 26
Troquet | S | **15e** 24
Trumilou | S | **4e** 20
Vagenende | S, T | **6e** 17
Vaudeville | S, T | **2e** 20
20 de Bellechasse | S | **7e** 20
Wepler | S | **18e** 20
Zébra Square | S, T | **16e** 16

PARKING

(V=valet, *=validated)

NEW Abeille | V | **16e** 23
A et M | V | **16e** 21
NEW Affable | V | **7e** -
Agapé | V | **17e** 24
Z Alain Ducasse | V | **8e** 28
Al Dar | V | **5e** 22
Z Ambassadeurs | V | **8e** 27
Z Ambroisie | V | **4e** 27
Antoine | V | **16e** 22
Z Apicius | V | **8e** 27
Arc | V | **16e** 16
Assaggio | V | **1er** 22
Astor | V | **8e** 24
Aub. Bressane | V | **7e** 22
Avenue | V | **8e** 16
Z Bar à Huîtres | V | **17e** 21
Bastide Odéon | V | **6e** 20
Benkay | V | **15e** 25

Bistro 121 | V | **15e** 22
Bistrot/Côté Flaubert | V | **17e** 21
Bistrot/Côté La Boutarde | V | **Neuilly** 21
Bistrot de Paris | V | **7e** 19
Boeuf Couronné | V | **19e** 23
Boeuf/le Toit | V | **8e** 18
Bouchon/L'Assiette | V | **17e** 22
Bouquinistes | V | **6e** 23
Brass. Flo | V | **10e** 19
Brass. Julien | V | **10e** 19
Brass. La Lorraine | V | **8e** 18
Café de la Jatte | V | **Neuilly** 18
Café/l'Esplanade | V | **7e** 18
Café du Commerce | V | **15e** 17
Café Lenôtre | V | **8e** 23
Café Terminus | V | **8e** 19
Cantine/Tontons | V | **15e** 17
Z Carré/Feuillants | V | **1er** 27
Caves Pétrissans | V | **17e** 23
Z Caviar Kaspia | V | **8e** 26
Céladon | V | **2e** 23
Chalet des Iles | V | **16e** 18
Z Chamarré Mont. | V | **18e** 26
NEW Chardenoux/Prés | V | **6e** 21
Chen Soleil d'Est | V | **15e** -
Chez Françoise | V | **7e** 20
Chez Fred | V | **17e** 19
Chez Georges | V | **17e** 22
Chez Jenny | V | **3e** 19
Chez Les Anges | V | **7e** 24
Chez Vong | V | **1er** 23
Chiberta | V | **8e** 24
Citrus Etoile | V | **8e** 24
Clocher Péreire | V | **17e** 24
Closerie/Lilas | V | **6e** 20
Comme/Savonnières | V | **6e** -
Comptoir Marguery | V | **13e** 21
Congrès Maillot | V | **17e** 20
Copenhague | V | **8e** 23
Costes | V | **1er** 18
Cou de la Girafe | V | **8e** 13
Z Cristal Room | V | **16e** 20
Derrière | V | **3e** 15
Dessirier | V | **17e** 24
Diep | V | **8e** 21
Z Divellec | V | **7e** 26
1728 | V | **8e** 21
NEW Dodin/Mark Singer | V | **17e** -
Dôme du Marais | V | **4e** 19
Drouant | V | **2e** 23
Ecaille de Fontaine | V | **2e** -
Ecailler du Bistrot | V | **11e** 25
El Mansour | V | **8e** 21
Enfants Terribles | V | **8e** 20
Z Epicure (Le Bristol) | V | **8e** 27
Fakhr el Dine | V | **16e** 25
Ferrandaise | V | **6e** 20
Findi | V | **8e** 21
Flandrin | V | **16e** 15
Flora Danica | V | **8e** 21
Flottes O. Trement | V | **1er** 21
Fontaine Gaillon | V | **2e** 21
Fouquet's | V | **8e** 20
Frédéric Simonin | V | **17e** -
Gallopin | V | **2e** 20
Gare | V | **16e** 18
Goumard | V | **1er** 23
Gourmand | V | **1er** 25
Gourmets/Ternes | V | **8e** 23
Grand Colbert | V | **2e** 19
Grande Armée | V | **16e** 16
Grande Cascade | V | **16e** 24
Z Grand Véfour | V | **1er** 28
Z Grand Venise | V | **15e** 26
Gourmand | V | **Neuilly** 18
Z Guy Savoy | V | **17e** 28
Z Hélène Darroze | V | **6e** 26
Z Hiramatsu | V | **16e** 27
Ile | V | **Issy-les-Moul.** 19
Itinéraires | V | **5e** 23
Jamin | V | **16e** 23
Jean | V | **9e** 26
Jean-François Piège | V | **7e** 27
Z Jules Verne | V | **7e** 23
KGB | V | **6e** 23
Kim Anh | V | **15e** 23
Kong | V | **1er** 16

Lao Lane Xang | V | **13e** 22
Lapérouse | V | **6e** 23
Z Lasserre | V | **8e** 27
Laurent | V | **8e** 25
Liza | V | **2e** 24
Luna | V | **8e** 26
Lyonnais | V | **2e** 22
Maison Blanche | V | **8e** 23
Maison Courtine | V | **14e** 20
Maison du Caviar | V | **8e** 25
Mama Shelter | V | **20e** 16
Marée | V | **8e** 23
Marée Passy | V | **16e** 22
Marius | V | **16e** 25
Marius et Janette | V | **8e** 23
Market | V | **8e** 22
Marty | V | **5e** 20
Maxan | V | **8e** 20
Maxim's | V | **8e** 20
Méditerranée | V | **6e** 22
Z Meurice | V | **1er** 28
Z Michel Rostang | V | **17e** 27
Minipalais | V | **8e** 21
Miroir | V | **18e** 21
Montalembert | V | **7e** 19
Moulin à Vent | V | **5e** 20
Murat | V | **16e** 17
Paul Chêne | V | **16e** 23
Pavillon Montsouris | V | **14e** 22
Petite Sirène* | **9e** 25
Petit Marguery | V | **13e** 23
Petit Marius | V | **8e** 20
Petit Pergolèse | V | **16e** 25
Petit Riche* | **9e** 22
Petit Victor Hugo | V | **16e** 19
Pétrus | V | **17e** 23
Pharamond | V | **1er** 18
Pichet de Paris | V | **8e** 22
Pierre/Palais Royal | V | **1er** 22
Z Pierre Gagnaire | V | **8e** 28
Z Pré Catelan | V | **16e** 26
Prunier | V | **16e** 24
Pur' | V | **2e** 24
Z Quinzième | V | **15e** 26
Ralph's | V | **6e** 17
Rech | V | **17e** 22
Relais d'Auteuil | V | **16e** 25
Z Relais Louis XIII | V | **6e** 26
Relais Plaza | V | **8e** 25
Réminet | V | **5e** 23
Romantica | V | **Clichy** 22
Rôtiss. d'en Face | V | **6e** 20
Saut du Loup | V | **1er** 13
Sébillon | V | **Neuilly** 22
Z Senderens | V | **8e** 26
Sensing | V | **6e** 23
NEW Shang Palace | V | **16e** 24
6 New York | V | **16e** 23
Sormani | V | **17e** 24
Stella | V | **16e** 21
Table d'Hédiard | V | **8e** 22
Table/Lancaster | V | **8e** 25
NEW Tablettes/Nomicos | V | **16e** 28
Z Taillevent | V | **8e** 29
Tang | V | **16e** 22
Terrasse Mirabeau | V | **16e** 26
Timgad | V | **17e** 22
Tong Yen | V | **8e** 22
Z Tour d'Argent | V | **5e** 25
39V | V | **8e** 23
Vernet | V | **8e** 24
Z Villa Corse | V | **15e** 21
Villaret | V | **11e** 23
Vin et Marée | V | **multi.** 21
Zébra Square | V | **16e** 16

PEOPLE-WATCHING

Absinthe | **1er** 21
NEW Affable | **7e** -
Z Alain Ducasse | **8e** 28
Z Ami Louis | **3e** 24
Anahi | **3e** 19
Arc | **16e** 16
Z Arpège | **7e** 27
Astor | **8e** 24
Z Astrance | **16e** 28
Z Atelier/Joël Robuchon | **7e** 27
Avenue | **8e** 16
Z Benoît | **4e** 23

Bistro Volnay | **2e** 21
Brass. Balzar | **5e** 18
Z Brass. Lipp | **6e** 18
Z Café de Flore | **6e** 16
Café/l'Esplanade | **7e** 18
NEW Camélia | **1er** -
Z 144 Petrossian | **7e** 24
Chateaubriand | **11e** 23
Chez Les Anges | **7e** 24
Chez Omar | **3e** 19
Z Cinq | **8e** 28
Cinq Mars | **7e** 21
Costes | **1er** 18
Cul de Poule | **9e** 20
Dali | **1er** -
Derrière | **3e** 15
Z Deux Magots | **6e** 17
Z Divellec | **7e** 26
Dôme | **14e** 22
Drouant | **2e** 23
Z Duc | **14e** 28
Z Epicure (Le Bristol) | **8e** 27
Etc. | **16e** 25
Ferme St-Simon | **7e** 21
Flandrin | **16e** 15
Fouquet's | **8e** 20
Gare | **16e** 18
Gauloise | **15e** 18
Georges | **4e** 17
Grande Armée | **16e** 16
Z Grand Véfour | **1er** 28
Z Guy Savoy | **17e** 28
Itinéraires | **5e** 23
Joséphine/Dumonet | **6e** 25
Kong | **1er** 16
Z Lasserre | **8e** 27
Maison Blanche | **8e** 23
Mama Shelter | **20e** 16
Market | **8e** 22
Méditerranée | **6e** 22
Minipalais | **8e** 21
Ombres | **7e** 21
NEW Opéra Rest. | **9e** 19
Pavillon/Lac | **19e** 19
Pavillon Ledoyen | **8e** 25
Petrelle | **9e** 25
Z Pierre Gagnaire | **8e** 28
Z Pré Catelan | **16e** 26
Prunier | **16e** 24
Z Quinzième | **15e** 26
Ralph's | **6e** 17
Relais Plaza | **8e** 25
Saturne | **2e** 22
Saut du Loup | **1er** 13
Z Senderens | **8e** 26
Sensing | **6e** 23
Société | **6e** 17
Sormani | **17e** 24
Square Trousseau | **12e** 19
Stresa | **8e** 22
Table/Lancaster | **8e** 25
Z Taillevent | **8e** 29
Tan Dinh | **7e** 22
Terrasse Mirabeau | **16e** 26
Tong Yen | **8e** 22
Z Tour d'Argent | **5e** 25
Voltaire | **7e** 22

POWER SCENES

NEW Abeille | **16e** 23
NEW Affable | **7e** -
Agapé | **17e** 24
Z Alain Ducasse | **8e** 28
Z Ambassadeurs | **8e** 27
Z Ambroisie | **4e** 27
Z Apicius | **8e** 27
Z Arpège | **7e** 27
Z Atelier/Joël Robuchon | **7e** 27
Aub. Bressane | **7e** 22
Bar/Théâtres | **8e** 17
Z Benoît | **4e** 23
Bistrot de Paris | **7e** 19
Bistrot d'Henri | **6e** 22
Brass. Balzar | **5e** 18
Z Brass. Lipp | **6e** 18
Z Café de Flore | **6e** 16
Z Carré/Feuillants | **1er** 27
Caves Pétrissans | **17e** 23
Z Caviar Kaspia | **8e** 26

Céladon | **2e**	23
Chen Soleil d'Est | **15e**	-
Cherche Midi | **6e**	22
Chez Les Anges | **7e**	24
Chiberta | **8e**	24
Cigale Récamier | **7e**	22
Clos/Gourmets | **7e**	25
Closerie/Lilas | **6e**	20
Copenhague | **8e**	23
Costes | **1er**	18
Z Cristal Room | **16e**	20
Dessirier | **17e**	24
Z Divellec | **7e**	26
Dôme | **14e**	22
Z Duc | **14e**	28
Z Epicure (Le Bristol) | **8e**	27
Etc. | **16e**	25
Ferme St-Simon | **7e**	21
Flandrin | **16e**	15
Fouquet's | **8e**	20
Frédéric Simonin | **17e**	-
Gare | **16e**	18
Gaya | **7e**	24
Georges | **4e**	17
Goumard | **1er**	23
Grande Cascade | **16e**	24
Z Grand Véfour | **1er**	28
Z Guy Savoy | **17e**	28
Il Vino | **7e**	22
Itinéraires | **5e**	23
Izakaya Issé | **1er**	23
Joséphine/Dumonet | **6e**	25
Z Jules Verne | **7e**	23
Z Lasserre | **8e**	27
Laurent | **8e**	25
Maison Blanche | **8e**	23
Marée | **8e**	23
Marius | **16e**	25
Marius et Janette | **8e**	23
Market | **8e**	22
Marty | **5e**	20
Z Meurice | **1er**	28
Z Michel Rostang | **17e**	27
Montalembert | **7e**	19
Mori Venice | **2e**	21
Oth Sombath | **8e**	23
Paul Chêne | **16e**	23
Pavillon Ledoyen | **8e**	25
Pavillon Montsouris | **14e**	22
Perron | **7e**	-
Petit Marguery | **13e**	23
Petit Marius | **8e**	20
Pétrus | **17e**	23
Pichet de Paris | **8e**	22
Pierre/Palais Royal | **1er**	22
Z Pierre Gagnaire | **8e**	28
Z Pré Catelan | **16e**	26
Prunier | **16e**	24
Z Quincy | **12e**	26
Ralph's | **6e**	17
Relais d'Auteuil | **16e**	25
Relais Plaza | **8e**	25
Sébillon | **Neuilly**	22
Z Senderens | **8e**	26
NEW Shang Palace | **16e**	24
Société | **6e**	17
Sormani | **17e**	24
Stella Maris | **8e**	25
Stresa | **8e**	22
Table/Lancaster | **8e**	25
NEW Tablettes/Nomicos | **16e**	28
Z Taillevent | **8e**	29
Tan Dinh | **7e**	22
Tante Marguerite | **7e**	22
Terrasse Mirabeau | **16e**	26
Tong Yen | **8e**	22
Z Tour d'Argent | **5e**	25
39V | **8e**	23
Tsé-Yang | **16e**	22
Vernet | **8e**	24
Violon d'Ingres | **7e**	25
Voltaire | **7e**	22

QUICK BITES

Z As/Fallafel | **4e**	23
Bar/Théâtres | **8e**	17
Baron Rouge | **12e**	18
Bistrot/Vins Mélac | **11e**	18
NEW Blend | **2e**	-

Bons Crus | **1er** 21
Brass. Printemps | **9e** 15
Breizh Café | **3e** 22
Z Café de Flore | **6e** 16
Café du Commerce | **15e** 17
NEW Camion Qui Fume | **Location Varies** -
Cave Schmidt | **15e** 23
Chez Marianne | **4e** 19
Cloche/Halles | **1er** 18
NEW Clocher/Montmartre | **18e** -
Clown Bar | **11e** 15
Cocottes | **7e** 24
Congrès Maillot | **17e** 20
Crémerie | **6e** 21
Cul de Poule | **9e** 20
NEW Dans les Landes | **5e** 23
Da Rosa | **6e** 21
Z Deux Magots | **6e** 17
Duc de Richelieu | **12e** 22
Ebouillanté | **4e** 22
Ecluse | **multi.** 17
Emporio Armani | **6e** 19
Ferdi | **1er** 21
Fines Gueules | **1er** 20
NEW Floréal | **10e** -
Z Frenchie | **2e** 26
Fumoir | **1er** 18
Garnier | **8e** 22
NEW Gyoza Bar | **2e** -
Juveniles | **1er** 15
Ma Bourgogne | **4e** 19
Maison du Caviar | **8e** 25
NEW Maison Mère | **9e** -
Mama Shelter | **20e** 16
Mauzac | **5e** 15
Mesturet | **2e** 16
Minipalais | **8e** 21
Mirama | **5e** 22
Murat | **16e** 17
Nemrod | **6e** 17
Papilles | **5e** 25
Petite Sirène | **9e** 25
Pinxo | **1er** 23
Pizza Chic | **6e** 21
Quedubon | **19e** 18
Rose Bakery | **9e** 22
Rubis | **1er** 19
Shu | **6e** 25
Table d'Hédiard | **8e** 22
Tsukizi | **6e** 22
NEW Verjus | **1er** -
Vin sur Vin | **7e** 21
NEW Yoom | **multi.** -

QUIET CONVERSATION

NEW Affranchis | **9e** -
Aimant du Sud | **13e** 21
Allobroges | **20e** 22
Ambassade/Auv. | **3e** 22
Assaggio | **1er** 22
Assiette | **14e** 19
Z Astrance | **16e** 28
NEW Atao | **17e** -
Z Atelier/Joël Robuchon | **7e** 27
Aub. Pyrénées | **11e** 24
Bellini | **16e** 21
Z Benoît | **4e** 23
Z Bigarrade | **17e** 27
Bistro Poulbot | **18e** 23
Bistrot/Côté Flaubert | **17e** 21
Bistrot/Côté La Boutarde | **Neuilly** 21
Bistrot d'Henri | **6e** 22
Bistrot du Peintre | **11e** 18
Bistro Volnay | **2e** 21
Bizan | **2e** -
Boeuf/le Toit | **8e** 18
Bon Saint Pourçain | **6e** 19
Bouchon/L'Assiette | **17e** 22
Bouillon Racine | **6e** 18
Brass. Flo | **10e** 19
Brass. Julien | **10e** 19
Z Brass. Lipp | **6e** 18
Brass. Mollard | **8e** 18
Café du Passage | **11e** -
Café Lenôtre | **8e** 23
Café Marly | **1er** 17

NEW Camélia | **1er**	–
Camélia | **Bougival**	21
Cartes Postales | **1er**	–
Z Caviar Kaspia | **8e**	26
Z 144 Petrossian | **7e**	24
Chardenoux | **11e**	23
Charpentiers | **6e**	20
NEW Chatomat | **20e**	–
Chez Géraud | **16e**	20
Chez Les Anges | **7e**	24
Chez René | **5e**	19
Chiberta | **8e**	24
Cigale Récamier | **7e**	22
NEW Clocher/Montmartre | **18e**	–
Clocher Péreire | **17e**	24
Clos/Gourmets | **7e**	25
Closerie/Lilas | **6e**	20
Concert/Cuisine | **15e**	–
Copenhague | **8e**	23
Corte | **1er**	–
Costes | **1er**	18
Coupe-Chou | **5e**	20
Z Coupole | **14e**	18
Crus/Bourgogne | **2e**	20
Cuizine | **11e**	–
Dali | **1er**	–
Da Rosa | **6e**	21
Daru | **8e**	19
Délices/Aphrodite | **5e**	20
Dessirier | **17e**	24
Desvouges | **5e**	–
Z Deux Magots | **6e**	17
Ebouillanté | **4e**	22
Ecaille de Fontaine | **2e**	–
El Mansour | **8e**	21
Epi d'Or | **1er**	19
Epigramme | **6e**	23
Escargot Montorgueil | **1er**	22
Fines Gueules | **1er**	20
Fins Gourmets | **7e**	18
Firmin le Barbier | **7e**	21
Flora Danica | **8e**	21
Flore en l'Ile | **4e**	17
Flottes O. Trement | **1er**	21
Z Fontaine de Mars | **7e**	22
Fougères | **17e**	27
Fourchette | **17e**	23
Gallopin | **2e**	20
Garnier | **8e**	22
Gaya | **7e**	24
Georgette | **9e**	17
Gli Angeli | **3e**	20
Goumard | **1er**	23
Gourmand | **1er**	25
Graindorge | **17e**	23
Huîtrier | **17e**	22
Isami | **4e**	25
Itinéraires | **5e**	23
Jean | **9e**	26
Joséphine/Dumonet | **6e**	25
Z Jules Verne | **7e**	23
Lapérouse | **6e**	23
Legrand Filles/Fils | **2e**	21
Lilane | **5e**	25
Macéo | **1er**	23
Maison Blanche | **8e**	23
Mansouria | **11e**	21
Marée | **8e**	23
Marlotte | **6e**	18
Marty | **5e**	20
Maxan | **8e**	20
Méditerranée | **6e**	22
Minipalais | **8e**	21
Montalembert | **7e**	19
Moulin/Galette | **18e**	20
Muscade | **1er**	–
NEW Neva | **8e**	–
Oto-Oto | **6e**	–
Z Oulette | **12e**	26
Pères et Filles | **6e**	17
Petite Chaise | **7e**	18
Petite Sirène | **9e**	25
Petit Lutetia | **6e**	17
Petit Marguery | **13e**	23
Petit Rétro | **16e**	18
Pierre/Palais Royal | **1er**	22
Z Pierre Gagnaire | **8e**	28
Polidor | **6e**	15

P'tit Troquet | 7e 22
Quai-Quai | 1er 18
Repaire/Cartouche | 11e 17
Rest. du Marché | 15e 21
Rest. du Palais Royal | 1er 20
Roi/Pot-au-Feu | 9e 19
Saotico | 2e -
Sarladais | 8e 23
Saturne | 2e 22
Saudade | 1er 16
Saut du Loup | 1er 13
Sébillon | **Neuilly** 22
Sot l'y Laisse | 11e 22
Soufflé | 1er 22
Z Spring | 1er 27
Stella Maris | 8e 25
Stresa | 8e 22
Table/Lancaster | 8e 25
Tan Dinh | 7e 22
Tante Louise | 8e 23
Tourbillon | 5e 24
39V | 8e 23
Trou Gascon | 12e 25
Tsé-Yang | 16e 22
Vin Chai Moi | 1er -
Vin sur Vin | 7e 21

ROMANTIC PLACES

NEW Abeille | 16e 23
Z Alain Ducasse | 8e 28
Allard | 6e 21
Z Ambassadeurs | 8e 27
Z Ambroisie | 4e 27
Z Arpège | 7e 27
Astor | 8e 24
Z Astrance | 16e 28
Bistro Poulbot | 18e 23
Bouillon Racine | 6e 18
Bouquinistes | 6e 23
Brass. Flo | 10e 19
Brass. Julien | 10e 19
Z Café de Flore | 6e 16
Café Lenôtre | 8e 23
Café Marly | 1er 17
Casa Olympe | 9e 23
Z Caviar Kaspia | 8e 26
Z 144 Petrossian | 7e 24
Chalet des Iles | 16e 18
Z Chamarré Mont. | 18e 26
Chardenoux | 11e 23
Chez Julien | 4e 21
Closerie/Lilas | 6e 20
Costes | 1er 18
Cottage Marcadet | 18e -
Coupe-Chou | 5e 20
Z Coupole | 14e 18
Z Cristal Room | 16e 20
Crus/Bourgogne | 2e 20
Délices/Aphrodite | 5e 20
Z Deux Magots | 6e 17
1728 | 8e 21
Dôme | 14e 22
El Mansour | 8e 21
Z Epicure (Le Bristol) | 8e 27
Epi d'Or | 1er 19
Fakhr el Dine | 16e 25
Flora Danica | 8e 21
Z Fontaine de Mars | 7e 22
Gavroche | 2e 24
Georges | 4e 17
Grande Cascade | 16e 24
Z Grand Véfour | 1er 28
Z Guilo-Guilo | 18e 27
Z Guy Savoy | 17e 28
Jardins de Bagatelle | 16e 20
Joséphine/Dumonet | 6e 25
Z Jules Verne | 7e 23
Lapérouse | 6e 23
Z Lasserre | 8e 27
Laurent | 8e 25
Ma Bourgogne | 4e 19
Macéo | 1er 23
Maison/Amér. Latine | 7e 21
Maison Blanche | 8e 23
Mansouria | 11e 21
Marty | 5e 20
Maxim's | 8e 20
Méditerranée | 6e 22
Z Meurice | 1er 28

Moulin/Galette | **18e**	20
Muscade | **1er**	-
Pavillon/Lac | **19e**	19
Pavillon Ledoyen | **8e**	25
Pavillon Montsouris | **14e**	22
Petrelle | **9e**	25
☒ Pré Catelan | **16e**	26
☒ Relais Louis XIII | **6e**	26
Rest. Paul | **1er**	18
Romantica | **Clichy**	22
Rughetta | **18e**	21
Sormani | **17e**	24
Square Trousseau | **12e**	19
Stella Maris | **8e**	25
Tan Dinh | **7e**	22
Timgad | **17e**	22
☒ Tour d'Argent | **5e**	25
☒ Train Bleu | **12e**	19
39V | **8e**	23
Trou Gascon | **12e**	25
Vernet | **8e**	24
Versance | **2e**	-

SENIOR APPEAL

A et M | **16e**	21
☒ Alain Ducasse | **8e**	28
Allard | **6e**	21
Allobroges | **20e**	22
Ambassade/Auv. | **3e**	22
☒ Ambassadeurs | **8e**	27
☒ Ambroisie | **4e**	27
☒ Ami Louis | **3e**	24
☒ Apicius | **8e**	27
☒ Arpège | **7e**	27
Assiette | **14e**	19
Astor | **8e**	24
Aub. Bressane | **7e**	22
Aub. Pyrénées | **11e**	24
Ballon des Ternes | **17e**	19
Beaujolais/Auteuil | **16e**	19
☒ Benoît | **4e**	23
Bistro 121 | **15e**	22
Bistro/Deux Théâtres | **9e**	21
Bistro St. Ferdinand | **17e**	19
Bistrot/Côté Flaubert | **17e**	21
Boeuf Couronné | **19e**	23
Boeuf/le Toit | **8e**	18
☒ Bofinger | **4e**	19
Bon Accueil | **7e**	23
Bon Saint Pourçain | **6e**	19
Bouillon Racine | **6e**	18
Bouquinistes | **6e**	23
Brass./l'Ile St-Louis | **4e**	19
Brass. Balzar | **5e**	18
Brass. Flo | **10e**	19
Brass. Julien | **10e**	19
☒ Brass. Lipp | **6e**	18
Brass. Mollard | **8e**	18
☒ Café de Flore | **6e**	16
Café Marly | **1er**	17
Cagouille | **14e**	23
Camélia | **Bougival**	21
☒ Carré/Feuillants | **1er**	27
Caves Pétrissans | **17e**	23
☒ 144 Petrossian | **7e**	24
Chardenoux | **11e**	23
Charpentiers | **6e**	20
Chez André | **8e**	22
Chez Denise | **1er**	23
Chez Fred | **17e**	19
Chez Gégène | **Joinville**	16
☒ Chez Georges | **2e**	23
Chez Georges | **17e**	22
Chez Géraud | **16e**	20
Chez la Vieille | **1er**	23
Chez Michel | **10e**	24
Chez René | **5e**	19
☒ Cinq | **8e**	28
Clos/Gourmets | **7e**	25
Closerie/Lilas | **6e**	20
Copenhague | **8e**	23
☒ Coupole | **14e**	18
Crus/Bourgogne | **2e**	20
Dessirier | **17e**	24
☒ Deux Magots | **6e**	17
☒ Divellec | **7e**	26
Dôme | **14e**	22
Drouant | **2e**	23
☒ Duc | **14e**	28

Z Epicure (Le Bristol) | **8e** 27
Epi d'Or | **1er** 19
Escargot Montorgueil | **1er** 22
Ferme St-Simon | **7e** 21
Fermette Marbeuf | **8e** 19
Fins Gourmets | **7e** 18
Flandrin | **16e** 15
Florimond | **7e** 25
Z Fontaine de Mars | **7e** 22
Fougères | **17e** 27
Fouquet's | **8e** 20
Gallopin | **2e** 20
Garnier | **8e** 22
Gauloise | **15e** 18
Gavroche | **2e** 24
Gaya | **7e** 24
Goumard | **1er** 23
Gourmand | **1er** 25
Graindorge | **17e** 23
Grand Colbert | **2e** 19
Grande Cascade | **16e** 24
Z Grand Véfour | **1er** 28
Z Guy Savoy | **17e** 28
Z Hélène Darroze | **6e** 26
Hide | **17e** 24
Huîtrier | **17e** 22
Itinéraires | **5e** 23
Jardins de Bagatelle | **16e** 20
Jean | **9e** 26
Joséphine/Dumonet | **6e** 25
Z Jules Verne | **7e** 23
Languedoc | **5e** 21
Z Lasserre | **8e** 27
Laurent | **8e** 25
Lyonnais | **2e** 22
Macéo | **1er** 23
Maison Courtine | **14e** 20
Marée | **8e** 23
Marlotte | **6e** 18
Marty | **5e** 20
Mémère Paulette | **2e** 23
Z Meurice | **1er** 28
Z Michel Rostang | **17e** 27
Moissonnier | **5e** 24
Moulin à Vent | **5e** 20
Pavillon Ledoyen | **8e** 25
Petite Chaise | **7e** 18
Petit Lutetia | **6e** 17
Petit Marguery | **13e** 23
Petit Niçois | **7e** 20
Petit Rétro | **16e** 18
Petit Riche | **9e** 22
Pichet de Paris | **8e** 22
Z Pied de Cochon | **1er** 19
Pierre/Palais Royal | **1er** 22
Z Pierre Gagnaire | **8e** 28
Polidor | **6e** 15
Z Pré Catelan | **16e** 26
Z Relais Louis XIII | **6e** 26
Relais Plaza | **8e** 25
Rest. du Marché | **15e** 21
Roi/Pot-au-Feu | **9e** 19
Sarladais | **8e** 23
Saudade | **1er** 16
Sébillon | **Neuilly** 22
Z Senderens | **8e** 26
Soufflé | **1er** 22
Z Taillevent | **8e** 29
Tante Louise | **8e** 23
Tante Marguerite | **7e** 22
Terminus Nord | **10e** 18
Thoumieux | **7e** 20
Z Tour d'Argent | **5e** 25
Z Train Bleu | **12e** 19
Trou Gascon | **12e** 25
Vagenende | **6e** 17
Vernet | **8e** 24
Vin sur Vin | **7e** 21
Voltaire | **7e** 22

SINGLES SCENES

Absinthe | **1er** 21
A et M | **16e** 21
Arc | **16e** 16
Astor | **8e** 24
Bar/Théâtres | **8e** 17
Baron Rouge | **12e** 18
Bistro/Deux Théâtres | **9e** 21
Bistrot/Vins Mélac | **11e** 18

Bistrot/Côté Flaubert | **17e** 21
NEW Braisenville | **9e** –
Brass. Balzar | **5e** 18
Brass. de la Poste | **16e** 22
Café Burq | **18e** 21
Z Café de Flore | **6e** 16
Café de la Jatte | **Neuilly** 18
Café de la Paix | **9e** 19
Café/l'Esplanade | **7e** 18
Café du Passage | **11e** –
Café Lenôtre | **8e** 23
Café Marly | **1er** 17
Café Ruc | **1er** 15
NEW Caffe Burlot/Costes | **8e** –
Cave Schmidt | **15e** 23
Chateaubriand | **11e** 23
Cherche Midi | **6e** 22
Chez Gégène | **Joinville** 16
Cinq Mars | **7e** 21
Closerie/Lilas | **6e** 20
Clown Bar | **11e** 15
Comédiens | **9e** 19
Costes | **1er** 18
NEW Dauphin | **11e** 22
Z Deux Magots | **6e** 17
Emporio Armani | **6e** 19
Enoteca | **4e** 22
Ferdi | **1er** 21
Z Frenchie | **2e** 26
Fumoir | **1er** 18
Grille St-Germain | **6e** 21
Kong | **1er** 16
Mama Shelter | **20e** 16
Murat | **16e** 17
Pinxo | **1er** 23
Rose Bakery | **3e** 22
Rubis | **1er** 19

SLEEPERS

(Good food, but little known)

Assaggio | **1er** 22
Bistro Poulbot | **18e** 23
Boucherie Roulière | **6e** 26
Bouchon/L'Assiette | **17e** 22
Brass. de la Poste | **16e** 22
Caffé dei Cioppi | **11e** 25
Cantine/Troquet | **multi.** 25
Chez Cécile | **8e** 25
Chez la Vieille | **1er** 23
Chez Ly | **17e** 25
Christophe | **5e** 24
Claude Colliot | **4e** 23
Clocher Péreire | **17e** 24
Cristal de Sel | **15e** 27
Duc de Richelieu | **12e** 22
Ebouillanté | **4e** 22
Ecume St-Honoré | **1er** 23
Etc. | **16e** 25
Famille | **18e** 23
Fougères | **17e** 27
Graindorge | **17e** 23
Grand Pan | **15e** 23
Hide | **17e** 24
I Golosi | **9e** 23
Jean | **9e** 26
Kai | **1er** 25
Kifune | **17e** 23
Kim Anh | **15e** 23
Lilane | **5e** 25
Luna | **8e** 26
Main d'Or | **11e** 22
Mémère Paulette | **2e** 23
Moissonnier | **5e** 24
Montagnards | **1er** 23
Opportun | **14e** 22
Oum el Banine | **16e** 22
Palanquin | **6e** 24
Petit Châtelet | **5e** 22
Petite Sirène | **9e** 25
Petrelle | **9e** 25
Pichet de Paris | **8e** 22
Pomponette | **18e** 23
Rest./Pergolèse | **16e** 25
Royal Madeleine | **8e** 23
Shu | **6e** 25
Sot l'y Laisse | **11e** 22
Stéphane Martin | **15e** 23
Terrasse Mirabeau | **16e** 26
Tourbillon | **5e** 24

Tsukizi | **6e**	22
Vernet | **8e**	24
Yen | **6e**	22

TASTING MENUS

Agapé | **17e**	24
NEW Agapé Substance | **6e**	25
Agrume | **5e**	24
Aida | **7e**	25
NEW Akrame | **16e**	23
Z Alain Ducasse | **8e**	28
Allobroges | **20e**	22
Z Ambassadeurs | **8e**	27
Z Apicius | **8e**	27
Z Arpège | **7e**	27
Astor | **8e**	24
Z Astrance | **16e**	28
Aub. Nicolas Flamel | **3e**	21
Avant Goût | **13e**	23
Z Bar à Huîtres | **3e**	21
Beurre Noisette | **15e**	25
Z Bigarrade | **17e**	27
Bistrot/Côté Flaubert | **17e**	21
Bistrot/Sommelier | **8e**	22
Bistro Volnay | **2e**	21
Bizan | **2e**	-
Café Le Moderne | **2e**	22
Camélia | **Bougival**	21
Z Carré/Feuillants | **1er**	27
Cartes Postales | **1er**	-
Céladon | **2e**	23
Z 144 Petrossian | **7e**	24
Z Chamarré Mont. | **18e**	26
Chen Soleil d'Est | **15e**	-
Z Chez L'Ami Jean | **7e**	25
Chez la Vieille | **1er**	23
Chez Les Anges | **7e**	24
Chez Marianne | **4e**	19
Chez Michel | **10e**	24
Chez Vincent | **19e**	23
Chiberta | **8e**	24
Chieng Mai | **5e**	22
Z Cinq | **8e**	28
Concert/Cuisine | **15e**	-
Copenhague | **8e**	23
Coulisses | **9e**	-
Z Cristal Room | **16e**	20
D'Chez Eux | **7e**	24
Dominique Bouchet | **8e**	25
Z Epicure (Le Bristol) | **8e**	27
Fables/Fontaine | **7e**	25
Fermette Marbeuf | **8e**	19
Ferrandaise | **6e**	20
Flottes O. Trement | **1er**	21
Fogón | **6e**	23
Fougères | **17e**	27
Frédéric Simonin | **17e**	-
Gaigne | **4e**	24
NEW Galopin | **10e**	-
Gazzetta | **12e**	24
Grande Cascade | **16e**	24
Z Grand Véfour | **1er**	28
Z Guy Savoy | **17e**	28
Z Hélène Darroze | **6e**	26
Z Hiramatsu | **16e**	27
Il Vino | **7e**	22
Itinéraires | **5e**	23
Jadis | **15e**	23
Jean | **9e**	26
Jean-François Piège | **7e**	27
Z Jules Verne | **7e**	23
KGB | **6e**	23
Kim Anh | **15e**	23
Kinugawa/Hanawa | **1er**	24
Lapérouse | **6e**	23
Z Lasserre | **8e**	27
Laurent | **8e**	25
Liza | **2e**	24
Maison Blanche | **8e**	23
Maxan | **8e**	20
MBC | **17e**	-
Z Meurice | **1er**	28
Z Michel Rostang | **17e**	27
Miroir | **18e**	21
Moulin/Galette | **18e**	20
Orient-Extrême | **6e**	23
Oth Sombath | **8e**	23
Z Oulette | **12e**	26
Z Passage 53 | **2e**	27

Passiflore | **16e** 23
Pavillon Ledoyen | **8e** 25
Petit Marguery | **13e** 23
Z Pré Catelan | **16e** 26
Prunier | **16e** 24
Pur' | **2e** 24
Z Quinzième | **15e** 26
Relais d'Auteuil | **16e** 25
Z Relais Louis XIII | **6e** 26
Réminet | **5e** 23
Rest./Pergolèse | **16e** 25
Romantica | **Clichy** 22
Saotico | **2e** -
Schmidt - L'Os/Moëlle | **15e** 23
Sensing | **6e** 23
Stella Maris | **8e** 25
NEW Sur Mesure | **1er** -
Z Table d'Eugène | **18e** 26
Table/Lancaster | **8e** 25
NEW Tablettes/Nomicos | **16e** 28
Z Taillevent | **8e** 29
Terrasse Mirabeau | **16e** 26
NEW Tintilou | **11e** -
Z Train Bleu | **12e** 19
Troquet | **15e** 24
Z Truffière | **5e** 26
NEW Verjus | **1er** -
Vernet | **8e** 24
Vin Chai Moi | **1er** -
Violon d'Ingres | **7e** 25
Z Yam'Tcha | **1er** 26

TRENDY

Afaria | **15e** 23
NEW Affable | **7e** -
Agapé | **17e** 24
NEW Agapé Substance | **6e** 25
Aida | **7e** 25
Alcazar | **6e** 18
Z Ami Louis | **3e** 24
Anahi | **3e** 19
Z Astrance | **16e** 28
Avenue | **8e** 16
NEW Braisenville | **9e** -
Brass. de la Poste | **16e** 22
Z Café de Flore | **6e** 16
Café/l'Esplanade | **7e** 18
Café des Musées | **3e** 20
Café du Passage | **11e** -
NEW Caffe Burlot/Costes | **8e** -
Cailloux | **13e** 22
Cantine/Quentin | **10e** -
Z 144 Petrossian | **7e** 24
Chateaubriand | **11e** 23
Cherche Midi | **6e** 22
Chéri Bibi | **18e** 20
Chez Julien | **4e** 21
Chez Les Anges | **7e** 24
Chez Omar | **3e** 19
Chez Paul | **11e** 22
Chez Prune | **10e** 15
Chez Ramulaud | **11e** -
Chez Vong | **1er** 23
Chieng Mai | **5e** 22
Cocottes | **7e** 24
Z Comptoir/Relais | **6e** 27
Costes | **1er** 18
Z Cristal Room | **16e** 20
Crudus | **1er** -
Cul de Poule | **9e** 20
NEW Dauphin | **11e** 22
Derrière | **3e** 15
Deux Amis | **11e** 21
NEW Entrée/Artistes | **11e** -
Famille | **18e** 23
Ferdi | **1er** 21
Fish La Boiss. | **6e** 21
Z Fontaine de Mars | **7e** 22
Fouquet's | **8e** 20
Z Frenchie | **2e** 26
Fumoir | **1er** 18
Gare | **16e** 18
Gazzetta | **12e** 24
Georges | **4e** 17
Gli Angeli | **3e** 20
Grande Armée | **16e** 16
Grand Pan | **15e** 23
Z Guilo-Guilo | **18e** 27
Hangar | **3e** 23

Ile | **Issy-les-Moul.** 19
KGB | **6e** 23
Kong | **1er** 16
Legrand Filles/Fils | **2e** 21
Maison Blanche | **8e** 23
NEW Maison Mère | **9e** –
Mama Shelter | **20e** 16
Market | **8e** 22
Martel | **10e** 21
Minipalais | **8e** 21
Miroir | **18e** 21
Mori Venice | **2e** 21
NEW Passage | **11e** –
Pavillon/Lac | **19e** 19
Pizza Chic | **6e** 21
Quai-Quai | **1er** 18
404 | **3e** 20
Z Quinzième | **15e** 26
Racines | **2e** 20
Ralph's | **6e** 17
Relais Plaza | **8e** 25
Rest. Manufacture | **Issy-les-Moul.** 22
Ribouldingue | **5e** 22
Rino | **11e** 25
Rose Bakery | **multi.** 22
Rughetta | **18e** 21
Saturne | **2e** 22
Sensing | **6e** 23
NEW Septime | **11e** 25
Sormani | **17e** 24
Z Spring | **1er** 27
NEW Square Gardette | **11e** –
Stresa | **8e** 22
Table/Lancaster | **8e** 25
Tong Yen | **8e** 22
NEW Verjus | **1er** –
NEW Vivant | **10e** 24
Voltaire | **7e** 22
Z Ze Kitchen Galerie | **6e** 25

VIEWS

Absinthe | **1er** 21
NEW Affable | **7e** –
NEW Affranchis | **9e** –
Antoine | **16e** 22
Arc | **16e** 16
Avenue | **8e** 16
NEW Bélisaire | **15e** 23
Benkay | **15e** 25
Bistro/Breteuil | **7e** 18
NEW Bistro/Gastronomes | **5e** 23
Bistrot Vivienne | **2e** 19
Bon Accueil | **7e** 23
Bouquinistes | **6e** 23
Bourguignon/Marais | **4e** 25
Brass./l'Ile St-Louis | **4e** 19
Brass. de la Poste | **16e** 22
Brass. du Louvre | **1er** 19
Z Café de Flore | **6e** 16
Café de la Jatte | **Neuilly** 18
Café de la Musique | **19e** 17
Café/l'Esplanade | **7e** 18
Café Lenôtre | **8e** 23
Café Marly | **1er** 17
Café Rouge | **3e** 19
Cagouille | **14e** 23
Cantine/Quentin | **10e** –
Cantine/Tontons | **15e** 17
Z Caviar Kaspia | **8e** 26
Chalet des Iles | **16e** 18
Z Chamarré Mont. | **18e** 26
Chantairelle | **5e** –
Chez Francis | **8e** 18
Chez Fred | **17e** 19
Chez Gégène | **Joinville** 16
Chez Julien | **4e** 21
Chez Léna et Mimile | **5e** 21
Chez Marie-Louise | **10e** –
Chez Paul | **13e** 22
Chez Prune | **10e** 15
Z Cinq | **8e** 28
Cloche/Halles | **1er** 18
Clos/Gourmets | **7e** 25
Copenhague | **8e** 23
D'Chez Eux | **7e** 24
Z Divellec | **7e** 26
Ecluse | **6e** 17
Z Epicure (Le Bristol) | **8e** 27
Fables/Fontaine | **7e** 25

Restaurant	Location	Rating
Fins Gourmets	7e	18
Firmin le Barbier	7e	21
Flora Danica	8e	21
Flore en l'Ile	4e	17
Z Fontaine de Mars	7e	22
Fontaine Gaillon	2e	21
Fouquet's	8e	20
Fumoir	1er	18
NEW Galopin	10e	-
Gare	16e	18
Georges	4e	17
Grand Café	9e	19
Grande Armée	16e	16
Grande Cascade	16e	24
Z Grand Véfour	1er	28
Gourmand	**Neuilly**	18
Hôtel Amour	9e	15
Ile	**Issy-les-Moul.**	19
Isami	4e	25
Jamin	16e	23
Jardins de Bagatelle	16e	20
Z Jules Verne	7e	23
Khun Akorn	11e	21
Kong	1er	16
Lapérouse	6e	23
Z Lasserre	8e	27
Laurent	8e	25
Legrand Filles/Fils	2e	21
Ma Bourgogne	4e	19
Main d'Or	11e	22
Maison/Amér. Latine	7e	21
Maison Blanche	8e	23
Market	8e	22
Méditerranée	6e	22
Minipalais	8e	21
Montalembert	7e	19
Moulin/Galette	18e	20
Muscade	1er	-
Ogre	16e	-
Ombres	7e	21
Parc aux Cerfs	6e	20
Pavillon Ledoyen	8e	25
Pavillon Montsouris	14e	22
Petit Châtelet	5e	22
Petite Cour	6e	20
Petit Marguery	13e	23
Petit Pergolèse	16e	25
Pharamond	1er	18
Z Pied de Cochon	1er	19
Z Pré Catelan	16e	26
Quai	7e	19
Quai-Quai	1er	18
Racines	2e	20
Rest. du Palais Royal	1er	20
Rest. Paul	1er	18
Romantica	**Clichy**	22
Rosa Bonheur	19e	16
Rotonde	6e	19
Saotico	2e	-
Saut du Loup	1er	13
Sébillon	**Neuilly**	22
Sola	5e	27
Square Marcadet	18e	-
Square Trousseau	12e	19
Table d'Hédiard	8e	22
Table/Lancaster	8e	25
Terrasse Mirabeau	16e	26
Z Tour d'Argent	5e	25
Z Train Bleu	12e	19
39V	8e	23
Trumilou	4e	20
Vaudeville	2e	20
Vin et Marée	1er	21
Wepler	18e	20

VISITORS ON EXPENSE ACCOUNT

Restaurant	Location	Rating
NEW Abeille	16e	23
Agapé	17e	24
Z Ambroisie	4e	27
Z Ami Louis	3e	24
Z Arpège	7e	27
Assaggio	1er	22
Assiette	14e	19
Z Atelier/Joël Robuchon	7e	27
Auguste	7e	24
Z Benoît	4e	23
NEW Camélia	1er	-
Z Carré/Feuillants	1er	27

Z Caviar Kaspia | 8e 26
Z Chamarré Mont. | 18e 26
Chen Soleil d'Est | 15e –
Chez Les Anges | 7e 24
Chiberta | 8e 24
Copenhague | 8e 23
Dessirier | 17e 24
Z Divellec | 7e 26
NEW Dodin/Mark Singer | 17e –
Dôme | 14e 22
Dominique Bouchet | 8e 25
Drouant | 2e 23
Z Duc | 14e 28
Etc. | 16e 25
Ferme St-Simon | 7e 21
Flora Danica | 8e 21
Fougères | 17e 27
Fouquet's | 8e 20
Frédéric Simonin | 17e –
Garnier | 8e 22
Gaya | 7e 24
Goumard | 1er 23
Z Grand Véfour | 1er 28
Z Guy Savoy | 17e 28
Z Hélène Darroze | 6e 26
Il Vino | 7e 22
Joséphine/Dumonet | 6e 25
Z Jules Verne | 7e 23
Kifune | 17e 23
Z Lasserre | 8e 27
Laurent | 8e 25
Maison Blanche | 8e 23
Mansouria | 11e 21
Marée | 8e 23
Marius | 16e 25
Maxim's | 8e 20
Z Michel Rostang | 17e 27
Oth Sombath | 8e 23
Z Oulette | 12e 26
Pavillon Ledoyen | 8e 25
Pétrus | 17e 23
Pierre/Palais Royal | 1er 22
Z Pierre Gagnaire | 8e 28
Z Pré Catelan | 16e 26
Z Relais Louis XIII | 6e 26
Relais Plaza | 8e 25
Z Senderens | 8e 26
NEW Shang Palace | 16e 24
Stella Maris | 8e 25
NEW Sur Mesure | 1er –
Table/Lancaster | 8e 25
NEW Tablettes/Nomicos | 16e 28
Z Taillevent | 8e 29
Tante Marguerite | 7e 22
Terrasse Mirabeau | 16e 26
Z Tour d'Argent | 5e 25
39V | 8e 23
Trou Gascon | 12e 25

WATERSIDE

Brass./l'Ile St-Louis | 4e 19
Chalet des Iles | 16e 18
Chez Gégène | **Joinville** 16
Chez Marie-Louise | 10e –
Chez Prune | 10e 15
Ecluse | 6e 17
Gourmand | **Neuilly** 18
Quai | 7e 19
Quai-Quai | 1er 18

WINNING WINE LISTS

Agapé | 17e 24
Z Alain Ducasse | 8e 28
NEW Albion | 10e –
Z Ambassadeurs | 8e 27
Z Ambroisie | 4e 27
Z Atelier/Joël Robuchon | 7e 27
Bistro/Vieux Chêne | 11e 23
Bistrot/Sommelier | 8e 22
Bistrot Paul Bert | 11e 21
Bistro Volnay | 2e 21
Bourguignon/Marais | 4e 25
Café Burq | 18e 21
Café Lenôtre | 8e 23
Cagouille | 14e 23
Z Carré/Feuillants | 1er 27
Cave Schmidt | 15e 23
Caves Pétrissans | 17e 23

Z 144 Petrossian | **7e**	24
Chez Géraud | **16e**	20
Z Cinq | **8e**	28
Comptoir Marguery | **13e**	21
Coupe Gorge | **4e**	-
Crémerie | **6e**	21
Dessirier | **17e**	24
Z Divellec | **7e**	26
Drouant | **2e**	23
Ecluse | **multi.**	17
Enoteca | **4e**	22
Z Epicure (Le Bristol) | **8e**	27
Ferme St-Simon | **7e**	21
Fines Gueules | **1er**	20
Fish La Boiss. | **6e**	21
Fogón | **6e**	23
Grande Cascade | **16e**	24
Z Grand Véfour | **1er**	28
Z Guy Savoy | **17e**	28
Z Hélène Darroze | **6e**	26
Il Vino | **7e**	22
Jeanne A | **11e**	-
Joséphine/Dumonet | **6e**	25
Z Jules Verne | **7e**	23
Z Lasserre | **8e**	27
Laurent | **8e**	25
Legrand Filles/Fils | **2e**	21
Macéo | **1er**	23
Marée | **8e**	23
Maxim's | **8e**	20
Z Meurice | **1er**	28
Z Michel Rostang | **17e**	27
Minipalais | **8e**	21
Oth Sombath | **8e**	23
Z Oulette | **12e**	26
Pavillon Ledoyen | **8e**	25
Petit Marguery | **13e**	23
Pierre/Palais Royal | **1er**	22
Z Pierre Gagnaire | **8e**	28
Quedubon | **19e**	18
Racines | **2e**	20
Z Relais Louis XIII | **6e**	26
Saudade | **1er**	16
Z Senderens | **8e**	26
Stella Maris | **8e**	25
Z Taillevent | **8e**	29
Tante Marguerite | **7e**	22
Z Tour d'Argent | **5e**	25
39V | **8e**	23
Trou Gascon | **12e**	25
NEW Verjus | **1er**	-
Vernet | **8e**	24
Vin sur Vin | **7e**	21
Yugaraj | **6e**	20

Wine Vintage Chart

This chart is based on a 30-point scale. The ratings (by U. of South Carolina law professor **Howard Stravitz**) reflect vintage quality and the wine's readiness to drink. A dash means the wine is past its peak or too young to rate. Loire ratings are for dry whites.

Whites	95	96	97	98	99	00	01	02	03	04	05	06	07	08	09	10
France:																
Alsace	24	23	23	25	23	25	26	22	21	22	23	21	26	26	23	26
Burgundy	27	26	22	21	24	24	23	27	23	26	26	25	26	25	25	-
Loire Valley	-	-	-	-	-	-	-	25	20	22	27	23	24	24	24	25
Champagne	26	27	24	25	25	25	21	26	21	-	-	-	-	-	-	-
Sauternes	21	23	25	23	24	24	29	24	26	21	26	25	27	24	27	-
California:																
Chardonnay	-	-	-	-	22	21	24	25	22	26	29	24	27	23	27	-
Sauvignon Blanc	-	-	-	-	-	-	-	-	-	25	24	27	25	24	25	-
Austria:																
Grüner V./Riesl.	22	-	25	22	26	22	23	25	25	24	23	26	25	24	25	-
Germany:	22	26	22	25	24	-	29	25	26	27	28	26	26	26	26	-

Reds	95	96	97	98	99	00	01	02	03	04	05	06	07	08	09	
France:																
Bordeaux	25	25	24	25	24	29	26	24	26	25	28	24	24	25	27	-
Burgundy	26	27	25	24	27	22	23	25	25	23	28	24	24	25	27	-
Rhône	26	22	23	27	26	27	26	-	26	25	27	25	26	23	27	-
Beaujolais	-	-	-	-	-	-	-	-	-	-	27	25	24	23	28	25
California:																
Cab./Merlot	27	24	28	23	25	-	27	26	25	24	26	24	27	26	25	-
Pinot Noir	-	-	-	-	-	-	26	25	24	25	26	24	27	24	26	-
Zinfandel	-	-	-	-	-	-	25	24	26	24	23	21	26	23	25	-
Oregon:																
Pinot Noir	-	-	-	-	-	-	-	26	24	25	24	25	24	27	24	-
Italy:																
Tuscany	25	24	29	24	27	24	27	-	24	27	25	26	25	24	-	-
Piedmont	21	27	26	25	26	28	27	-	24	27	26	26	27	26	-	-
Spain:																
Rioja	26	24	25	22	25	24	28	-	23	27	26	24	24	25	26	-
Ribera del Duero/ Priorat	25	26	24	25	25	24	27	-	24	27	26	24	25	27	-	-
Australia:																
Shiraz/Cab.	23	25	24	26	24	24	26	26	25	25	26	21	23	26	24	-
Chile:	-	-	-	-	24	22	25	23	24	24	27	25	24	26	24	-
Argentina:																
Malbec	-	-	-	-	-	-	-	-	-	25	26	27	26	26	25	-